Sustainability, Participation & Culture in Communication

Sustainability, Participation & Culture in Communication
Theory and praxis

Edited by Jan Servaes

intellect Bristol, UK / Chicago, USA

First published in the UK in 2013 by
Intellect, The Mill, Parnall Road, Fishponds, Bristol, BS16 3JG, UK

First published in the USA in 2013 by
Intellect, The University of Chicago Press, 1427 E. 60th Street,
Chicago, IL 60637, USA

A catalogue record for this book is available from the
British Library.

Cover designer: Edwin Fox
Copy-editor: MPS Technologies
Production manager: Tim Mitchell
Typesetting: Planman Technologies

ISBN 978-1-84150-661-6

Printed and bound by 4edge Ltd, UK

Contents

Part II: (New) Media For Social Change

Part III: Culture and Participation

Part IV: Health Communication

Contents

List of Acronyms

AIDS:	Acquired Immune Deficiency Syndrome
AU	African Union
BCC:	Behavior Change Communication
BRAC:	Bangladesh Rural Advancement Committee
CCA	Culture Centered Approach
CfD or C4D:	Communication for Development
CDSC:	Communication for Development and Social Change
CSC:	Communication for Social Change
CSO:	Civil Society Organization
CSSC:	Communication for Sustainable Social Change
CSSC&D:	Communication for Sustainable Social Change and Development
DVD:	Digital Versatile/Video Disc
ECA:	Ethnographic Content Analysis
EFTA:	European Fair Trade Association
FAO:	Food and Agriculture Organization
FGD:	Focus Group Discussions
GAID:	Global Alliance for ICT and Development
GED:	Gender Development Index
GEM:	Gender Equity Measure
GFATM:	Global Fund to Fight AIDS, Tuberculosis, and Malaria
GLTB:	Gay, Lesbian, Transgender, and Bisexual
GNH:	Gross National Happiness
GNP:	Gross National Product
HDI:	Human Development Index
HIV:	Human Immunodeficiency Virus
HIV/AIDS:	Human Immunodeficiency Virus/Acquired Immune Deficiency Syndrome
HPI:	Human Poverty Index
ICTs:	Information and Communication Technologies
ICTD:	Information and Communication Technologies for Development
IMF:	International Monetary Fund
INEXSK:	Infrastructure, Experience, Skills, Knowledge
IT:	Information Technology
ITU:	International Telecommunications Union

KAP: Knowledge, Attitude, and Practice
MDGs: Millennium Development Goals
M&E: Monitoring and Evaluation
NEWS: Network of European Worldshops
NGO: Non-Governmental Organization
NICT: New Information and Communication Technologies
NWICO: New World Information and Communication Order
PBS: Public Broadcasting Service
PEPFAR: United States of America President's Emergency Plan for AIDS Relief
PPP: Public-Private Partnership
PSA: Public Service Advertisement
R&D: Research and Development
RME: Research, Monitoring, and Evaluation
RTC: Right to Communicate
SCOT: Social Construction of Technology
STI: Sexually Transmitted Infections
TB: Tuberculosis
UDHR: Universal Declaration of Human Rights
UN: United Nations
UNAIDS: Joint United Nations Programme on HIV/AIDS
UNCDP: United Nations Capital Development Programme
UNCRC   United Nations Convention on the Right of the Child
UNCSTD: United Nations Commission on Science and Technology for Development
UNCTAD: United Nations Conference on Trade and Development
UNDP: United Nations Development Programme
UNESCO: United Nations Educational, Scientific, and Cultural Organization
UNFCCC: United Nations Framework Convention on Climate Change
UNFPA: United Nations Population Fund
UNICEF: United Nations Children's Fund
UNIFEM: United Nations Development Fund for Women
USAID: United States Agency for International Development
WB: World Bank
WCC: World Council of Churches
WFTO: World Fair Trade Organization
WHO: World Health Organization
WTO: World Trade Organization
WWF: World Wildlife Fund
ZANLA: Zimbabwe African National Liberation Army
ZANU: Zimbabwe African National Union
ZAPU: Zimbabwe African People's Union
ZIPRA: Zimbabwe People's Revolutionary Army

List of Figures and Tables

Chapter 1

Introduction: The Kaleidoscope of Text and Context in Communication

Jan Servaes

A new 2012 United Nations (UN) report on sustainable development estimates that the world will require at least 50 percent more food, 45 percent more energy, and 30 percent more water by 2030 if it is to keep pace with population growth, projected to reach nearly 9 billion by 2040. The report by a special 22-member international panel (United Nations Secretary-General's High-level Panel on Global Sustainability, 2012) calls for sustainable development indicators that factor in poverty, inequality, science, and gender equality. The aim is to build on the Millennium Development Goals, which will be assessed in 2015, and replace them with Sustainable Development Goals. "We need to chart a new, more sustainable course for the future, one that strengthens equality and economic growth while protecting our planet," said Ban Ki-moon, the UN Secretary-General, on January 30, 2012, at the release of the report. Also, the 2012 Global Environmental Outlook report by the United Nations Environment Programme (UNEP), which was published in preparation for the Rio+20 World Summit on the Environment, concludes that the world continues to speed down an unsustainable path despite over 500 internationally agreed goals and objectives to support the sustainable management of the environment and improve human well-being (for more details, see Tran, 2012, and UN News Centre, 2012).

Earlier, in October 2011, when the seventh billion person was welcomed on our planet, the United Nations Development Program (UNDP) issued a warning that our planet could only cater to a maximum of 4 billion people if they all expected the standard of living that Hollywood presents as the American way of life. "This world of plenty and poverty cannot be sustained," Ban Ki-moon stressed. "We need to marshal all forces to power progress in a way that protects our planet and promotes the welfare of all people" (UN News Centre, 2011).

One way in which the planet has shown its discomfort is through what is being referred to as global warming. NASA's Goddard Institute for Space Studies (GISS) in New York, which monitors global surface temperatures on an ongoing basis, released in early 2012 an updated analysis that shows temperatures around the globe in 2011 compared to the average global temperature in the mid-twentieth century. The comparison shows how the earth continues to experience warmer temperatures than several decades earlier. The average temperature around the globe in 2011 was 0.51°C warmer than the mid-twentieth-century baseline. The global average surface temperature in 2011 was the ninth warmest since 1880, according to NASA scientists. The finding continues a trend in which nine of the ten warmest years in the modern meteorological record have occurred since the year 2000 (NASA, 2012).

Obviously, apart from the global warming deniers and a few nutters and fruitcakes who occupy political debates (Jacoby, 2009), everybody agrees that something needs to be done. The question remains: what?

The so-called GEO-5 (UNEP, 2012) report outlines ways in which the race for development need not be at the expense of the environment or the populations that rely upon it. Indeed, many of the projects that the publication analyzes prove that development can be boosted through better understanding the value of natural resources.

Above all, a redefinition of wealth that goes beyond gross domestic product to a more sustainable metric could boost the quality of life and well-being of all communities, especially those in developing nations.

The report makes the following specific recommendations:

– More reliable data are needed to make informed decisions about environmental resources and to measure progress toward meeting internationally agreed goals.
– There is a need for clear long-term environment and development targets and for stronger accountability in international agreements.
– Capacity development to support environmental information, especially in developing countries, needs to be stepped up significantly.
– Changes need to be both short- and long-term, and combine technology, investment, and governance measures along with lifestyle modifications grounded in a mindset shift toward sustainability- and equity-based values.
– Transformation requires a gradual but steadily accelerating transition process. Some successful policy innovation is already happening but needs to be mainstreamed.
– International cooperation is essential, since environmental problems do not follow national boundaries. Global responses can play a key role in setting goals, generating financial resources, and facilitating the sharing of best practices.
– Even though national and regional responses have shown success, a polycentric governance approach is needed to attain effective, efficient, and equitable outcomes.
– Improving human well-being is dependent on the capacity of individuals, institutions, countries, and the global community to respond to environmental change.

Also, at the 2012 edition of the World Economic Forum in Davos, Switzerland, the background report on the global risks our world faces clearly stated that three common crosscutting observations emerged from the varied groups of experts consulted (World Economic Forum, 2012: 49):

– Decision-makers need to improve understanding of incentives that will improve collaboration in response to global risks.
– Trust, or lack of trust, is perceived to be a crucial factor in how risks may manifest themselves. In particular, this refers to confidence, or lack thereof, in leaders, in the systems that ensure public safety, and in the tools of communication that are revolutionizing how we share and digest information.

– Communication and information sharing on risks must be improved by introducing greater transparency about uncertainty and conveying it to the public in a meaningful way.

In other words, communication is increasingly being considered to be crucial in effectively tackling today's major problems.

Sustainability for whom and for what?

The focus in this book is on Communication for Sustainable Development and Social Change (CSSC) in both theory and practice. Perspectives on sustainability, participation, and culture in communication changed over time in line with the evolution of development approaches and trends and the need for effective applications of communication methods and tools to new issues and priorities. Communication in sustainable development has started to address the specific concerns and issues of food security, rural development and livelihood, natural resource management and environment, poverty reduction, equity and gender, and Information and Communication Technologies (ICTs). However, more analysis, discussion and research is needed.

In the last twenty years, Sustainable Development has emerged as one of the most prominent development paradigms. In 1987, the World Commission on Environment and Development (WCED) concluded that "sustainable development is development that meets the needs of the present without compromising the ability of future generations to meet their own needs." Sustainable development is seen as a means of enhancing decision-making so that it provides a more comprehensive assessment of the many multi-dimensional problems society faces (Elliott, 1994; Lele, 1991; Taylor, 1996). What is required is an evaluation framework for categorizing programs, projects, policies, and/or decisions as having sustainability potential.

There are three dimensions that are generally recognized as the "pillars" of Sustainable Development: economic, environmental, and social. "The essence of sustainability therefore, is to take the contextual features of economy, society, and environment – the uncertainty, the multiple competing values, and the distrust among various interest groups – as givens and go on to design a process that guides concerned groups to seek out and ask the right questions as a preventative approach to environmentally and socially regrettable undertakings" (Flint, 2007: IV).

Over the years different perspectives – based on both 'Western' and 'Eastern' philosophical starting points (see Servaes & Malikhao, 2007a & b) – have resulted in a more holistic and integrated vision of Sustainable Development. At the same time, a unifying theme is that there is no universal development model. Development is an integral, multi-dimensional, and dialectic process that differs from society to society, community to community, context to context. In other words, each society and community must attempt to delineate its own strategy to Sustainable Development starting with the resources and "capitals" available (not only physical, financial, and environmental but also human, social, institutional, etc.) and by considering needs and views of the people concerned.

Sustainable Development implies a participatory, multi-stakeholder approach to policy making and implementation, mobilizing public and private resources for development and making use of the knowledge, skills and energy of all social groups concerned with the future of the planet and its people. Within this framework, communication and information play a strategic and fundamental role by (a) contributing to the interplay of different development factors, (b) improving the sharing of knowledge and information, and (c) encouraging the participation of all concerned.

In the social and communication sciences, development has traditionally been associated with "development problems" that occurred in "developing countries." It is only since the late 1980s and early 1990s that the concept of development was gradually replaced by social change to highlight the global and universal importance of the issue (Servaes, 2011).

The study of communication for development and social change has therefore been through several paradigmatic changes. From the modernization and growth theory to the dependency approach and the multiplicity or participatory model, these new traditions of discourse are characterized by a turn toward local communities as targets for research and debate, on the one hand, and the search for an understanding of the complex relationships between globalization and localization, on the other. The early twenty-first-century "global" world, in general as well as in its distinct regional, national, and local entities, is confronted with multifaceted economic and financial crises but also those of social, cultural, ideological, moral, political, ethnic, ecological, and security. Previously held traditional modernization and dependency perspectives have become more difficult to support because of the growing interdependency of regions, nations, and communities in our globalized world.

The conclusion we can draw from late-twentieth- and early twenty-first-century reconceptualizations and reorientations of development and social change is that while income, productivity, and gross national product (GNP) are still essential aspects of human development, they are *not* the sum total of human existence. Hence, the current attempts to shift the debate toward Sustainable Development Goals, a Human Development Index, and Gross National Happiness indicators. Just as this has important implications for the way we think about social change and development, so too does it present opportunities for how we think about the role and place of communication in development and social change processes.

One world, multiple cultures

The above history has been summarized in "Communication for Development. One World, Multiple Cultures" (Servaes, 1999), a textbook that is currently out of print and under revision for another edition. We distinguished between three general development paradigms (modernization, dependency, and multiplicity), which were narrowed down to two communication paradigms: diffusion versus participatory communication.

In general, Social Change (or development) can be described as a significant change of structured social action or of the culture in a given society, community, or context. Such a broad definition could be further specified on the basis of a number of "dimensions" of social change: space (micro, meso-, macro), time (short, medium, long-term), speed (slow, incremental, evolutionary vs. fast, fundamental, revolutionary), direction (forward or backward), content (sociocultural, psychological, sociological, organizational, anthropological, economic, and so forth), and impact (peaceful vs. violent). For more details, see Servaes (2008, 2011).

The field of communication for social change is vast, and the models supporting it are as different as the ideologies that inspired them. However, generally speaking we see two approaches: one aims to produce a common understanding among all the participants in a development initiative by implementing a policy or a development project, that is, the top-down model. The other emphasizes engaging the grassroots in making decisions that enhance their own lives, or the bottom-up model. Despite the diversity of approaches, there is a consensus in the early twenty-first century on the need for grassroots participation in bringing about change at both social and individual levels. Bessette (2004), Bhambra (2007), Chambers (2005; 2008), Escobar (2008), Fals Borda (1991), and Max-Neef (1991), among others, promote this perspective.

The study of communication for development and social change uses a combination of methodologies, often in mixed and integrated ways: quantitative, qualitative, and participatory. Often one starts with a basic quantitative study to set the stage for more qualitative and participatory investigations. Within each, more complex and specific methods can be identified. While a triangulated form of mixed methods is often considered ideal, there remains a substantial gap between the theory and practice of Communication for Development and Social Change (CDSC), as once again confirmed by Lennie and Tacchi (2010: 4):

The evaluation of Communication for Development (C4D) needs to be based on an appropriate combination of qualitative and quantitative techniques, complementary approaches and triangulation, and recognition that different approaches are suitable for different issues and purposes. However, there is often a lack of appreciation, funding and support for alternative, innovative Research, Monitoring and Evaluation (RME) approaches among management and mainstream M&E specialists in the UN. Commitment to participatory processes is often rhetoric rather than meaningful or appropriate practice. Funders tend to place greater value on narrow, quantitative measurement-oriented approaches and indicators that do not sufficiently take the complexity of culture and the context of C4D and development initiatives into account.

(Lennie & Tacchi, 2010: 4) (see also Alvarez, 2011; and Whaley et al., 2010)

Several of the authors contributing to this volume have referred to the above typologies as a starting point for their own deliberations and explorations. In this book we basically wish to elaborate and problematize the relevance and specifics of a participatory communication perspective within the multiplicity paradigm. This is not an easy task, because, as we have argued elsewhere (e.g., Servaes, 2007, 2008) our world has become increasingly complex and difficult to synthesize within traditional models and schemata. Therefore, each chapter in this volume should be looked at as an inherently limited contribution to a rather complex – by certain standards even chaotic – understanding of today's world. Another way of looking at it would be to use the symbol of a mosaic or kaleidoscope, which, while focusing on certain colors and shapes, makes it difficult to focus on the whole.

Sustainability indicators

In order to provide some guidance to the reader, we reproduce a framework for the assessment of sustainability that forms part of an ongoing research project at our SBS Center "Communication for Sustainable Social Change" (see Servaes et al., 2012a & b).

Based on a review of the literature, the four sectors of development or social change for which we have developed our indicators are Health, Education, Environment, and Governance. We selected eight indicators for each of the sectors of development (see Table 1.1): actors (the people involved in the project, who may include opinion leaders, community activists, tribal elders, youth, etc.), factors (structural and conjunctural), level (local, state, regional, national, international, global), development communication approach (behavioral change, mass communication, advocacy, participatory communication, or communication for sustainable social change – which is likely a mix of all of the above), channels (radio, ICT, TV, print, Internet, etc.), message (the content of the project, campaign), process (diffusion-centered, one-way, information-persuasion strategies, or interactive and dialogical), and method (quantitative, qualitative, participatory, or in combination).

For each indicator, we developed a set of questions designed to specifically measure the sustainability of the project. We defined "sustainability," for example, by analyzing whether the channels are compatible with both the capacity of the actors and the structural and conjunctural factors. If they are, the project will have a higher likelihood of being sustainable in the long run. We asked to what extent was the process participatory and consistent with the cultural values of the community? Was the message developed by local actors in the community, and how was it understood? Our research shows that the more local and interactive the participation – in levels, communication approaches, channels, processes, and methods – the more sustainable the project will be. We further analyzed each of the indicators in the context of sustainability for each project.

Below, we identify the primary sector and indicators, which each contributor (using the chapter number in the table) has selected for analysis and argument in his/her chapter.

Table 1.1: Sectors of development and main indicators for each chapter.

Sectors of development addressed in chapters

Health	Education	Governance	Environment
13, 14, 15, 16, 17, 18	7, 8, 9, 11, 12	4, 6, 7, 8, 9, 10	2, 5, 8, 12

Indicators for sustainability addressed in chapters

Actors		5, 6, 7, 9, 10, 11, 12, 15
Factors	Structural	2, 3, 7
	Conjunctural	4, 5, 11, 12
Level	Local	2, 11, 12
	National/Regional	2, 5, 7, 9, 10, 16
	International/Global	2, 3, 4, 8
Development Communication Approach	- BCC Behavioral Change Communication	12, 15
	- MC Mass Communication	3, 9, 11, 15, 17
	- AC Advocacy	11, 12
	- PC Participatory Communication	5, 10
	- CSSC Communication for Sustainable Social Change	2, 7, 9, 10
Channels	Face to Face	7, 9
	Print	7, 9, 11, 13
	Radio/Television	14, 16, 18
	ICT	
	Wireless Phone	3, 4, 7, 8
	Internet	4, 15
Process	Persuasion Strategies	5, 11, 13
	One-Way Transmission	8, 9, 17
	Interactive Dialogue	2, 16
Methods	Quantitative	13, 17, 18
	Qualitative	7, 8, 18
	Participatory	11
	Mixed Methods	2
Message	Was it developed by the community?	2, 8 , 9, 13, 16, 17, 18
	Was it received?	
	Was it understood?	

Four themes, seventeen cases

Four key themes, which together constitute the essence of our current understanding of the role and place of communication in social change processes, have been used to structure the organization of this volume: sustainability and globalization, (new) media for social change, culture and participation. The fourth theme is health communication, as the focus on health-related problems seems to be one of the dominant concerns in the field of Communication for Social Change.

Adinda Van Hemelrijck kicks off with a state-of-the-art assessment of the ongoing debate regarding the effectiveness of aid, and more specifically, how to measure its impacts and make evidence-based arguments about what works and what does not. The debate has culminated, once again, in the age-old war over methods. The fight is between logical positivism and interpretative relativism, and the "scientific" way of collecting hard evidence versus the more participatory approach producing soft(er) qualitative data. While recognizing the depth and importance of the methodological debate, she argues, it appears to be more productive to move beyond the dispute and make the best use of all worldviews in an integrated, flexible, and responsive manner. She then explains how her former employer, Oxfam America, used this proposition to develop a rights-based approach to impact measurement and learning, based on the understanding that fighting poverty and injustice requires fundamental systemic-transformational changes, and consequently, a methodological fusion that can capture complexity and present it in a way that can meet and influence stakeholders' different worldviews.

Van Hemelrijck talks about Oxfam America's approach to impact measurement and learning, which in essence is about "empowerment" considered as both the means and the ends of development. She describes how she believes impact measurement can be meaningful and doable, and what kind of monitoring, evaluation, and learning systems are needed. She also attempts to unpack the key aspects that will define its success and the main organizational, cultural, and contextual challenges to be anticipated, illustrated through the particular case of Oxfam's program on smallholders' productive water rights in Ethiopia, which can be considered as emblematic of a range of possible issues we may or may not encounter in other programs.

From the arguments developed in Van Hemelrijck's chapter, it is a logical and easy step to make the connection to the first set of contributions on sustainability and globalization. As local realities are influenced and shaped by the wider system, while at the same time are also influencing their wider environment and thus the larger system, the root causes of poverty and injustice are multi-dimensional, varying across different contexts but entrenched in wider and more complex interdependencies.

Toks Oyedemi opens this section with a broad and critical overview of Information and Communication Technologies (ICTs) for development. It asserts that ICT for development and social change has evolved as a global agenda on a number of levels.

Firstly, the potentials of ICTs in government activities, healthcare services, education and other sectors, and the limited penetration of certain technologies, make it paramount that sustainable social change agendas include extending access to ICTs. Consequently, governments and nongovernmental agencies focus on access to ICT as a global agenda for development and social change.

Secondly, the theoretical discourse of development and the framings of technology in this discourse lead to an ideological construct that elevates technology for development as a global agenda evident in generic models of ICT for development. These framings influence the crafting of a global policy agenda, such as universal service, to confront a global divide with implementations of ICTs for development projects.

Critically, the rhetoric of ICT for development hides an underlying global agenda of neoliberalism, evident in the collaboration of private enterprises with public-service institutions, and the Public-Private Partnerships (PPPs) between ICT companies and governments and many international development agencies. Technology corporations are building telecenters, providing software and equipment in the ICT4D projects in the developing world in an effort to bridge the "digital divide" that describes a "global market" of over 70 percent of the world's population without access to the Internet. However, many projects lack sustainability, beneficiaries lack skills to utilize technologies, and there is indiscriminate proliferation of telecenters in the developing world with a resultant consequence on cultural ideologies.

Irrespective of this market agenda and numerous critiques of ICTs for development, the failure to invest in ICT applications and networks will exacerbate existing global and local inequalities. Oyedemi concludes that the task is to rethink approaches toward an ethical implementation of ICTs for sustainable social change.

Tokunbo Ojo problematizes this further for the African context. He studies the diffusion of mobile phones and ICTs for development in the Sub-Saharan African region within the global discourse of telecommunication reform, globalization, and trade. The concerns expressed more than three decades ago in the debate on the New World Information and Communication Order (NWICO) are, according to Ojo, still having far-deepening ramifications for African countries, in view of the ongoing process of commercialization of ICTs and mobile phones for development. This is, Ojo contends, one of the reasons for Africans and their governments not to take the new ICTs for development agenda and the international regimes that accompany it as a given. To maintain their own cultural sovereignty and production capacities, they need to understand the culture of ICTs and its relevance to their own development plans on their own terms, not the terms imposed by external forces.

Fadia Hassan's chapter extends the conversation on community into the business practice of fair trade, which boasts of being an ethical entrepreneurial force that places its ideological focus on creating sustainable and fair communities that directly connect producers and consumers. Fair trade claims to bridge wage discrepancies, retailers' goals and consumer concerns for social and environmental responsibility. The extent to which it is indeed effective in creating such a sustainable community within varied cultural and economic contexts in Bangladesh is explored and analyzed in this chapter.

The businesses' efficacy in "fair" community building, which they claim to be their key goal, one that deviates from a so-called isolating mainstream "capital-centric" consumer society development model is studied in detail. Global fair-trade organizations like Aarong, Bangladesh, and Bibi Productions that are located (and originated) outside the Global North/West are investigated and analyzed. Aarong is a fair-trade business, developed by the famed Bangladeshi nongovernmental organization, the Bangladesh Rural Advancement Committee (BRAC), employing a participatory model that attempts to create a "fair" and "sustainable" community. Through an exploration of the Fair-Trade Consumer Culture in Bangladesh, the fixed notion of the trade concept is challenged and the need for a new framework that is more inclusive and appropriate to the geopolitical context of Bangladesh emerges, one that can revolutionize the applicability of the term beyond its current state.

In what ways is the term fair-trade negotiated and redefined in this specific cultural and geopolitical context? What are the challenges that are faced in the construction of such an idyllic vision of community? Is fair trade successful in creating community cohesiveness and sustenance? To what extent does it facilitate the development of inclusionary networks among producers, retailers, and consumers, in line with the dream of constructing the idyllic "global village," but in this case, an idyllic national community? Has fair trade given a new meaning to production and consumption ethics for both the producers and the consumers? Is the term stable and fixed as it flows from the producer to the consumer, across borders and cultures? These are the questions that Fadia Hassan attempts to answer.

Rachel Stohr starts with a dialectical approach and begins the process of theorizing and exploring the control-resistance dialectic in the discourse on globalization of the World Trade Organization (WTO). She highlights the relationship between communication and social change by exploring the WTO's discourse of globalization. Much valuable research demonstrates the harmful effects of globalization, but few studies have explored the rhetorical tactics with which powerful international financial institutions simultaneously control and resist public discourses about this phenomenon. Exploring the tension-laden relationship between power and discourse, Stohr argues, helps us to understand that power relations are fluid and that communication can facilitate the process of reclaiming and reappropriating power to promote sustainable economic development.

The section on (new) media for social change presents three interesting and timely case studies. Emily Polk focuses on the recent revolution in Egypt, which has amplified a debate among scholars, activists, journalists, bloggers, and policy makers about the significance of social media in instigating lasting social and political change. She argues first that social media cannot be analyzed as a singular phenomena but rather must be understood in the context of all of the conditions that made the revolt possible and, secondly, that while the youth have been given credit for leading the uprising via social media, it was in fact their emphasis on the physical public sphere and their successful cultivation and management of the relationship between the digital and physical publics that made the success of the uprising possible.

The chapter offers a brief summary of public sphere theory – digital and physical – followed by the Egyptian context; provides a historical analysis of the revolution, including how activist groups used social media to mobilize; uses Actor Network Theory as a framework to explore how the relationship between the digital and physical public spheres was successfully cultivated and sustained via on-the-ground organizing and online coordination throughout the uprising. Finally, while it is still impossible to know whether the revolt and the uprisings that preceded and proceeded it in the Middle East will lead to sustainable democratic social change, it builds upon Gurstein's (2011) analysis of lessons learned during the uprising in Egypt in order to better understand and contextualize the relationship between the digital and physical public spheres.

Song Shi analyzes two Chinese ICT projects: the Connecting Every Village Project and the Civil Society Organization (CSO) Web 2.0 Project. He argues that the Connecting Every Village Project is primarily in line with the modernization paradigm and diffusion model, whereas the CSO Web2.0 Project is a more participatory project. In his analysis of the Connecting Every Village Project, Shi shows that although the modernization theories were originally meant to analyze development issues of developing countries and the relations between developed and developing countries, they are also applicable in the study of development issues of less-developed regions and relations between less-developed regions and relatively developed regions within one country. Secondly, by analyzing the relation between the two projects, Shi explores the relations between participatory and diffusion models in the specific context of Internet use and development in China in the INEXSK model proposed by the United Nations Commission on Science and Technology for Development (UNCSTD).

Shi's conclusions are significant both from a theoretical and practical perspective. On a theoretical level, little research has addressed the applicability of modernization paradigm theories in the study of regional development issues within one country. More importantly, no research has addressed the relation between participatory paradigm projects and modernization paradigm projects in a specific context. On a practical level, it is widely agreed that telecommunication and the Internet are important components in development projects in different communities and countries. This chapter assesses the increasing popularity of telecommunication and Internet and their significant role in the development of less-developed regions in China. This study ends with recommendations for policy makers, practitioners, and development workers on ICT development in China and other developing countries.

From Liberation to Oppression tracks the deterioration of freedom of the press, freedom of speech, and freedom of expression in the 30 years following Zimbabwe's independence in 1980. Verity Norman also analyzes possible explanations for certain independent performance spaces, such as Harare's highly politicized Book Café, that have been left untouched by the state watchdogs. In this oppressed state where independent media is crushed, political plays shut down, and independent activists are arrested, why are performers in this small, lively café allowed to speak out against the government and raise their voices about issues that are usually discussed in whispers? Why has this performance space not been threatened or closed down? Why have its performers not been arrested? What is it that exempts them from what has become common treatment for individuals who dare to publicly challenge Mugabe's rule? Are these artists an authentic voice of dissent, and are they effecting change in their community? Or, as a community, do they have such a limited reach that the government is able to dismiss them as unimportant or insignificant and simply appealing to the Zimbabwean bourgeoisie?

After a decade of guerilla warfare, the "Second Chimurenga" led by Zimbabwe's President Robert Mugabe and the militant Zanla and Zipra, Mugabe emerged as the first democratically elected president of the people of Zimbabwe – their liberator. However, in today's Zimbabwe, Mugabe continues to use the same machinations of oppression used by the British settlers who claimed their Unilateral Declaration of Independence back in 1965. State watchdogs, namely the police and the army, continue to harass and arrest artists and activists alike when they raise questions about the injustice inflicted on the Zimbabwean people. Part 1 of this chapter tracks the emergence of Mugabe and the ruling Zanu-PF as oppressors of the people. This section also includes an analysis of how media laws and communication practices have run parallel to the well-documented and much publicized socioeconomic and political collapse in Zimbabwe.

The second part of this chapter explores the arts activism movement that emerged during the height of Zimbabwe's economic collapse, with a specific focus on spoken word and hip hop as a participatory medium of protest. The chapter includes a study of Harare's grassroots hip hop movement, which centers around the Book Café and is led by two hip hop activists – Comrade Fatso and Outspoken – and their youth-focused NGO, Magamba Cultural Activists Network. Verity Norman also analyzes Harare's popular Book Café as a site of protest.

This chapter and study is rooted in a framework that considers the work of Foucault (1982) and engages in the discourse around the United Nations' Declaration of Human Rights, and the human right to freedom of speech and expression within that context. Verity Norman draws her conclusions from personal observations and involvement in the arts community in Zimbabwe, as well as two 1.5-hour semi-structured interviews with spoken-word activist, Outspoken, and informal conversations with Book Café performers and patrons. She spent two years working closely with artist-activists in Zimbabwe, from 2006 to 2008, and has continued to collaborate with partners in this community following her move to the United States. Despite the danger involved with publicly speaking truth to power in Zimbabwe, these artists continue their struggle against injustice, using words as their only weapon. It is fair to say that this has been an ongoing journey of struggle and inspiration.

In the section on Culture and Participation, Boonlert Supadhiloke opens by tracing the evolution of Human Rights and its associated Right to Communicate, with particular reference to people's participation, and examines their applications in the democratic development process through various case studies in Thailand. The results show that, although the concepts of human rights and the right to communicate have long existed in

Thailand, the public came to be aware of them only after the 1932 democratic revolution when Thailand changed from an absolute to a constitutional monarchy.

However, the application of the right to communicate, particularly in the participatory process, has always been very limited in Thailand. This was particularly true in the democratization of mass media and national politics. In media democratization, the government's efforts to liberalize the broadcasting industry by allowing citizens to participate in the national public-service broadcasting and community broadcasting had come to a standstill after the 1997 Constitution was abolished by a military coup on September 19, 2006. However, the democratization process has often been marked by a low rate of people's participation due largely to lack of adequate education and limited freedom to express public opinions. For example, in the referendum for adoption of the new Constitution on August 19, 2007, almost half of the 45 million eligible voters abstained from casting their votes. In the general election in November 2007, a large number of people also did not go to polls due to their limited access to information. Had the people's right to communicate been put to work, their participation could have been raised, thus enhancing democracy in Thailand.

Increasingly, communication scholars have called for the examination of the role of participatory processes in the realm of development and social change outside so-called formal democratic electoral procedures. Challenging the top-down conceptualizations of traditional development communication projects, these scholars have noted the importance of engaging with local communities in projects of development, eliciting genuine participation in the development of solutions. A critical engagement with the literature on participatory communication approaches illustrates the multiple tensions and contradictions that play out in the various commitments/agendas of the participating actors within the discursive space, particularly as it relates to the negotiations of relationships between the community and the outside actors. Further, there is the constant effort to match the rhetoric of participation to the actual practices on the field. The chapter by Lalatendu and Dutta builds on the literature on participatory communication and child participation and examines the tenets of participation through the theoretical framework of a culture-centered approach and how it might impact sustainable change through a case study of the child participation project "The Child Reporters" in Koraput in the state of Orissa, India. The framework of a culture-centered approach locates participatory processes at the intersections of structure, culture, and agency, examining the ways in which dominant structures erase the voices and agency of the subaltern sectors, thus creating points of entry for listening to the hidden voices. Lalatendu and Dutta listen and engage with the voices of the Koraput child reporters and underscore the importance of participation in bringing about social change.

The chapter by Park and Richardson describes university communication courses that were transformed into community-led partnerships in New Orleans after Hurricane Katrina. It begins by discussing the theoretical framework that informed and guided this project, situating it in US history as well as within the communication field. Using social justice-oriented participatory communication pedagogy, this chapter describes how community needs can be addressed while enhancing student learning. The role of universities as potential change agents is given a thoughtful analysis, which addresses the complex power relations constraining many relief projects.

The rebuilding of New Orleans was quickly politicized, with many influential groups opposed to rebuilding certain sections of the city. Volunteers who responded to community needs during this turbulent period often faced resistance from local and national authorities, including the police, the local Catholic church, the federal government, and university personnel. The community-led pedagogy created under these circumstances quickly evolved into a social-justice oriented model of participatory communication, grappling with the challenges of rebuilding large impoverished sections of the city, including African-American and white neighborhoods of lower socioeconomic status. The majority of residents were homeless, scattered across the United States, with many unable to return and rebuild due to financial constraints and a lack of government support. Under these conditions, the courses often partnered with a local nonprofit relief organization, founded by a small number of activists to represent and advocate for marginalized communities in the immediate and extended aftermath of the levee failure. Together, guided by community needs, which at the beginning of the relief processes consisted of requests for volunteers to gut houses and remove debris, the communication courses and the nonprofit group designed several years worth of national communication campaigns to attract volunteers and material donations. By creating extensive media lists, news releases, radio announcements, websites, feature stories, competitions, and volunteer "goodbye-thank you" packets, which provided templates returning volunteers could use to contact their local media for further exposure and recognition, the students gained valuable media experience.

These campaigns not only created hands-on learning opportunities for students, in terms of practical applications for integrated communication skills, but they also cultivated an activated understanding of oppression and power relations that few students experience in their lifetimes. Perhaps most importantly for the students, these partnerships cultivated a sense of empowerment and agency after they saw the fruits of their labor. During the three years of its existence, the project generated over $1.2 million of rebuilding supplies and pro-bono labor from over five thousand volunteers. Given this combined material and educational success, the chapter suggests that similar partnerships of course/nonprofit/community offer a potential model for consideration in other communication programs, and suggests that a rethinking of the communication field may be necessary if one believes that educational institutions should address community needs and problems. This chapter shows that communication professors can harness academia for the public interest, at the classroom level, with highly effective media-skill instruction, without sacrificing the rigor of sociological and critical analysis.

This approach, although complicated by political forces, can directly address forms of oppression and injustice. The enormous challenges in the rebuilding of New Orleans eventually led to the demise of this unique partnership between the nonprofits, communication courses and community needs. However, with a detailed understanding of the historical implications of this case study, we hope that change agents will be able to better navigate the pressures associated with any politicized relief work under future circumstances. Communication departments can and should embrace more roles as potential community change agents, not only during crisis situations but also in "non-crisis" situations, as well as through experiential and community-led pedagogies. Perhaps a re-envisioning of the communication field and the role of public universities can more positively impact crises and non-crisis community needs around the world (for more ideas along these lines, see Kennedy, 2008; and Nagy-Zekmi and Hollis, 2012).

Print media plays an important role in setting the public agenda, mobilizing public opinions (framing), and influencing decision-makers to offer possible solutions around gender and racial disparity, health equity/inequity and other social issues experienced by people who are homeless. Many factors influence how this type of social issue is communicated or framed by the media: for example, the social-cultural and political context may be the reason for certain stories on homelessness. The newspapers' ownership and their historical context can also influence the amount and type or emphasis of coverage of this specific social issue. A factor less studied is the gender of the journalists and whether this is a variable in the framing of societal issues such as homelessness. Richter, Burns, Mogale, and Chaw-Kant present findings on whether the gender of the journalists influenced agenda setting or framing of disparity, health equity/inequity, and other social issues faced by individuals or families who are homeless.

The chapter starts with a background overview of the key concepts of the media's framing of homelessness as a social or societal issue and the arguments that arise around the gender of the journalist and how this might influence the outcomes of homelessness communication to the public. The focus of this chapter is the description, analysis, and discussion of the results of a case study based in Alberta, Canada. In this case, gender is investigated as a variable in the media's framing and influence concerning homelessness as a social issue and as part of cultural awareness or an "awareness culture."

In the news media, the gender of journalists has been linked to gender representation in news stories that can lead to biases, for example, male journalists tend to quote male subjects. If men are the constant contributors of news coverage concerning key societal issues and women are repeatedly underrepresented, an inaccurate reflection of those societal issues will be presented. In contrast, female journalists are more likely to advocate for women, address issues specifically affecting women, and use female sources. Thus, gender does matter in story sourcing. Although the media professionals are key players in "framing" the homeless and their situation, decision-makers, researchers, and others also have a role in creating a social constructionist frame of homelessness. How are our beliefs and construction of social issues formed or caused? Some would argue that people, whether female or male, are influenced by those things that align with their own social or personal interests. With this view, the gender of the journalists might influence how a social issue such as homelessness is framed, which in turn can be either supportive or nonsupportive of the homeless.

The study revealed no significant difference between the gender of the journalist and the general story themes they addressed. However, some of the findings suggest some key gender-specific trends. More female journalists reported on housing-related issues, family challenges, and socioeconomic impacts. In contrast, male journalists tended to report on government reductions in social programs and social assistance. The different types of stories could impact the readers in very different ways, especially considering the different genders of the readers.

For the media to truthfully portray our society and to produce reporting that is complete and diverse, it is important that the news reflects the world as seen by women and men in an equal and equitable manner. This is how we construct our notion of reality of today's homelessness issues. Homelessness crosses over all gender, age, and other demographic and social boundaries.

Richter, Burns, Mogale, and Chaw-Kant note that the social constructionist frame of the homeless is fluid and dynamic and the framing of homelessness might shift with changes in not only the environmental context, but also with the changes in employment in the media profession where more women may accept positions traditionally given to men. As more women become involved in all levels of media organization as reporters, senior editors, and media decision-makers, the stories will reflect these changing roles and experiences. Homelessness is a problem with societal, community, family, and individual roots. The media and the journalists, regardless of gender, will frame stories in a positive or negative light, thus promoting debate regarding social issues and influencing or supporting existing public perceptions. This traditional media practice is culturally acceptable, and gender may not enter into the public's analysis of the story as written.

One conclusion from the study is that women should be involved at all levels of the media organization as reporters, senior editors, and media decision-makers. A gender balance would provide a broad spectrum of communication on social issues such as homelessness. The nature of how a social issue is framed in the media needs more attention. More gender-based research is needed on individual-level effects of communication and media framing of social issues.

The fourth set of chapters, focusing on health communication, is opened by Patchanee Malikhao who explores different views on "globalization" and its implication on culture. The interaction between global and local cultures, especially in the case of Thailand, and the consequences for HIV/AIDS policy and prevention, which resulted in a change of sexual norms and practices, is being explained. The change of the Thai sexual norms and practices, due to the so-called contemporary globalization period, is being analyzed. HIV/AIDS prevention strategies through media campaigns, sex education, and community approaches are being discussed regarding the dynamic interaction of globalization and Thai culture.

As already argued by Oyedemi, Ojo, and Stohr, development agencies have gained prominence in a global context characterized by the erosion of the nation state. In Africa in particular, institutions such as the World Bank, the IMF, and USAID have an overt social change goal and significantly shape education and health. In the latter area, development agencies edict public health policies and allocate significant resources to infrastructures and equipment. This increasing role deserves attention from scholars because such interventions are far from being innocuous and are connected to larger ideological, cultural, and socioeconomic dimensions. The study by Joelle Cruz examines fifteen health success stories on the USAID website for Senegal. It uses critical discourse analysis as a method and features two overarching themes: illness and health. The framing of illness and health fit into underdevelopment, a disease-ridden space, and development, an illness-free site. Therefore, Cruz encourages us to question the implications of social change initiatives.

The chapter by Katrina Phillips and Betty Chirchir considers a participatory communication project designed to challenge the personal and professional harm of HIV/AIDS stigma among health workers in Kenya. In particular, it focuses on lessons learnt in using DVD-led training as a catalyst to deep discussion, reflection, and consensus on change in complex health and social issues.

TB or tuberculosis is the most common opportunistic infection among persons living with HIV and AIDS. Current estimates place up to 59 percent of TB patients in Kenya as coinfected with HIV. Ministry of Health policy in Kenya is to cross-test for TB and HIV. Working with the Ministry of Health, the Center for Disease Control and Prevention, GAP-Kenya funded a project to encourage the uptake of cross-testing at hospitals and clinics. Kenya-based Mediae was commissioned by Danya International to develop the communication strategy and media materials.

Initial situational research presented at a stakeholder meeting revealed two key points. Firstly, a confident health worker aware of his or her own HIV status appears to be far more comfortable and successful when counseling patients to test for HIV or TB. Secondly, there was considerable stigma about HIV/AIDS among health workers, to the extent that many did not know their own status or, if found positive, would not seek treatment. Together these two findings illustrated the clash of two contexts: personal fears versus professional demands as public health providers and communicators.

The stakeholders agreed that health workers within their work environment (and by extension, their families and patients) would become the primary target group of the communication strategy – with the objectives of improving their own health, their confidence at work, and their professional communication skills, ultimately leading to increased uptake in cross-testing for TB and HIV.

Tailor-made media for the project included a storyline in Makutano Junction, a popular Kenyan television edutainment series reaching 6.5 million viewers each week; local vernacular radio call-in programs with experts in the studio responding to listeners; SMS contact numbers for television and radio audiences seeking further information; and the main focus of this chapter, DVD-led awareness training for health workers.

The DVDs were produced to feature clips from the TV drama series plus specifically scripted scenarios with locally well-known actors, interviews with professional health workers and some patients, together with a handbook for each group session participant to take away. The DVD works as a catalyst, leading group discussion through experiences of HIV stigma, discrimination, testing, disclosure and communication skills. It is an interactive and participatory form of group communication, using humor, drama, and personal experience to open what may be difficult discussions, leading to a commitment to change that is owned by the participants themselves.

This chapter explores the effectiveness and potential of using DVD-led discussion in communication for social change, tackling a complex issue such as stigma in a way that challenged the silence around it, leading to open discussion and agreement of the need to change by the participants. It also calls for greater recognition of the value of funding longer-term impact evaluation of communication for social change projects.

From a similar case-based perspective, Jyotika Ramaprasad summarizes the results of an effectiveness test for a public-service announcement (PSA) that presents benefits of a couple testing together for HIV. Based on a community's identification of the need for messages encouraging couple testing, so as to enable disclosure of a partner's HIV status in a counseling setting, a text with voiceover PSA was created. It was then evaluated in the same community in Uganda, using a pre-post design. Results indicated effectiveness of the PSA in changing beliefs about disclosure, discordancy, and the importance and benefits of couple testing, as well as intent-to-test together as a couple. The use of this individual level intervention is then situated within the communication for social change theories. The author suggests that as per the new thinking about "social change communication," such interventions are a useful part of a mix of approaches that together provide a holistic approach in this field.

The last case by Tilly Gurman focuses on Latina adolescents and telenovelas. Latinos are currently the largest ethnic minority population in the United States. Countless studies illustrate that although Latina adolescents are less likely to engage in sex compared to other adolescents, they are nevertheless disproportionately affected by negative sexual health outcomes, including teen births and sexually transmitted infections (STIs), including HIV/AIDS. In the United States, the vast majority of HIV-positive Latinas were exposed through heterosexual contact.

Mutual monogamy is considered an effective strategy for the prevention of STIs, while infidelity may increase an individual's risk. Previous studies have documented that Spanish-language soap operas, also known as telenovelas, contain large amounts of infidelity, with little emphasis on safer sex. Moreover, for programs popular among Latino adolescents, telenovelas contain more infidelity compared to English-language programs. Because Spanish-language telenovelas are among the highest rated programs among Latina adolescents in the United States, it is likely that Latina adolescents who watch telenovelas will be exposed to messages reinforcing infidelity.

It is widely believed that adolescents can learn vicariously about sexual behavior by observing what television characters say and do. As a result, it is imperative to understand how telenovelas portray infidelity in order to tailor effective sexual health communication programs for Latina adolescents.

The study by Tilly Gurman employed ethnographic content analysis (ECA), a qualitative methodology that facilitates discovery specific to the who, what, where, and why of mass-media depictions. Grounded in social cognitive theory, this ECA explored the treatment of infidelity in twenty episodes of popular telenovelas that aired primetime on the Univision network between February 28, 2006, and April 17, 2006. These episodes were identified from a larger quantitative content analysis, which compared sexual content of English- and Spanish-language television programs popular among Latino adolescents in the United States, as identified by Nielsen ratings. This larger study reported a high frequency of infidelity within telenovelas, with little mention of sexual risk or responsibility. Of particular interest in the current study was the role of infidelity alongside the evolution of the individual narratives for the four female lead characters.

Study findings illustrated that infidelity was practically inevitable, with all four leading female characters having engaged in infidelity. At the same time, infidelity resulted in largely negative consequences. Female leads that engaged in infidelity for selfish reasons and turned away from religion or tradition experienced tragic and fatal outcomes. Even the female leads that ultimately enjoyed happy endings needed to repent and engage in self-sacrifice, such as enduring physical suffering and public humiliation. Happy endings were only experienced by the female characters that turned to religion for guidance and ascribed to more traditional gender roles.

These findings suggest important implications for Latina adolescent health. First, given their popularity, telenovelas should be used in sexual health interventions to initiate discussions about monogamy and sexual health with Latina adolescents. For example, these interventions should incorporate information about condoms, since it is likely that telenovelas will not mention them as a way to prevent STIs. Second, media literacy interventions could teach adolescent Latinas to critically interpret portrayals of infidelity, gender roles, and sexuality. In combination with comprehensive sexuality education, such media literacy interventions can empower Latina adolescents to become advocates for their own sexual health while teaching them the skills to become critical consumers of mass-media content. Finally, parents or other adults may also use telenovelas as a starting point from which to initiate discussion about the depiction of sexual health issues and how they coincide with their own family's values.

References

Alvarez Nobell, Alejandro (2011). *Measurement and Evaluation in Communication* (in Spanish). Malaga: Institute for Research in Public Relations (IIRP).

Bessette, G. (2004). *Involving the Community: A Guide to Participatory Development Communication.* Penang: Southbound/IDRC.

Bhambra, G. K. (2007). *Rethinking Modernity. Postcolonialism and the Sociological Imagination.* London: Palgrave Macmillan.

Chambers, R. (2005). *Ideas for Development.* London: Earthscan.

——— (2008). *Revolutions in Development Inquiry.* London: Earthscan.

Elliot J. (1994). *An Introduction to Sustainable Development*. London: Routledge.

Escobar, A. (2008). *Territories of Difference: Place, Movements, Life, Redes*. Durham: Duke University Press.

Fals Borda, O. (1991). *Knowledge and Social Movements*. Santa Cruz, CA: Merrill Publications.

Flint, W. (2007), *Sustainability Manifesto. Exploring Sustainability: Getting Inside the Concept.* Retrieved on December 17, 2011 *from http://www.eeeee.net/sd_manifesto.htm.*

Foucault, M. (1982). The Subject and Power. *Critical Inquiry*, 8 (4), 777–795.

Gurstein, M. (Feb. 23, 2011). Egypt: From the Iron Rule of Tyranny to the Iron Law of Oligarchy: Can ICT Change the Rules? *Gurstein's Community Informatics. Retrieved on March 2, 2011 from http://gurstein.wordpress.com/2011/02/23/applying-the-ict-lessons-of-revolt-to-the-institutional-challengesof-reconstruction-they-overthrew-hosni-mubarek-now-can-they-overthrow-robert-michels/.*

Jacoby, Susan (2009). *The Age of American unreason*. New York: Vintage Books.

Kennedy, T. (2008). *Where the Rivers meet the Sky: A Collaborative Approach to Participatory Development*. Penang: Southbound.

Lele, S. (1991). Sustainable Development: A Critical Review. *World Development*. 19 (6), 607–621.

Lennie, June & Tacchi, Jo (2010). *Evaluating Communication for Development: Trends, Challenges and Approaches*. Draft report on a literature review and consultations conducted for the project: UN Inter-agency Research, Monitoring and Evaluation Resource Pack for Communication for Development Programs, New York: UNICEF, December 3.

Max-Neef, Manfred (1991). *Human Scale Development: Conception, Application and Further Reflections*. New York: The Apex Press.

Nagy-Zekmi, Silvia & Hollis Karyn (eds.) (2012). *Global Academe: Engaging Intellectual Discourse*. New York: Palgrave Macmillan.

NASA (2012). NASA Finds 2011 Ninth-Warmest Year on Record. Retrieved on January 25, 2012 from http://www.nasa.gov/topics/earth/features/2011-temps.html, January 19.

Servaes, Jan (1999). *Communication for Development: One World, Multiple Cultures*. Cresskill, NJ: Hampton Press.

——— (ed.) (2007). Communication for Development: Making a Difference – a WCCD Background Study, in *World Congress on Communication for Development: Lessons, Challenges and the Way Forward*. Washington, DC: World Bank, 209–292 (ISBN 0-8213-7137-4).

——— (ed.) (2008). *Communication for Development and Social Change*. Los Angeles; London; New Delhi; Singapore: Sage (ISBN 9780761936091).

——— (2011) Social Change, *Oxford Bibliographies Online* (OBO). New York: Oxford University Press, pp. 58. Retrieved on January 25, 2012 from http://www.oxfordbibliographiesonline.com/display/id/obo-9780199756841-0063

Servaes, Jan & Malikhao, Patchanee (2007a). Communication and Sustainable Development, FAO, Communication and Sustainable Development: Selected Papers. Rome: FAO, pp. 1–38 (ISBN 978-92-5-105883-1).

——— (2007b). Communication and Sustainable Development, J. Servaes & S. Liu (eds.), *Moving Targets. Mapping the Paths between Communication, Technology and Social Change in Communities*. Penang: Southbound, pp. 11–42.

Servaes, Jan, Polk, Emily, Song Shi, Reilly, Danielle, & Yakupitijage, Thanu (2012a). Sustainability Testing for Development Projects, *Development in Practice*, Oxfam-Routledge, 22 (1) (February), pp. 18–30. Retrieved on February 15, 2012 from http://www.developmentinpractice.org/

—––––– (2012b), Towards a Framework of Sustainability Indicators for 'Communication for Development and Social Change' Projects, *The International Communication Gazette*. 74 (2), 99–123.

Taylor, Lance (1996). Sustainable Development: An introduction. *World Development*, 24 (2), 215–225.

Tran, Mark (2012), Put Planet and Its People at the Core of Sustainable Development, Urges Report. *The Guardian*, January 30. Retrieved on January 30, 2012 from http://www.guardian.co.uk/global-development/2012/ jan/30/planet-people-sustainable-development-report.

United Nations Environment Programme (UNEP) (2012). *Global Environmental Outlook GEO5: Environment for the Future We Want*. New York: United Nations Environment Programme.

United Nations Secretary-General's High-level Panel on Global Sustainability (2012). Resilient People, Resilient Planet: A Future Worth Choosing, New York: United Nations (eISBN: 978-92-1-055304-9).

UN News Centre (2011). World Must Welcome 7 Billionth Citizen with Sustainable Future, Says Ban. October 11. Retrieved on October 25, 2011 from http://www.un.org/apps/news/story.asp?NewsID=40011&Cr=sustainable+development&Cr1=.

—––––– (2012). The High-level Panel on Global Sustainability presents its report to the Secretary-General on 30 January 2012 in Addis Ababa. Retrieved on January 30, 2012 from http://www.un.org/gsp/report.

Whaley, Denise, Weaver, Liz, and Born, Paul (2010). *Approaches to Measuring: Community Change Indicators*. Waterloo, ON: Tamarack. www.tamarackcommunity.ca.

World Commission on Environment and Development (1987). *Our Common Future*. Published as Annex to General Assembly document A/42/427, Development and International Co-operation: Environment. New York: United Nations.

World Economic Forum (2012). *Global Risks 2012* (7th edition). An Initiative of the Risk Response Network. Geneva: WEF.

Chapter 2

Powerful Beyond Measure? Measuring Complex Systemic Change in Collaborative Settings

Adinda Van Hemelrijck

Introduction

Over the past two decades, there has been considerable debate regarding the effectiveness of aid and its contributions to development. The demand for rigorous performance and impact measurement for making evidence-based arguments has increased significantly. As a result, the debate has revivified the old paradigm war over methods (Patton, 2008:420–421). Recognizing the depth and importance of the methodological debate, perhaps it would be more apposite and fruitful to move beyond the dispute and make better use of all worldviews in an integrated, flexible, and responsive manner. A comprehensive approach is needed for addressing the aid effectiveness challenge: one that produces different kinds of evidence over a longer period of time, sheds light on the development issues from different perspectives, and builds arguments that can convince development actors to commit to their respective roles more responsibly (Fowler, 2007, 2008; Guba & Lincoln, 1989; Khagram et al., 2009; Mertens, 2009; Patton, 2008, Servaes, 2007).

In this chapter,[1] I argue that in order to provoke the right conversations among key players in the development process about what works, what doesn't, why, and what are plausible alternatives; the data must be meaningful, useful, and respond to their information and learning needs. In other words, the approach should be primarily focused on evidence-based learning. At Oxfam America, this proposition led to a rights-based and systems-thinking approach to impact measurement and learning, based on the understanding that fighting poverty and injustice calls for fundamental systemic changes. To measure these changes, a methodological fusion is required to capture the attendant complexities and present them in a way that can meet and influence stakeholders' different worldviews. This is where communication for sustainable social change and development (CSSC&D) comes into play: it provides a conceptual and methodological framework for encouraging stakeholders to engage meaningfully in the development process from their own perspectives, and to be accountable to learn and act upon, or behave in accordance with, what they have learned in dialogue and collaboration with others.

This chapter explores Oxfam America's approach to program design and impact measurement and learning from a CSSC&D perspective, which in essence is about the means and ends of empowerment. Impact measurement can be both meaningful and feasible; this chapter attempts to unpack the key aspects that define its success, and elaborates briefly on the methodological implications from a culture and sustainability perspective. The approach is illustrated with a practical example: Oxfam America's program on smallholders' productive water rights in Ethiopia. By comparing theory with practice, underlying principles and assumptions are revealed and important challenges identified. Hopefully this will foster a dialogue between academics and professionals that can help Oxfam and other international agencies find more sophisticated and knowledge-based answers.

A rights-based and systemic approach to development

Context and background

At the end of the twentieth century, more than 50 percent of the six billion people on earth earned less than $2 a day, 30 percent less than $1 a day. The statistics triggered a worldwide debate over the effectiveness of aid: it didn't seem to work as expected, didn't reach the poor, and turned out to carry many negative side effects (François et al., 2006).

In the post-Soviet international environment, a more persistent call emerged for broader democracy, good governance, ownership and partnership, donor coordination, demand-driven aid, and a greater focus on human development.[2] In the 1990s, a new development paradigm and a new system of global governance based on international law began to emerge. While in the 1970s and 1980s, the focus was predominantly on technological modernization, economic growth,[3] and structural adjustment[4] – with the interdependency[5] and basic needs[6] approaches as alternative critiques – poverty reduction, sustainable development, and human rights now rose to the top of the international development agenda (Coolsaet, 2006; Develtere, 2005; Fowler, 2003; Robb, 2004).

The essential beliefs or assumptions underlying this new paradigm or model were that:

(a) States and markets are each other's necessary complements, and well-functioning institutions are necessary for sustainable growth and development[7] (Bourguignon, 2004; Roche, 2012; Wallace et al., 2007).

(b) Economies grow and develop best and more sustainably[8] when all people equally participate in, benefit from, and take responsibility for growth (Edwards, 2011; Edwards & Hulme, 1992; Rowlands & Eade, 2003).

(c) Poverty is more than simply insufficient income, but is also the inability to choose, attain, and sustain a decent living standard. Poverty is complex and systemic, caused by multilevel and multidimensional exclusion and marginalization (Green, 2008; Kakwani & Silber, 2007; Kanbur & Lustig, 2001; Sen, 1999).

(d) All people are responsible citizens who have the right to development that includes dignity, well-being, equality, freedom, and self-determination. People have fundamental and universal human rights, which are codified in international laws and treaties and should be enshrined in moral and ethical norms that govern human societies

(Chambers, 2008a; Cornwall, 2004; Green, 2008; Kakwani & Silber, 2007; Kanbur & Lustig, 2001; Sen, 1999; Toye, 2011).

(e) Poor individuals, families, households, and communities are meant not just to benefit from but also to be enabled by development to live and act as responsible and dignified citizens (Gaventa, 2002; Green, 2008; Johnson, 2003; Offenheiser & Holcombe, 2003).

(f) Understanding the local sociocultural and political-economic context is imperative for effectively and sustainably addressing the key determinants of poverty (Chambers, 2008a, 2009, 2011a, 2011b; Groves & Hinton, 2004; Wallace et al., 2007; Woolcock, 2009).

(g) Local realities are influenced and shaped by wider and global systems, though local dynamics also influence the broader systems. Development is shaped by trends and processes occurring at multiple interacting levels, manipulated by global policies (Jupp et al., 2010; Mayoux, 2007; Mayoux & Chambers, 2005).

Based on these assumptions, it is argued that sustainable and human development should entail a wide variety of strategies that focus simultaneously on the equal distribution of economic growth and opportunities, on gender justice and human rights, environmental protection, strengthening local institutions, and democratic governance and market inclusion at multiple levels. This requires new types of partnerships (including private-public) and the active engagement of multiple legitimate stakeholders who weigh the objectives and observe the relationships from different perspectives (Green, 2008; Khagram et al., 2009). Those who are living in poverty should be viewed as the primary constituents, and the primary agents, of development. The focus of aid should be on creating opportunities, expanding choices, and enlarging freedoms through building capacities, rather than increasing income through economic growth and providing services in response to poor people's basic needs (Chambers, 2009, 2011b; Lucas & Longhurst, 2010; Roche, 2012). Interventions should be designed based on sound multidisciplinary and context-specific analyses, recognizing the crucial role of local culture, networks, and institutions to cope with market failures, and mobilizing communities as the primary stakeholders[9] of development. Therefore, interventions need to be better aligned and selectively more tuned to the objectives of their primary stakeholders and constituents (Chambers, 2008a; Edwards, 2011; Green, 2008; Kanbur & Lustig, 2001; Sen, 1999).

In today's neoliberal context and after nearly five years of triple crisis (e.g., food, energy, and financial), it appears as if the new concept and paradigm of development is interminably in flux. While poverty continues growing, development issues such as growth, well-being, rights, and equality are becoming more complex. Local and global perspectives are making room for multidimensional, multilevel, and multiscalar systems-thinking approaches that build on a more dynamic and complex interrelational view of poverty and related development issues. This trend challenges traditional ways of measuring and explaining aid and development. Alternative approaches to impact measurement and learning are needed that can help key stakeholders better understand what it means to engage in development in a world characterized by multiple crises and power shifts culminating in higher degrees of uncertainty and unpredictability (Bawden, 2010; Chambers, 2011a, 2011b; Groves & Hinton, 2004; Khagram et al., 2009).

Development as rights and empowerment

By enforcing the application of the rights principles enshrined in international agreements, conventions, and laws, sustainable and human development practice became increasingly more rights-oriented (Cornwall & Nyamu-Musembi, 2005; Fowler, 2003; Johnson, 2003; Servaes, 2005; Uvin, 2004).

The rights-based approach to development generally builds on the belief that poverty and injustice have to be considered essentially as rights issues that are convoluted by the multilevel nature of rights violations and moral obligations. The problems people face are not the "natural" human conditions; they are the consequences of complex sociopolitical relationships, structures, and local-to-global market mechanisms that sustain and (re) generate inequality and injustice. This cannot be fixed by short-term interventions or the scaling-up of technical solutions. The symptoms can be fought temporarily (as famine is by food aid, or the lack of water by digging wells), but its root causes require more fundamental and sustainable systemic changes (Cornwall, 2004; Fowler, 2008; Green, 2008).

From a rights perspective, development is the process whereby people become increasingly aware of their rights, learn from their own and others' experiences, appreciate the global processes of change engulfing them, grow in their ability to adapt and cope with change, face challenges with dignity and perseverance, learn how to harness opportunities in a respectful and sustainable manner, and acquire the ability to access and influence institutions to claim their rights, and hold development actors accountable. Development can therefore be understood as freedom or empowerment: the ability of people to influence the wider system and take control of their own lives (Annan, 2005; Fowler, 2003; Khan, 2004; LEAD, 2008; United Nations, 2003, 2004; Van Hemelrijck, 2009).

The human rights approach adds an ethical and moral dimension to development based on human dignity. It presents a powerful proposition for applying an expanded, more relational notion of accountability, building on the principle that all development actors have the duty to respect and protect the individual and collective rights of legitimate rights-holders, who are equally obligated to conform to law and respect others' rights. Backed by international law, a strong legal-normative basis is provided for poor people to make claims on their development status, and hold to account duty-bearers such as state governments, private sector, civil society, and other development actors (including Oxfam) for enhancing their rights. This can be challenging when complex power dynamics are at play and people are threatened and have limited or no access to adequate legal services and other local institutions to protect them. Broader support from within and outside their societies is needed to demand accountability and justice: local and global citizens, public leaders, media, and other societal and international actors have the moral obligation to demand fairness, equality, democratic governance, and respect for human rights. They, too, are part of the rights and relational accountability framework (Eyben, 2008; Gready, 2008; Green, 2008; Nyamu-Musembi, 2005; Offenheiser & Holcombe, 2003).

Communication for development in Oxfam's rights-based programs

From a rights perspective, participation is seen as more than just an instrument for effective grassroots intervention. It is concerned with "who is in control" and is meant to broaden people's power and influence in the priority-setting, creation, and analysis of systemic solutions. Grassroots-level participation[10] can be scaled and people's influence broadened through social mobilization,[11] coalition-building,[12] and advocacy.[13] In this rights-based approach, multiple spaces are created for poor people to meaningfully engage by applying communication strategies and methodologies that are commonly delineated as CSSC&D. This field of work is generally defined as a well-planned, evidence-based, long-term, and participatory process that seeks to empower poor people to shape their own lives, culture, and development; influence attitudes and opinions among citizens; and promote democratization and participation at local, national, and global levels (Bakewell et al., 2005; Gaventa, 2006; Gaventa & Cornwall, 2006; Hickey & Mohan, 2004; McKee & Aghi, 2000; Puddephatt et al., 2009).

Using such a rights and empowerment perspective, Oxfam America has developed a programming approach that is similar to CSSC&D. Different, however, from more standard models is its purposeful design to deliver impact that is defined and measured as "empowerment" in the sense of (LEAD, 2008; Van Hemelrijck, 2009, 2010):

a significant and sustainable change in power relations that enables excluded and marginalized people to realize their rights to access and manage the resources, services and knowledge they need for strengthening their livelihoods, improving their well-being, and influencing and holding accountable the institutions that affect their lives.

Only long-term collaborative efforts persistently focused on a specific rights issue and simultaneously working at grassroots, civil society, and various governance levels can hope to realize such impact. This is why Oxfam America and its partners develop ten–fifteen years programs that build upon a sophisticated knowledge of the local context and drive on a broader coalition for deploying strategic interventions synergistically geared to achieve a common impact goal. These interventions typically include grassroots community mobilization, market inclusion and private sector engagement, movement building, policy and advocacy work, and rights monitoring and impact research.

This is very similar to what is defined as "collective impact" (Kania & Kramer, 2011:39): "long-term commitments by a group of important actors from different sectors to a common agenda for solving a specific social problem." The opposite is described as "isolated impact" (Ibid:38): "an approach oriented toward finding and funding a solution embodied within a single organization, combined with the hope that the most effective organizations will grow and replicate to extend their impact more widely." Collective impact requires more than ad hoc or voluntary collaboration (such as in networks and multistakeholder initiatives), or a narrow contractual or technical partnership (such as in traditional service provision and grants of construction project). Furthermore, it requires "a systemic approach to social impact that focuses on the relationships between organizations and the progress toward shared objectives" (Ibid:38). Contrasting with the more donor-driven "isolated impact" approach that seeks "to isolate that grantee's individual influence from all other variables" (Ibid:38) in order to demonstrate attribution, it is further argued that collective impact initiatives require shared impact measurement and learning systems for effectively generating and demonstrating greater impact collectively realized (Blewden, 2010; Chambers et al., 2009; Kania & Kramer, 2011).

Impact measurement and learning in Oxfam America's rights-based programs

In Oxfam America's program approach, rights and empowerment can only be realized through collaborative commitments that are long term, persistently focused on a collective impact goal, apply a systemic approach, and build a shared impact measurement and learning system. This section will elaborate on how Oxfam America has conceptualized impact measurement and learning in its rights-based programs by trying to address the following questions:

How can we scale up grassroots participation, broaden people's influence, and build coalitions for attaining larger and wider impacts without causing a loss of focus, intent, rigor, legitimacy, and validity? How can we possibly measure these impacts, and learn about the thorny rights and power issues that are dependent on so many conditions and behaviors of individuals and institutions, beyond any single actor's control? How can we measure its impacts in ways that reinforce poor people's empowerment, and help partners and key stakeholders understand more about the process by which systemic change occurs, its likelihood of occurring, and their collective contributions?

Understanding and measuring empowerment

In Oxfam America's programs, impact is defined and measured as both the ends and the means of empowerment. Drawing upon critical-realist theory, interpretivism, constructivism, gender studies, and rights-based theory, empowerment in terms of its "means" is understood as an ongoing and combined process of (a) expanding poor people's individual and collective agency, (b) changing their social institutions, and (c) reconfiguring the broader societal relationships (Mosendale, 2005; Van Hemelrijck, 2009). From an evaluative perspective it implies looking at changes in the behavior of the key change agents and their interactions and relationships that are shaping the system:

(a) *Agency* (individual and collective) refers to people's capabilities or power to act consciously and purposefully: their ability to analyze their lives and relationships, understand the wider system, make conscious decisions to change things, purposefully make choices, define and claim their values and goals, and consequently act upon these. It implies a self-directed process that encompasses identity, knowledge, motivation, capacities, and resources needed to realize and sustain one's development and well-being. It builds on people's beliefs and sense of dignity, and is shaped through social interaction (Gaventa & Cornwall, 2006; Hickey, 2009; Huesca, 2008; Kabeer, 1999; Krznaric, 2007; Rosengren, 2000).

(b) *Institutions* (formal and informal) are the norms, values, laws, rules, regulations, conventions, routines, and structures that shape people's status, attitudes, and beliefs, their roles and their participation in decisions. Institutions form the basic interpretative and regulatory frameworks for human behavior, and strongly affect whether and to what extent people have access to resources, knowledge, and services, and can use them to exercise agency and assert their rights. Institutions are not static, but evolve constantly as they are contested and adapted through social interaction processes (Bastiaensen et al., 2002; Brinkerhoff, 2005; Huesca, 2008; Rosengren, 2000).

(c) *Societal relationships* encompass the many ways in which different social actors expand (or limit) their reach and influence through complex webs of social networks, professional associations, nongovernmental organizations and independent media (together called *civil society*). They form the intermediaries through which power can be contested or expanded and new spaces for participation can be created. Through these societal relationships, poor women and men can acquire power and access the institutions for negotiating their interests and asserting their rights (Bastiaensen et al., 2002; Huesca, 2008; Kabeer, 2005; Krznaric, 2007; Rosengren, 2000).

People's agency builds from the social and cultural construction of their individual and collective identities and the shared norms and values about what is wrong or right. Through social interaction, people construct new interpretations of reality, create new patterns of behavior, and discover new choices and solutions that better serve their individual and collective needs and interests. However, the favored and the marginalized have different views of the issues that need to be addressed, the forces that cause the problems, and the solutions that must be pursued. The dominant (including development) discourses in society tend to maintain the status quo and favor those already in power. Changing societal relationships, therefore, is about changing the way these dominant discourses are shaped and contested, and thus how different social actors communicate and relate to one another; and how poor individuals and groups can activate social networks, build alliances and movements, and influence powerful elites (Eyben et al., 2006; Foucault & Rabinow, 1984; Gaventa, 2006; Huesca, 2008; Kabeer, 2005; Rosengren, 2000).

In terms of its ends, empowerment can be understood as the expansion of an individual's or group's ability to make transformative life choices where this ability was previously curtailed. Greater freedom, equality, and self-determination result from combined changes in agency, institutions, and societal relationships (Alsop & Heinsohn, 2005; Narayan-Parker, 2002, 2005; Rosengren, 2000; Sen, 1999). From an evaluative perspective, this implies looking at new patterns of social, societal, and institutional behavior and interaction that create new and equal opportunities for poor women and men (i.e., systems change), and the extent to which poor women and men effectively are seizing these new opportunities (i.e., impacts on poor people's lives).

Complex systems-thinking in impact measurement and learning

Complex systems-thinking generally refers to a more holistic approach as compared to a rather reductionist linear-thinking approach. It tends to be more comprehensive, dynamic, and inclusive in its analysis of social change and development processes by taking into account the complexity of the multiple interacting parts, angles, and variables that has often unpredictable outcomes. Phenomena and patterns of interactions and behaviors are emergent from "tensions of difference" inherent to the system they are part of. Systemic change is caused by the synergistic interplays between its parts, created by these tensions. A system therefore can never be merely the sum of its parts, and consequently its parts can never be understood apart from the system (Bawden, 2010; Chambers, 2008b; Flood, 2006; Hawe et al., 2009; Midgley, 2007).

Complex systems-thinking in rights-oriented impact measurement implies a serious attempt to capture the full complexity of the rights and empowerment issues under concern. In Oxfam America's programs, changes in agency, institutions, and societal relationships are measured to help partners and stakeholders understand the system's dynamics and discover new patterns that can help them shape systemic solutions. The assumption is that persistent collaborative efforts are needed for realizing systemic change, for which collective learning is essential (Aragón & Giles Macedo, 2010; Guijt, 2008a, 2008b; Kania & Kramer, 2011; Williams & Imam, 2007). The purpose of impact measurement is, therefore, primarily to serve and strengthen these collaborative efforts (rather than donor interests) and empower poor people to hold partners and stakeholders accountable to help realize their rights (Eijkemans & Das, 2009; Guijt et al., n.d.; Hawe et al., 2009; Van Ongevalle et al., 2012). This highlights the importance of robust impact measurement and learning systems, which can:

(a) reveal the complex systemic changes or emergent patterns of interaction and behavior at different levels and at different moments in time, and make them understandable (without fragmenting or overly simplifying things);

(b) proactively produce convincing arguments showing partners and key stakeholders that they are part and thus can influence the system, and that together they are more likely to do so and achieve their goals;

(c) create the appropriate spaces at various levels for ongoing constituency feedback and dialogue between key stakeholders, through which collaborative learning can occur, and new options for alternative action and behavior can be developed;

(d) thwart a digression into a classical broad sector approach, and keep partners and key stakeholders sharply focused on a particular impact goal and the diverse, mostly cross-sectoral leverage points crucial to arrive at this goal;

(e) deal with the unpredictability of changing contexts, changing alliances, unstable partnerships, and transforming power configurations due to shifting interests and influence of stakeholders;

(f) remain simple, flexible and cost-effective enough to last for many years.

Oxfam America's programs incorporate shared impact measurement and learning systems designed to produce evidence of systemic change toward achieving its collective impact goals over the longer term. Rather than trying to attribute results to a single intervention, these systems attempt to build the case for plausible contributions and promote dialogue among key stakeholders and partners about the dynamics leading to the desired systemic changes (LEAD, 2008). Two elements are critical for this (Aragón & Giles Macedo, 2010; Keystone Accountability, n.d.-a; Nitipaisalkul, 2007; Oswald & Taylor, 2010; Woolcock, 2009):

1. Making the program's change hypothesis or Theory of Change explicit in a way that helps partners and stakeholders understand the complex systemic changes presumably needed for realizing the aspired impact goal and get to know its underlying assumptions; and

2. Directing impact measurement toward collaborative and evidence-based learning *against* the Theory of Change.

Theory of change

In mainstream development practice, a Theory of Change is often used as the summary of a program's or project's intervention logic (mostly identical to the Logical Framework method) that starts from what the organization does or wants to do, identifies the results that may come out of this, and uses evaluation to learn whether the actions are leading to the expected results. Such an approach tends to be unaware of its underlying assumptions and blind to developments outside the intervention logic. This makes it difficult to discover and explain unpredictable, nonlogical systemic changes, and to remain open to viable alternatives for action (ActKnowledge & The Aspen Institute, 2003; Davies, 2005; Eyben, 2012; Funnell & Rogers, 2011; Jacobs et al., 2010; James, 2012; Keystone Accountability, n.d.-b).

In Oxfam America's approach, a Theory of Change takes the collective impact goal as its starting point, and visualizes a plausible pathway of systemic change that works backward from that goal. This helps partners and stakeholders gain a bird's-eye view of the changes needed in the system. It suggests, and makes explicit how partners and stakeholders believe change might happen. No actions are suggested or defined[14] – only the hypothetical changes anticipated at interrelated levels (local, intermediate, national, and regional or international). It serves as a working hypothesis that is regularly updated when new conditions and ways of interaction are emerging and influencing the system. The Theory of Change doesn't need to be perfect but good enough to make the complexity of systemic change and its dynamics comprehensible for partners and key stakeholders. This implies an emergent modeling through iterative reflection and learning, for helping participants explore or probe plausible hypotheses and understand the changes occurring in certain circumstances (Anderson, n.d.; Funnell & Rogers, 2011; Midgley, 2007:17; Williams & Hummelbrunner, 2010). The context, relationships, partner capacities, and program levels and conditions are different in every program area and time frame, but the Theory of Change should keep partners and key stakeholders focused on the program's impact goal and serve as the basis for ongoing dialogue about what constitutes systemic change and how to arrive at that.

Evidence-based learning

Evidence-based and collaborative learning against the Theory of Change is facilitated by connecting indicators to key points in the change model. There is no clear-cut, one-to-one relationship between indicators and aspired changes, since presumably they can only say something meaningful about systemic change if they are measured as a system. Variables perceived as relevant for measuring a particular indicator at one point in time may be inadequate or obsolete later, as a complex system's characteristics are expected to be constantly changing (Guijt, 2008b; Jupp et al., 2010; Midgley, 2007). The variables or questions for measuring the indicators have to be determined and regularly reviewed in close collaboration with the key stakeholders, through iterative impact research, monitoring, and reflection.

Iterative impact research helps partners and stakeholders discover changes in patterns of behavior and interaction, assess their own individual and collective contributions to these changes over time, and analyze the influence of trends and conditions in the broader context. Baseline and subsequent impact evaluations conducted every three to four years are complemented with more narrowed and specialized impact studies. These focused studies should examine the questions, causalities, or gaps in the Theory of Change that are most pertinent at particular moments, analyzing issues as open and embedded subsystems interacting and changing with their environments. Assessing these interactions helps partners and stakeholders better understand to what extent the systemic change is sustainable. Feedback from constituents is essential for ongoing monitoring of the aptness and effectiveness of stakeholders' or responsible actors' responses to sustainability issues occurring. The evidence collected over the program's lifetime must create a coherent and credible picture of the complex realities and changes in the system at large, as viewed and experienced by the different stakeholders. Therefore, the methodology must be rigorous and consistent, using mixed methods and creating space for equal participation (Funnell & Rogers, 2011; Jacobs et al., 2010; Keystone Accountability, n.d.-b; Mertens, 2009; Midgley, 2007).

Involving all key stakeholders – including poor people – in the process of selecting, validating, and making sense of the evidence produced on an annual basis, and reflecting critically on how and to what extent the achievements foment systemic change, is part of the process of ongoing change modeling and learning against the Theory of Change. Poor people's understanding of how the system can be influenced presumably will increase if they actively participate in these cognitive and critical reflection processes (Chambers, 2007, 2008b; Fowler, 2007; Freeman, 2010; Mayoux, 2007; Mayoux & Chambers, 2005).

Methodological implications from a culture and sustainability perspective

Impact baseline and evaluation, from a systems-thinking perspective, is an ongoing and adaptive challenge. It requires methodological innovation, thinking beyond the restraints of mainstream logical positivism, and making hard compromises rooted in a sophisticated understanding of the politics of knowledge in the development process. While rigorously evaluating and comparing changes over time and space, impact measurement must permit collaborative and iterative learning, integral participation, and inclusion in the analysis of progress/regress regarding systemic change (Eijkemans & Das, 2009; Freeman & Vasconcelos, 2010; Guijt et al., n.d.; Hawe et al., 2009). Methods are rigorous if they consistently generate valid and reliable data that speaks to the indicators and questions in the program's Theory of Change, modeled collaboratively with partners and key stakeholders (Funnell & Rogers, 2011; Khagram et al., 2009; Khagram & Thomas, 2010). This implies setting boundaries while dealing with its political vagaries, since "the business of setting boundaries defines both the knowledge to be considered pertinent and the people who generate that knowledge" (Midgley, 2007:21).

Boundary judgments are deeply normative, particularly when it comes to impact evaluation. The process of boundary setting tends to maintain the status quo by constraining the pursuit of values and views important to the less powerful in determining what knowledge is valid. Researchers communicate, create, and attribute value and meaning, and interact with the embedded power structure and thus take part in the system that is investigated (Midgley, 2007:15). The purpose of involving external researchers in impact measurement is, therefore, not so much to obtain objective evidence, than to provide a critical analysis of the observed state of play, and challenge partners and stakeholders on the value judgments made. Mertens (2009:72) argues that if such value judgments "exclude the views of the non-majority communities, then it serves to support the status quo and disallows challenges to power distributions. Hence, culturally unexamined constructions of validity can serve as collaborations of oppression and discrimination."

Researchers' own notion of validity is influenced by the biases and assumptions of their disciplinary specializations and methodological preferences.[15] Patten (2008:396–397) makes a distinction between overall evaluation validity and the more narrow conceptions of validity in scientific investigation and qualitative research. Evaluation validity includes both scientific *and* sociocultural methodological rigor and competences, and implies credibility and relevance of selected evaluation metrics, methods and data for the different stakeholders involved. His and others' conclusion is that researchers need to acknowledge and properly deal with all sorts of value judgments and power issues that pervade the decisions around the research design, which can be done by (Chen et al., 2011; Greene, 2011; Julnes, 2011; Mertens, 2009; Patton, 2008):

(a) critically analyzing and debating the power relations involved,
(b) critically reflecting on and making explicit one's own power and value judgments,
(c) extensively and rigorously triangulating data sources,
(d) embracing methodological pluralism, which implies a strategic use of mixed methods (quantitative and qualitative) that deals with assumptions and biases,
(e) facilitating inclusive design and validation of research findings and interpretations, and
(f) consciously creating equal space for primary stakeholders to participate.

Mixed methods are also needed for rigorously comparing data over time and in space, and must be inclusive of stakeholders' different views and perceptions, allowing for critical analysis, sociocultural critique, and dialogue between the stakeholders (Chambers, 2007, 2008b; Cornwall, 2002; Creswell & Clark, 2010; Freeman, 2010; Servaes, 2008; Woolcock, 2009). Appropriate sampling and extensive cross-checking of all data sources prevent selection bias, enhance inclusiveness, and stimulate the dialogue between different views and interpretations. What is measured, for what purposes, with what evidence, at what moment in time, must be negotiated and validated with all key stakeholders. In cases where a true and equal dialogue between key stakeholders is not possible, safe spaces must be created separately where poor people can speak out freely (Gaventa, 2006; Guba & Lincoln, 1989; Khagram et al., 2009; Mertens, 2009; Mertens et al., 2010; Patton, 2008).

The case of smallholders' productive water rights in Ethiopia

Context and background

Almost 90 percent of Ethiopia's population is rural: 87 percent are smallholders with less than two hectares of land. They are dependent on rainfall for crop production and cattle breeding, and are extremely vulnerable to recurrent and chronic drought, declining soil fertility, and unfair competition for natural resources. They have limited access to markets, financial institutions, and technical resources. There are almost no alternatives for employment in other sectors such as industry or services. Rapid population growth, acute environmental degradation and desertification, limited mobility, fluctuating agricultural markets, and the impact of climate change further exacerbate their situation. This has created a trend of increasing food insecurity and extreme poverty among rural Ethiopians in the past three decades (Davis et al., 2010; Gebreselassie, 2004; Regassa et al., 2010; TANGO International, 2010).

The official government appeal, released in February 2011 (Government of Ethiopia, UN Country Team in Ethiopia, & UN Office for the Coordination of Humanitarian Affairs, 2011), indicated that 2.8 million people require drought-related food aid, in addition to the 7.5 million chronically food-insecure people dependent on the government's Productive Safety Net assistance. Due to La Nina that hit merely south of the country, this number has increased up to 3.2 million by June 2011 and 4.5 million by the end of that year (Government of Ethiopia, UN Country Team in Ethiopia, & UN Office for the Coordination of Humanitarian Affairs, 2012). Every year billions of dollars from big donors like the EU and USAID are pumped into food aid and water rationing in response to drought and famine emergencies. As a result, three decades of continuous food aid has created an aid dependency syndrome, "one of the problems that hinder personal and collective motivations to challenge poverty and to find ways to get out of the prevailing despair situation" (Gebreselassie, 2004).

While water won't solve the whole problem, its lack is a key constraint to poverty reduction and food security in Ethiopia. Water can increase small farmers' and herders' productivity and income by 25 percent or more. In contrast, farmers with limited or no access to water are unable to reinvest in farm inputs, irrigation, and other technologies to cope with recurrent drought and other threats. They sell their livestock and timber, further contributing to soil erosion and reduced crop and livestock production. Moreover, the Ethiopian government can reallocate land that is not properly utilized by smallholders for productive purposes, redistributing it among communities and other investors (Federal Democratic Republic of Ethiopia (FDRE), 1997; TANGO International, 2010; Taye Assefa & Yamahbarawi tenat madrak (Ethiopia), 2008).

Despite the many efforts made in the past 10 years by the Ethiopian government and other development actors, the problems remain considerable. Ethiopia has abundant water resources, which are largely unexploited, yet water availability varies significantly across different parts of Ethiopia, and the diversity of agro-ecological conditions, ethnic identities, cultural institutions, and livelihood strategies makes it difficult to find one-size-fits-all solutions. The development of water resources for smallholder agriculture and cattle breeding must be firmly grounded in local contexts. This entails greater risks, higher costs, and greater unpredictability in the outcomes of those investments that are seeking massive replication at scale, which increase donors' and investors' reluctance to invest (Awulachew & International Water Management Institute, 2007; Emana et al., 2007; Oxfam, 2009; TANGO International, 2010).

The prevalent responses – massive food aid or scalable "silver-bullet" solutions – cannot solve the deeper problems. Fundamental systemic changes are required that can address smallholders' motivations and capacities, increase their equitable access, restore trust between communities, and advance the sustainable distribution and management of land and water. Scope for greater impact is provided by the Ethiopian government's new five-year Growth & Transformation Plan (GTP). The GTP focuses on increasing smallholders' productivity and food security through integrated and concerted efforts. High priority is given to the expansion of small-scale irrigation, watershed conservation, and the sustainable management of natural resources by smallholder communities, with due investments in the capacity-strengthening of farmers and pastoralists, and the development of appropriate government support structures at all levels, particularly locally (Federal Democratic Republic of Ethiopia (FDRE), 2010a, 2010b).

A flexible, evolving Theory of Change

Oxfam America and its partners have developed a long-term program that aims at enabling vulnerable rural communities in moisture-stressed areas in Tigray, Amhara, and Oromia Regional States to access, use, and manage productive water resources in an equitable and sustainable manner, in order to improve their food security and strengthen their rural livelihoods (Oxfam America, 2009).

The program strategy is development around a Theory of Change that was conceptualized through a series of bilateral negotiations, collective workshops, and consultation rounds with partners and key stakeholders in 2009–2010. The diagram below (see Figure 2.1), depicting the Theory of Change, shows the full complexity of the envisioned systemic changes (albeit without the differences in local culture, livelihood style, political economy, and hydro-ecology that determine the design and management of the water systems). The theory illustrated in the diagram builds on the core proposition of co-investment involving communities, NGOs, and government in the development of small-scale water systems, and visualizes the necessary institutional and regulatory changes needed at the local, regional, and federal levels. Improvements in smallholders' capacity, awareness, and organization, and the expansion of women's influence and leadership, presumably will lead to better governance of the water systems, increased productivity, better access to markets and services, and higher revenues. Allegedly, this will enable smallholders to reinvest in their water systems and cooperative business enterprises, which over time will create new opportunities for adapting and strengthening their livelihoods. If successful, this will produce a new rural landscape in which communities take greater charge of decisions involving water rights protected by law, women's water interests hold equal status with those of men, and smallholders gain greater confidence to start new businesses.

Gaps and assumptions in the Theory of Change were identified and discussed in a two-day, multistakeholder workshop in February 2010 in Addis Ababa. Because of its complexity

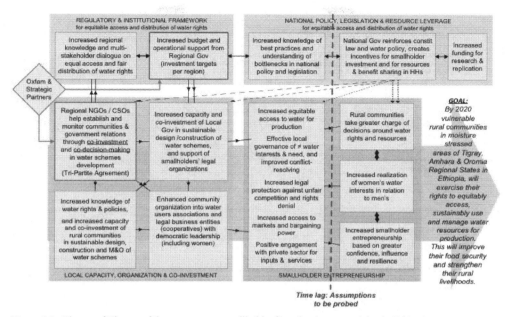

Figure 2.1: Theory of Change of the program on smallholders' productive water rights in Ethiopia.

and densely worded presentation, an alternative drawing had to be developed as a tool for helping the participants capture the complexity and further sculpt the Theory of Change. The illustration[16] below (see Figure 2.2) was created for this purpose. It shows the complexity and challenges of the program, the opportunities for change as well as the constraints, the gaps, and the cracks in the larger system. It provoked conversations around questions such as: "Why are there cracks in the pillars?" "What are the women and men doing at the top or foot of the pillars?" "How are these pillars connected – should they operate in silos or rather in collaboration?" "What elements should be tracked in order to know if the system is changing?"

Sixty-five people from the three regional states attended the workshop, which included women and men from the farmer and herder communities, local organizations and NGOs, government offices involved at the local, regional, and federal levels, research institutes, various Oxfam affiliates, and other international organizations. A special facilitation approach with iterative design called the Scan-Focus-Act model[17] was applied, and special methods were used for fostering authentic and equal dialogue. This was fairly new and unconventional for the Ethiopian context as its society tends to be quite hierarchical. Common practice in Ethiopian high-level workshops is long speeches and plenary discussions dominated by government officials, ministers, engineers, and scientists. The expert views of the urban technocratic and political elite about natural resource development and management can be significantly different though from the practical knowledge that farmers and herders

Figure 2.2: Tool for change modeling with key stakeholders.

hold. In this workshop, no speeches were delivered, and PowerPoint presentations, which tend to enlarge the distance between expert-presenter and participants, were abandoned. Everybody was encouraged to share knowledge and personal views, actively listen to each other, learn and appreciate the different perspectives, and discover common ground and shared commitment. The conversations were held mainly in three local languages (Oromo, Tigrinya, and Amharic) with occasional translations to English in plenary sessions. At the

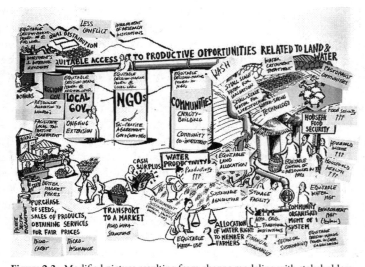

Figure 2.3: Modified picture resulting from change modeling with stakeholders.

end of the two days, impact indicators, mutual roles and responsibilities, and ways for moving forward were identified and agreed. The modified picture in Figure 2.3 was endorsed as the stakeholders' shared model for a Theory of Change, which will be used as the basis for developing local change models with the communities, reflecting local contexts and conditions in each of the water systems.

Measuring and reflecting on complex systemic change

Since there is no linear relationship between anticipated changes or aspired program outcomes and indicators – they interact and measure systemic change in a dynamic way – a programmatic impact baseline was established on a core set or system of thirteen indicators measuring the value proposition of coinvestment in the Theory of Change (Mapedza & Wichelns, 2010; TANGO International, 2010). Impact evaluation against the baseline three to four years later will reveal whether this proposition contributed to systemic change. Statistically random sampling and surveying did not work, given the complexity of the system and the high degree of variability across different localities and regions. Instead, case studies were conducted in three selected sites, with comparative case studies in each, in combination with institutional analysis and secondary data review. The primary research was implemented by a team of local anthropologists, led by a rural and urban planning scientist and coordinated by a senior principal economist, with support from several thematic advisors of the IWMI[18] (International Water Management Institute). Research findings were validated first by the communities through focus group discussions, and subsequently with all stakeholders and partners in a validation workshop held in Addis Ababa in June 2010.

Impact research and evaluation is complemented by an annual impact monitoring, reflection, and reporting cycle. On an annual basis, key stakeholders are invited to reconvene for making sense of the various data streams, reflecting on changes observed against the Theory of Change, and advising program partners on possible strategy adjustments. The first Annual Impact Reflection (AIR) was held in June 2011 in Shashemene (Oromia Regional State). The two-day workshop hosted 58 people from local stakeholders, of which nearly half were members of the communities from the various intervention locations across the region, and nearly 23 percent were women. The Scan-Focus-Act model[19] that was used for designing and facilitating the change modeling workshop in Addis Ababa the year before was also applied here but adapted to local cultural practice. A professional facilitator-consultant with local background was hired and formerly trained in this facilitation model. Prior to the workshop he conducted a field level assessment on the 2010 partner reports and perceptions of changes in the intervention area, and consulted with the various local stakeholders. He trained and guided four traditional Oromo Geda leaders (three men and one woman) to facilitate the workshop:

  – two "Abba Murtiis" (leaders) who facilitated the debates and discussions, endorsed decisions based on popular consensus, and summarized key points of agreement; and

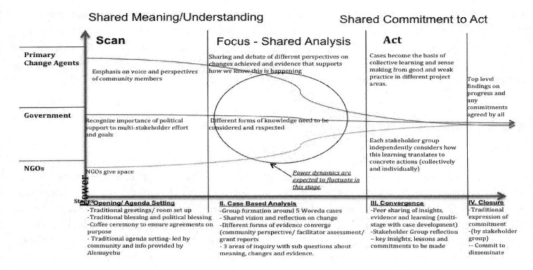

Figure 2.4: AIR workshop design.

– two "Qortuus" (opinion leaders) who acted as catalysts, instigated wider discussion, and ensured equal space for participation irrespective of age, sex, and status.

The first scanning stage of the workshop emphasized the voice and perspectives of the community members in this process by opening with a traditional cultural practice of news exchange in a dramatized way, e.g., news from the different locations about the local situations of peace, rainfall, livestock, and health within the communities and neighborhoods, followed by a traditional way of "agenda-setting" that is kicked off with the opening question "Maaliif akkana baanee?" meaning "why is this gathering organized?" The workshop was officially endorsed by a representative of the regional government and blessed by means of a traditional coffee ceremony.

What we have discovered

This last section presents the challenges Oxfam America faces with the impact measurement and learning system in its program in Ethiopia. Although every program and every sociocultural and sociohistorical context differs, this case is emblematic of what may be encountered in Oxfam America's nine other long-term programs around the world. The challenges are inherent to a new systems-thinking approach to rights-oriented impact measurement and learning.

Creating spaces for meaningful participation in impact measurement and learning

A rights-based approach seeks to enlarge people's scope and potential influence; it pushes participation and empowerment far beyond the narrow decisions and actions of grassroots interventions. Participation must, therefore, be relevant to the reality in which people are living, while encouraging them to think beyond their own context – to imagine a different view of both past and future. It implies using methods that are culturally sensitive and can meet people's worldviews yet can facilitate a sociocultural and sociohistorical critique of power (Chambers & Pettit, 2004; Eyben et al., 2006; Freire, 1974; Gaventa & Cornwall, 2006; Gledhill, 2009, Parks, 2005).

The challenge is to create spaces where people can truly shape and voice their opinions and negotiate their terms of engagement, beyond condescending tokenism. This calls for explicit strategies that structure various levels and spaces of collaborative learning, systematically collect people's feedback, and consciously include the voices of those with less power. Guijt (2008:23) identifies three levels of learning – farmer group level, organizational, and societal learning – that largely coincide with the three "means" of empowerment – changes in agency, institutions, and societal relationships. Oxfam America attempts to formalize such strategies for meaningfully engaging communities, civil society, and other powerful actors in a process of collaborative learning against a shared Theory of Change, through the annual impact measurement and reflection cycle. This involves facilitating processes in which poor or disadvantaged people themselves can construct their own physical and imagined spaces for meaningful engagement, shifting the way actors communicate and interact, and thus changing the dominant discourses that shape how people view themselves in relation to others.

The caveat is that the process can easily turn into a mechanistic token exercise, in which stakeholders reach collaborative agreements without taking concrete responsibility for addressing fundamental inequalities. In Ethiopia, there are many community gatherings, consultations, and multistakeholder workshops. People tend to be very vocal concerning the issues; they are aware of what is happening around them, and understand how localized politics serve central power. But an empowering approach encouraging them to question the status quo and call for collective action remains largely inapt as a strategy in current rural Ethiopia. Community gatherings must be officially authorized, law[20] restricts spontaneous social-political mobilization, and people's memory of a violent past, combined with three decades of food aid, has undermined their resilience and confidence. It is widely understood that fundamental change stems from motivation, trust, sense of responsibility, and active citizenship. Despite the government's efforts to create stability, build capacities, and strengthen its structures for dealing with the multiple problems in rural areas, real change though must grow in people's hearts and minds (Cornwall, 2002; Gaventa, 2002; Gaventa & Cornwall, 2006; Green, 2008; Guijt, 2008a).

The long-term measurement and learning systems in Oxfam America's programs attempt to address this challenge. But how do we really know that these systems contribute to empowerment, particularly where an empowering strategy seems inappropriate? And what competencies are needed to manage the complex multilevel and multistakeholder learning processes and understand the methodologies involved?

Managing diverse and unstable relationships

A program's stakeholders and partners typically have varying interests, information needs, status and influence, capacities, learning abilities, communication styles, and diverging perceptions of and allegiances to a program's collective impact goal. A few of these actors are homogeneous or stable entities in themselves (Eyben, 2008; Funnell & Rogers, 2011; Guijt, 2008a; Hadad et al., 2010; Kania & Kramer, 2011).

These different relationships and engagements cannot be regulated and controlled in a standard contractual manner; they must be enabled in a way that allows for redefining the power balance. In Ethiopia, the program's impact measurement system is managed by a program governance group composed of a steering committee and four working groups (co-learning, co-strategizing, shared accountability, and co-funding). Partner directors constitute the steering committee, which is tasked with the overall strategic management of the program, using the products emerging from impact measurement and learning. Partners' managers and experts drive the working groups, and along with stakeholders, are expected to develop a strategy for their thematic area and to monitor its implementation. A major challenge for Oxfam America and its partners is managing the fluid relationships involved in a flexible and strategic manner. This requires competencies beyond those most program managers are trained in: they must also understand how to mediate differences, negotiate priorities, and clarify roles and responsibilities without formalized agreements. Program managers must know who to negotiate within groups without clear forms of leadership and commitment. They also must understand organizational change and exchange processes, and deal with resistance and drawbacks in a tactical manner (Aragón, 2010; Fisher, 2010; Guijt, 2008a; Herasymowych et al., 2007; Patton, 2008; Roper et al., 2003).

Dealing with managers' and donors' anxiety over complexity and uncertainty

The complexity of systemic change and the focus on less tangible more interactive and behavioral aspects of water resource management makes it difficult to discern the causal relationships and impacts of particular interventions. As a result, among the challenges we face in Ethiopia is whether the key players will remain dedicated over time to the systemic changes that are hard to measure, and whether sufficient funding can be secured for elements of the program with indirect and muddled outcomes.

The long-term and systems-thinking perspective makes most policy makers, fundraisers, and donors uneasy. They often must deal with decision-making deadlines that are tied to restricted administrative, budgetary, and fiscal timeframes. Despite the widespread acknowledgment of the need for longer term more systemic and collective impact approaches focusing on root causes, a few donors, foundations, or social investors are willing to support impact measurement and learning efforts that cannot quickly show clear attributable results (Edwards, 2011; Eijkemans & Das, 2009; Gready, 2009; Kania & Kramer, 2011; Watson, 2006).

In their daily routine, local program managers prefer approaches that simplify their requirements and challenges; they don't like fuzzy relationships and uncertain outcomes. Although Oxfam's approach attempts to confine complexity and uncertainty by using a Theory of Change, the methodology remains counterintuitive to most development practitioners. Committed to achieving predetermined targets, they are tempted to adhere to approaches that can prove unambiguous success. This forms a particular challenge in Ethiopia, where staff and managers are incessantly approached by social entrepreneurs and philanthropies eager to test and scale new ideas.

Summary and a way forward

From a rights perspective, sustainable development is a normative, nonlinear, and rather complex process requiring systemic changes with multiple stakeholder engagements at multiple levels. It is bound to a concept of empowerment that demands accountability to the poor for achieving sustainable change, and requires poor people's participation in the development process. CSSC&D provides a conceptual and methodological framework for encouraging people to engage meaningfully, enlarge their power and influence, and create an institutional environment that enables them to assert their rights. Oxfam America and its partners develop long-term programs that apply a systemic approach using CSSC&D and focus on achieving a collective impact goal defined and measured as empowerment.

Earlier in this chapter, we posed three tough questions regarding the advancement of such a rights-based collective impact approach:

1. How can we scale grassroots participation, broaden influence, and build coalitions without causing a loss of focus, intent, rigor, legitimacy, and validity?
2. How can we measure the impacts and learn about thorny rights and power issues that are beyond any single actor's control?
3. How can we measure impacts in a way that reinforce poor peoples' empowerment and help key stakeholders understand more about the process by which systemic change occurs?

Impact measurement must support the partners' and stakeholders' joint commitment to realizing a collective impact goal by using a methodological approach that helps them comprehend the system's complexity and their contributions to systemic change. Evidence is, therefore, collected on indicators, questions, and knowledge gaps pertaining to a collectively developed Theory of Change that reflects a plausible pathway for systemic change. Produced over time, this evidence creates a coherent and credible picture of the complex realities and changes in the system as viewed and experienced by the different stakeholders. The methodology must be rigorous and consistent, using mixed methods and creating space for equal participation (Servaes & Frissen, 1997). It should enable people themselves to rediscover, redefine, and reconstruct their views of the world, themselves in relation to others, the changes that are required, and the ways these changes can be assessed. If this impact measurement and learning approach succeeds in shaping and scaling public debate about power distribution and people's rights, then this presumably prepares the ground for sustainable systemic change resulting in greater freedoms and equality. Sustainability is furthered by evidence-based social, societal, and institutional learning in a collaborative setting (Byrne, n.d.; Chambers, 2008b; Guijt, 2008a, 2008b; Mertens, 2009; Wadsworth & Patton, 2011).

Most of Oxfam America's program measurement and learning systems were developed through a long participatory design process, and have now established an impact baseline. In a few years, an assessment of these systems will likely tell us more about what the real challenges are – challenges that can not only put the systems at risk but also may offer Oxfam America the unique opportunity to make a truly innovative breakthrough in the impact measurement and aid effectiveness debate. What I think needs to be probed and researched in the coming years, is precisely how these systems fundamentally can contribute to changing views, practices, and attitudes of people, their organizations, networks, and institutions – thus to empowerment itself – while at the same time producing robust evidence of these impacts. The answers we have found have suggested new questions that will carry us forward:

- How can the measurement of empowerment reinforce empowerment, and how can we measure that?
- What processes must be in place to enable key stakeholders to meaningfully engage in critical reflection and collaborative learning?
- What are the risks of engaging primary stakeholders in a public debate around rights and empowerment, and how can we mitigate these?
- What kinds of competencies are needed for dealing with complexity, risk, and uncertainty?
- And finally, how can we ensure methodological rigor and consistency, coherence in the evidence produced, and institutionalization of the knowledge acquired over a program's lifetime?

References

ActKnowledge & The Aspen Institute. (2003). *SCOPE: How Much Should a Good Theory Account For?* New York: The Aspen Institute Roundtable on Comprehensive Community Initiatives.

Alsop, R. & Heinsohn, N. (2005). *Measuring Empowerment in Practice: Structuring Analysis and Framing Indicators* (Policy Research Working Paper No. WPS3510). Policy Research Working Paper. World Bank.

Anderson, A. A. (n.d.). *The Community Builder's Approach to Theory of Change. A Practical Guide to Theory Development*. New York: The Aspen Institute Roundtable on Community Change.

Annan, K. A. (2005). *In Larger Freedom: Towards Development, Security and Human Rights for All*. New York: Secretary-General of the United Nations.

Aragón, A. O. (2010). A Case for Surfacing Theories of Change for Purposeful Organisational Capacity Development. *IDS Bulletin*, 41(3), 36–46.

Aragón, A. O. & Giles Macedo, J. C. (2010). A "Systemic Theories of Change" Approach for Purposeful Capacity Development. *IDS Bulletin*, 41(3), 87–99.

Awulachew, S. B. & International Water Management Institute (2007). *Water Resources and Irrigation Development in Ethiopia*. Colombo, Sri Lanka: International Water Management Institute.

Bakewell, O., Harris-Curtis, E., & Marleyn, O. (2005). *The Implications of Adopting Rights-based Approaches for Northern Ngos: A Preliminary Exploration*. Occasional Paper Series, p. 76. INTRRAC/South Research.

Bastiaensen, J., Herdt, T. D., Vaessen, J., & Management, U. I. A. I. of D. P. (2002). *Poverty, Institutions and Interventions: A Framework for an Institutional Analysis of Poverty and Local Anti-poverty Interventions*, University of Antwerp, Institute of Development Policy and Management.

Bawden, R. (2010). The Community Challenge: The Learning Response, in: Blackmore, C. (ed.). *Social Learning Systems and Communities of Practice*. Springer.

Blewden, M. (2010). Developing Evaluation Capacity and Use in the New Zealand Philanthropic Sector: What Can Be Learnt from the US Experience? *Evaluation Journal of Australasia*, 10(1), 8–16.

Bourguignon, F., Gertler, P., Kress, D., Manning, R., & Gottlieb, J. (2006). When Will We Ever Learn? Improving Lives through Impact Evaluation. *Development*, May, 1–95.

Bourguignon, Francois (2004). *The Poverty-Growth-Inequality Triangle* (Working Paper No. 125). Indian Council for Research on International Economic Relations, New Delhi, India.

Brinkerhoff, D. W. (2005). *Organisational Legitimacy, Capacity and Capacity Development* (Discussion paper No. 58A). Capacity, Change and Performance. Maastricht: European Centre for Development Policy Management.

Byrne, A. (n.d.). Working toward Evidence-based Process: Evaluation that Matters. Communication for Social Change Consortium, MAZI.

Chambers, R. (2007). *Who Counts? The Quiet Revolution of Participation and Numbers*. Brighton: University of Sussex, Institute of Development Studies.

——— (2008a). *Poverty Research Methodologies, Mindsets and Multidimensionality*. Brighton: University of Sussex, Institute of Development Studies.

——— (2008b). *Revolutions in Development Inquiry*. London: Earthscan.

——— (2009). So That the Poor Count More: Using Participatory Methods for Impact Evaluation. *The Journal of Development Effectiveness*, 1(3), 243–246.

———— (2010, November). A Revolution Whose Time Has Come? The Win-Win of Quantitative Participatory Approaches and Methods. *IDS Bulletin,* 2010 41 (6).

———— (2011a, February 10). *Whose Paradigm Counts? Guest Post 1.* Aid on the Edge of Chaos. Retrieved from http://aidontheedge.info/2011/02/10/whose-paradigm-counts/

———— (2011b, February 15). *Whose Paradigm Counts? Guest Post 2.* Aid on the Edge of Chaos. Retrieved from http://aidontheedge.info/2011/02/15/whose-paradigm-counts-2/

Chambers, R., Karlan, D., Ravallion, M., & Rogers, P. (2009). *Designing Impact Evaluation: Different Perspectives* (Working Paper No. 4). 3ie Working Paper series. New Delhi: International Initiative for Impact Evaluation (3ie).

Chambers, R. & Pettit, J. (2004). Shifting Power to Make a Difference, in Groves, L. C. & Hionton R. B. (eds.), *Inclusive Aid: Changing Power and Relationships in International Development.* London: Earthscan, pp. 137–162.

Chen, H. T., Donaldson, S. I., & Mark, M. M. (2011). Validity Frameworks for Outcome Evaluation. *New Directions for Evaluation,* 2011(130), 5–16, doi:10.1002/ev.361.

Coolsaet, R. (2006). *Macht en waarden in de wereldpolitiek. Actuele vraagstukken in de internationale politiek.* Gent: Gent Academiapress.

Cornwall, A. (2002). *Making Spaces, Changing Places: Situating Participation in Development.* Institute of Development Studies.

———— (2004). *What Is the "Rights-Based Approach" All About? Perspectives from International Development Agencies.* Institute of Development Studies.

Cornwall, A. & Nyamu-Musembi, C. (2005). Why Rights, Why Now? Reflections on the Rise of Rights in International Development Discourse. *IDS Bulletin,* 36(1), 9–18.

Creswell, J. W. & Clark, V. L. P. (2010). *Designing and Conducting Mixed Methods Research.* SAGE.

Davies, R. (2005). Scale, Complexity and the Representation of Theories of Change Part II. *Evaluation,* 11(2), 133–149.

Davis, K., Swanson, B., Amudavi, D., et al. (2010). *In-depth Assessment of the Public Agricultural Extension System of Ethiopia and Recommendations for Improvement.* (IFPRI Discussion paper No. 01041). Addis Ababa: IFPRI Eastern and Southern Africa Regional Office.

Develtere, P. (2005). *De Belgische Ontwikkelingssamenwerking.* Leuven: Davidfonds.

Edwards, M. (2011). *Thick Problems and Thin Solutions: How NGOs Can Bridge the Gap.* FUTURE CALLING – THINK PIECE. The Hague: HIVOS, p. 18.

Edwards, M. & Hulme, D. (1992). *Making a Difference. NGO's and Development in Changing Worlds.* London: Save the Children, Earthscan.

Eijkemans, C. & Das, P. (2009). Measuring Results in the Development Sector. Issues and Challenges Moving from External Design and Evaluation Towards Shared Learning. *Contextuals,* (6).

Emana, B., Chemeda, D., Berisso, T., & Senbeta, G. (2007). *Impacts of Water and Irrigation Programs in Ethiopia and Capacity Building Needs of Stakeholders.* (Formative program evaluation report). Addis Ababa: Oxfam America, SID Consult.

Eyben, R. (2008). *Power, Mutual Accountability and Responsibility in the Practice of International Aid: A Relational Approach.* Brighton: University of Sussex, Institute of Development Studies.

———— (2012, March 11). *Theories of Change: Breaking out of the Results Agenda.* The Big Push Forward. Retrieved from http://bigpushforward.net/archives/1419#more-1419.

Eyben, R., Harris, C., & Pettit, J. (2006). Introduction: Exploring Power for Change. *IDS Bulletin*, 37(6), 1–10.

Federal Democratic Republic of Ethiopia (FDRE) (1997). *Federal Rural Land Administration Proclamation. Proclamation No. 89/1997*. Federal Negarit Gazeta.

Federal Democratic Republic of Ethiopia (FDRE) (2009). *Proclamation to Provide for the Registration and Regulation of Charities and Societies, Proclamation No. 621/2009*. Federal Negarit Gazeta.

Federal Democratic Republic of Ethiopia (FDRE) (2010a, November). *Growth and Transformation Plan 2010/11-2014/15. Volume 1: Main Text*. Ministry of Finance and Economic Development.

Federal Democratic Republic of Ethiopia (FDRE) (2010b, November). *Growth and Transformation Plan 2010/11-2014/15. Volume 2: Policy Matrix*. Ministry of Finance and Economic Development.

Fisher, C. (2010). Between Pragmatism and Idealism: Implementing a Systemic Approach to Capacity Development. *IDS Bulletin*, 41(3), 108–117.

Flood, R. L. (2006). The Relationship of "Systems Thinking" to Action Research, in Rdason, P. & Bradbury, H. (eds.), *Handbook of Action Research: The Concise Paperback Edition.*SAGE.

Foucault, M. & Rabinow, P. (1984). *The Foucault Reader*. Pantheon Books.

Fowler, A. (2003). *International Development Frameworks, Policies, Priorities and Implications. A Basic Guide for NGOs*. Oxfam Canada / Oxfam Quebec.

——— (2007). Civic Driven Change and International Development: Exploring a Complexity Perspective. *Contextuals*, (7), 61.

——— (2008). Connecting the Dots. Complexity Thinking and Social Development. *The Broker Articles*.

Freeman, M. (2010). *Critical Social Theory and Evaluation Practice: New Directions for Evaluation*. San Francisco: Wiley/Jossey-Bass.

Freeman, M. & Vasconcelos, E. F. S. (2010). Critical Social Theory: Core Tenets, Inherent Issues. *New Directions for Evaluation*, 2010(127), 7–19.

Freire, P. (1974). *Education for Critical Consciousness*. New York: Continuum International Publishing Group.

Funnell, S. C. & Rogers, P. J. (2011). *Purposeful Program Theory: Effective Use of Theories of Change and Logic Models*. New York: John Wiley & Sons.

Gamble, J. (2008). *A Developmental Evaluation Primer*. Canada: The J. W. McConnell Family Foundation (on the Sustaining Social Innovation Initiative).

Gaventa, J. (2002). Exploring Citizenship, Participation and Accountability. *IDS Bulletin*, 33(2), 1–14.

——— (2006). Finding the Spaces for Change: A Power Analysis. *IDS Bulletin*, 37(6), 23–33.

Gaventa, J. & Cornwall, A. (2006). Challenging the Boundaries of the Possible: Participation, Knowledge and Power. *IDS Bulletin*, 37(6), 122–128.

Gebreselassie, S. (2004). *Food Insecurity and Poverty in Ethiopia: Evidence and Lessons from Wollo*. Addis Ababa: EEA/Ethiopian Economic Policy Research Institute.

Gledhill, J. (2009). *The Rights of the Rich versus the Rights of the Poor*, in Hickey, S. & Mitlin, D. (eds.), *Rights-Based Approaches to Development: Exploring the Potential and Pitfalls* . Sterling, VA: Kumarian Press, pp. 31–46.

Government of Ethiopia, UN Country Team in Ethiopia, & UN Office for the Coordination of Humanitarian Affairs (2011). *Humanitarian requirements 2011.* Joint Government and Humanitarian Partners' Document. Addis Ababa: UN Office for the Coordination of Humanitarian Affairs.

Government of Ethiopia, UN Country Team in Ethiopia, & UN Office for the Coordination of Humanitarian Affairs (2012). *Humanitarian requirements 2012.* Joint Government and Humanitarian Partners' Document. Addis Ababa: UN Office for the Coordination of Humanitarian Affairs.

Gready, P. (2008). Rights-Based Approaches to Development: What Is the Value-Added? *Development in Practice,* 18(6), 735–747.

——— (2009). Reasons to Be Cautious About Evidence and Evaluation: Rights-Based Approaches to Development and the Emerging Culture of Evaluation. *Journal of Human Rights Practice,* 1(3), 380–401.

Green, D. (2008). *From Poverty to Power: How Active Citizens and Effective States Can Change the World.* (M. Fried, ed.). Boston: Oxfam Publishing.

Greene, J. C. (2011). The Construct(ion) of Validity as Argument. *New Directions for Evaluation,* 2011(130), 81–91.

Groves, L. C. & Hinton, R. B. (2004). *Inclusive Aid: Changing Power and Relationships in International Development.* London: Earthscan.

Guba, E. G. & Lincoln, Y. S. (1989). *Fourth Generation Evaluation.* Los Angeles: SAGE.

Guijt, I. (2008a). *Seeking Surprise: Rethinking Monitoring for Collective Learning in Rural Resource Management.* Wageningen: Wageningen Universiteit.

——— (2008b). *Critical Readings on Assessing and Learning for Social Change: A Review.* Sussex: Institute of Development Studies at the University of Sussex.

Guijt, I., Brouwers, J., Kusters, C., Prins, E., & Zeynalova, B. (n.d.). *Evaluation Revisited: Improving the Quality of Evaluative Practice by Embracing Complexity. Conference Report. (May 20–21, 2010).* Retrieved May 10, 2012, from http://evaluationrevisited. wordpress.com/

Haddad, L., Lindstrom, J., & Pinto, Y. (Nov 2010). The Sorry State of M&E in Agriculture: Can People-Centred Approaches Help? *IDS Bulletin,* 2010 41(6), 6–25.

Hawe, P., Bond, L., & Butler, H. (2009). Knowledge Theories Can Inform Evaluation Practice: What Can a Complexity Lens Add? *New Directions for Evaluation,* 2009(124), 89–100.

Herasymowych, M., Hawkins, J. H., & Senko, H. (2007). *Navigating Through Complexity: Systems Thinking Guide.* Alberta: MHA Institute, Incorporated.

Hickey, S. (2009). Rethinking Agency, Rights, and Natural Resource Management, in Hickey, S. & Mitlin, D. (eds.), *Rights-based Approaches to Development: Exploring the Potential and Pitfalls.* Sterling VA: Kumarian Press.

Hickey, S. & Mohan, G. (2004). *Participation: From Tyranny to Transformation? Exploring New Approaches to Participation in Development.* London: Zed Books.

Huesca, R. (2008). Tracing the History of Participatory Communication Approaches to Development: A Critical Appraisal, in Servaes, J. (ed.), *Communication for Development and Social Change.* Los Angeles: SAGE Publications.

Jacobs, A., Barnett, C., & Ponsford, R. (2010). Three Approaches to Monitoring: Feedback Systems, Participatory Monitoring and Evaluation and Logical Frameworks. *IDS Bulletin*, 41(6), 36–44.

James, C. (2012). *Theory of Change Review – A Report Commissioned by Comic Relief.* Comic Relief.

Johnson, U. (2003). *Human Rights Approach to Development Programming.* Nairobi: UNICEF.

Julnes, G. (2011). Reframing Validity in Research and Evaluation: A Multidimensional, Systematic Model of Valid Inference. *New Directions for Evaluation*, 2011(130), 55–67.

Jupp, D., Ali, S. I., & Barahona, C. (2010). *Measuring Empowerment? Ask Them: Quantifying Qualitative Outcomes from People's Own Analysis: Insights for Results-Based Management from the Experience of a Social Movement in Bangladesh.* Stockholm: Swedish International Development Cooperation Agency (Sida).

Kabeer, N. (1999). Resources, Agency, Achievements: Reflections on the Measurement of Women's Empowerment. *Development and Change*, 30(3), 435–464.

———— (2005). *Inclusive Citizenship: Meanings and Expressions.* London: Zed Books.

Kakwani, N. & Silber, J. (2007). *The Many Dimensions of Poverty.* Basingstoke: Palgrave Macmillan.

Kanbur, S. M. R. & Lustig, N. (2001). *World Development Report. 2000/2001 Attacking Poverty.* Oxford: Oxford University Press/World Bank.

Kania, J. & Kramer, M. (2011). *Collective Impact.* Stanford CA: Stanford Social Innovation Review.

Keystone Accountability (n.d.-a). *Impact Planning, Assessment and Learning – An Overview.* IPAL Guides. Keystone Accountability.

Keystone Accountability (n.d.-b). *Developing a Theory of Change A Framework for Accountability and Learning for Social Change. A Keystone Guide.* IPAL Guides. Keystone Accountability.

Khagram, S., Thomas, C., Lucero, C., & Mathes, S. (2009). Evidence for Development Effectiveness. *The Journal of Development Effectiveness*, 1(3), 247–270.

Khagram, S. & Thomas, C. W. (2010). Toward a Platinum Standard for Evidence-Based Assessment by 2020. *Public Administration Review*, 70, S100–S106.

Khan, H. (2004). *Development as Freedom.* Tokyo: CIRJE, Faculty of Economics, University of Tokyo.

Krznaric, R. (2007). *How Change Happens: Interdisciplinary Perspectives for Human Development.* Boston Oxfam.

Lacayo, V. (2007). *What Complexity Science Teaches Us about Social Change.* Orange NJ: MAZI.

Laerman, R. (1997). *Sociale systemen bestaan: Een kennismaking met het werk van Niklas Luhmann.* Leuven: Acco.

LEAD (2008, December). *ROPE II. Rights-Oriented Programming for Effectiveness: Designing and Evaluating Long-Term Programs.* Oxfam America.

Leeuwis, C. (2004). *Communication for Rural Innovation. Rethinking Agricultural Extention.* Oxford: Blackwell Publishing.

Lucas, H. & Longhurst, R. (2010). Evaluation: Why, for Whom and How? *IDS Bulletin*, 41(6), 28–35.

Mapedza, E. & Wichelns, D. (2010). *Evaluating Baseline Indicators Pertaining to Oxfam America's Water Program in Ethiopia.* International Water Management Institute, Oxfam America.

Mayoux, L. (2007). *Evaluation and Impact Research for Rights-Based Development. Issues and Challenges.* Paper presented to Oxfam America Impact Evaluation Workshop, September 17–21, 2007, Lima, Peru. Boston: Oxfam America.

Mayoux, L. & Chambers, R. (2005). Reversing the Paradigm: Quantification, Participatory Methods and Pro-poor Impact Assessment. *Journal of International Development*, 17(2), 271–298.

McKee, N. & Aghi, M. (2000). *Involving People, Evolving Behaviour.* Penang: Southbound.

Mertens, D. M. (2009). *Transformative Research and Evaluation.* New York: Guilford Press.

Mertens, D. M., Bledsoe, K. L., Sullivan, M., & Wilson, A. (2010). *Utilization of Mixed Methods for Transformative Purposes.* In SAGE Handbook of Mixed Methods in Social & Behavioral Research. Los Angeles: SAGE

Midgley, G. (2007). *Systems Thinking for Evaluation. Systems Concepts in Evaluation. An Expert Anthology.* Point Reyes, CA: EdgePress of Inverness.

Mosendale, S. (2005). *Strategic Impact Inquiry on Women's Empowerment.* Atlanta: CARE International.

Narayan-Parker, D. (2002). *Empowerment and Poverty Reduction: A Sourcebook.* Washington DC World Bank Publications.

——— (2005). *Measuring Empowerment: Cross-Disciplinary Perspectives.* Washington DC: World Bank Publications.

Nitipaisalkul, W. (2007). *Theories of Change: A "Tipping Point" for Development Impact?"* (Knowledge Brief No. 3). Impact. Barton (Australia): Hassall & Associates International's (HAI) Development Impact Group.

Nyamu-Musembi, C. (2005). Towards an Actor-Oriented Perspective on Human Rights, in: Kabeer, N. (ed.). *Inclusive Citizenship: Meanings and Expressions.* London: Zed Books.

Offenheiser, R. C. & Holcombe, S. H. (2003). Challenges and Opportunities in Implementing a Rights-Based Approach to Development: An Oxfam America Perspective. *Nonprofit and Voluntary Sector Quarterly*, 32(2), 268–301.

Oswald, K. & Taylor, P. (2010). A Learning Approach to Monitoring and Evaluation. *IDS Bulletin*, 41(6), 114–120.

Oxfam America (2009). *Water Program in Ethiopia. Program Strategy Paper 2010–2020.* Oxfam America.

Pankhrest, H. (2008). *Situational Analysis of Vibrancy of Water Sector: Ethiopia.* Addis Ababa CARE.

Parks, W. (2005). *Who Measures Change? An Introduction to Participatory Monitoring and Evaluation of Communication for Social Change.* South Orange, NJ: Communication for Social Change Consortium.

Patton, M. Q. (2008). *Utilization-Focused Evaluation.* Los Angeles: SAGE Publications.

Peet, R., Hartwick, E., & Hartwick, E. R. (2009). *Theories of Development: Contentions, Arguments, Alternatives.* New York: Guilford Press.

Puddephatt, A., Horsewell, R., & Menheneott, G. (2009). *Discussion Paper on the Monitoring and Evaluation of UN-assisted Communication for Development Programs. Recommendations for Best Practice Methodologies and Indicators* (Background Paper for the 11th UN Inter-Agency

Round Table on Communication for Development (March 11–13, 2009)). Washington DC: UNDP - World Bank/Global Partners & Associates.

Regassa, S., Castillo, G., & Givey, C. (2010). *The Rain Doesn't Come on Time Anymore. Poverty, Vulnerability and Climate Variability in Ethiopia.* Addis Ababa: Oxfam International.

Robb, C. (2004). Changing Power Relations in the History of Aid. *Inclusive Aid: Changing Power and Relationships in International Development.* London: Earthscan, pp. 21–41.

Roche, C. (2012, April 18). *Has the Focus on Results Damaged Aid's Potential to Support Long Term Transformation?* The Big Push Forward. Retrieved from http://bigpushforward.net/archives/1446

Roper, L. E., Pettit, J., & Eade, D. (2003). *Development and the Learning Organization: Essays from Development in Practice.* Oxford: Oxfam.

Rosengren, K. E. (2000). *Communication: An Introduction.* London: SAGE.

Rowlands, J. & Eade, D. (2003). *Development Methods and Approaches: Critical Reflections: Selected Essays from Development in Practice.* Oxford: Oxfam.

Sen, A. K. (1999). *Development as Freedom.* Oxford Oxford University Press.

Servaes, J. & V. Frissen (1997). *De interpretatieve benadering in de communicatiewetenschap. Theorie, methodologie en case-studies.* Leuven: Acco.

Servaes, J. (1999). *Communication for Development. One World, Multiple Cultures.* Cresskill: Hampton Press.

––––––– (2003). *Approaches to Development. Studies on Communication for Development.* Paris: UNESCO.

––––––– (Oct 2005). *Mapping the New Field of Communication for Development and Social Change. Paper Represented to the Social Change in the 21ˢᵗ Century Conference.* Queensland University of Technology.

––––––– (2007). Harnessing the UN System into a Common Approach on Communication for Development. *International Communication Gazette,* 2007(69), 483–507.

––––––– (2008). *Communication for Development and Social Change.* Los Angeles: SAGE Publications.

TANGO International (2010). *Water Program Impact Baseline Literature Review.* Boston: Oxfam America.

Taye Assefa & Yamahbarawi tenat madrak (2008). *Digest of Ethiopia's National Policies, Strategies and Programs.* Addis Ababa: Forum for Social Studies.

Toye, J. (2011). Poverty Reduction, in: Cornwall, A. & Eade, D. (eds.). *Deconstructing Development Discourse: Buzzwords and Fuzzwords.* Rugby: Practical Action.

United Nations (2003). *The Human Rights-Based Approach to Development Cooperation: Towards a Common Understanding among the UN Agencies.* New York: UNDP.

United Nations (2004). *Human Rights and Poverty Reduction: A Conceptual Framework.* Geneva & New York.

Uvin, P. (2004). *Human Rights and Development.* Sterling VA Kumarian Press.

Van Hemelrijck, A. (2000). *Naar een evaluatiekader voor de beoordeling van ontwikkelingseducatie bij NGO's. Executieve samenvatting. Onderzoeksrapport. Evaluatiekader. Annexes.* KUBrussel: Research Centre Communication for Social Change.

———— (2009). *LEAD Measurement Note on Empowerment in Rights-Based Programming. Implications for the Work of Oxfam America* (Internal measurement note). Boston: LEAD, Oxfam America.

———— (2010). *A Rights-based Systems Approach to Impact Measurement & Learning.* Presented at the Evaluation Revisited: Improving the Quality of Evaluative Practice by Embracing Complexity (May 20-21, 2010), Utrecht (The Netherlands).

Van Ongevalle, J., Maarse, A., Temmink, C., Boutylkova, E., & Huyse, H. (2012). *Dealing with Complexity through Planning, Monitoring & Evaluation (PME). Mid-term Results of a Collective Action Research Process* (Praxis Paper No. 26). PSO, HIVA.

Wadsworth, Y. & Patton, M. Q. (2011). *Building in Research and Evaluation: Human Inquiry for Living Systems.* Walnut Creek CA Left Coast Press.

Wallace, T., Bornstein, L., & Chapman, J. (2007). *The Aid Chain: Coercion and Commitment in Development NGOs.* Rugby Practical Action Pub.

Watson, D. (2006). *Monitoring and Evaluation of Capacity and Capacity Development* (Discussion paper No. 58B). A theme paper prepared for Capacity, Change and Performance (p. 32). Maastricht: The European Centre for Development Policy Management.

Williams, B. & Hummelbrunner, R. (2010). *Systems Concepts in Action: A Practitioner's Toolkit.* Stanford CA Stanford University Press.

Williams, B. & Imam, I. (2007). *Systems Concepts in Evaluation: An Expert Anthology.* Point Reyes, CA: EdgePress of Inverness.

Wolfensohn, J. D. (2004). *Development and Poverty Reduction: Looking Back, Looking Ahead: Prepared for the 2004 Annual Meetings of the World Bank and IMF October 2004.* Washington, DC, USA: World Bank.

Woolcock, M. (2009). Toward a Plurality of Methods in Project Evaluation: A Contextualised Approach to Understanding Impact Trajectories and Efficacy. *The Journal of Development Effectiveness,* 1(1), 1–14.

Notes

1 The argument presented in this chapter reflects the personal views of the author, and does not represent Oxfam America's official position.

2 UNDP conceptualized and promoted a vision of human development in its first Human Development Report in 1990.

3 The modernization or growth model perceived development purely in terms of economic growth. This top-down governmental development approach aimed to change traditional agrarian into industrialized modern societies through technocratic interventions focused on technological innovation, managerial efficiency, and growth of GNP. Communication was perceived as a unidirectional and top-down process, using mass media to transmit modernistic ideas to those who were thought to be trapped in the traditionalist past (McKee & Aghi, 2000; Peet et al., 2009; Servaes, 1999, 2008).

4 Cf The Washington Consensus (http://en.wikipedia.org/wiki/Washington_Consensus).

5   The dependency model was a critique of the modernization approach and analyzed the unequal power balances between countries in the North and South, implicit in geopoliticized funding and information streams and labeled it cultural imperialism. It accurately described global inequalities between developed and developing countries but failed to take into account the power imbalances keeping communities trapped in poverty within developing countries (Develtere, 2005; McKee & Aghi, 2000; Robb, 2004; Servaes, 1999, 2008).

6   The basic needs approach, often characterized as the growth-with-equal-distribution model, attempted to compensate for the failure of the prevailing growth model to address people's basic needs beyond income, including issues like health, nutrition, education, and livelihood. It focused on poverty issues in rural area, particularly the obsolete community institutions and farmer organizations, and the lack of appropriate extension service delivery. Interventions were directed at capacity-building and training using participatory communication and education methods (Develtere, 2005; Groves & Hinton, 2004; McKee & Aghi, 2000; Servaes, 1999, 2008).

7   The financial and economic crisis in 1997–1998 in East Asia demonstrated that the weaknesses of political, economic, and financial institutions could threaten or undo the development progress made by market liberalization and rapid growth (Wolfensohn, 2004).

8   Growth and development should be sustainable so that it "meets the needs of the present without compromising the ability of future generations to meet their own needs." This often-quoted definition of sustainable development comes from the Brundtland report *Our Common Future*, published in 1987 by Oxford University Press (http://en.wikipedia.org/wiki/Sustainable_Development).

9   A stakeholder is any individual, group, or organization who is affected or can affect the achievements of development efforts. Stakeholder approaches have become increasingly important because of the accelerated globalization process of the past decades (Patton, 2008, pp. 62–63). Primary stakeholders are the women and men, and their families and communities, who are living in poverty and injustice, and therefore are the primary focus of the development efforts.

10 Grassroots participation is concerned with communication for social change that "seeks to engage and empower communities and networks to influence or reinforce social norms and cultural practices to create an environment that supports long-term sustainable change. It is human resource intensive and often requires investment over longer periods of time. Its results are usually measured in terms of processes and shifts in social norms or power relationships" (Puddephatt et al., 2009, p. 4).

11 Social mobilization is defined by the UNICEF Global Communication Team in 1998 as "a process of bringing together all feasible and practical intersectoral social partners and allies to determine felt-need and raise awareness of, and demand for, a particular development objective. It involves enlisting the participation of such actors, including institutions, groups, networks and communities, in identifying, raising, and managing material resources, thereby increasing and strengthening self-reliance and sustainability of achievements" (McKee & Aghi, 2000, p. 208).

12 Coalition-building can be considered as part of social mobilization as defined above.

13 A useful working definition of advocacy is given by Servaes (2008, p. 208): "Advocacy for development is a combination of social actions designed to gain political commitment, policy support, social acceptance and systems support for a particular goal or program. It involves collecting and structuring information into a persuasive case; communicating the case to decision-makers and other potential supporters, including the public, through various interpersonal and media channels; and stimulating actions by social institutions, stakeholders and policy-makers in support of the goal or program." (see also Servaes, 2003)

14 A program's actions or interventions are presented in an operational document called the Program Implementation Plan (PIP). A program's Theory of Change is benchmarked in three to four years that helps partners and stakeholders sequence outcomes to achieve the collective impact goal and its strategic objectives. The PIP lays out strategic interventions for the nearby three to four years benchmark outcomes, and thus forms a practical guide for action. The PIP also links interventions through the benchmark outcomes with the impact indicators on the Theory of Change.

15 The critique of qualitative methods is that they replace the rigorous collection and analysis of data as "scientific facts" with biased opinions and anecdotal data. Quantitative methods are criticized as structured sets of questions and preset quantitative measures that impose "a reality which may not exist in the minds of the people" validating the researchers' reality more than that of the people (Chambers, 2008b; McKee & Aghi, 2000, p. 93; Mertens, 2009; Patton, 2008).

16 The illustration was created by Lucia Fabiani (lucia@mattersolutions.eu), who is a member of Matter Solutions (see next endnote).

17 The facilitation approach was designed and implemented by Daniel Newman (dan@ mattersolutions.eu) who is the Principle of Matter Solutions (http://www.mattersolutions.eu/ method), an organization based in Rome and specialized in facilitation of large and diverse groups of people in complex situations. The Scan-Focus-Act model enables participants to understand context and develop a common language before diving deep to stress test various options, eliminate alternatives, and drive toward a detailed design of the desired solution. Matter is a member of the MGTaylor valueweb™ (http://www.mgtaylor.com).

18 IWMI is a non-profit research organization with an East Africa regional office based in Addis Ababa (see: http://eastafrica.iwmi.org/). Its mission is to improve the management of land and water resources for securing food, livelihoods and environment. The IWMI was selected by the program partners for its autonomy, long-term stability, and strategic importance and influence on policy in the domain of water resource management.

19 The facilitation approach of Matter Solutions (http://www.mattersolutions.eu/method) – see Endnote 17.

20 In February 2009, the Ethiopian government issued the *Proclamation to Provide for the Registration and Regulation of Charities and Societies*. Known as the Civil Society Law, it prohibits international organizations (like Oxfam), and local NGOs who secure more than 10 percent of their annual revenue from foreign sources from participating in the socio-political advancement of human rights [Federal Democratic Republic of Ethiopia (FDRE), 2009]. Oxfam America maintains its rights-oriented approach by focusing on capacity-strengthening and collaboration, building tactical alliances with change agents within the ministry of agriculture and its regional bureaus, and facilitating an ongoing dialogue between key stakeholders.

Chapter 3

The Global Agenda: Technology, Development, and Sustainable
Social Change

Toks Dele Oyedemi

Background

The academic and state policy engagements with communications in sustainable social change are consequence of the acknowledgment that varieties of communication interventions are visibly making impacts in social transformation. These communication interventions are continuously influenced by many socioeconomic, political, and technological factors. Particularly, the dynamic developments around new communication technologies play major role in communication for social change programs.

This chapter attempts a broad overview of Information and Communication Technologies (ICTs) for development and sustainable social change. It discusses the rationalization and potentials of technology in social change agendas and revisits the theoretical discourse of development while engaging the theoretical framings of technology in this discourse. Critically, this chapter notes the rhetoric of ICTs for development hides an underlying global agenda of neoliberalism. It identifies different critiques of ICTs for development, and argues that irrespective of these critiques, the failure to invest in ICT applications and networks will exacerbate the huge inequalities in many nations and between developed and developing nations. There is a need to rethink the ICTs for development approaches toward an ethical implementation of technologies for development and sustainable social change.

The history of human civilization is a history of technology. Technology shapes society, culture, nature, and every scientific and socioeconomic revolution of human histories. Kirkpatrick (2008) asserts that technology to human is synonymous to language, since there is no human civilization without language; human society without technology is as inconceivable as one without language. Technologies[1] are harbingers of cultural and social revolution. The invention of writing changed the way human communicate and store information, the Gutenberg printing press heralded the first information revolution (Drucker, 1997), a revolution that not only changed the pattern of access to information, but also sparked a transformation in culture, religion, knowledge creation, and dissemination. Also revolutionary were the inventions of radio, television, telegraph, telephone, the computer, and the Internet.

Since technology fosters development, progress, and efficiency, and facilitates social and cultural participations, it engenders academic, political, and economic discourses about its critical role in human development and sociability. Some advancements made in developed regions of the world have been ascribed to the applications of technological innovations in all economic and social activities. The current discourse of technology addresses how similar advancements and development may be achieved in developing countries, where access to ICTs is low. It gives rise to the study of how ICTs can aid development and social change among the majority of world's populations that reside in Africa, Asia, Latin America, the Caribbean, and in regions of the world where poverty and lack of access to social services that hinder human well-being are conspicuously present.

Consequently, *ICTs for Development* (ICTD) becomes a global agenda for international activities around the application of technology to confront many social issues. ICT for development is the use of ICTs to improve the social, cultural, economic, and political development of people, with a goal of engendering social change. It involves the applications of communication technologies in providing the necessary information and externalities that can lead to and improve the well-being of people and communities mostly in developing countries. ICTs are seen as necessary tools in the twenty-first century, as they enhance the speed of information and communication, and provide access to relevant social services to people who are connected to these technologies. It is believed that the lack of access to ICTs can exacerbate the development gap between and within nations. In the past decade, there has been an enormous rise in development agendas and programs geared toward the use of ICTs for development. Many countries in the world have crafted national policies to address the need for the spread of ICTs for their national developments.

International non-governmental agencies (NGOs), development agencies, and nonprofit organizations have devoted a big slice of their development agendas to ICTD. Examples of this abound: The United Nations has a number of its agencies working on ICT and development issues: the UN ICT Task Force and Global Alliance for ICT and Development (GAID) work with stakeholders in many sectors toward the use of ICTs to achieve many internationally agreed development agendas, including the Millennium Development Goals (MDGs); UNESCO actively focuses on the use of ICTs for community development, which resulted in the program for establishing Multipurpose Community Centers, and other initiatives. Other UN agencies, such as United Nations Development Programme (UNDP), the Food and Agriculture Organization (FAO), International Telecommunications Union (ITU), and the World Bank through *Info*Dev also focus on ICTs for development. Many state-owned international development agencies, such as the USAID (US), CIDA (Canada), DANIDA (Denmark), and SIDA (Sweden), have projects supporting ICTs for development in developing countries. Apart from all these international organizations, many regional institutions in Asia, Latin America, and Africa are also actively involved in the area of ICTs for development. National governments are developing policies around extending the use of ICTs for their national development goals. It is estimated that billions of dollars are spent annually for this global development agenda. Technology corporations are working in partnership with governments and NGOs in extending access to the 70 percent of the world population who are unconnected, thereby serving a global market agenda under a more pleasant framing of ICTs for development. ICTs for development has become a global agenda and a major policy goal for development in many developing nations.

Rationale for ICTs in development

The rationale for the global attention for the use of ICTs for development is explicable. ICTs are known to provide access to information in many sectors of human development. They have the potential to confront poverty and facilitate public and private sector activities in areas such as public administration and government, urban and rural development, transport, healthcare, education, environment, agriculture, commerce, and business (Mansell & Wehn, 1998; Mansell, 1999; Harris, 2004; Franklin, 2006; Sein & Harindranath, 2004). The notion of the use of technology in development has engendered debates in the academic and government policy discourses. Critics have questioned the appropriateness of ICTs to address issues of poverty and other social issues that the developing world encounters. The argument points to the question of why so many financial investments are expended on "bridging the digital divide," rather than bridging a nutritional, educational, opportunity, or health care divide. As Hosman & Fife (2008) note, this argument is the core essence of the "bread vs. broadband debate." Considering that there are more urgent basic needs of water, housing, food, education, fighting diseases, and poverty to be met in developing countries, why devote attention to technology?

Understandably, this argument is justified, but the bread vs. broadband dichotomy is a weak one. Basic needs and the utilization of technology are not an either/or position, as Hosman & Fife (2008) assert, "from a long-term historical perspective, economic development has been a story of technological change – both invention and application. To claim that development without technology is possible is to turn a blind eye to reality" (p. 53). The rationale for the investment in the application of ICTs for development agendas is hinged on the accrued benefits that technology offers in addressing the social issues confronting many developing countries:

ICTs and poverty
This is one of the most contentious themes, and it raises a critical question: can technology help alleviate poverty? To understand the role of ICTs in confronting poverty, it is essential to understand the definition and nature of poverty. There are about 1 billion people living on less than US$1 a day, with 2.6 billion – 40 percent of the world's population – living on less than US$2 a day. More than 80 percent of the world's population lives in countries where income differentials are widening. This is relevant considering that income distribution influences the rate at which economic growth translates into poverty reduction. Around 10 million children die each year before the age of five, the vast majority from poverty and malnutrition (UNDP-HDR, 2007).

However, poverty measurement based on income inequality provides only a glimpse of the picture; it does not address the complete pattern of poverty. In addition to income inequality, key features of poverty include powerlessness, voicelessness, vulnerability, the deprivation of basic capabilities, lack of access to education, to health care, to natural

Table 3.1: First-order and second-order resources for poverty alleviation.

First-order resources	Second-order resources
Food	Postsecondary education
Clothing	Economic literacy
Shelter	Information technology
Housing	Ability to accumulate assets
Primary and secondary education	Soft skills
Health care	
Childcare	

Source: Servon, (2002:20).

resources, to land and credit, lack of capability for political participation, and so forth (Harris, 2004; Franklin, 2006; World Bank, 2000). In a broader approach, the deprivation of necessary information and knowledge needed to participate in all levels of society and to confront issues that hinder well-being is a reflection of poverty (Sen, 1992, 1999; Servon 2002). Servon (2002) provides a theoretical mapping of the role of technology in addressing poverty by identifying two levels of resources needed to engage poverty: the first-order and second-order resources (Table 3.1).

Most of the resources in the first-order category keep the poor in a survival mode, but do not help take them out of poverty. The second-order resources provide the skills and materials to get people out of poverty. Clearly, technology with the skills it offers and the information it provides enhances the knowledge and intelligence necessary to confront poverty. Technology can influence poverty alleviation by creating marketable skills among the poor, making it possible to impart knowledge and skills to children of poor parents and break a generational circle of poverty. It provides information to fight child malnutrition; it connects individuals, groups, enterprises, communities, and governments faster. Technology speeds up production process, and facilitates financial transaction[2] (Chowdhury, 2000; Urquhart et al., 2008). The advent of mobile phone banking is making impacts on poverty alleviations in many developing countries. It allows for fund transfer, bank saving accounts, and opportunity for customers to earn interest on their savings and access credit and insurance services (Wakefield, 2010).[3] Thomas (2008) notes that access to information through ICTs can help in alleviating poverty in many developing countries. Access to information is a human rights issue, because with proper information people can mobilize themselves and strive for their own development; they can also gain access to resources provided by government. Thomas argues further, "access to information is an important right for it can become the basis for the enjoyment of related rights and securities: in education, shelter, access to food grain and employment opportunities" (p. 34). Undoubtedly, access to health care, shelter, economic opportunities, education, water, food, and many other basic needs is important for development, equally important is access to information technologies.

ICTs and government

The growth in e-government allows many public administration information and government services to be accessed online. Many government offices are increasingly making their services available online, cutting the bureaucratic bottlenecks that often plague government activities. Gradually more people in developing countries can fill and download forms online, and accessed information about government services. This has reduced the amount of time people physically spend in line, the cost of accessing government information, and it also increases productivity on the part of the government.

ICTs and education

The use of ICTs in education is greatly enhancing the extension of education to many people who are geographically located away from urban areas where most postsecondary institutions are located. According to UNESCO, only about three percent of young people in sub-Saharan Africa and seven percent in Asia attend some form of postsecondary education, as compared to about 58 percent in industrialized countries as a whole, and 81 percent in the United States (Harris, 2004). In sub-Saharan Africa, 75 percent of secondary-school-age children are not enrolled in secondary school (UNESCO, 2009). ICTs can help in extending education to many in the developing countries. The use of e-learning in distance education has, without doubt, provided access to education for many people, and improved the productivity of many educators in the educational systems, not only in the developed countries, but increasingly in many developing regions of the world.

ICTs and health

ICTs are critical in the health sector and in many health-related development projects. ICT applications are valuable resources in the medical field; they support exchanges of information between health professionals in urban sites and those in rural sites. ICTs are fundamental for the healthcare systems to meet many obligations, to deliver care, pursue research, educate medical students, treat patients, and monitor public health (Ajuwon & Rhinet, 2007). ICT applications facilitate telemedicine, where medical information is transferred via communication networks for remote medical procedures. There are many examples of this: in 2003, doctors in a South African hospital were able to perform a critical operation on a patient with live instructions from another doctor in Hanover, Germany. This was done through a networked robotic technology and videoconferencing (Green, 2003); a British doctor, who was volunteering in DR Congo, used text message instructions from a colleague in the United Kingdom to perform a life-saving operation on a boy (BBC, 2008); and ICTs are used daily in may healthcare facilities. ICTs in health extend beyond the clinical aspect to preventive campaigns. ICTs have been very useful in the dissemination of information and in providing relevant resources for health-related campaigns. For example, a text messaging project, called Project Masiluleke, was set up in South Africa to try to counter the fact that only 5 percent of the population has been tested for HIV. The goal of this project is to tackle the problem of slowing the progress of HIV in a country with an estimated 6 million people living with HIV by encouraging people to seek testing and treatment. This project, scheduled to send one million free text messages a day to encourage people to be tested and treated, has shown considerable success. Trials of the system showed that calls to counselors at the National Aids helpline increased by 200 percent when messages were broadcast (Praekelt Foundation, 2008).

Other potential benefits of ICTs include: promoting local entrepreneurship – by helping to develop financial capital, human capital, and social capital of people and communities; building capacity and capability of individuals; enriching culture; supporting agriculture; encouraging social and political participation;, enhancing creative innovations; and facilitating social network. If access to ICTs is important for social and economic developments, the global dispersion of ICTs is appalling, more than half of human population is yet to be touched by some of these technologies, see Table 3.2 and Figure 3.1. This makes it paramount that development agendas include extending access to ICTs. Although there has been a slight growth in access to the Internet with over a quarter of the world's population having connection to the network, as shown in Figure 3.1, this access rate is highly skewed with most Internet subscribers residing in North America and Europe. If social, cultural, and economic benefits accrue to the regions of the world with access to modern communication technologies, the task is to extend the application of these technologies to the regions of the world with most human population, who also happen to have the world's highest rate

Table 3.2: ICT penetration in selected countries with large population.

Countries	Population	Cell phone per 100 inhabitants	Household with computers	Internet users per 100 inhabitants	Fixed broadband subscribers per 100 inhabitants
China	1.3 B.	47.95	31.80	22.28	6.23
India	1.1 B.	29.36	4.44	4.38	0.45
USA	311 M.	86.79	72.46	74.00	23.46
Indonesia	227 M.	61.83	6.42	7.92	0.18
Brazil	191 M.	78.47	31.17	37.52	5.26
Pakistan	176 M.	49.74	9.80	10.45	0.09
Bangladesh	160 M.	27.90	2.24	0.35	0.03
Nigeria	151 M.	41.66	12.01	15.86	0.04
Russia	141 M.	141.11	40.00	32.00	6.56

Source: ITU ICTeye (2008).

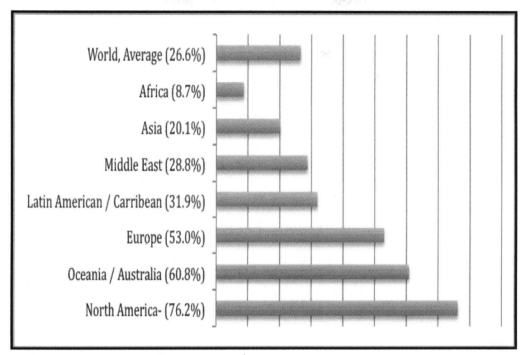

Figure 3.1: World Internet penetration rates by geographical regions.
Source: Internet World Stats – http://www.internetworldstats.com/stats.htm

of poverty and inequality. In addition, these regions also have the highest rate of gender inequalities, population without access to healthcare services and education, and many other developmental challenges. This provides a critical rationale for why development programs are geared toward exploring how ICTs can help in achieving human well-being as encapsulated in the United Nations Millennium Development Goals (MDGs).

Theoretical framing of ICT and development

The conceptual framework of development is centered around three main theoretical approaches: modernization or modernist perspective, dependency, and a third approach that has been framed differently, but with a focus on people-centered development. The modernist perspective sees the developing countries as lacking resources to transform from traditional societies to a modern developed society. In order to achieve this transformation, there is a need to transfer the technology and the expertise of the developed nations to these countries. Development in this approach is a construct that defines the massive transfer of capital, ideology, technology, and know-how (Servaes, 1999). To be developed, developing nations need to emulate the western nations who have utilized the power of technology. This theoretical framing, originating from the development communication scholarship, is notable in the works of Daniel Lerner (1958); Walt Rostow (1960); Everett Rogers (1962); and Wilbur Schramm (1964). It continues to shape many development projects. The modernist/diffusionist approach to development projects is exemplified by transfer of technology and diffusion of innovations to the underdeveloped communities. It is often in a top-down process without input and participation from the receiving communities.

Dependency approach posits that underdevelopment and poverty are caused by the very process that made developed countries rich. The core argument is that underdevelopment is a result of the modernist approach to development, and that developed countries explored the poor countries during colonization, and now through trade and other socioeconomic configurations that benefit the developed nations. The dependency approach originated as a response to the modernist paradigm of development, and argues that the reliance of developing nations on technology and ideology of the developed nations further slows down their own development. Critics, such as Herbert Schiller (1992) and Armand Mattelart (1994), address the role of multinational corporations in ICT transfer to developing nations from this theoretical perspective. They see this transfer as global extension of market, with ICTs strengthening the position of the developed countries in the world system (Leye, 2007).

A third theoretical approach is a class of different theories that focuses on a participatory and people-centered approach to development, an approach that is human-centered, bottom-up (rather than top-down) and grassroots-based. Examples of this conceptual thinking are the multiplicity approach by Jan Servaes (1999), another development developed by the Dag Hammarskjöld Foundation of Sweden, *conscientização* by Paulo Freire, capability and functioning approach by Amartya Sen. These theories may be categorized within human development approach. The human development approach reflects Amartya Sen's (1999) framing of development as freedom to enhance an individual's potential and choices to attain economic, social, political, and cultural well-being. Development is seen as confronting obstacles that hinder people's functioning, ability to participate in a society, and the ability to expand one's choices. In contrast to the modernist and dependency approaches, development here is multidimensional with a focus on issues of freedom and justice from the relationship of tension between the individual and society, while addressing the many faces of power, culture, and ideology (Servaes, 1999). Sein & Harindranath (2004) identify key features of the human development approach: enabling choices in education, health, and standard of living; building a democratic society marked by involvement, participation, and transparency; and better management of behavior and customs, based on a better understanding of culture.

Development in this approach is measured by many factors and series of indices collectively identified as the *Human Development Index* (HDI). This measurement defines UNDP's approach to the assessment of global development. The key elements are: (1) HDI, which includes life expectancy at birth, level of education, and GNP per capita; (2) Gender Development Index (GDI), which uses the HDI to measure differences between men and women; (3) Gender Equity Measure (GEM), which addresses the possibilities of women to be part of the decision-making in economics and politics; and (4) Human Poverty Index (HPI), which studies the standard of living in a country. These measurement tools provide some of the mechanisms to engage inequality and other socioeconomic injustices that hinder human development. From these theoretical framings of development, ICTs are subsequently conceptualized as playing a key role in addressing these development challenges toward achieving social change.

In framing technology and development, the core theoretical perspectives can be described as the deterministic approach, a dystopia view, and a structuralist approach. The deterministic approach is a utopian view that sees ICTs as a way for developing countries to leapfrog development, that ICTs open window of opportunities, and offer solution to many social and economic problems. Predominant in this view is the technology determinism approach. This approach implies that technology has effects on society, that society defines itself along technological innovations, and that technology is a force that shapes society. Seminal works in this argument can be seen, for example, in the works of Marshall McLuhan and Ithiel de Sola Pool. ICTs for development in the technology determinism framework take a modernist and diffusionist approach. This is seen in the way that technologies are being transferred to rural and poor locations where adequate knowledge and skills to utilize these technologies are absent. It is an approach that assumes that with the transfer of technology and its diffusion, the rural, the poor, and the uneducated will gradually apply this technology to transform their social well-being. In a pattern of similar arguments made by Daniel Lerner (1958) and Wilbur Schramm (1964) about the mass media, technology is reified as a "mobility multiplier."

On the other hand, a social determinism approach, which is derived from the theoretical framework of *social construction of technology* (SCOT), argues that technology is shaped by culture, politics, and economics, and that social consequence shapes technological innovations. SCOT is a response to the technology determinism argument. SCOT is derived from the social constructivist approach that elaborates the sociology of technology and the social context of human-technology relations. The argument for a sociological and constructivist approach to technology has been eloquently discussed in the works of Bruno Latour, and the seminal work of Bijker et al. (1987). This approach in ICTD addresses the regulatory and policy context of ICT in development, recognizes the impact that cultural context makes in the adoption and use of technology, and studies how different social groups and actors shape and engage technology in confronting their problems. It can also be applied to studies that focus on developing skills and literacy in order to adequately utilize technology.

A dystopia view sees technology as a wrong resource in addressing the social conditions of the poor. It argues that attention to development issues regarding the poor should be geared toward providing water, health care, jobs, electricity, and so on. The common parlance in this approach is that "the poor cannot eat computer," or that the poor needs bread not broadband. The third approach is a structuralist perspective, which argues that ICTs lead to improvement and innovations in society, and at the same time recognize that society, and its sociopolitical structures, also has consequences in shaping technology. Scholars in this approach may also take a poststructuralist, culturalist, postmodernist, and a multidimensional understanding that ICTs provide externalities that can help people function, improve their well-being, and provide opportunities for economic and social benefits (Castells, 2004, 2007; Warschauer, 2003; Mansell, 2002; Servon, 2002; Mossberger et al., 2003).

Beyond this theoretical classification, the most popular framing of technology and development is the concept of digital divide. The term originated in the United States in the 1995 Department of Commerce's study called *Falling Through the Net*. This was a series of studies emphasizing the limited rate of Internet penetration amongst poor and rural Americans. However, by the end of the 1990s and early 2000s, the term became a global concept in framing technology and development. It became prominent in many national and international policy discourses on access to new communications technologies. The term describes the gap or the divide that exists between those with access to technologies and those without. Digital divide reflects the divides between the information rich and information poor, the technology "Haves" and the "Have Nots," and thus argues for policy efforts to bridge this gap. Many social critics, economists, development experts, and communication scholars have questioned the narrow conceptual framework of the digital divide, citing its focus on physical access to technology rather than other relevant forms of divides such as skills and usage (cf. van Dijk, 2005). The digital divide framing influenced development agendas and many technology policy discourses, such as universal service and universal access policies.

As a result of these framings, a global ideology of technology, development, and social change was engendered. These framings, first of all, elevate the rhetoric of development to a signifying mode, a signifier for a state of "modernity," where, as Sosale (2004) notes, modernity is seen as adoption of new technologies, modern style of living based on Western behaviorism and positivism, rational thinking over nature, and where alternative way of living based on traditional concept is seen as less desirable. Sosale (2004) argues that the rhetoric of development becomes a dominant way of defining, mapping, and classifying the world. Technology is embraced as an index of development, to be developed, thus becomes a global agenda that is achievable through adopting a Western ideology of a techno-social and economic configuration that dominates national polities. This ideology became internalized in the consciousness of "the developing," and institutionalized in government policies, and in the development agendas of international agencies and foundations. The global ideology of technology and development hides the neoliberal agendas of multinational corporations working in tandem with international agencies in the ICTs for development programs in developing nations. Consequently, this ideology makes technology natural and normal for culture, and also creates the rationalization that technology is what is actually needed to make society better.

The dominant models of ICT for development

There are various ICTD projects initiated all over the developing world; they are supported and funded by national governments, development agencies, and multinational corporations. These projects operate under generic approaches that have become dominant models of implementing ICTs for development.

The telecenter approach

Telecenters are facilities strategically located to provide public access to ICTs. These technologies usually include, but not limited to: telecommunication services, such as telephone, fax, e-mail, Internet; office equipment, such as computer, printers, and photocopiers; and multimedia equipment, such as radio, TV, and video. Many varieties of telecenters are available depending on the services provided. For example, multipurpose community telecenters provide a gamut of services beyond the ones listed above. They offer, in addition, training workshops, seminar rooms for meetings, videoconferencing, and access to distance education services. Telecenters can function as community multipurpose facilities, where everything related to communication and training is available; in this sense, telecenters goes beyond access to telephony or computers.

Originating in Sweden in 1985, telecenters have become popular in many ICTs for development projects (Oestmann & Dymond, 2001). Many projects that focus on enhancing access to ICTs have adopted the establishment of telecenters as a key strategy. Many developing countries have initiated telecenter project as part of national telecommunication policy and development agendas. Telecenters provide many advantages, and perhaps these are the contributing reasons for their popularity as development strategy. Telecenters provide the means of delivering public communication services to rural and remote location/ people without incurring large investment. By doing this, telecenters are helping to:

- Develop rural and remote infrastructure.
- Provide rural regions with better public services and improved local administration.
- Generate employment and foster socioeconomic development.
- Integrate relatively isolated communities into the national and international information network and thus accelerate exchange of private goods and services.
- Transfer expertise in a number of areas, such as agriculture, to and from the community.
- Give local producers access to market information, thus reducing the need for middlemen and increasing rural incomes (ibid:4).

Most commonly used services at the telecenters usually include people making phone calls, photocopying, printing, typing services, bookkeeping, and the Internet. In many developing countries, problems that usually arise from the use of the telecenters centered around illiteracy (especially computers skills), language problems (as most Internet contents are in English language), lack of awareness and the culture of technology use, high cost of Internet connections, and poor quality connections.

Capacity training approach

ICT capacity building is the process of developing the human capital to apply ICTs. It can be seen as the acquiring of human and cultural capital through the attainment of new skills or knowledge (Urquhart et al., 2008). ICT capacity building is implemented by providing necessary skills for the ICT intervention to be successful; this can be training in how to use the technologies at the telecenters located in the communities or schools, and the building of human capital by the use of the ICT infrastructure itself. It also includes developing the human capital to manage the appropriate resources necessary for an environment of the application of technology in a country's development through policy and improved regulatory process. This aspect of capacity building is identified as critical for successful implementations of ICTs in developing countries. A key feature of ICTs for development is the crafting and proper implementation of appropriate policies. This is one critical area that is missing in many developing countries. The establishment of telecenters for development usually starts with policy objectives, the implementations of ICTs in education, in economic development, in government, and in all spheres of a country's political and economic sectors starts with policy and appropriate regulation in the ICT sector. Consequently,

> effective policy-making and regulation, informed by global best practice but adapted to specific needs and context of a country and region, are critical element in expanding affordable access to, and effective use of, information and communication technologies and services as tools of broad-based development and poverty reduction in developing countries.
>
> (*info*Dev, 2008)

Policy making is a critical area in ICTs for development; challenges facing ICTD in many developing countries are due to:

- A "copy and paste" approach to policy, whereby policy frameworks utilized in developed countries are adopted by developing nations without taking into cognizance the dynamics of the issues confronting developing countries, which are, in most parts, different from those in the developed nations.
- The fact that the ICT sector is a very dynamic area, it constantly changes due to the increasingly changing nature of the technologies; policies that are geared toward ICTD need to be flexible and adaptable to the technological changes.
- Many developing nations are confronted with a shortage of skilled policy makers in this area.
- Many capacity training projects geared toward a one-off training approach do not adequately meet the need in developing countries for policy making. In addition, some of these training projects are usually based in the West, and hence they are very expensive for policy makers in developing nations to attend.

Realizing this shortage of capacity in the sector, development agencies, NGOs, foundations, and national governments have funded many capacity training projects in the developing world, some of these are shown in Table 3.3.

Table 3.3: Some projects funded by donor agencies with focus on ICT policy capacity training.

Project	Sponsor
African Technology Policy Studies	IDRC
Catalyzing Access to ICTs in Africa	DFID, SIDA
Building Digital Opportunities	DFID
Pro-Poor Pro-Market Policy and Regulation	IDRC
Regional ICT Support Program	European Union
Research ICT Africa Network	IDRC
African Information Society Initiative	UNECA, Danish Cooperation, GTZ
NetTel@Africa	USAID, SIDA, DFID
ScanICT Project	UNECA, IDRC, Norwegian Aid
African ICT Policy Monitor	APC, UNDP, Open Society Institute
Information Technology Centre for Africa	UNECA, Korean Government

*Source: info*Dev (2008).

NGOs and multinational corporation partnerships

The fact that about 70 percent of the world's population is not connected to the Internet is seen as a global social issue and addressing it has been constructed as a global agenda. For many multinational technology corporations, reaching this people offers opportunity for extension of market and economic benefits under a social agenda of development. Constrained by government bureaucracy and lack of fund to implement ICTD projects in developing countries, the private sector is allowed to partner the states and international agencies in many programs. The notion is that the private sector would target the untapped markets in developing countries with low-cost technologies and services. This is seen as a win-win situation by increasing the well-being of the poor, getting them connected to technologies while increasing profit for the private sector (Kuriyan, et al., 2008; Hosman & Fife, 2008). This approach, referred to as "Bottom of the Pyramid" approach (Prahalad, 2005), is a framework of targeting the four billion poor people who are located in bottom of the economic pyramid. It is an approach that aims to address social issues with a business model that benefits the private corporations and the poor at the same time.

The private corporations' involvements in the multilateral system have increased over the years. For instance, in the UN system it has been addressed as an almost unavoidable practice with the dwindling of financial contribution by member states, which has led to financial stress. The United Nations has welcomed collaboration with private enterprises with an accompanied ideological shift to neoliberalism – and its elements of privatization and private involvement in the UN development agendas (Leye, 2007). Public-Private Partnerships (PPPs) between ICT companies and governments of developing nations are also increasing with support from many international agencies, such as USAID, UN, and the World Bank. Technology corporations, such as Microsoft, Intel, and Cisco, are now in partnerships with development agencies in "bridging the digital divide." These corporations are setting up telecenters, providing software and equipment in the ICTD agenda in the developing world. An example is the 50 × 15 initiative by the global microprocessor manufacturer, AMD, which seeks to enable affordable, accessible Internet connectivity and computing capabilities for 50 percent of the world's population by the year 2015 (see *http://50x15.amd.com/en-us/*).

Critique of the dominant models of ICTD

Although necessary for development, ICT is not a panacea for all development problems. Many ICTD projects are implemented in a manner that access to technology is seen as an end instead of a means of achieving other social change goals. Consequently, having physical access to technology is erroneously perceived as achieving a development objective (Heeks, 1999). This *garment of Jesus*[4] ideology elevates technology as instant universal cure for all development problems; that a mere physical access to ICTs will miraculously eliminate poverty, inequalities, and other social problems. The attention placed on certain forms of ICT – namely, computer and the Internet – may overlook other essential medium like radio that has a higher penetration in developing countries. Many ICT projects have been criticized for lacking sustainability; once donor fund is expended, the projects seem to expire, and many communities with ICT project lack the skills to offer technical support for sustainability (Hosman & Fife, 2008). Other critics, such as Oyelaran-Oyeyinka & Adeya (2004), argue that many benefits of ICTs are not adequately tapped in developing countries; they cite the instance of lack of credit system, which affects the use of e-commerce in many African countries. In addition, information that these technologies provide is foreign to many communities, Internet content projects a different culture and different language that may make information irrelevant to many.

Scholars have criticized the indiscriminate establishment of telecenters in many communities in the developing world (Benjamin, 2001a, 2001b; Dagron, 2001; Bailur, 2008). This view highlights the failure of many telecenter projects, establishing telecenter in an area with many social problems usually rendered the projects "white elephants." Others, such as Leye (2007), point to a neodependency view, arguing that establishment of telecenters in developing countries is a form of development that is manipulated by corporate giants and development agencies to maintain the dependency of developing countries on the West, a resurrection of the modernization paradigm of development. Dagron (2001) observes that thousands of telecenters have been established globally and millions of dollars invested in buying computers and ensuring Internet connectivity; however, "every time we are to mention the successful experiences, the same five or six places come to mind" (p. 86).

The implementation of many ICTD projects has been criticized for its modernist and diffusionist approach. An approach that resonates the criticism of technology transfer, not merely as economic and political ideologies, but as a form of cultural process pushed forward through Western ideology, and at its extreme, an imperialist agenda mediated through the culture of technology (Martin-Barbero, 1993; Garcia-Canclini, 1995). The diffusionist approach to development assumes that external forces can stimulate development, whether through transfer of technology or the communication of information for behavioral change. However, contrary to findings on the ground, proponents and supporters of the diffusionist school believe it can still be the best approach to telecenters (Rogers & Shukla, 2002; Roman, 2003). Many ICTs for development projects have adopted this approach in the establishment of telecenters. The frameworks for the telecenters are often crafted away from the beneficiaries, in government bureaucratic systems, and from international agencies' offices in the West, in a top-down framework. Armed with funds, technological equipment, and communication technologies, the "apostles" of telecenters enter rural areas. They solicit for a building to house the equipment, or build a new one with approval of local communities who are eager to know how these technologies will change their lives.

Benjamin (2001a, 2001b), assessing the first wave of telecenters in South Africa, notes that the telecenter program was a top-down program that unintentionally created dependency and stifled local adaptation and ownership, and that a top-down planning commonly found in telecenter projects is very unlikely to achieve sustainable bottom-up social change. In contrast to the diffusionist top-down ICT initiatives, researchers have argued for an adoption of a participatory framework that attempts to guide projects by involving communities in the process, and based on their needs (Srinivasan, 2006). This approach is hinged on what many scholars have argued, that development initiatives must begin with grassroots communities and organizations (Servaes, 1999; Jacobson, 2003; Huesca, 2008).

For the NGOs, it raises a dilemma in the implementations of development projects with a methodological balance acting to address the need to respect the voices of communities, and the needs of donors – including multinational corporations. It is critical to unveil the techno-deterministic and utopian rhetoric of technology as agents of social, economic, and political developments, and reveals the pattern of capitalism and neoliberalism in development agendas. This is a pattern that benefits transnational corporations. Neoliberalism with its market agenda has infiltrated global telecommunications sector and national communication policies. Consequently, telecommunications services are treated as marketable services as seen in the WTO GATS agreements. As a result, we are witnessing an era of the corporatization of development, brought about by a widespread belief that there are no alternatives to neoliberal imperative and that development will come about through the forces of the market (Leye, 2007). Microsoft's partnership with UNESCO in bridging the digital divide is an example of this process. It should be seen in the light that many government institutions and NGOs around the world are gradually applying Free and Open Source Software (FOSS); Microsoft's partnership with UNESCO is thus an attempt by this software giant to secure its grip on the global software market. Consequently, Microsoft's development initiative of corporate social responsibility ensures activities that tie people, businesses, and organizations to its software (ibid.).

Many other issues of appropriate content, language, skills, and many more also raise concerns in ICTD. However, as Mansell (1999) asserts, ICT applications do not offer the panacea for social and economic development problems. Nevertheless, the risks of not participating in the technology, development, and social change phenomenon are enormous. The failure to invest in some of the ICT applications and network services will exacerbate the huge inequality between rich and poor countries, and between peoples in the developed and the developing regions of the world.

Rethinking ICTs for development: Toward sustainable social change

Technology plays an important role in social development, and the application of technology for development and social change agendas has significance. The critical issue is to engage how technology can be ethically adopted for sustainable social change. Technology gap and inequalities cannot be left to the free market alone, and neither should technology be seen as a universal remedy for all development problems. ICT-based programs for development can only be achieved through a combination of ethical issues of citizen's rights, human rights, freedom of expression and participation, elevating the concept of global social justice, and democratic principles. To achieve sustainable benefits from ICTs in development, there is a need to rethink development activities and recognize that ICT is just one ingredient of a solution to development challenges (Harris, 2004). Development strategies should follow a process of identifying the social problem, study what information is needed to confront this challenge, and what technology is best suited for a particular context to deliver this information. Unfortunately, most development initiatives erroneously start from the technology stage. An ethical approach to achieve sustainability in ICTD also includes:

Education and technology
In order to break a generational circle of poverty, education is identified as a key component of poverty alleviation program. Tying ICT to education, especially for children of the poor, will offer the skills and externalities that can break the circle of poverty and offer potentials for sustainability in ICT use for social change. ICT should not only be made available in schools for children, but technology skills should form part of the educational curricula. As a result, perennial problems of lack of local and relevant contents in home languages in ICT applications may finally be circumvented. ICT can also help to extend access to education for millions.

Recognizing that access to technology of information and communication is a right – human rights of citizens. In as much as access to information is considered fundamental human rights, it is also essential to recognize the rights to have access to the media that provide information. A number of countries are beginning to assert this notion in their constitutional framework. Finland has made access to broadband Internet a legal right of all citizens (Reisinger, 2009); France has also made efforts in recognizing access as basic rights (Bremner, 2009). Developing countries need to be proactive and begin to address access issue from a human rights perspective; the price of not doing so will stall progress and further exacerbate development gap and inequalities in these countries. For many developing countries, making access to ICT a basic right may raise concerns about a culture of entitlement, which may financially constrain the capacity of these countries to make access available for all. However, a legal or constitutional framework that recognizes access to communication technologies as basic rights, for instance, will be useful in monitoring the market operations of communication corporations and oblige governments to create programs and policies that make this right possible.

ICT projects must be established by adopting a bottom–up approach, which includes the democratic participation of beneficiaries. This enhances mechanisms for sustainability. Projects developed from the stipulated needs of a community usually tend to be more successful than an indiscriminate pattern of transferring technology. Employing grassroots participatory approach to the establishment and operation of technology access centers augurs sustainability of the centers. Using action-based, participatory, and ethnographic approaches to the study of ICT projects gives voice to the local beneficiaries and empowers them. Their "voices" and participation can improve the sustainability and relevance of projects. It is important to craft appropriate ICT policy that not only tackles access, but also how to encourage use, address skills development, gender inequality in the technology environment, and the ethical intervention of market forces and private partnerships in building technology infrastructure.

It is possible to engage ICTs for development that is community and people centered; it is feasible for technology to aid development and sustainable social change agendas in developing nations, and technology can be shaped to compliment social, cultural, political, and economic developments of majority of the world's population located in the bottom of the socioeconomic pyramid.

References

Ajuwon, G. & Rhinet, L. (2007). The Level of Internet Access and ICT Training for Health Information Professionals in Sub-Saharan Africa. *Health Information and Libraries Journal*, 25, 175–185.

Bailur, S. (2008). Deconstructing Community Participation in Telecenter Projects. *Development Informatics Working Paper series*. Paper #31. Retrieved on December 5, 2008 from http://www.sed. mnchester.ac.uk/idpm/research/publications/wp/di/index.htm

BBC. Surgeon Saves Boy's Life by Text. Retrieved on December 12, 2008 from http://news.bbc. co.uk/2/hi/health/7761994.stm

Benjamin, P. (2001a). The Gaseleka Telecentre, Northern Province, South Africa, in Latchem, C. & Walker, C. (eds.), *Telecentres: Case Studies and Key Issues*. Vancouver: Commonwealth of Learning.

———— (2001b). Telecenters in South Africa. *Journal of Development Communication*, 2(12), 1–6.

Bijker, W., Hughes, T., & Pinch, T. (1987). *The Social Construction of Technological Systems: New Directions in the Sociology and History of Technology*. Cambridge, MA: MIT Press.

Bremner, C. (2009). Top French Court Rips Heart out of Sarkozy Internet Law. Retrieved on December 11, 2009 from *http://technology.timesonline.co.uk/tol/news/tech_and_web/article6478542.ece*

Castells, M. (2004). Informationalism, Networks, and the Network Society: A Theoretical Blueprint, in Castells, M. (ed.), *The Network Society: A Cross-cultural Perspective*. Northampton, MA: Edward Elgar.

———— (2007). Communication, Power and Counter-power in the Network Society. *International Journal of Communication*, 1, 238–266.

Chowdhury, N. (2000). Poverty Alleviation and Information/Communication Technologies. Towards a Motif for the United Nation ICT Task Force. Retrieved on November 1, 2009 from http://www.eb2000.org/short_note_19.htm

Dagron, A. G. (2001). Prometheus riding Cadillac? Telecenters as the promised flame of knowledge. *Journal of Development Communication*, 2(12), 85–93.

Drucker, P. (1997). The Second Revolution. *New Perspective Quarterly*, 14(2), 20.

Franklin, M. (2006). Suggested Best Practice for Pursuing Development and Poverty through National ICT Strategies. *Journal of Eastern Caribbean Studies*, 31(4), 85–104.

Garcia-Canclini, N. (1995). *Hybrid Cultures: Strategies for Entering and Leaving Modernity*, trans. Christopher, L. Chiappari & Silvia L. Lopez. Minneapolis: University of Minnesota Press.

Green, J. (2003). Long Distance Op Puts SA on Medical Map. Retrieved on December 6, 2008 from http://www.iol.co.za/index.php?set_id=1&click_id=31&art_id=vn20030219050855781C418394

Harris, R. W. (2004). Information and Communication for Poverty Alleviation. United Nations Development Programme's Asia-Pacific Development Information Programme (UNDP-APDIP). Retrieved on November 1, 2009 from www.apdip.net/publications/iespprimers/eprimer-pov.pdf

Heeks, R. (1999). *Information and Communication Technologies, Poverty, and Development*. Development Informatics Working Paper, University of Manchester, Manchester, UK.

Hosman, L. & Fife, E. (2008). Improving the Prospects for Sustainable ICT Projects in the Developing World. *International Journal of Media and Cultural Politics*, 4(1), 51–69.

Huesca, R. (2008). Tracing the History of Participatory Communication Approaches to Development: A critical Appraisal, in Servaes, J. (ed.), *Communication for Development and Social Change*. Thousands Oaks, CA: SAGE.

InfoDev. (2008). Building Local Capacity for ICT Policy and Regulation: A Needs Assessment and Gap Analysis for Africa, the Caribbean, and the Pacific. *infoDev Working Paper #16*.

Jacobson, T. (2003). Participatory Communication for Social Change: The Relevance of the Theory of Communicative Action, in Kalbfleisch, P. J. (ed.), *Communication Yearbook 27*. International Communication Association. Mahwah, NJ: Lawrence Erlbaum Associates.

Kirkpatrick, G. (2008). *Technology and Social Power*. New York, NY: Palgrave Macmillan.

Kuriyan, R., Ray, I. & Toyama, K. (2008). Information and Communication Technologies for Development: The Bottom of the Pyramid Model in Practice. *The Information Society*, 24, 93–104.

Lerner, D. (1958). *The Passing of Traditional Society: Modernizing the Middle East.* New York, NY: Free Press.

Leye, V. (2007). Unesco, ICT Corporations and the Passion of ICT for Development: Modernization Resurrected. *Media, Culture & Society*, 29, 972–993.

Mansell, R. (1999). Information and Communication Technologies for Development: Assessing the Potentials and the Risks. *Telecommunications Policy*, 23, 35–50.

––––––– (2002). From Digital Divides to Digital Entitlements in Knowledge Societies. *Current Sociology*, 50, 407–426.

Mansell, R. & Wehn, U. (1998). (eds.) *Knowledge Societies: Information Technology for Sustainable Development.* New York: Oxford University Press.

Martin-Barbero, J. (1993). *Communication, Culture and Hegemony: From the Media to Mediations*, trans. Elizabeth Fox & Robert A. White. London: SAGE.

Mattelart, A. (1994). *Mapping World Communication: War, Progress, Culture.* Minneapolis, MN: University of Minnesota.

Mossberger, K., Tolbert, C. J., & Stansbury, M. (2003). *Virtual Inequality: Beyond the Digital Divide.* Washington, DC: Georgetown University Press.

Oestmann, S. & Dymond, A. (2001). Telecentres – Experiences, Lessons and Trends, in Latchem, C. & Walker, C. (eds.), *Telecentres: Case Studies and Key Issues.* Vancouver: Commonwealth of Learning.

Oyelaran-Oyeyinka, B. & Adeya, C. N. (2004). Internet Access in Africa: Empirical Evidence from Kenya and Nigeria. *Telematics and Informatics*, 21, 67–81.

Praekelt Foundation. (2008). *Project Masiluleke.* Retrieved on November 5, 2008 from http://www.praekeltfoundation.org/spotlight.html

Prahalad, C. K. (2005). *The Fortune of the Bottom of the Pyramid: Eradicating Poverty through Profits.* Delhi: Wharton School Publishing.

Reisinger, D. (2009). Finland Makes 1Mb Broadband Access a Legal Right. Retrieved on November 2, 2008 from *http://news.cnet.com/8301-17939_109-10374831-2.html*

Rogers, E. & Shukla, P. (2001). The Role of Telecenter in Development Communication and the Digital Divide. *Journal of Development Communication*, 2(12), 26–31.

Rogers, E. (1962). *Diffusion of Innovations.* New York: The Free Press.

Roman, R. (2003). Diffusion of Innovations as a Theoretical Framework for Telecenters. *Information Technologies and International Development*, 1(2), 53–66.

Rostow, W. W. (1960). *The Stages of Economic Growth: A Non-communist Manifesto.* Cambridge: University Press.

Schiller, H. (1992). *Mass communication and American empire.* Boulder, CO: Westview.

Schramm, W. (1964). *Mass Media and National Development: The Role of Information in the Developing Nations.* Paris & California: UNESCO and Stanford University Press.

Sein, M. K. & Harindranath, G. (2004). "Conceptualizing the ICT Artifact: Towards Understanding the Role of ICT in National Development." *The Information Society*, 20, 15–24.

Sen, A. (1992). *Inequality Reexamined.* Cambridge, MA: Harvard University Press.

––––––– (1999). *Development as Freedom.* New York, NY: Knopf.

Servaes, J. (1999). *Communication for Development: One World, Multiple Cultures.* Cresskill, NJ: Hampton.

Servon, L. J. (2002). *Bridging the Digital Divide: Technology, Community, and Public Policy*. Malden, MA: Blackwell.

Sosale, S. (2004). Toward a Critical Genealogy of Communication, Development, and Social Change, in Semanti, M. (ed.), *New Frontiers in International Communication Theory*. New York, NY: Rowan & Littlefield.

Srinivasan, R. (2006). Where Information Society and Community Voice Intersect. *The Information Society*, 22, 355–365.

Thomas, P. (2008). Communication and the Persistence of Poverty: The Need for a Return to Basics, in Servaes, J. (ed.), *Communication for Development and Social Change*. Thousands Oaks, CA: SAGE.

UNESCO (2009). Educational For All (EFA) Global Monitoring Report 2009; *Overcoming Inequality: Why Governance Matters*. Retrieved on November 1, 2009 from http://unesdoc. unesco.org/images/0017/001776/177683e.pdf.

United Nations Development Programme (2007). Human Development Report (HDR). Retrieved on May 7, 2009 from http://hdr.undp.org/en/reports/global/hdr2007–2008/news/ latinamerica/

Urquhart, C., Liyanage, S., & Kah, M. (2008). ICTs and Poverty Reduction: A Social Capital and Knowledge Perspective. *Journal of Information Technology*, 23, 203–213.

Van Dijk, J. (2005). *The Deepening Divide: Inequality in the Information Society*. Thousand Oaks, CA: SAGE.

Wakefield, J. (2010). Mobile Banking Closes Poverty Gap. Retrieved on June 4, 2010 from http:// news.bbc.co.uk/2/hi/technology/10156667.stm

Warschauer, M. (2003). *Technology and Social Inclusion: Rethinking the Digital Divide*. Cambridge, MA: MIT Press.

World Bank. (2000). *World Development Report: Attacking Poverty*. Retrieved on November 7, 2009 from http://www.worldbank.org/poverty/wdrpoverty/index.htm

Notes

1   Technology as applied here refers to information and communication technologies. It is used interchangeably with ICTs throughout this chapter.

2   For instance, at a rudimentary level, cell phone has become a major source of money transfer in many sub-Saharan African communities. Through text messages encoded with specific numbers, rural dwellers can receive and transfer fund across the country. This has become a source, of not only receiving money from family members in the cities, but a form of payment for services and goods. See example of M-Pesa in Kenya: http://www.safaricom. co.ke/index.php?id=257

3   With the increasing penetration of cell phone in developing countries, mobile banking is becoming popular in these regions. However, some challenges are encountered in mobile banking services, especially in rural areas. There are issues of fraud, monitoring agents that provide access to cash, illiteracy, and lack of knowledge on how the system works. See http:// news.bbc.co.uk/2/hi/technology/10156667.stm

4   This is a reference to a miraculous healing recorded in Mathew, 9: 20 (New American Standard Bible):

And a woman who had been suffering from a hemorrhage for twelve years, came up behind Him and touched the fringe of His cloak; for she was saying to herself, "If I only touch His garment, I will get well." But Jesus turning and seeing her said, "Daughter, take courage; your faith has made you well." At once the woman was made well.

Unfortunately, the issue of access to technologies with reference to poverty, inequalities, economic opportunities, social and political development, and participation is more complex. They are not problems that can be solved miraculously by mere physical access to computer and the Internet. The solution is far more complex than a mere contact or access to technologies.

Chapter 4

ICTs and Mobile Phones for Development in Sub-Saharan African Region[1]

Tokunbo Ojo

W ith the advancement in communication technologies in the last two decades, there has been a renewed interest in information and communication technologies (ICTs) as "an icon for modern development" (Heeks, 1999:15). ICTs, along with mobile telephony, are now being touted as the leapfrogging technologies that will allow "the least developed countries (LDC) to skip the industrial phase and move directly to the post-industrial one" (Wong, 2000:170). Since many of these LDCs are in the sub-Saharan African region, this has led to a new missionary zeal in which transnational companies are working with international developmental agencies in initiating "developmental projects" in the region. In addition to this, governments of these African countries are also privatizing their telecommunication sectors in line with the Washington Consensus Group[2]'s demands and requirements of the World Trade Organization (WTO) for the free flow of information. Being underpinned by market-friendly regulatory framework, there is question of sustainability, accessibility, and equity. Can market-driven reforms and diffusion of telephony technologies foster equity and accessibility for citizens?

This chapter problematizes the diffusion of mobile phones and ICTs for development in the sub-Saharan African region within the global discourse of telecommunication reform, globalization, and trade.

Background of sub-Saharan Africa's telecommunication development

The advent of the electric telegraph in the nineteenth century[3] changed the landscape of international communication in a similar way that the printing press[4] changed the global literacy and communication in the fifteenth century. The electric telegraph stimulated the internationalization of communication and the growth of international trade and investment (Thussu, 2000). As Read (1992) documented:

> The decade from 1870 to 1880 saw the successive inaugurations of communication links between the English coast and the Dutch East Indies (Batavia), the Caribbean network, the line from the British West Indies to Australia and China, the networks in the China and Japanese seas, the cable from Suez to Aden, communication between Aden and British India, the New Zealand cables, communication between the east and south coasts of Africa, and the cable from Hong Kong to Manila (cited in Thussu, 2000:16).

The development of these telecommunication networks and undersea communication cables came at the height of colonization. These telecommunication networks and undersea cable outlets became "an essential part of the new imperialism" (Headrick, 1981:163). It was this period that telecommunications were introduced to colonized African countries by Britain, France, Germany, and European colonialists. It was meant to maintain political control over the colonies as well as to advance economic interests of the colonial empire.

Since the colonialists' primary goal of building the networks was for the control and the exploitation of "the peoples and resources of the African continent" (M'Bayo, 1997:350), they built the telecommunication infrastructures only in the selected capital cities and major urban areas, especially those closer to coastal line. The consequences of this are that "the external telecommunications in almost all of Africa are better developed than [local] telecommunications infrastructures" (M'Bayo, 1997:350). As a result of the way that the telecommunication trunks and hubs were laid in the continent, it is extremely difficult to make local calls within the borders of many African countries more than five decades after they achieved independence from their colonial masters (Britain, France, Portugal, and Belgium).

The old colonial communication networks and information flows still stand because "almost all (94%) of inter-African telecommunications traffic [still] transits through metropolitan centers outside the continent, such as London or Paris" (Winseck, 1997:353; cf. Turan, 1989). This means that the local phone from a landline phone, in most cases, has to be routed through the communication networks of the former colonial "masters" or third-party networks first before travelling through inner-city networks, of which many are still analog and "are operating at saturated capacity or are highly unreliable, especially in the rainy season" (Jensen, 1999:184).

The postcolonial governments of many African countries have done relatively little to improve the inherited telecommunication systems due to factors that include the following:

- lack of continuous capital investment in communication infrastructures;
- investment inefficiencies in human development and appropriate technologies;
- inadequate private sector involvement;
- foreign exchange scarcity;
- poor management incentives;
- insufficient regional development; and
- political instability in many countries in the postindependence era (Gebreab, 2002).

It is estimated that it would cost over US$28 billion to improve fixed-line teledensity level in the region (Iridium, 1997:8, cited in M'Bayo, 1997). Such a huge investment in the wire line or fixed-line services is not considered cost-effective because it might not increase accessibility to all and sundry in urban and rural areas. It is, therefore, believed that the continent will be better served now and in the future if the investment is greatly diverted to the wireless system (Teledesic, 1996). Based on this assumption, more attentions are being given to the telephony and mobile phone systems at the expense of the stagnated fixed-line system. In the last five years, there has been a significant boom in the mobile phone subscriptions within the continent. The International Telecommunications Union (ITU) has consistently adjudged Africa as the world's fastest growing market for mobile phone since 2007.

Mobile phone as an alternative?

While indeed the mobile phones and telephony offer alternative option, there are inherent old problems such as the unreliable network connectivity and poor quality services that are manifesting within this "alternative" approach. Obijiofor (2008) recounted customers' frustrations and poor quality service that the MTN Nigeria[5], which has a near monopoly of the Nigerian mobile phone market, offers, as thus:

> Anyone who was in Nigeria in December 2007 and much of January 2008 would have experienced the worst telecommunications service provided by a company since the introduction of mobile telephony in Nigeria. Here are some of the bizarre experiences. You dial a mobile phone number and the call goes to an unintended receiver. You speak with someone on your mobile phone and you hear other people discussing on the same line. This is not something that is associated with mobile phone business in this age of new technologies.
>
> With MTN Nigeria, anything is possible. You dial a mobile phone number and before you complete the dialing, one of the following messages flashes across your mobile phone screen: "Call end. No response"; Call end. Dropped"; Call end. No answer", etc. Add to these the phenomenon of your receiver's voice dropping off constantly. In the first decade of the 21st century, customers of MTN Nigeria should not have to put up with this nonsense.

Many customers now have two or more mobile lines as a way to mitigate the problem, which is partly rooted in the poor telecommunication infrastructures within the country and in the whole continent. This obviously raises questions about the accuracy of the ITU's statistical figures that there are over 246 million mobile subscribers in Africa, especially in view of the fact that about 65 million of these subscribers are in Nigeria.

What is organically emerging from this is the short-term solution that the diffusion of mobile phones presents. This short-term solution masks the historical imbalance and structural inequalities in the national and global communication systems that were the subjects of the New World Information and Communication Order (NWICO) debate in the late 1970s and 1980s. As it might be recollected, the major concerns that led to the demand for the NWICO were:

- An unequal distribution of information: owing to the socio-technological imbalance there was a one-way flow of information from the "centre" to the "periphery," which created a wide gap between the "haves" and "have-nots";
- An unequal power in production: the information rich were in a position to dictate terms to the information poor, thus creating a structure of dependency with widespread economic, political, and social ramifications for the poor societies;
- The dominance of Western media: this vertical flow (as opposed to a desirable horizontal flow of global information) was dominated by the Western-based transnational corporations;
- The commercialization of media: information was treated by the transnational media as a "commodity" and subjected to the rules of the market;
- An extension of the global economic and social inequality: the entire information and communication order was a part of international inequalities that created and sustained mechanisms of neocolonialism (Masmoudi, 1979:172–173, cited in Thussu, 2000).

More than three decades after, these outlined concerns are still having far-deepening ramifications for African countries, in view of the ongoing process of commercialization of ICTs and mobile phone for development.

Market reforms and new frontiers

The global telecommunication market reforms and ICT industry since the early 1990s have shown an increasing privatization and transnational companies' dominant take-over of the industry. This trend is exacerbated by the World Trade Organization (WTO)'s 1997 Basic Telecommunication Agreement, which perceives privatization and deregulation of the telecommunications sector as "a precondition to the foreign direct investment (FDI), economic growth" and an avenue for a political integration in the globalized world economy (Hills, 1998:459). This new wave of liberalization and privatization is rooted in the economic assumption that opening up the market to the private sector would herald efficiency, faster service, and competition.

Since the agreement came into effect, almost all African countries have now introduced market-focused reforms in their telecommunications sector; with each country at different stages of the reform process (Gebreab, 2002; Wilson & Wong, 2003; Ojo, 2004). While these reform processes have been lauded by international financial institutions (World Bank) and ITU, the hard reality is these reforms are being undertaken in relative policy vacuum and "in advance of substantive restructuring of operations" (Mustafa et al., 1997). In consequence, the reforms seem overcomplicated and are proving ineffective "in promoting improvements in sector performance" in many countries across the continent (Mustafa et al., 1997:xi).

For instance, in Ghana, telecommunication reforms are still in the transition stage more than a decade after the reform process started. The licensed private enterprises in the fixed-line phone market are not fulfilling the conditions of their licenses, as mutually agreed to when they became strategic investors in the country's telecommunication market. These conditions include service extension to the rural areas and upgrading of network infrastructure in interior parts of the country. So far, licensees are reneging on their commitments, out of the fear that their investments would not yield maximum returns. This is the shortcoming of the market-based development, which is touted as "the magic wand" for the telecom problems of developing countries (Alhassan, 2007). South Africa's experience with another private operator, Telkom, also gives credence to this that telecommunication privatization is not yielding huge benefits in terms of access, fair price, and competition as theorized within the neoliberal telecommunication reform policies.

After a decade of reform (from 1996 to 2006), South Africa's objectives of accelerated development plans and provision of affordable access to communication resources have been disappointing – "at worst a medium-term failure" – with the end result being a private monopoly controlled by the licensee Telkom in place of the previous state monopoly (Horwitz & Currie, 2007; Gillwald, 2005). Being the *Shylock* of the markets (Ya'u, 2004), "Telkom[6] has clearly used its monopoly (in fixed line) to its advantage: since the year 2000, its operating profit margin increased from R1.54 billion to just over R9 billion in the fiscal year ending in 2007" (Ponelis & Britz, 2008:221). As opposed to the much-anticipated equity, fair competition, better prices, and quality service provision, telecommunication costs in South Africa are currently among the most expensive in the world (South Africa Foundation, 2005; Ponelis & Britz, 2008).

Across the continent, many of the licensed companies in both fixed and mobile telephony are operating in what could be considered as near-monopolies; with MTN, Vodacom, and Celtel[7] being the "Goliaths" of African mobile telephony alongside with Orange-France Telecom. The reform has allowed these companies to acquire "massive new freedom of maneuver in their attempts to reintegrate markets for labour power, goods and service, and thus to pursue on a global scale" (Schiller, 2010a:132). In other words, as one form of monopoly (state monopolies) ended, another one has emerged. The new monopoly is largely made up of consortium of transnational telecommunication companies, private foreign investors, and national elites within the continent.

At the global level, privatization and deregulation have fostered "a concentration of capital, growth of transnational corporations and forms of industrial oligopolization" that have excluded large numbers of individuals, social groups, local business entrepreneurs, and nation-states from the envisioned inclusive network economy and global public sphere (Hamelink, 1997:117). The 2008 OECD study of the ICT industry, which encompasses telecommunication services, information communication (IT) software, internet services, communication equipment, and semiconductor and electronics, revealed that approximately 78 percent of the world's top 250 ICT firms[8] are only located in nine countries – United States[9] (99 companies), Japan (40 companies), Chinese Taipei (19 companies), Canada (7 companies), France (7 companies), United Kingdom (6 companies), Korea, (6 companies), Netherlands (5 companies), and Germany (5 companies). The annual revenues of many of these companies, in some cases, are "bigger than the size of individual national economies, such as those of Malawi, Angola, Bangladesh, Bolivia, Bulgaria, Ireland, Kenya, Malaysia, New Zealand, or Pakistan" (Boyd-Barrett, 2010:143).

More than a decade after the WTO's 1997 Basic Telecommunication Agreement, the countries of origins of global top ten companies have not changed much, as Table 4.1 shows. With the exception of two new companies from Mexico and Spain that have joined the rank of global ten companies, companies from the United States, China/Hong Kong, Japan, United Kingdom, France, and Germany are still the dominant forces on the list in 2011, as they were in 1997. As opposed to a competitive and inclusive open market, the "invisible free hand of the market" has *reregulated*, not deregulated, the market to suit the hegemonic financial locales of the world.

The significant change from the 1997 list and 2011 list in Table 4.1 is that only three of the companies in the top ten in 1997 remain on the top ten list in 2011. The Dot.Com bust of the early 2000s and global financial crises of 2009/2010 affected the operations and the continued existence of many of the companies that dominated the telecommunication market in the mid-1990s. For instance, in the aftermath of global and European financial crises, Italian Telecom that was in the top ten ranking in 1997 dropped down to number eighteen in 2011. MCI WorldCom was acquired by Verizon Communications in 2005, following the Dot.Com bust. As one frontier is closed, another one is opened.

Several mergers and acquisitions of formerly public-owned telecommunication enterprises and small start-up companies between 1997 and 2010 have led to emergence of some new transnational telecommunication companies. Telefonica is an example of these

Table 4.1:   Top ten companies in global telecommunication services.

1997		2011	
Companies	**Country**	**Companies**	**Country**
AT&T	United States	China Mobile	Hong Kong & China
MCI Worldcom[10]	United States	AT&T	United States
Deutsche Telekom	Germany	Vodafone Group	United Kingdom
DGT	China	Telefonica SA	Spain
Hong Kong Telecom	Hong Kong & China	Verizon Communications	United States
KDD	Japan	AMX	Mexico
France Telecom	France	NTT DoCoMo	Japan
Sprint	United States	Deutsche Telekom	Germany
VSNL	India	Nippon Telegraph & Telephone	Japan
Telecom Italia	Italy	France Telecom-Orange[11]	France

Source: Financial Times (2011); OECD (2008); Thussu (2006).

new transnational companies. Prior to 1997, Telefonica's business was mainly confined to Spain. However, with the global expansion opportunity that WTO agreement presented, it expanded its global reach and captured most of the Latin American markets that opened up as a result of deregulation and privatization process.

In a similar vein, mergers and acquisitions have helped companies such as AT&T and France Telecom-Orange to consolidate their global market shares and maintain their top ranking. France Telecom-Orange, in particular, has made a lot of acquisitions and inroad in Africa, especially in Francophone African countries[12] that were France's colonies in the colonial era, to stay afloat. Outside of Europe, Africa is its second largest market. In the quest for more African markets, it is building a 12,000-km submarine fiber-optic cable that would extend from the coast of Gabon to France. The planned routes of connection, which is shown in Figure 4.1, are along the coastal lines. At the completion of this project – "African Coast to Europe (ACE)" – in late 2012, about twenty countries[13] will be connected on these trade routes and communication links.

From the strategic business standpoints, these trade routes and communication links are "deliberately designed to maintain centers of power and to overcome international comparative disadvantages" (Melody, 1993:66) in the global communication, as it was the case during the colonial era when telecommunication infrastructures were laid across the metropolitan cities of the colonies. For example, long after the colonial rule is over, politically and economically, "Britain still benefits substantially from its historically established communication links with its former colonies" (Melody, 1993:66).

The present evolving global reforms, primarily under the guidance of WTO, is creating a similar structural concentration of world's wealth and technological resources in the confine of a few multinational companies and countries with comparative advantages in the international trade and technological development (UNCTAD, 2004; UNDP, 2005; Kegley & Blanton, 2009). For African countries, this means that they are locked into a new relationship of structural dependency that the new globalizing reforms and trade relation present. In particular, those African countries on the trade routes might not be able "to develop progressive social and economic policies" (Mohammadi, 1997:89) for the benefit of their populations and local business enterprises as a result of the systemic transnationalization of the communication resources.

The systemic transnationalization of communication networks creates dialectic conditions for these countries when exercising their sovereignty power when it comes to policy and regulatory framework for their telecommunication sectors. For instance, before making any regulatory change, they have to do "the cost-benefit calculus of many policy choices that they must take," in the context of structural features of global economy, and rules and trade sanction of the WTO[14] (Hanson, 2008:158–160). In addition to the tension of balancing private interest with public interest, they also have to work out a model of reconciling global interest with national interest. The implication of this is the absence of room for the citizens' communication needs, as the market further "strengthens existing conditions of social inequity," and spatial economic inequality (Hamelink, 1997:117). These

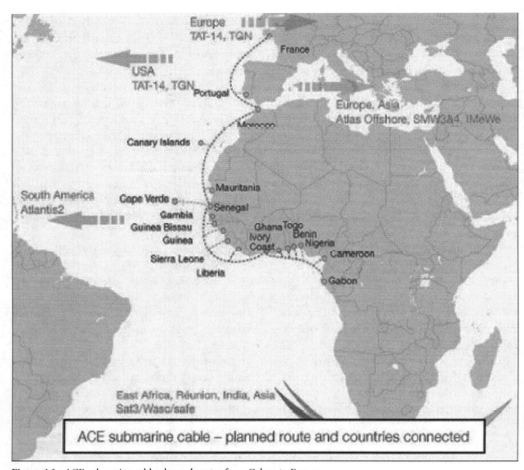

Figure 4.1: ACE submarine cable planned routes from Gabon to France.
Source: France Telecom-Orange (2008).

are the inherent complications and the spatial bias[15] in the present global communication structure.

From the critical school of thought in the political economy of communication, these emerging ICT and telecommunications systems are examples of what Herbert Schiller called "media-cultural imperialism," which is a subset of the general system of imperialism (Schiller, 2010b:247). Imperialism, as Schiller defined it, is "a system of exploitative control of people and resources" (Schiller, 2010b:250). As it was the case in the Agrarian period and industrialization era, Africa, its people and resources are once again being exploited in this present age of digitalization. The raw materials such as

Columbite-tantalite (Coltan as a short form) that are used for the productions of digital technologies, which range from mobile phones to computer chips and video cassette recorders (VCRs), are taken from Africa at relatively cheap price or in exchange for war ammunitions for rebels in countries such as Congo. These raw materials are taken to West as well as China, processed, and are then returned back to the continent for consumption. In their diverse varieties, they are branded as disruptive technologies, technologies of freedom, and technologies of social change with the power of leapfrogging the continent's development process.

To this end, they are taken as given and signs of modern development by Africans and their leaders in line with the dominant global discourse of quantitative-based development, which Washington Consensus Group and United Nations heavily promote in their assessment of national e-readiness and global information-based economy. The consequence of this is that the subtle replication of the unequal way that Africa was integrated into the global system at the mercantilist phase of early capitalism between the sixteenth century and eighteenth century, which in turn fostered "a good part of the later 'backwardness' of the continent" and underdevelopment (Amin, 2002:43) that ICTs must leapfrog.

Paradoxically, Africans and their leaders are consuming themselves to "death." Money, which could have gone into saving, health care, education, or food production, is being spent on the consumption of the ICTs applications and services. On the annual basis, many African countries pay billions of dollars as proprietary licensing fees[16] and service delivery fees for software such as Microsoft offices suite and Oracle package. For instance, Nigeria pays approximately US$1 billion annually in the form of licensing software, delivery support, and technical support fees to transnational companies and their local subsidiaries and partners, according to Chris Uwaje, President of the Institute of Software Practitioners of Nigeria (Ayantokun, 2011). This is more than what the country spends on education and health services in the last five years.

Sharra (2010) indicated that, in Malawi, one government agency spends almost US$67 million (about MK 10 billion in the local currency) on the software license fees annually. This is a significant portion of the country's annual budget, which as at 2008/2009 was $US1.6 billion (MK 227.2 billion in local currency). He notes:

> Worse still, there are several other Malawian government and corporate entities that are spending hard earned taxpayer money and scarce forex paying for these software license fees. To illustrate this, much of the costs of running the telecentres the government is constructing across the country are going toward software licenses for proprietary software. ... The telecommunications industry itself sends out billions of kwacha every year paying these kinds of fees to developed countries (Sharra, 2010: online).

Like their governments, many Africans spend an average of 10 to 17 percent of their monthly incomes on mobile phone services. This is almost twice the amount that people in the OECD

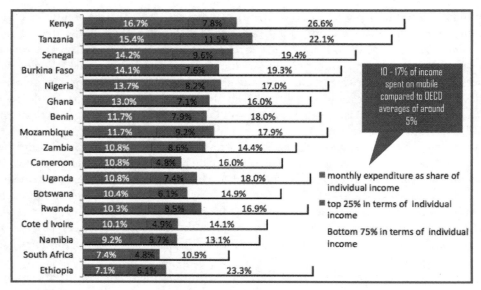

Figure 4.2: Percentage income and spending on mobile phones.
Source: Gillwald (2009).

countries spend monthly on their mobile phone services. Figure 4.2 shows more detailed spending figures in proportion to the monthly income.

These trends compound the disequilibria of development. It is culture of consumerism, not a creative knowledge production that stimulates long-term sustainable development. This is an indictment of local policy makers and stakeholders who subordinated national planning and people to the global agenda and technical experts that seek to "develop" people and societies through ICTs and electronic communication gadgets. If crucial intervention is not made soon, what is left of Africans might be "consumed in turn by the industrial machine which churns out the latest novelty, one which, to complete the cycle of illusion … and therefore of a dynamic, contemporary world culture. Is this perhaps what is meant by development?" (Soyinka, 1994:209).

Where do we go from here?

This is one of the reasons that Africans and their governments should not take the new ICTs for development agenda and the international regimes that accompany it as given. To maintain their own cultural sovereignty and production capacities, they need to understand the culture of ICTs and its relevance to their own development plans on their own terms, not the terms imposed by the external forces. Questions and issues underpinning the ICTs for development agenda are not merely economic ones. "They are also socio-cultural and political" in nature (Graham, 2001 as cited in Shade, 2003:114).

In lieu of the current model of adopting communication technologies and reform policies strictly on intuition and "the wish to be seen as modern" (Adamolekun, 1996:26), the emphasis should be on the development of human and social capabilities. These include "(1) general education and technical competencies, (2) the institutions that influence abilities to finance and operate modern organizations, and (3) the political and social factors that influence risks, incentives, and personal rewards including social esteem" (Mansell, 2001:56 – *numeric number added*). With human development in terms of technical innovation, creativity, social knowledge, and empowering local manufacturing expertise, Africans will be able to develop and utilize a new generation of ICTs in accordance with their cultural norms, social realities, and national development goals (Ojo, 2006; Adeya & Cogburn, 2001).

About 45 percent of the continent's current populations are under the age of 15. This "Africa's youthfulness can become a plus if it is seen as a potential, a pointer to a long-term solution to the ICT problem" (Sonaike, 2004:57). Any long-term developmental plans that fail to take into consideration this young generation is bound to fail. It is to this degree that the future policy intervention should be predated on self-determination ethos, cultural values, human capabilities, and dignity instead of the "catch-up thesis."

References

Adamolekun, W. (1996). The Information Superhighway and Traditional Communication: Where We Stand. *Africa Media Review*, 10(2), 22–36.

Adeya, C. N. & Cogburn, D. L. (2001). Globalisation and the Information Economy: Challenges and Opportunities in Africa, in Nulens, G., Hafkin, N., Audenhove, L. V., & Cammaerts, B. (eds.), *The Digital Divide in Developing Countries: Towards an Information Society in Africa*. Brussels: VUB University Press, pp. 77–112.

Alhassan, A. (2007). Broken Promises in Ghana's Telecom Sector. *Media Development*, 3. Retrieved on February 1, 2009 from http://www.waccglobal.org/lang-en/publications/media-development/46-2007-3/459- Broken-promises-in-Ghanas-telecom-sector.html

Amin, S. (2002). Africa: Living on the Fringe. Monthly Review, March. Retrieved on January 31, 2009 from http://www.monthlyreview.org/mar2002.htm

Ayantokun, O. (2011). Foreign Software Licensing: Nigeria loses $1bn annually. *Nigerian Tribune*, March 29. Retrieved on June 23, 2011 from http://www.tribune.com.ng/index.php/ tele-info/19585-foreignsoft ware-licensing-nigeria-loses-1bn-annually-

Boafo, K. S. T. (1991). Communication Technology and Dependent Development in Sub-Saharan Africa, in Gerald Sussman & John A. Lent (eds.), *Transnational Communications: Wiring the Third World*. Newbury Park, London and Delhi: SAGE, pp. 103–124.

Boyd-Barrett, O. (2010). Media Imperialism Reformulated, in Daya Kishan Thussu (ed.), *International Communication: A Reader*. New York/London: Routledge, pp. 139–153.

Financial Times. (2011). FT Global 500 2011. Retrieved from http://media.ft .com/cms/ 33558890-98d4-11e0-bd66-00144feab49a.pdf.

France Telecom-Orange. (2008). Orange Partners ACE, a New Submarine Fibre-optic Cable that Will Connect 20 African Countries to Broadband Internet. *Press Release*, December 11.

——— (2007). *Annual Report*. Paris: France Telecom-Orange.

Gebreab, F. (2002). Getting Connected: Competition and Diffusion in African Mobile Telecommunications Markets. *World Bank Policy Research Working Paper 2863*. Washington DC: World Bank.

Gillwald, A. (2005). Good Intentions, Poor Outcomes: Telecommunications Reform in South Africa. *Telecommunications Policy*, 29, 469–491.

——— (2009). ICT Policy and Regulatory Frameworks: the status and challenges of SADC countries. A Presentation made at the e-Parliaments: Concepts, Policy and Reality Conference on 12 October 2009 in Cape Town, South Africa.

Hamelink, C. J. (1997). International Communication: Global Market and Morality, in Mohammadi, A. (ed.), *International Communication and Globalization*. Thousand Oaks, CA: SAGE, pp. 92–118.

Hanson, E. C. (2008). *The Information Revolution and World Politics*. Lanham, Maryland: Rowman & Littlefield.

Headrick, D. (1981). *The Tools of Empire: Technology and European Imperialism in the Nineteenth Century*. New York: Oxford University Press.

Heeks, R. (1999). Information and Communication Technologies, Poverty and Development. *Development Informatics*, Working Paper Series, Number 5. Manchester, UK: Institute for Development Policy and Management.

Hills, J. (2002). *The Struggle for Control of Global Communications: The Formative Century*. Urbana and Chicago: University of Illinois Press.

——— (1998). Liberalization, Regulation and Development. *Gazette: The International Journal for Communication Studies*, 60(6), 459–76.

Hoff, D. (2006). South African Cellular Wars in Nigeria. *International Journal of Emerging Markets*, 1(1), 84–95.

Horwitz, R. B. & Currie, W. (2007). Another Instance Where Privatization Trumped Liberalization: The Politics of Telecommunications Reform in South Africa—A Ten-Year Retrospective. *Telecommunications Policy*, 31(8–9), 445–462.

Kegley, C. W. & Blanton, S. L. (2009). *World Politics: Trends and Transformations, 2009–2010*. Belmont, CA: Wadsworth Publishing.

Jensen, M. (1999). Sub-Saharan Africa, in Tawfik, M. (ed.), *World Communication and Information Report 1999–2000*. Paris: UNESCO, pp. 180–196.

Mansell, R. (2001). The Deep Structure of Knowledge Societies, in Liss Jeffrey (ed.), *Vital Links for a Knowledge Culture: Public Access to New Information and Communication Access*. Strasbourg: Council of Europe Publishing, pp. 55–73.

M'Bayo, R. (1997). Africa and the Global Information Infrastructure. *Gazette: The International Journal for Communication Studies*, 59(4–5), 345–364.

Melody, W. H. (1993). On the Political Economy of Communication in the Information Society, in Janet Wasko, Vincent Mosco & Manjunath Pendakur (eds.), *Illuminating the Blindspots:*

Essays Honoring Dallas W. Symthe. Norwood, New Jersey: Ablex Publishing Corporation, pp. 63–81.

Mohammadi, A. (1997). Communication and the Globalization Process in the Developing World, in Mohammadi, A. (ed.), *International Communication and Globalization*. Thousand Oaks, CA: SAGE, pp. 67–89.

Mustafa, M., Laidlaw, B., & Brand, M. (1997). *Telecommunication Policies for Sub-Saharan Africa*. World Bank Discussion Paper, No.353, Washington: World Bank.

Obijiofor, L. (2008). MTN: It's Time to Go. *Guardian Newspaper*, January 25. Retrieved on February 1, 2009 from http://www.nigeriavillagesquare.com/articles/levi-obijiofor/mtn-it-s-time-to-go-3.html

OECD. (2008). *Information Technology Outlook*. Paris: OECD.

Ojo, T. (2004). Old Paradigm and Information and Communication Technologies for Development Agenda in Africa: Modernization as Context. *Journal of Information Technology Impact*, 4(3), 139–150.

———— (2006). Communication Networking: ICTs and Health Information in Africa, *Information Development*, 22(2), 94–101.

Ponelis, S. R. & Britz, J. J. (2008). To Talk or not to Talk? From Telkom to Hellkom: A Critical Reflection on the Current Telecommunication Policy in South Africa from a Social Justice Perspective. *The International Information & Library Review*, 40, 219–225.

Read, D. (1992). *The Power of News: The History of Reuters, 1849–1989*. Oxford: Oxford University Press.

Schiller, D. (2010a). World Communications in Today's Age of Capital, in Daya Kishan Thussu (ed.), *International Communication: A Reader*. New York/London: Routledge, pp. 122–135.

Schiller, H. (2010b). Not Yet the Post-Imperialist Era, in Daya Kishan Thussu (ed.), *International Communication: A Reader*. New York/London: Routledge, pp. 247–260.

Shade, L. R. (2003). Here Comes the Dot Force! The New Cavalry for Equity? *Gazette: The International Journal for Communication Studies*, 65(2), 105–118.

Sharra, S. (2010). Malawi Has an App for That: Charting a Developing Nation's IT Future. July 25. Retrieved on July 28, 2010 from http://mlauzi.blogspot.com/

Sonaike, S. A. (2004). The Internet and the Dilemma of Africa's Development. *Gazette*, 66(1), 41–61.

South Africa Foundation. (2005). Telecommunication Prices in South Africa: An International Peer Group Comparison. Occasional Paper No. 1, April. Melrose Arch, Johannesburg: Genesis Analytics (Pty) Ltd.

Soyinka, W. (1994). Culture, Memory and Development, in Ismail Serageldin & June Taboroff (eds.), *Culture and Development in Africa*. Washington DC: The World Bank, pp. 201–218.

Stiglitz, J.E. (2003). *Globalization and Its Disconnects*. New York: W.W. Norton.

Teledesic. (1996). Teledesic's Global Network to Help African Continent Achieve Broadband Connectivity. Retrieved on February 18, 2009 from http://www.allbusiness.com/trade-development/economic-development/7267920-1.html

Telkom. (2007). *Telkom Corporate Profile*. Pretoria, South Africa: Telkom.

Thussu, D. (2000). *International Communication: Continuity and Change*. London: Arnold.

—— (2006). *International Communication: Continuity and Change* (2nd ed.). London: Arnold.

Turan, O. (1989). Reflections on the Methods to be Used for Establishing Tariffs between Countries in Africa" Telecommunications Journal, 56(1), 48–50.

UNCTAD (United Nations Conference on Trade and Development). (2004). *World Investment Report 2004: The Shift toward Services.* New York: United Nations.

UNDP. (2005). *Human Development Report.* New York: UNDP/Oxford University Press.

Wilson, E. J. & Wong, K. (2003). The Status of the Information Revolution in Africa. *Telecommunications Policy*, 27(1–2), 155–177.

Winseck, D. (1997). The Shifting Contexts of International Communication: Possibilities for a New World Information and Communication Order, in Bailie, M. & Winseck, D. (eds.), *Democratizing Communication? Comparative Perspectives on Information and Power.* Cresskill, NJ: Hampton Press Inc, pp. 343–375.

Wong, K. (2000). Leapfrogging Development: The Political Economy of Telecommunications Restructuring. *Journal of Communication*, 50(2), 170–171

Ya'u, Y. Z. (2004). The New Imperialism and Africa in the Global Electronic Village. *Review of African Political Economy*, 31(99), 11–29.

Notes

1 The sub-Saharan African region is a geopolitical region that is in the south of the Sahara desert. The region, which spans three linguistic zones (Anglophone, Francophone, and Lusophone), has a population of about half a billion. The region is "occupied by 41 independent states that, with the exception of Ethiopia and Liberia, emerged from a long period of colonial administration only in the late 1950s and the 1960s" (Boafo, 1991:103).

2 Washington Consensus Group is made up of the International Monetary Fund (IMF), the World Bank and the US Treasury Department. They are tagged 'Washington Consensus' Group because of the usual "consensus between the IMF, the World Bank, and the US Treasury about the 'right' policies for developing countries" (Stiglitz, 2003:16).

3 The telegraph was invented in 1837 by Samuel Morse.

4 Johann Gutenberg invented the printing press in the fifteenth century. The printing press radically changed the means of communication in Europe with the massive publication of books and translation of the Bible in different languages. Prior to the invention of the printing press, books and the Bible have only been in the domains of elites and priests. But things changed radically when there were publications of books in millions from the printing presses in major European cities. As a result of this development, the average citizen got access to the Bible and read it on his/her own without having to seek the permission of the priests. The hierarchical societal structure of access to knowledge, exemplified by Bible and books, was demolished.

5 MTN Nigeria is subsidiary of the MTN Group, which operates in about 21 countries in Africa and the Middle East.

6   Among many South Africans, the Telkom is connotatively known as "Hell-kom." Some of the disappointed customers have taken their frustrations to the cyberspace by setting up www. hellkom.co.za, which has become a public sphere for the customers and citizens to express their views on poor access to telecommunication in South Africa. The site's implicit goal is to pressurize the Telkom and South Africa government for accessible telecommunication resources and better quality of service. This is necessary in view of the fact that the South African government is the largest shareholder in Telkom, with approximately 40 percent shares (Telkom, 2007; Ponelis & Britz, 2008).

7   These companies are active from coast to coast across the continent (Hoff, 2006).

8   In 2006, these companies generated combined revenue of US$3,375 billion.

9   The very strong market presence and dominance of the US-originated transnational companies in the industry led further credence to the argument that WTO and the market-friendly agreement only "created the opportunity for the worldwide integration of domestic and international communication networks under a US-led oligopoly" (Hills, 2002:1).

10 In 2005, Verizon Communications acquired MCI WorldCom.

11 It became France Telecom-Orange in 2000, following its $US40 billion acquisition of Orange UK mobile phone operator.

12 Francophone countries that the France Telecom has made acquisitions since 1997 include Togo, Cameroon, Senegal, Niger, Central Africa Republic, Gabon, Ivory Coast, Guinea, and Guinea Bissau. It also is expanding its acquisition quest to other Anglophone parts of the continent. In 2007, it purchased 51 percent stake in Telkom Kenya, which has over 280,000 fixed mobiles as well as a new license for mobile phone services operation (France Telecom-Orange, 2007).

13 The twenty countries that will be connected when at the completion of the project are: Gabon, Cameroon, Nigeria, Benin, Togo, Ghana, Ivory Coast, Liberia, Sierra Leone, Guinea, Guinea Bissau, Senegal, Gambia, Cape Verde, Mauritania, Canary Islands, Morocco, Spain, Portugal, and France.

14 Under the rules of the WTO, certain government policies that could protect local industry and enhance industrial development in Africa and many developing countries are prohibited. These include "local content and technology transfer requirements for foreign investments" (Hanson, 2008:162). This is simply to ensure an "uninterrupted" flow of trades, and internationalization of production of goods and services. You can see more case studies on the WTO rules and the national policies here: http://www.wto.org/english/res_e/booksp_e/casestudies_e/casestudies_e.htm.

15 The recently enacted "buy America and American Acts" of the US government illuminate the inherent bias and unequal power relation in the global structure. These Acts, which are meant to protect American local industry and ensure the country's fast recovery from the present global recession, contradict every tenet of "free flow of trade gospel" that is preached to African governments and the rest of the world by the US and the Washington Consensus Group (the World Bank, the WTO, the IMF, and the US Treasury Department). For more than two decades, the US and the Washington Consensus Group have been vilifying similar "Acts" in many developing countries and considering them to be an "antithesis" to global trade and progressive development.

16 African governments and corporate entities could save a lot of money through the adoption of the open-source software. With the exception of handful such as the governments of South Africa and Zimbabwe, many of them do not see the need for open-source software. They are cajoled by the branding and names of Microsoft, Adobe, Oracle, and others. This attraction to "big brand names" is partly due to the corporate philanthropy programs of Microsoft, CISCO, and Oracle in the continent.

Chapter 5

Fair-Trade Practices in Contemporary Bangladeshi Society:
The Case of Aarong

Community Development, Cultural Revival, and Sustainability
through a Participatory Approach

Fadia Hasan

Introduction

Through the lens of development communication (Servaes, 1999, 2008) and diverse economies (Gibson-Graham, 2006, 2008), I engage in the topic of production, consumption, and community by exploring the business concept called fair trade, one that claims of being an ethical and community focused alternative that brings together a diversity of producers, retailers, and consumers in the global market (Dickson & Littrell, 1999). Fair trade as a business concept is theoretically constructed to promote a lifestyle principle that aids in community building in all its different stages of production, distribution, and consumption. I investigate the growing presence of the so-called "alternative" business spaces, specifically fair-trade organizations in the global arena. Based on extensive qualitative fieldwork, this study specifically focuses on the flourishing fair-trade sector in Bangladesh, exploring and analyzing the ways in which the practice has been localized and implemented in the region and the extent to which this kind of market-based approach is successful in contributing to effective participatory communication, community development, and sustenance.

Fair trade claims being an ethical entrepreneurial force that places its ideological focus on "paying producers as much as possible" rather than "as little as possible" (Dickson & Littrell, 1999:5). The idea is of creating a community, where not only the producers and consumers are linked economically, but with a higher purpose of forming a bond that is both materially and communally beneficial. Even though there is not one determining body of fair-trade certification, certain global (mostly Western/Northern) organizations have gained reputation and strength in claiming authority over the standards of fair-trade certification, which collectively are referred to as FINE – Fairtrade Labelling Organizations International (FLO), International Fair Trade Association, now the World Fair Trade Organization (WFTO), Network of European Worldshops (NEWS!), and European Fair Trade Association (EFTA). Their idea of what is "fair" is widely held normative in the measurement and comparison of the principle around the world (Dickson & Littrell, 1999).

To elaborate on the premise of this chapter, I engage in the discussion of communication, community, and fairness as envisioned by fair trade and connect it to my research findings in the fair-trade sector in Bangladesh. Some of the questions at stake are: In what ways is the term fair trade negotiated and redefined in the specific cultural and geo-political context of Bangladesh? Is fair trade successful in creating fair community communication, cohesiveness, and sustenance? To what extent does it facilitate the development of inclusionary networks among producers, retailers, and consumers, in line with the dream of constructing the idyllic "global village" (McLuhan, 1962), in the case of Bangladesh, an idyllic national community? Is the term stable and fixed as it flows from the producer to the consumer, across borders and cultures? Is fair trade in its current form perpetuating the very setbacks of a capitalist system through its market-based approach, by creating a new face of it … alternative capitalism?

In order to address these questions in the Bangladeshi context, I will analyze the country's fair-trade movement through a case study of the largest Bangladeshi fair-trade organization called, Aarong. Aarong is developed by BRAC, formerly the acronym of Bangladesh Rural Advancement Committee. This fair-trade organization in theory employs a participatory and performative development approach or what Servaes (1991) calls the multiplicity paradigm where interaction and communication must be dialogic, interactive, and sustained to attempt to create a "fair" and "sustainable" community. Multiplicity paradigm has its origins in the 1980s and it stemmed from diverse geo-political sites that focused on connecting the local, national, regional, and the global by emphasizing on localized, culture-based participatory approaches that yield sustainable results. Local issues are at the core of such a paradigm and participatory models are at the heart of it.

Fair trade, like the multiplicity paradigm, holds the promise of a better connection between producers, consumers, and their locality to develop an intimate chain and better communication. My work investigates how well theory and praxis connect in the context of the fair-trade sector in Bangladesh, the organization's impact in the overwhelmingly Euro-Ameri-centric field of fair trade and the extent to which the organization creates new, fairer terms of trade by following the principles of participatory, performative communication, and development practices. My analysis will not be complete without recommendations of a more inclusive – "fairer" fair-trade model, which could be potentially achieved by bringing about changes to the existing business model at Aarong.

Fair trade: mainstream understandings

Fair trade was developed as an alternative to production practices that often heavily isolate producers from consumers, products from their cultural context that thrive in sustaining income inequalities (Dickson and Littrell, 1999). It claims to bridge "artisans' needs for income, retailers goals for transforming trade and consumers' concerns for social responsibility through a compatible, non-exploitative and humanizing system of international exchange" (Dickson & Littrell, 1999:4). The roots of the specific terminology of "fair trade" comes from a prominent US-based retail store called Ten Thousand Villages, which is a globally renowned fair-trade retail not-for-profit organization with 200 or more branches in the United States and Canada (Dickson & Littrell, 1999). Ten Thousand Villages was initially called SELFHELP, a humanitarian-oriented entrepreneurial project of the

Mennonite Central Committee (MCC). The organization changed to its current name to match its mission of providing "vital, fair income to Third World people by marketing their handicrafts and telling their stories in North America" (Citing Website: Ten Thousand Villages, Retrieved April 2009, from tenthousandvillages.com).

The 50-year journey of Ten Thousand Villages was spearheaded by Edna Ruth Byler, who was volunteering in her Mennonite community and through her work, travelled to Puerto Rico, where she met women living in poverty and strife. Through her social work she discovered that the women were producing quality linen needle-work and ready-made products, ones that had the potential of being very popular in the United States. Six years later, Byler along with her colleague, Ruth Lederach, imported some of these Puerto Rican handicrafts and took them to a Mennonite World Conference in Switzerland and sold them there, becoming the first recorded person in the global West/North to actually trade "fairly" across nations (Hockerts, 2005; Dickson & Littrell, 1999; Citing Website: Ten Thousand Villages, Retrieved April 2009, from tenthousandvillages.com).

Following this experiment, their first shop was opened in Akron, Pennsylvania, U.S.A. in 1958, which has now taken the shape of the iconic Ten Thousand Villages. From humble beginnings, Ten Thousand Villages has grown to be a prominent, international social entrepreneur, even though it does not in any way match the diversity and volume of Aarong's productive output. However, in 1981, the term "fair trade", in the western vocabulary, was coined based on Byler's vision and work (Hockerts, 2005). It brought Western/Northern attention toward creating social entrepreneurs working to empower and provide fair, economic opportunities to artisans in the developing world.

Aarong at a glance

In scale, Aarong is an exemplary alternative "lifestyle" store, one that is unmatched by any in the larger global context, with only Ten Thousand Villages (North America) and Fabindia (India) following a similar trajectory. Aarong, the largest, most successful, and prominent NGO retail operation in Bangladesh, spearheaded the fair-trade trend and debatably the idea of social entrepreneurship in postindependent Bangladesh. The term "social entrepreneurship" made popular by entrepreneur Bill Drayton has its origins in the 1960s, which stems from the idea of creating sustainable yet profitable business models. Social entrepreneurship is concerned with profits as well as societal progress and is considered by many to be the predecessors of green business initiatives that have proliferated in the last decade (Tueth, 2010).

Established in 1978, Aarong works with the main goal of Bangladeshi cultural, arts, and crafts revival from around the country. Aarong is "a diverse representation of 65,000 artisans, 85% of whom are women", a "foundation upon which independent cooperative groups and family-based artisans market their craft, in an effort to position the nation's handicraft industry on a world platform" (Aarong Official Site, www.aarong.org). It provides employment to rural Bangladeshi women, a segment of population that is underrepresented in the formal monetized sector of the national economy. This South Asian nation is one of the most densely populated countries in the world (150 million and rising), with an almost equal women's population (Citing Website: Bangladesh Bureau of Statistics Official Site, Retrieved Feb 2012, from www.bbs.gov.bd).

Aarong states that one of its main aims is to reach women in rural as well as low-income urban areas who have many potential income-generating skills, and give them an opportunity of being self-earning and self-sufficient agents. Aarong claims to work with the idea of reviving and conserving the cultural traditions, techniques, and products that these women (and men) have inherited from their rich familial artisan heritage and to enable financial stability and prosperity for everyone associated with the chain of production (Citing Website, Aarong Official Site, Retrieved May 2009, from www.aarong.org).

Aarong in many ways can be called Bangladesh's first green superstore, due to the wide array of goods that is designed, produced, and sold under one brand name. Their ever-expanding multiple food, apparel, jewelry, accessory, home goods and décor lines, cosmetics, and so on are all locally designed, produced, and distributed. In many regards, it is a green and sustainable option for Bangladeshis, recreating the magic of high quality Bangladeshi goods for frequent, national consumption in an age of mechanized international (and displaced) mass production. One of the key strengths of *Aarong* is that it supports the skills of the locality, by encouraging women (and men) to join the formal monetized sector of the economy in a role that they are comfortable in performing. Following what seems to be some of the principal tenets of the multiplicity paradigm, Aarong's approach can aid in building cultural defense for marginalized communities one that relies on community participation and bottom-up movements from the grassroots to action, rather than having top-down, vertical, external direction, which follow the traditional modernizing, diffusion of innovations model (Servaes, 1991, 1999, 2008).

The organization works also with an asset-based approach, focusing on the "haves" rather than the "have-nots" of the locality, hence taking, what Gibson-Graham (2006) calls a performative approach through their diverse economies project. Aarong does not force their producers into a career path that requires years of new, complex training in unfamiliar and foreign fields that often require a major lifestyle or knowledge shift. This process enables local cultural and skill conservation along with income generation. Apart from the wages that the workers receive as compensation for their skilled labor, the organization gives their employees access to education, health care, and legal aid, which aids them in making more informed choices about their lives (Citing Website: BRAC Official Site, Retrieved April 2009, from www.brac.net; Citing Website: Aarong Official Site, Retrieved April 2009, from www.aarong.com). In many ways, the current model of Aarong does go some steps forward in creating a fairer system of communication, trade, and commerce that combines cultural revival with income generation. However, despite all the positives, the core of their business model still operates within the constructs of centralized capitalism – or creates a new kind of alternative capitalism (or green capitalism). This centralized business format again mimics a top-down model that limits the communication flows from all directions to be manifested in the institutional level and just aids in maximizing the company's profit returns, which benefits a few select group of people at Aarong, instead of evenly benefitting the chain of producers in different stages of production. This significantly confines the potentials of making the chain of production more inclusive, equitable, fair, and sustainable.

Methodology

Multiple research methods have been employed in this qualitative study to examine the fair-trade sector in Bangladesh, specifically Aarong. This chapter is a product of a combination of participant observation of the Dhaka branches of Aarong, 67 one-on-one interviews of consumers and producers, semiotic/textual analysis of the company's website and its in-store advertisements and promotions along with studying the literature (articles and book-chapters) on the organization that have already been published.

Aarong officially claims that its primary objective is not about generating profit, but of establishing an ethical economic exchange by creating a safe and dynamic space for dialogue and communication among the members of the organization at all levels. Through participant observation, along with detailed interviews with the administrative team, this study attempts to determine the extent to which these ideals and goals were highlighted and established in the field. Furthermore, interviews with the main headquarter office team of Aarong were conducted to get the "producer" perspective on the matter (even though they were not the "producers" in the Marxist sense, but in the Capitalist sense), and to examine the meaning they attach to the production of the commodities that are sold nationally and regionally under the tag of fair trade. The purpose of the mixed-method research was to achieve greater clarity on Aarong's mission, purpose, and claims.

Aarong: Theoretical conflicts

As mentioned earlier, this project's backbone is a rereading of Marxist trajectories following the Diverse Economies approach and combining it with the Multiplicity Paradigm that can be applied to question whether a universal, essential definition of fair trade is indeed necessary and if the mainstream incarnation of the trade principle is truly helpful in building a "fair" and sustainable world. Participatory models rely on community participation, the movement from the grassroots to action, rather than having top-down direction, which follow the traditional modernizing, diffusionist model (Servaes, 1991, 2008). In this paradigm, interdependence is emphasized between and among external and internal sources (Wildermeersch, 1999) and targets development processes from poststructuralist and postmodernist frameworks, which highlight that there is no objective reality, no universal formula, "no universal path to development" (Servaes & Malikhao, 2008:163). Local issues are at the core of participatory models as they target issues such as women's economic empowerment, maternal mortality, poor health care, preservation of local industries, sustenance, equal employment opportunities, to name a few, in the Bangladeshi context. Coming to the theoretical core, the urgent question is whether fair trade can be reestablished both in institutional practices and regulations and understood in other geo-political contexts, such as Bangladesh. I propose that this goal can be achieved, but only by reimagining the community and by changing the rules of the game to one that yields similar returns to a larger group of people in all sectors of the production process rather than a small group of business executives.

Through an ontological reframing of the economy as a diversity of class processes (and subjectivities) in a continual process of becoming (Agamben, 1993) and by generating noncapitalist practices that create possibilities for a new imaginary and new economies is "one way to enact a counterhegemonic project" (Gibson-Graham, 2006:78). Based on the Marxian discourse of the economy, we are led to the possibility of a community economy, one that highlights the social production of the economy in nonessential ways. Gibson-Graham write, "In post-structuralist thought there are no depths to plumb for the subject's true essence or identity; rather the subject is understood as always in the process of becoming, being shaped in a multitude of ways by various discourses and practices." (2006:3). This not only illuminates the coming of a community, that is always in the process of transformation, definition, and redefinition, but also brings into the picture the futility of being fixed, immutable, and essential, in constructing of what fair trade is, in a global economic context. In addition, it provides a space for communities to actively communicate and participate in creating the economy they want to live in, by generating value through the process of production and bringing it to fruition through the process of fair exchange (Gibson-Graham, 2006).

The contribution of Aarong in the field of fair trade challenges a universal, Euro-centric definition of the term to some extent. But in order to achieve true fairness, the artisans, the active producers of the products must be active in communicating and negotiating their needs and compensation, which is not an option in the top-down, centralized system of Aarong, which favors vertical rather than horizontal communication and sustainability practices. In their business model, like many other global fair-trade giants, the terms and conditions of trade are restricted by an alternative capitalistic structure, an inconsistent reality of a large number of fair-trade global organizations.

Structural limitations of the global fair-trade sector

Despite fair trade's purposeful communication and communally orientated vision, it is not devoid of limitations. Fair trade in its traditional understanding creates the illusion of being solely a Western/Northern, interventionist project, which often uses the same rhetoric of fair-trade policy developed in the 1980s (Linton et al., 2004) and it employs, what I call, a politics of saving in relation to the less-developed world. Furthermore, it applies what I also term, the spectacle of poverty to support and sustain their rhetoric of politics of saving. By spectacle of poverty, I am speaking to the meanings that are continually being constructed by using imagery of less privileged "others" from faraway lands and sentimental, compelling language about global poverty as selling points of the fair-trade brands. In the Northern/ Western branding of fair trade, there is a conscious effort being made to directly connect the stark images of "others" to consumption, community development, and sustainability. It is not to say that all of the construction of this rhetoric is for effect; however, I attempt to bring to the forefront the need for a more nuanced representation of the complexities that are at play in this chain of trade.

By constructing the term, politics of saving, I refer to the construction of an overhyped and much-misleading international rhetoric, which propagates the idea of the global North seeking to improve the lives of the people in the South, a support without which the Southern economies would collapse. This idea reinforces and perpetuates the same imperialistic, old-fashioned modernizing stereotypes of the East-South as being inadequate, dependent, and chaotic and unable to manage itself until the rational, superior, and in this case "fair" North/ West intervenes into its matters. This is quite consistent with the modernizing model, which is aligned with western scientific traditions of positivism and behaviorism, as well as the socio-cultural-economic traditions of enlightenment, neoliberal economics, which holds the west as the torchbearer of progress. Following this myopic, ideological trajectory, Western/ Northern nations become the ideal, which underdeveloped nations must strive to become a facsimile of (Servaes, 2002). Without denouncing outright the contributions of institutions and organizations from the global North that have made positive differences in the lives of workers from around the world, the question remains if fair trade can be conceived of in other ways that challenges this age-old "center" and "periphery" imperialistic tension.

By having a Euro-Ameri-"centric" point of reference, fair trade as it stands now in the mainstream is limited and problematic, since it largely focuses on Western/Northern interventions into non-Western/Southern regions, ignoring substantial efforts like Aarong that stem out of the so-called "periphery." The social perceptions of this model is constructed and manipulated to reinforce the inequality and economic instability in the global south, which undeniably exists; however, there needs to be greater caution practiced in the representation of the so-called "periphery" through this economic medium. This overemphasis on the North/West limits the scope of exposure of the alternative economic models that stem from the global South, an example being, Bangladesh's fair-trade movement and organizations that developed out of largely local initiatives and countless other initiatives and movements that are mushrooming in Latin America, Africa, and other parts of Asia (Citing Website: Fair Trade Action Network, Retrieved Jan 2012, from www. fairtradeaction.net/world). Greater global attention needs to be on the movements from all geo-political locations, as only then will the multiplicity of the concept be realized. There will be scope for comparison and contrast between models, which eventually creates the possibility of true, fair, and sustained community building.

The tendency to narrowly concentrate on only certain geo-political locations and industries in the fair-trade realm results in the perpetuation of a fixed nature of the term, one that is fraught with issues of essentialism. By essentialism I am referring to economic approaches or practices, in this case, fair trade that is reductive of its diverse natures, achievements, and potentials in varied cultural, national, and political contexts. In its current form, fair trade is limited and problematic as it overemphasizes one region over the other, which again neatly tries to package the story of the idyllic global community made possible by western intervention such as Ten Thousand Villages, instead of also bringing into light like projects from the global periphery.

Although Aarong still works within the capitalist structure of trade, albeit a green and/ or alternative one, in many ways, Aarong's successful and large-scale operation as a fair-trade giant within Bangladesh sans any foreign support upsets the notions of "core" and "periphery" in the global sphere and generates conversation on fair trade operating within the so-called "periphery." It brings into light the important work that is being done within a locality to sustain itself. This is a narrative that has been understudied, underdocumented, and rendered invisible in fair-trade mapping around the world, which closes down infinite possibilities that emerge from comparative dialogue, initiative, and action. It is timely and important to highlight such projects because they unsettle fixed, narrow, and misleading ideas about economic practices in the global arena. It participates in what St. Martin (2009) describes as countermapping or the setting of conditions that provide a "parallel and spatial analogue" (St. Martin, 2009:4) creating new possible realities that were not thought possible previously in certain spaces and situations. St Martin argues that countermapping "is an effective method of reclaiming material resources for those who have been dispossessed, but it works to counter particular forms of economic subjectivity and space" (St. Martin, 2009:8).

Even though Aarong is still operating within the frameworks of capitalism (alternative and/or green) and a more inclusive and fair model is desired of it (which will be the main focus of discussion hereforth), still the existence of it is in opposition to the representation of economies of the global South, which are always positioned in a place of need and intervention from the global North, rather than focusing on active agents within the bounds of the so-called "peripheral" nation-state.

Aarong: Need for a shift?

To focus on the strengths of the organization, a very encouraging aspect of Aarong is its cultural revival model that provides opportunities for marginalized artisan communities around the country to thrive. Based on the archival research as well as my own interviews conducted with administrative producers at Aarong, the need for a holistic rural revival and advancement program was required in postindependent Bangladesh in 1971 (Citing Website: United Nations Official Site, Retrieved Jan 2012, from www.un.org). BRAC and subsequently Aarong was developed by Founder Sir Fazle Hasan Abed with the vision of mobilizing the human potential of a nation, which still has the majority of its population living in rural areas with highly sophisticated life-skills (BRAC Official Site, www.brac.net).

The vision of the organization was to create sustainable national development, by focusing on the assets of a nation that has been ravaged by war, by relying on nothing but its own skills and merits. The idea was to urge the locality to produce and reap its own rewards, instead of depending on the North-South trade alliance, which increases dependency outside of your own locality as well as escalating unfair, marginal returns to labor. Sir Abed's initiatives were intelligent and inspirational for an emerging nation struggling to recover from a devastating war; however, the model was bound by the very trade process of capitalism, only reduced to a specific national locality, rather than a North-South alliance. Community development and fairness in Aarong is governed by the capitalist, market-based approach of localized economic exchange. On one hand, interdependence in production and consumption is inevitable in the current form of globalized economic scenario.

However, the imbalance and unfairness of the so-called fair-trade system stems from the inadequate and disproportionate compensation for the producers', artisans', and laborers' skills, which do not utilize horizontal, participatory communication strategies. The dominant players of the fair-trade sector in the North (and also in the South, like Aarong) form very insular decision-making bodies. Therefore, even within fair-trade arrangements like these organizations, communication and community result from the vertical rather than horizontal integration that is formed through a top-down exchange, where the people higher up in the vertical ladder benefit from disproportionately higher monetary returns than the "productive," labor class in the bottom. A large number of prominent fair-trade organizations, including major global players such as Ten Thousand Villages, Fab India, and so on, still operate in the framework of a market-based, capitalistic model of the boss-employee hierarchical dichotomy, and disappointingly so, Aarong is no exception.

Despite their efforts in creating a green, fair-trade and culturally conscious organization, these current fair-trade organizations' approach to community building, sustenance, and establishing fairness in the chain of trade seems quite incomplete and inadequate as they still operate within an unequal, capitalist framework. Power is still centralized, and it is this "center" that dictates the wages of the physical producers of the commodities, who are in the "periphery" of the localized economy. Hence, they are not only creating an "alternative" capitalism but they are also duplicating the model of "core" and "periphery" within the localized context, to institutionalize even more power structures within a region. With such un-"fair"-ness at stake, a model that gives dignity to all forms of labor is urgently required to make such projects truly "fair," communication and community driven, and in line with their theoretical claims as fair-trade businesses. Moving to a cooperative model of business may just be the only solution to reach that goal, an example being, the widely celebrated, large-scale success of Mondragon Initiative in Spain (Ellerman, 1984; Whyte & Whyte, 1989; Gates, 1991; Rothschild & Allen-Whitt, 1986). The initiative had humble beginnings as a solidarity business model in the post Spanish Civil War era, which has grown to be the seventh largest Spanish company in 2010 (Mondragon Initiative Official Site, mondragon-corporation.com).

As important as it is for efforts like Aarong to be mapped internationally from the global "periphery," it is more important for such organizations that are such massive successes from marginalized geo-political locations to lead the way in challenging unequal business ethics. They should be torchbearers and advocates of ideas and practices of true fairness by reestablishing more fair, more sustainable, and more ethical trade parameters for the national as well as international fair-trade community of artisans that are the hearts, souls, and fingers of its products. This will lead the way for others to emulate for true community fostering and sustenance that is beneficial to a large group of people across the chain of production, distribution, and consumption. The coming of such a fair community is directly related to the need of the people to have a democratic voice and right in negotiating and establishing a fair compensation for their labor, rather than following the rules set up by someone higher up in the economic and social ladder, which is ultimately driven by increased profit returns rather than well-being for all.

The theme of the coming community came up during my interview with Anam (pseudonym), one of the Marketing and Outreach heads of BRAC Bangladesh, who has been working in the organization from 1997. He said,

> Relief is not a permanent solution. At the beginning when this project was envisioned, we thought that we would be able to dictate how we can alleviate Bangladesh from poverty, by following more of a traditional, top-down approach. Very quickly BRAC learned that an integrated approach to community building, one that involves a participatory model approach, where BRAC does not dictate a solution, but instead, focusing on putting the community involvement at the core, is the best way of bringing this about. By taking this approach a solution is constantly emerging, in relation to changing contexts, the only model that has any hope of working in this ever-changing world (Anam, personal interview, 17 June 2009).

This was a major development in my findings, since it highlighted the blurry connections between theory and praxis and brought to the surface the inconsistencies and contradictions in their understanding of communication and community development and sustenance between theory and praxis. Aarong's executive was speaking about the failure of top-down approaches that fail to take note of localities and their assets and hinder communication between different levels, which most modernizing paradigms of development favor. Aarong prides itself in following a localized, culturally driven, participatory, and performative communication and development model; however, on a deeper level, the organization's claim was not substantiated by praxis, as they were creating a new kind of politically correct capitalist structure. In praxis, there is a premium being made on the skills and outputs of the diverse artisans' of Bangladesh by deciding and controlling the "fair" value of their labor, which does not provide dignity to the diversity of labor processes.

Fair trade and diverse cultural contexts

Despite being the largest fair-trade retail business in Bangladesh, the brand image that *Aarong* aggressively promotes within the country is one that downplays its social links in its national advertisements and publicity campaigns. This is an approach that is in sharp contrast to that of its North American counterparts, such as Ten Thousand Villages, which takes every opportunity to remind customers of its ethical business model (Hasan, forthcoming). In Ten Thousand Villages' aggressive campaign to promote the ethic of fair trade, there is no stone left unturned to visually market the rhetoric of the privileged Western/Northern intervention into nonprivileged non-Western/Southern projects, to create the image of the idyllic global village.

During my interview with one of the marketing heads of Aarong, Anam (pseudonym), I asked him what the marketing team wants Aarong to represent to its consumers, one that spans across a range of socio-economic and cultural backgrounds in Bangladesh. He commented, "We want to reach consumers with wide differences in income, education and taste. Our products should not only show the variation of price and styles, but also needs to be approachable to people of various levels of thought." I further asked him the reason for their conscious disassociation from representing the concept of fair trade in their promotion and publicity, a tactic much celebrated by western connoisseurs of the model. He replied,

> Well, we don't want to sell poverty. We do not want poverty to be the excuse for selling our products. People know that our products are locally produced, they all bear our cultural stamp, starting from our food line, to cosmetic line to the children's clothing line, they all bear the stamp of being Bengali. Plus, it is very difficult for people to come to terms with the western term "fair-trade". It seems too tricky for us. This term has very little space in the consumer imagination of Bangladesh, because it seems like a foreign concept to them, as it seems to make a *spectacle of poverty* (Anam, Personal Interview, 27 June 2009).

This is a rather curious comment, as it complicates the understanding and stability of fair trade as a commercial practice from a non-Western/Northern location, urging people to think about it in a new way. Anam also mentioned the importance of constructing the right language to design Aarong's shopping experience, which only in the last decade is waking up to the idea of home-grown local and/or national brands. He said that for Aarong to have a more approachable, widespread, mass-appeal, their strategy was to consciously move away from a "serious, savior-type image" but instead highlight the contemporary and trendy spirit of the store, even though it adheres to all mainstream fair-trade principles.

Anam was concerned about the way meaning was constructed around the language of poverty, to justify the "fairness" of trade. He said that the organization's team was very careful about linking the language around poverty and consumption as is routinely done in the West. They found it complex in the Bangladeshi context of branding. Anam insisted that the clientele in Bangladesh are aware of the products being handmade and local, unlike the West, since this is not an unusual phenomenon in Bangladesh, where the handmade tradition is alive and in some cases cheaper than mass-produced goods in all sectors of the economy. His team did not feel the need to explicitly use poverty, since, according to their market research and the specific cultural context, he was certain that the consumers are already aware of the artisans. He also mentioned that the invisibility of labor in other modes of Western/Northern non-fair-trade production processes drives this obsession to make a spectacle of poverty out of their interpretation of the fair-trade movement. He insisted that this type of marketing would not be applicable to the Bangladeshi understanding of artisanry, craftsmanship, or consumption.

I found that to be a clever, nuanced, yet somewhat valid perspective, one that again challenges the mainstream and monotheistic understanding of fair trade. His comment raises an important point about representation; however, it also undermines in the public eye the role and the rights of producers, one that is at the core of fair-trade theory, making the need for protecting the labor and giving it dignity all the more crucial. I was vocal to him about the importance of finding a way to represent the labor force behind the organization in their advertisements, which did not reduce them to a spectacle of poverty. But one that generates multiplicity in understanding and encourages a deeper understanding of a highly skilled labor force that is capable of sustaining itself and flourishing in the right economic arrangement where they are able to communicate and create their terms of trade and sustainability.

Anam continued by saying that the inapplicability of the term also stems from the stubbornly set universal nature of the term. He put emphasis on the high skills of the artisans of Bangladesh, which does not need the sympathy of consumers, rather, needs a platform where their rich skills would find a prominent platform. I could not agree more with the team in regards to the skills of the labor; however, I have disagreements about their economic arrangements that control and limit the economic well-being of the labor class. During my 2009 research session, I had earnestly requested his team to find a way to give visibility to the workers, which his team promised they would look into for their next yearly campaigns. Interestingly enough, their 2011 national advertising billboards have tastefully featured some of the artisans along with their featured products, which is an encouraging trend and change in the positive direction.

Overall, the tension inherent to the fair-trade term around poverty was echoed by all the administrative producers I interviewed in Bangladesh. The team at Aarong said that a frequent issue that arises is exclusiveness, and how the conception of fair trade is still so limited that in many ways they have to invent the wheel in the Bangladeshi context to stick true to the performative, participatory model. The invisibility of owning the term in their national public campaigns and the discomfort in using it in creating narratives around social and economic sustainable development is evident, one that creates hindrances in building fair communities in the actual sites of the grassroots in Bangladesh. Anam further added,

I do not want to sell at the expense of poverty, I do not want people to feel sorry about the poor majority and buy the products as aid, I want them to be moved by the beauty, quality and value of the product, and be convinced of its uniqueness, something that should make them make the right consumer choice, one that in turn sustains very local important industries, that are being threatened by power-looms and mass-production. I prefer to spend more time in constructing great products and a sound business model rather than one that wastes its time in focusing on naming a phenomena (Anam, Personal Interview, Jun 23 09).

As complex as it is, there are inconsistencies in the theory and praxis of the matter, as the physical producers of the products are rendered silent in the decision-making. The physical producers should be consulted about how they want to be represented in a marketing campaign that connects the producers and the consumers. Not undermining the vital role of administrative producers, their language leads me to think that they are claiming ownership of these products that are produced by artisans who are not getting compensated fairly for it, hence perpetuating this unequal and displaced production ethic that is common in non-fair-trade contexts.

Irrespective of being a major fair-trade organization in a different geo-political region from the so-called "center," Aarong is unfortunately not creating new rules of a fair-trade structure. They are not only abiding by the rules of capitalism, they are helping sustain new faces of it. They are entities that are depriving the producers' involvement of democratically deciding their "fair" compensation, which sustains a flawed model, one that goes against the true potentials of a performative, participatory model that is characterized by people as being the very nucleus of development. It is truly the people, in this case the artisans along with the office heads, who should be the collective controlling actors, with strong emphasis on the local community and culture who are actively working toward the decentering of and redistribution of power (Servaes, 2008).

Fair trade: Need for a shift?

A salient aspect of Aarong is their engagement with the local community in Bangladesh to preserve and sustain cultural traditions of goods. However, based on the above analysis, there needs to be a shift in the actual practices of the terms of trade by addressing different issues surrounding transparency and communal cooperation (Gibson-Graham, 2006). Projects like Aarong go some distance in developing the basic alternative economy framework within Bangladesh. They do take the asset-based approach of using the strength of the local grassroots to build their company; however, their structure does not permit a fair return to the labor involved in the company's large-scale projects. Pertaining to our discussion, Gibson-Graham (2006) create a discourse of community economy based on the idea of interdependence and active participation: both community and economy are seen as constituted by social relations that are intertwined with one another, which leads to our inter-(intra)-reliance and codependence.

Gibson-Graham also emphasize the importance of ethical community building and how citizens can and should be allowed to effectively engage in such decision-making, one that is not exclusive and hierarchical. Recognizing this crucial interdependence allows for rethinking and redefining economic discourse and decision-making. This is a significant component of fair trade (in theory), one that not only links the producer directly to the consumer, but by doing so, attempts to create a chain of well-being for the wider, (often) in this case, the national community.

As I stated earlier, for Aarong and other like organizations, moving to a kind of cooperative style of business may be the direction of achieving fairer trade, one that values every member's role in the organizations with equal returns, which is consistent to the vision of equality, effective communication, and community engagement presented above. Maybe the Mondragon Cooperative Initiative could provide inspiration for the transformation of the current fair-trade structure of Aarong into one that places "priority of labour over capital, the emphasis on the dignity of work and the need for worker solidarity" (Ellerman, 1975).

Cultural context and the understanding of fair trade as it operates in the Bangladeshi context is essential to this redefinition, one that connects the producer and consumer in a truly ethical, fair manner instead of a forced relationship as it stands now. Focusing attention on the complexity of fair trade within national boundaries, within the ever-the-more complex global "periphery" is a necessity for this shift. As it stands now, Aarong has created its own localized version of "north" and "south" within Bangladesh, something that should be redefined to achieve true fairness. The goal should be for a model that shares the economic and social rewards with all its workers instead of concentrating on an elite few. In its current state, it is an alternative system that sustains capitalism, like many other fair-trade giants around the world, which does not reach to the depth of the potentials of fair trade as an ethical and fair concept.

Conclusion

Fair-trade theory has to take new directions in order to avoid blatant universalism, a key weakness of the modernization paradigm. The framework has to embrace the multifacetedness and diverse contextual possibilities of the practice of fair trade as a practical and ethical tool in varied settings and efforts must be made to countermap the fair-trade initiatives from around the world. The theoretical languages of Servaes (2002, 2008) and Gibson-Graham (2000, 2006, 2008) provide solid foundations of operation and sustenance in a complex and multifaceted globalized world. A workable multiplicity paradigm and active social participation is needed for community sustenance, one that connects organized institutional infrastructure to the grassroots in localities without losing the focus of that integral connection, democratization, and participation in the international, regional, national, and local levels.

This project brings into attention that there is no substitute to a model that engages the local community to address their own, localized issues. Aarong works with the grassroots, low-income communities, and it was evident that building an inclusive community that connects the skills and beauty of Bangladesh to the consumer is important to them. However, the important aspect of the fair compensation of labor is sidelined. But for an organization of their stature, they should be redefining mainstream fair-trade ideas and practices and developing a new language of connection, communication, and sustenance in their own terms that is more ethical and truly fair. A great deal of work is needed by such dynamic organizations to truly live up to the theoretical standards of fairness in production and consumption that benefits a larger group of people, instead of mimicking capitalist models, or creating their own versions of it, like so many other major fair-trade organizations around the world. As laid out in my research, progress *has* been made by these organizations in creating a performative, participatory, culturally inclined model of business. By creating new rules, Aarong can not only expand, but also redefine the traditional focus of (community) development and communication and be the torchbearer of what a truly sustainable business venture looks like.

References

Aarong Official Site (2011). Retrieved from www.aarong.com

Agamben, G. (1993). *The Coming Community*. Minneapolis: University of Minnesota Press.

Bangladesh Bureau of Statistics (2011). Retrieved from www.bbs.gov.bd/

Bourdieu, P. (1984). *Distinction: A Social Critique of the Judgement of Taste*. Cambridge, MA: Harvard University Press.

BRAC Official Site (2011). Retrieved from www.brac.net/

Carpentier, N., Lie, R., & Servaes, J. (2003). Community Media: Muting the Democratic Media Discourse? *Continuum: Journal of Media & Cultural Studies*, 17(1), 51–68.

Cameron, J. and Gibson, K. (2005). Participatory Action Research in a Post-Structuralist Vein. *Geoforum*, 36, 315–331.

Csikszentmihalyi, M. and Rochberg-Halton, E. (1981). *The Meaning of Things: Domestic Symbols and the Self*. New York: Cambridge University Press.

Cycon, D. (2007). *Javatrekker: Dispatches from the World of Fair Trade Coffee*. White River Junction, VT: Chelsea Green.

Dickson, M. A. & Littrell, M. A. (1999). *Social Responsibility in the Global Market*, Ames, IA: Sage.

——— (1995). Marketing Ethnic Apparel and a Social Cause through Alternative Trade. *Proceedings of the fifth international conference on marketing and development*.

——— (1998). Consumers of Ethnic Apparel from Alternative Trading Organizations: A Multifaceted Market. *Clothing and Textiles Research Journal*, 16(1), 1–10.

Ellerman, D. P. (1975). The 'Ownership of the Firm' is a Myth. *Administration and Society*, 7(1), 27–42.

——— (1984). Entrepreneurship in the Mondragon Cooperatives. *Review of Social Economy*, XLII, 272–294.

———— (1997). *The Democratic Corporation.* Beijing: Xinhua Publishing House.

Fair Trade Action Network (2011). Retrieved from www.fairtradeaction.net/world

Franke, R. W. (2003). The Mararikulam Experiment: Women Owned Cooperatives in Kerala, India. *GEO,* (May–June), 8–11.

Gates, J. (1998). *The Ownership Solution.* London: Penguin.

Gibson-Graham, J. K. (2006). *A Postcapitalist Politics.* Minneapolis: University of Minnesota Press.

———— (2006). *The End of Capitalism (As We Knew It): A Feminist Critique of Political Economy.* Minneapolis: University of Minnesota Press, pp. 1–23.

———— (2008). Diverse Economies: Performative Practices for 'Other Worlds. *Progress in Human Geography,* 32(5), forthcoming.

Hockerts, K. (2005). The Fair Trade Story. *Sustainability Case Writing Competition* 2005.

Holt, D. (1998). Does Cultural Capital Structure American Consumption? *Journal of Consumer Research, Inc.,* 25(1), 1–25.

Law, J. & Urry, J. (2004). Enacting the Social. *Economy and Society* 33(3), 390–410.

LeClair, M. (2006). Fighting the Tide: Alternative Trade Organizations in the Era of Global Free Trade. *World Development* 30(6), 949–58.

Lincoln, A. (2003). Alternative Work Spaces, in Leyshon, A., Lee, R., & Williams, C. C. (eds.), *Alternative Economic Spaces.* London: Sage Publications, pp. 107–127.

Linton, A., Chia, C., Liou, Y., & Shaw, K. A. (2004). A Taste of Trade Justice: Marketing Social Responsibility via Fair Trade Coffee. *Globalizations,* 1(2), 223–246.

Littrell, M. A. & Dickson, M. A. (1997). Exploring Labor Issues with Case Studies from Fair Trade Organizations, in McCoart, J. (ed.), *An Academic Search for Sweatshop Solutions.* Arlington, VA: Marymount University, pp. 59–63.

Maxwell, J. A. (2004). *Qualitative Research Design: An Interactive Approach* (2nd ed.). Washington, DC: Sage Publications.

McKee, N., Manoncourt, E., Yoon, C.S. & Carnegie, R. (2000). *Evolving People, Involving Behaviour.* Penang, Malaysia: South Bound.

McLuhan, M. (1962). *The Gutenberg Galaxy: The Making of Typographic Man* (1st ed.). Toronto, CA: University of Toronto Press; reissued by Routledge & Kegan Paul.

McMichael, P. (2006). *Development and Social Change.* USA: Pine Forge Press.

Morgan, D. L. (1997). *Focus Groups as Qualitative Research* (2nd ed.). Thousand Oaks, CA: Sage.

Morris, N. (2003). A Comparative Analysis of the Diffusion and Participatory Models in Development Communication. *Communication Theory,* 13(2), 225–248.

Mukerji, C. (1983). *From Graven Images: Patterns of Modern Materialism,* Ch. 1. Patterns of Modern Materialism, New York: Columbia University Press.

Nancy, J. L. (1992). *The Inoperative Community.* Minneapolis: University of Minnesota Press.

Rothschild, J. & Allen-Whitt, J. (1986). *The Cooperative Workplace.*Cambridge, MA: Cambridge University Press.

Servaes, J. (1991). Europe 1992: A Single Market for Producers and/or Consumers? *Telematics & Informatics,* 8(3), 127–133.

———— (1999). *Communication for Development: One World, Multiple Cultures.* Cresskill, NJ: Hampton Press.

—— (2002). *Communication for Development. One World, Multiple Cultures,* Hampton Press, Cresskil.

—— (2008). *Communication for Development and Social Change.* New Delhi, India: Sage Publications.

Servaes, J., & Malikhao, P. (2008). Development Communication Approaches in an International Perspective, Servaes J. (ed.), *Communication for Development and Social Change,* London–New Delhi: Sage, pp. 158–179.

Singhal, A. (2008). Where Social Change Scholarship and Practice Went Wrong? Might Complexity Science Provide a Way out of this Mess? *Communication for Development and Social Change,* 2(4), 1–6.

Sloan, D. (2003). *Culinary Taste: Consumer Behaviour in the International Restaurant Sector* (1st ed.). Great Britain: Butterworth-Heinemann.

St. Martin, K. (2009). Toward a Cartography of the Commons: Constituting the Political and Economic Possibilities of Place. *Professional Geographer.* 61 (4), 493–507.

Ten Thousand Villages (2011). Retrieved from www.tenthousandvillages.com

Tueth, M. (2010). *Fundamentals of Sustainable Business: A Guide to the Next 100 Years.* Hackensack: World Scientific Publishing Co.

Wildemeersh, D. (1999). Transcending the Limits of Traditional Research: Toward an Interpretive Approach to Development Communication and Education. In: Jacobson, T.L. & Servaes, J. (eds.), *Theoretical Approaches to Participatory Communication,* Cresskill, NJ: Hampton Press, pp. 211–227.Whyte, W. F. & Whyte, K. K. (1989). *Making Mondragón.* Ithaca, NY: ILR Press.

Chapter 6

Asserting Contested Power: Exploring the Control-Resistance Dialectic in the World Trade Organization's Discourse of Globalization

Rachel Stohr

Introduction

The transformationalist thesis of globalization posits globalization as a central driving force behind the rapid social, economic, and political changes that are taking place in contemporary society (Held et al., 1999). While the term continues to be contested, there are many uses of the word that are widely accepted, including a process that symbolizes "the intensification of world-wide social relations which link distinct localities in such a way that local happenings are shaped by events occurring many miles away and vice versa" (Giddens, 1990:86). Communication is central to the process of globalization. Beck (2000:12) argued that globalization is created and maintained through communication:

> The globalization process lies in the empirically ascertainable scale, density, and stability of regional-global relationship networks and their self-definition through the mass media, as well as of social spaces and image flows ... a world horizon characterized by multiplicity and non-integration which opens out when it is produced and preserved in communication and action.

In addition to being a communicative phenomenon, globalization is an ideological process that is inseparable from that of economic development. According to Appadurai (2000:3):

> Globalization is inextricably linked to the current workings of capital on a global basis: in this regard, it extends the earlier logics of empire, trade, and political dominion in many parts of the world. Its most striking feature is the runaway quality of global finance, which appears remarkably independent of traditional constraints of information transfer, national regulation, industrial productivity, or 'real' wealth in any particular society, country, or region.

International finance is a key symbol of globalization. Today, neoliberal ideology permeates global markets and multilateral financial institutions, such as the World Trade Organization (WTO), the International Monetary Fund (IMF), and the World Bank, reinforce neoliberal discourses that function to justify economic policies that typically prize corporate wealth over economic and social equality. Neoliberalism facilitates the restructuring of social relations in accordance with the demands of unrestrained global capitalism (Bourdieu,

1998). It has "led to an increasing division between rich and poor, increasing economic insecurity and stress for even the 'new middle' classes, and an intensification of the division of labor" (Fairclough, 2003:5). Neoliberal discourses shape the many manifestations of globalization.

Henceforth, my references to "globalization" encompass the process of instituting a new global economy that "has to do with certain fundamental disjunctures between economy, culture, and politics which we have barely begun to theorize" (Appadurai, 1990:2). I focus on the inherently communicative nature of globalization and begin the process of theorizing such disjunctures as they are articulated in the World Trade Organization's (WTO's) discourse of globalization. Theorizing discourses of globalization demands attention to numerous and complex dialectical tensions. Traditional theories of the convergence-divergence dialectic, for example, treat "the increasing intensification of economic, political, cultural, and social interconnectedness as neutral phenomena" (Stohl, 2005:230). As neoliberal discourses permeate global society, communication researchers must move away from such traditional theories and explore tension-filled relations to expose the fragile nature of seemingly great power that operates in complex, often hidden, ways. Neoliberalism is perhaps powerful because it is so many things at once – often constituted as much by what it is not (e.g., state regulation and intervention) than what it is (Ong, 2006). Communication-centered theories of globalization should therefore "capture the oppositional and dialectic forces that simultaneously obliterate, maintain, and maximize homogeneity/heterogeneity within the global system" (Stohl, 2005:244). Doing so highlights the role of communication in addressing contemporary social problems, promotes more socially responsive understandings of communication, and highlights its transformative potential.

In this chapter, I highlight the relationship between communication and social change by analyzing the WTO's discourse of globalization. Much valuable research demonstrates the harmful effects of globalization, but few studies have explored the rhetorical tactics with which powerful international financial institutions simultaneously control and resist public discourses about this phenomenon. Exploring the tension-laden relationship between power and discourse helps us to understand that power relations are fluid, and that communication can facilitate the process of reclaiming and reappropriating power to promote sustainable economic development. Because discourse is socially constructed, it can be deconstructed and reconstituted to facilitate global social change. Communication researchers can do this through attention to global economic injustice and social issues. Thus, my analysis of the WTO's discourse of globalization demonstrates how discursive structures "enact, confirm, legitimate, reproduce, or challenge relations of power and dominance in society" (Van Dijk, 2002:146).

Deetz (1992) discussed the concept of "discursive closures," which are produced when certain discourses are privileged over others. Powerful organizations, such as the WTO, typically seek to maintain power by controlling public discourses that reify hegemony, defined as "dominant cultural motifs which reinforce inequality and which short-circuit attempts at critical thinking" (Smith, 2001:39). Foucault (1976:98) argued that power "is something that circulates ... it is never localized here or there, never in anybody's hands, never appropriated as commodity". Marginalized discourses are not destined to remain marginalized indefinitely. Rather, "discursive openings" in which to challenge dominant, hegemonic discourses can be created within the tension-filled space of control and resistance.

Marx (1977:78) described his philosophical approach to overturning material structures of oppression when he argued:

> At times people complain in frustration that they lack the means to achieve their ends, or alternatively that they can justify their corrupt methods of work by the lofty aims they pursue. For dialectics, means and ends are a unity of opposites and in the final analysis, there can be no contradiction between means and ends – when the objective is rightly understood, the material conditions [means] for its solution are already present.

Communication that promotes social change can function to expose the fragile nature of power, thereby deconstructing oppressive discourses and combating global structural inequities. I employ a dialectical approach in my analysis and highlight the control-resistance dialectic that is present in the WTO's discourse of globalization. A dialectical approach to discourse analysis explores ongoing contradictions that constitute processes by which organizations shape practices, focusing less on meanings of specific discourses and "more on their interpretive struggles among discourses and practices" (Mumby, 2005:24). Because we do not often think of the powerful as resisting, my analysis offers a transformative understanding of how powerful institutions not only work to control public discourses, but must also simultaneously work to resist alternate, or counterdiscourses that contest their power.

By doing so, the WTO (and other international financial institutions) show that organizations are shaped by power and the regulation of discourse (Weedon, 1987). Power, though, is malleable. And the roles of the "powerful" and "powerless" are in constant contestation (Murphy, 1998); a dialectical approach to discourse analysis, then, demonstrates "the capacity of the weak, in the regularized relations of autonomy and dependence that constitutes social systems, to turn their weakness back against the powerful" (Giddens, 1982:39). To follow, I provide a brief description of the WTO, its major critiques, and my method of discourse analysis.

The WTO

The WTO was established in 1995 by the Uruguay Round negotiations that took place from 1986 to 1994. Its membership comprises 153 countries, according to its website. The functions of the WTO are: (a) administering WTO trade agreements, (b) providing a forum for trade negotiations, (c) handling trade disputes, (d) monitoring national trade policies, (e) providing technical assistance and training for developing countries, and (f) cooperating with other international organizations (WTO.org, 2010). The WTO represents itself as a "negotiating forum" and "set of rules" whose principal purpose is to "help trade flow as freely as possible – so long as there are no undesirable side effects – because this is important for economic development and well-being" (WTO.org, 2010).

The WTO claims that it "promotes peace," fair rules that "make life easier for all," and handles disputes "constructively" (WTO.org, 2008a). Additionally, the organization asserts that "free trade raises incomes, stimulates economic growth, cuts the cost of living, and provides consumers with a greater number of quality choices" (WTO.org, 2010). Proponents of the neoliberal economic model tend to accept these claims as truth and contend that the privatization of most goods and services, the control of inflation, and the specialization of national economies promote overall prosperity and worldwide economic development (Krugman, 2002). Despite its claims, critics of the WTO argue that trade liberalization and deregulation worsen the living and working conditions in developing nations.

Economic, cultural, and political critiques of the WTO

Critics of the WTO economic policy center their arguments on a variety of economic, cultural, and political issues. First, those critics concerned primarily with global economic inequality focus on the recent changes that have occurred in the relationships among corporations, states, and citizens (Falk, 1999). Neoliberalism promotes the free market and typically decries state regulation (Aune, 2001). Critics of the neoliberal economic model assert that the policies created and enforced by international financial institutions, privilege the profit interests of corporations over those of working people, exacerbate already considerable income differentials, and increase poverty in developing nations (Millen et al., 2000).

Such institutions follow a neoliberal economic model (Eltanaway, 2008) and implement Structural Adjustment Programs (SAPs) that, according to their proponents, are meant to promote economic growth in developing nations. Such programs, however, are typically "informed by an intellectual and ideological climate dominated by the United States" (Shah, 2005). And while free market capitalists contend that the poor in developing nations will benefit from the "trickle-down effect," the benefits of SAPs have failed to reach the poor as predicted (Eltanaway, 2008). Economic critiques of the WTO thus center on a rejection of the notion that free trade benefits all people and nations equally.

Next, cultural critiques of globalization denounce its production of increasing cultural homogenization. In critical communication research, culture "has always been understood as a site of struggle through which the social order is maintained, challenged, produced, and reproduced, in the performance of various social relations of equity and inequity" (Shome & Hegde, 2002). Cultural critiques of the WTO focus on how free market rhetoric of globalization as a means to economic growth is used as a warrant for attendant cultural changes. Such rhetoric is more "pervasive than the hegemonizing tendencies of empires yore, the present cultural globalization being a stronger superimposition on the regional cultural hegemonies wrought by these past empires" (Goonatilake, 1995:227).

When discourses become normative, they operate as "an ideology, a system of values, and an authoritative presence thoroughly inscribed into popular consciousness since colonial times" (Gopal et al., 2003:237). According to Papa et al. (2006:78), "in the exercise of power, certain 'truths' emerge and become the taken-for-granted knowledge base within a social system". Western cultural hegemony informs the WTO's discourse of globalization. Such oppressive discourses are created by institutions of power, produced by experts, and eventually accepted as conventional wisdom by the public (Foucault, 1972). Cultural critiques of the WTO thus focus on the need to disrupt hegemonic systems that result from the spread of neoliberal ideology.

Finally, those concerned with political issues of governance, transparency, and representation contend that transnational corporate power is undemocratic because it is subject neither to national sovereignty nor to global publics (Giddens, 2000). Deetz (2007) argued that organizations are inherently value-laden and free market choices fail to represent the interests of the people. To combat the neoliberal ideology that undergirds the WTO's economic policy, proponents of global democracy advocate collective resistance to the top-down model of globalization, loosely termed "globalization from below" because, according to Falk (1999:150):

Substantive democracy, unlike backlash politics ... seeks a politics of reconciliation that maintains much of the openness and dynamism associated with globalization from above, while countering its pressures to privatize and 'marketize' the production of public goods. In effect, the quest of substantive democracy is to establish a social equilibrium that takes full account of the realities of globalization in its various aspects.

Critics of unrestrained capitalism argue that transnational corporations threaten democracy by wielding coercive power across the globe (Gopal et al., 2003), and "have no accountability to nation-states and their electorates" (McMurtry, 1998:140). Political critiques of the WTO thus focus on how the organization must be made more democratic, transparent, and accountable to citizens in all nations affected by its trading system.

Method of analysis

To draw insights into the WTO's discourse of globalization, I conducted a generative type of critical discourse analysis (CDA), which describes discourse as representing some part of the world from a particular angle (Fairclough, 2003). Specifically, I analyzed publicly available information on the WTO's website, such as its mission statement, various press releases, newsletters, and other official documents produced by the organization to establish a consistent discursive pattern. I identified and subsequently explored the emergent paradoxical theme of control and resistance in WTO discourse by paying close attention to specific words and semantic relations between words. During this stage, I determined which themes are highlighted, minimized, and/or omitted by the WTO when describing its multilateral trading system. For example, the coherence of the WTO's assertion that it "promotes fairness" is dependent on a semantic relationship of hyponymy between "trade liberalization" and "fairness" (WTO.org, 2010). To liberalize trade is thus to establish a fair system. Such meaning relations are unique to certain discourses (Fairclough, 2003).

Next, I identified the perspective, or point of view, from which these meanings are represented in WTO discourse. The process of presenting information from a particular angle is known as "framing" (Huckin, 1997). By exploring how organizational discourse is framed, I sought to gain insights into the WTO's implicit and explicit justifications for its exertion of power over the global economy. Through this process of iterative data collection, my discourse analysis yielded two recurring themes: (1) WTO discourse as both control and resistance, and (2) the perpetuation of neoliberalism.

The WTO's discourse of globalization

Discourse as control

Based on my analysis of its published mission statement, various press releases, newsletters, and other official documents, I found that the WTO controls the discourse of globalization by presenting itself as a neutral body and globalization as a neutral process. The WTO represents itself as merely a neutral body that oversees international trade negotiations. In its publications, trade liberalization and deregulation are presented as inevitable realities of an increasingly interconnected world. According to the WTO, these realities necessitate an international institution that can oversee trade negotiations among each of its so-called equal member nations. The WTO represents itself as a "member-driven" organization without which countries would lack an objective forum from which to "thrash out their differences on trade issues" (WTO.org, 2008a). The discursive tactic of presenting both itself and the process of globalization as neutral enables the WTO to control public discourses in order to facilitate and legitimate the process of globalization and the spread of neoliberalism across the global economy.

Discourse as resistance

In addition to controlling public discourses by presenting itself and globalization as neutral, the WTO resists alternate (bottom-up) discourses of globalization by reframing its critiques as "misunderstandings" on the part of its critics. In its publications, the WTO first recognizes and subsequently dismisses various economic, cultural, and political critiques about the way its multilateral trading system works. Doing so, however, requires that the organization acknowledge criticisms in an effort to circumvent them.

In an official document entitled, *10 common misunderstandings about the WTO*, available for download on its website, the WTO reframes the following criticisms as "common misunderstandings" (WTO, 2008b):

1. The WTO dictates policy
2. The WTO is for free trade at any cost
3. Commercial interests take priority over development
4. Commercial interests take priority over the environment
5. Commercial interests take priority over health and safety
6. The WTO destroys jobs, worsens poverty
7. Small countries are powerless in the WTO
8. The WTO is the tool of powerful lobbies
9. Weaker countries are forced to join the WTO
10. The WTO is undemocratic

In this document, the organization briefly elaborates on each criticism, explaining that they are likely the result of misconceptions on the part of the public about the way its multilateral trading system operates. This discursive tactic of reframing criticisms as misunderstandings functions to trivialize and dismiss criticism (and those who offer it), as well as to deny the need for any corrective action. Still, in acknowledging these ten "misunderstandings," the WTO demonstrates its recognition of the public's perception that its approach to global economic development lacks a human rights perspective.

Its discourse of globalization as an example of both control and resistance reflects the WTO's precarious position in the global economy. This position is one of great, but fragile and increasingly contested power. As awareness among global publics about the harmful effects of globalization grows, the WTO is being met with collective resistances that span national borders. Mullard (2003:4) argued:

There are at present major problems of political accountability, transparency, and involvement. Oligarchy, elites, the narrowing of political spaces, political parties, bureaucracy, and experts are at present defining the nature of the democratic process. Globalized resistances, cosmopolitan connections, and global citizens are still merging as forms of new resistances.

As my analysis has shown, resistance works in concert with control. Recognizing the dialectical tensions associated with globalization might illuminate the potential of communication to deconstruct dominant discourses. Doing so is possibly the first step to affecting global social change.

The perpetuation of neoliberalism

The WTO's discourse of globalization also perpetuates neoliberalism across the global economy. Two rhetorical tactics are central to the perpetuation of neoliberalism: (1) framing neoliberalism as neutrality, and (2) framing neoliberalism as democracy. Together, these tactics illustrate how the WTO's discourse of globalization is framed to justify its exertion of power over the global economy.

Neoliberalism framed as neutrality

The WTO represents itself as a neutral body that objectively assists governments in making trade agreements and resolving trade disputes. The frame or perspective through which globalization is represented in WTO discourse is one of neutrality. However, my analysis reveals that the WTO adopts an ideological commitment to neoliberalism, which assumes that "the most effective form of capitalist economy is one based upon 'liberalized' markets, where trade and the movement and investment of capital, prices, employment and so forth are subject only to market forces, without the 'interference' of state regulation" (Fairclough, 2006:40). While the WTO asserts a commitment to enforcing its members' decisions, which are reached by what it describes as consensus, and espouses values of fairness and objectivity, the organization's values are inherently partial. As such, the WTO favors policies that benefit capitalist systems and consumers, a category in which all people are assumed to belong:

> [The WTO] gives consumers more choice, and a broader range of qualities to choose from. Look around and consider all the things that would disappear if all our imports were taken away from us. Imports allow us more choice – both more goods and services to choose from, and a wider range of qualities. Even the quality of locally-produced goods can improve because of the competition from imports (WTO.org, 2008a).

The organization's commitment to promoting "fair trade" and ensuring transparent trade conditions is therefore intrinsically ideological. The WTO does not, in fact, take a neutral stance on trade policy. Rather, it actively endorses trade liberalization and deregulation by discursively masking the Western ideographs of "choice" and "competition" as neutral and inevitable realities of the global economy. According to Mullard (2003:81):

> At present, globalization has become interchangeable with the policy choice of neoliberal perspectives on individualism and markets. To neoliberals the new globalized economy represents the triumph of liberal thinking. The market confirms the freedom of individual choice and competition. The globalized economy offers more choices, cheaper prices, and higher living standards. The role of the government should be confined to de-regulation policies of the labor market, and the privatization of state monopolies and the provision

of incentives for private pensions and health insurance. Globalization leads to the reinvention of government.

Its ideological perspective on globalization reflects the WTO's commitment to neoliberalism. By framing neoliberalism as neutrality, the WTO attempts to mask its ideological commitments, and normatizes free market capitalism under the guise of "fair trade." In short, the organization's discourse of globalization reflects its commitment to perpetuating neoliberal discourses that promote the notion that all people benefit from the integration of free markets into the global economy (Steger, 2005).

Neoliberalism framed as democracy

The WTO also frames neoliberalism as democracy. My analysis of its published mission statement, various press releases, newsletters, and other official documents reveals that this rhetorical tactic also functions to justify the organization's power over the global economy. Moreover, my analysis reveals that its implicit and explicit justifications stem from a perceived threat to its power by collective resistances who organize around global democracy. As both a preemptive measure and a response, then, the WTO asserts its expertise on international finance by justifying its multilateral trading system as democratic. However, its discourse of globalization is one that represents and reinforces a very particular type of democracy: liberal democracy, which serves as a means for the preservation of individualism and "depends heavily on the idea of private property, held both by individual and corporate persons" (Barber, 1984:110). Democracy, from this perspective, is constituted by capitalism.

For example, in a 2003 statement that is representative of its position on the relationship between globalization and democracy, the WTO director general stated:

Trade growth is key for economic growth and poverty reduction. We must recognize the obligation we have to live up to, not only as trade negotiators but also as representatives of governments that have committed themselves to meet the Millennium Development Goals and other vitally important international development initiatives. Increased market access and a strong, rules-based trading system also have a key role to play in enhancing financial stability and generating sustainable solutions to problems of foreign debt. Restricting trade increases the risk of financial crisis and debt problems occurring, and it contributes to the length and difficulty of the economic adjustment that is needed when they do. Advancing the trade negotiations has become all the more important in the light of slow economic growth that is now affecting all regions of the world economy. A boost to economic confidence is urgently needed – a sign that developed and developing country governments alike are committed to opening their markets to competition and setting about correcting structural economic weaknesses that will raise long-term growth prospects and create the conditions for renewed economic prosperity (WTO.org, 2003).

Thus, as it asserts the authority to represent the economic interests of its member nations and their citizens, the WTO does so from a particular point of view. By framing neoliberalism as democracy, the organization turns citizens into consumers. Under the guise of democracy, it promotes the liberalization of commodities and capital, which typically represents the interests of corporations, not people. By presenting corporate interests as citizen interests, the WTO attempts to ascertain democratic legitimacy that is typically conferred only upon elected bodies. The organization legitimates its power over the global economy with rhetorical tactics that function to assert authority to dominate the perspectives of others (Foss & Griffin, 1995).

Furthermore, my analysis reveals that its assertion of democratic legitimacy results from a perceived threat posed to its power by the very people it claims to represent, illustrating the WTO's paradoxical position as both a great global entity and an organization that is aware that its power is transient. Collective resistances to its top-down economic development model continue to challenge the WTO's authority over the global economy and expose its undemocratic decision-making and lack of transparency (Seneviratne, 1999). The tension in its discourse between asserting power and responding to a perceived threat to its power positions the WTO and its critics in fluid roles of "the powerful" and "the disempowered."

Discussion

In this chapter, I have argued for the need to explore the rhetorical tactics with which powerful international financial institutions, such as the WTO, simultaneously control and resist public discourses about globalization. In particular, I have highlighted the control-resistance dialectic in the WTO's discourse of globalization. Exploring the dialectical tension of control and resistance that is present in WTO discourse elucidates the fluid nature of power relations within the global economy. To more effectively challenge unjust global power relations, communication researchers and social change activists must continue to explore the ways discursive structures simultaneously reproduce and challenge dominance in society (Van Dijk, 2002).

My CDA responds to Fairclough's (2006) and Appadurai's (1990) calls to begin theorizing discourses of globalization by exploring the tensions between and within contested discourses. Specifically, exploring the discursive tactics with which the WTO simultaneously controls and resists public discourses associated with globalization is important to understand both the process and the economic, cultural, and political consequences of globalization. A central contribution of my analysis is the exploration of how social actors fix discourses and their meanings in ways that control and resist extant power relations. A dialectical approach to discourse analysis also demonstrates the ways in which "discursive openings" from which to challenge existing power relations are created within the tension-filled space of control and resistance. The insights yielded from my analysis support Mumby's (1997; 2005) assertion that, in contrast to previous research that has developed around an implicit duality of control and resistance, a dialectical approach better illustrates its mutually constitutive relationship. In addition, a dialectical approach to discourse analysis captures the paradoxical forces that produce, reproduce, and challenge dominant neoliberal discourses that permeate the global economy.

The control-resistance dialectic that is present in the WTO's discourse of globalization highlights the organization's position of great power and great vulnerability. This discursive opening provides a space for communication that facilitates social change, empowerment, transparency, and global democracy. For example, collective resistances and social movement organizations that took part in the 1999 "Battle of Seattle" challenged the WTO's authority over the global market, and continue to inspire globalization from below. This type of collective action illustrates how global citizens are creating discursive openings with which to contest dominant, hegemonic discourses and reclaim marginalized ones.

Moreover, my analysis demonstrates that communication constitutes reality and that discourse is often used to legitimate authority and justify the exercise of power. Discourse constructs organizational authority; it is "a way of knowing or a perspective for understanding" organizations (Putnam & Fairhurst, 2001:79). As evidenced in this chapter, power is revealed through self-serving discourse that "produces, maintains, and/or resists systems of power and inequality through ideology and hegemony" (Mumby, 2001:91). In its exercise of power, however, the WTO also exposes its susceptibility to collective resistances, implicitly acknowledging that power never remains within the clutch of "the powerful" forever.

The control-resistance dialectic that is present in WTO discourse draws our attention to the ability of the marginalized to resist the powerful by challenging dominant discourses, and de- and reconstructing oppressive discursive structures. While powerful international financial institutions construct, perpetuate, and attempt to control discourses that reinforce their positions of power, alternate discourses can expose and undermine unjust power relations throughout the world. Communication constructs and transmits power, and can expose, challenge, and assist in transforming systems of oppression.

It is important to note that in responding to its critics and globalization from below efforts, the WTO reasserts its legitimacy and authority over the global economy. The successful employment of this rhetorical tactic raises questions about the extent to which challenging power triggers even stronger reassertions of it. Because the powerful will not easily relinquish their control, collective resistances must devise and employ long-term plans in order to affect meaningful change from the bottom-up. Future research in this area should explore the many ways in which challenging powerful financial institutions results in the reassertion of their authoritative power on a global scale, and the most effective tactics with which collective resistances can organize for social change in an age of continued globalization.

Nevertheless, my analysis has implications for social change efforts among both local and global collective resistances. Social movement organizations can work together to deconstruct oppressive discourses and structures, and use communication to affect economic and social change throughout the world. Specifically, my analysis reveals that the control-resistance dialectic in WTO discourse creates a discursive space from which the "weak" may resist the "powerful," and challenge dominant discourses and systems of oppression. In many cases, this process begins simply by changing the way we speak to be more mindful of global social issues, and voicing these concerns in public fora. While doing so does not guarantee change, not doing so most certainly guarantees failure.

In reframing the arguments of its critics, for instance, the WTO acknowledges the yet unrealized power among the people to affect new, empowering sustainable development policy throughout the world. According to Fairclough (2006:164):

The way in which globalization develops depends upon a dialectical relation between existing structures and tendencies and successful strategies and, as part of that, successful discourses. This is how the (re)construction of the social world comes about, and how discourses contribute to the construction (of non-discursive elements or 'moments') of the social world, i.e. have causal effects upon the social world.

With this analysis, I began the process of theorizing the effects of the globalization process on the fundamental disjunctures between economy, culture, and politics. Exploring the tensions in discourses of globalization helps us to understand that "any contemporary theory for organizing for social change must account for the struggles and tensions that surface as people act together to accomplish individual and collective goals" (Papa et al., 2006). The marginalized can and must work within the tension-filled space of control and resistance to overturn oppressive discourses and structures, thereby reclaiming their collective power. In exploring the discursive tensions that are present within dominant discourses of globalization, I hope that future research in this area will incorporate a dialectical approach to discourse analysis to highlight the ways in which paradoxical dialectic forces simultaneously reify and resist relations of power in the global economy.

References

Appadurai, A. (1990). Disjuncture and Difference in the Global Cultural Economy. *Public Culture*, 2(2), 1–24.

——— (2000). Grassroots Globalization and the Research Imagination. *Public Culture*, 12, 1–19.

Aune, J. (2001). *Selling theFree Market*. New York: Guild Press.

Barber, B. (1984). *Strong Democracy: Participatory Politics for a New Age*. Berkeley, CA: University of California Press.

Beck, U. (2000). *What is Globalization?* Cambridge, UK: Polity Press.

Bourdieu, P. (1998). *On Television*. New York, NY: New Press.

Deetz, S. (1992). *Democracy in an Age of Corporate Colonialization*. New York: Hampden Press.

——— (2007). Corporate Governance, Corporate Social Responsibility, and Communication, in May, S., Cheney, G., & Roeper, J. (eds.), *The Debate over Corporate Responsibility*. New York: Oxford University Press, pp. 267–278.

Eltanaway, N. (2008). Pots, Pans, & Protests: Women's Strategies for Resisting Globalization in Argentina. *Communication and Critical/Cultural Studies*, 5, 46–63.

Fairclough, N. (2003). *Analyzing Discourse: Textual Analysis for Social Research*. London: Routledge.

——— (2006). *Language and Globalization*. New York, NY: Routledge.

Falk, R. (1999). *Predatory Globalization: A Critique*. Cambridge, UK: Polity Press.

Foss, S. K. & Griffin, C. L. (1995). Beyond Persuasion: A Proposal for an Invitational Rhetoric. *Communication Monographs*, 62, 2–18.

Foucault, M. (1972). *The Archaeology of Knowledge*. New York: Harper and Row.

——— (1976). *Power/Knowledge*. New York, NY: Pantheon.

Giddens, A. (1982). *Profiles and Critiques in Social Theory*. London: MacMillan Press.

——— (1990). *The Consequences of Modernity*. Cambridge: Polity Press.

——— (2000). *Runaway World: How Globalization Is Reshaping Our Lives*. London: Routledge.

Goonatilake, S. (1995). The Self Wandering between Cultural Localization and Globalization, in Nederveen, J. & Parekh, B. (eds.), *The Decolonialization of Imagination*. London: Zed Books, pp. 225–239.

Gopal, A., Willis, R., & Gopal, Y. (2003). From the Colonial Enterprise to Enterprise Systems: Parallels between Colonization and Globalization, in Prassad, A. (ed.), *Postcolonial Theory and Organizational Analysis: A Critical Engagement*. New York: Palgrave Macmillan.

Grant, D., Hardy, C., Oswick, C., & Putnam, L. (2004). Introduction: Organizational Discourse: Exploring the Field, in Grant, D., Hardy, C., Oswick, C., & Putnam, L. (eds.), *The Sage Handbook or Organizational Discourse*. London: SAGE.

Held, D., McGrew, A., Goldblatt, D., & Perraton, J. (1999). *Global Transformations: Politics, Economics and Culture*. Stanford, CA: Stanford University Press.

Huckin, (1997). Critical Discourse Analysis, in Miller, T. (ed.), *Functional Approaches to Written Text: Classroom Applications*. Washington, D.C.: United States Information Agency.

Krugman, P. (2002). *The Great Unraveling: Losing Our Way in the New Century*. New York: W. W. Norton.

Marx, K. (1977). *A Contribution to the Critique of Political Economy* (trans. Ryazaskaya, S. W.). Wappinger Falls, NY: Beekman Publishers.

McMurtry, J. (1998). *Unequal Freedoms: The Global Market as an Ethical System*. Toronto: Garamond Press.

Millen, J. V., Irwin, A., & Kim, J. Y. (2000). Introduction: What Is Growing? Who Is Dying? in Millen, J. V., Irwin, A., Kim, J. Y., & Gershman, J. (eds.), *Dying for Growth: Global Inequality and the Health of the Poor*. Monroe, ME: Common Courage Press, pp. 3–10.

Mullard, M. (2003). *Democracy, Citizenship, and Globalization*. New York: Nova Science Publishers.

Mumby, D. K. (1997). The Problem of Hegemony: Rereading Gramsci for Organizational Communication Studies. *Western Journal of Communication*, 61, 343–375.

————— (2001). Power and Politics, in Jablin, F. M. & Putnam, L. L. (eds.), *The New Handbook of Organizational Communication*. Thousand Oaks, CA: SAGE, pp. 585–623.

————— (2005). Theorizing Resistance in Organization Studies: A Dialectical Approach. *Management Communication Quarterly*, 19, 19–44.

Murphy, A. G. (1998). Hidden Transcripts of Flight Attendant Resistance. *Management Communication Quarterly*, 11, 499–535.

Ong, A. (2006). *Neoliberalism as Exception: Mutations in Citizenship and Sovereignty*. Durham, NC: Duke University Press.

Papa, M. J., Singhal, A., & Papa, W. H. (2006). *Organizing for Social Change: A Dialectical Journey of Theory and Praxis*. Thousand Oaks, CA: SAGE.

Putnam, L. L. & Fairhurst, G. T. (2001). Discourse Analysis in Organizations, in Jablin, F. M. & Putnam, L. L. (eds.), *The New Handbook of Organizational Communication*. Thousand Oaks, CA: SAGE, pp. 78–136.

Seneviratne, K. (1999). Democracy, Transparency Don't Exist at the WTO. *Third World Network*. Retrieved April 4, 2010, from www.twnside.org.sg/trade_7.htm

Shah, A. (2005). Structural Adjustment—Major Cause of Poverty. *Global Issues*. Retrieved April 3, 2010, from www.globalissues.org/article/3/structural-adjustment-a-major-cause-of-poverty.

Shome, R. & Hegde, R. (2002). Culture, Communication, and the Challenge of Globalization. *Critical Studies in Media Communication*, 19, 172–189.

Smith, P. (2001). *Cultural Theory*. Malden, MA: Blackwell Publishers Inc.

Steger, M. (2005). *Globalism: Market ideology meets terrorism*. Lanham: Rowman and Littlefield.

Stohl, C. (2005). Globalization Theory, in May, S. & Mumby, D. K. (eds.), *Engaging Organizational Communication Theory and Research: Multiple Perspectives*. Thousand Oaks, CA: Sage pp. 223–261.

Van Dijk, T. (2002). Critical Discourse Analysis, in Goldberg, D. & Solomos, J. (eds.), *The Blackwell Companion to Racial and Ethnic Studies*. Oxford: Blackwell, pp. 95–120.

Weedon, C. (1987). *Feminist Practice and Poststructuralist Theory*. New York, NY: Basil Blackwell Ltd.

WTO.org (2010). *About*. Retrieved on March 25, 2010 from http://www.wto.org/about.

————— (2008a). *10 Benefits of the WTO Trading System*. Retrieved on March 25, 2010 from http://www.wto.org/english/thewto_e/whatis_e/10ben_e/10b00_e.htm.

————— (2008b). *10 Common Misunderstandings*. Retrieved on March 25, 2010 from http://www.wto.org/english/thewto_e/whatis_e/10mis_e/10m00_e.htm.

————— (2003). *Documents*. Retrieved on March 25, 2010 from http://www.wto.org/documents.

Chapter 7

Revolutions, Social Media, and the Digitization of Dissent:
Communicating Social Change in Egypt

Emily Polk

Introduction

The revolution in Egypt amplified a debate among scholars, activists, journalists, bloggers, and policy makers about the significance and value of social media in instigating and sustaining social and political change. Among the varying spectrum of analysis and observation – from those who argue that too much credit is being given to the influence of social media sites like Facebook and Twitter [Gladwell, 2010; Morozov (via Empire), 2011], to others who credit the actions organized on these sites with Mubarak's resignation, several normative ideas appear to have emerged. The first takes a historical perspective: Popular revolutions occur as a consequence of social, political, and economic injustice and the people who revolt have always used and will always use the communication tools available to them to organize and mobilize. The popular tool of today is social media. The second idea follows the first and focuses specifically on Egypt: Social media as a tool in the context of the Egyptian uprising served two purposes. Firstly, it was a source of mobilization, organization, and coordination that let protestors know the next action steps – when and where to meet, what to do, and how to do it, including opportunities to get help if injured. Secondly, it immediately made public to the world, via personal accounts, photos, and videos, the specific details of what was happening on the ground: the actions of the police, military, and government, in addition to the numbers of protesters present and numbers wounded and killed.

Both of these points focus on the use of social media during an uprising – a time period when a revolution causes the dismantling of a regime and new possibilities for social change emerge. It is a distinct and important time for analysis – but it is not to be confused with the process that follows – that of nation building. Now that we are more than a year out from Egypt's famous revolution, it is important to distinguish between the use of social media for dismantling regimes and the use of social media for building democracy. I would argue that they are quite different. Although I touch on latter at the end of this chapter, the majority of my analysis focuses on the former.

Hani Morsi, a popular blogger who lives in Egypt, echoes many in the debate about the role of social media when he asks: "Is it about amplifying the dissenting voices and calling media attention to what is downplayed by state-controlled traditional media as insignificant, foreign interest driven and isolated action by rouge factions? Or is the real value in the community organizing efforts and the planning and coordination tools made possible by using digital activism?" (Morsi, 2011).

Depending on the context and circumstance, the significance of social media can be found in both. However, this chapter seeks to expand that analysis using actor-network theory by approaching the question of the role of social media less as a singular analysis of its value as a "new" tool, a digital public sphere independent of the physical public sphere, and more on the relationship between the two public spheres (the virtual space of online organizing and activism and the physical space of public squares as sites of protest) and the conditions that make that relationship possible. It explores how communication between the two spheres may govern the trajectory of social and political revolutions. The success (or failure) of such revolutions today may depend on this relationship between the two public spheres. It seems to be an old and outdated debate to argue the extent to which the Internet "matters" or which public sphere is more influential. A more nuanced analysis must explore not whether new media caused the revolution or who has access to it, but rather: What is the relationship *between* new media and the people in the streets, what conditions made this relationship possible, and how can it be built and sustained in the context of social change?

This chapter can be divided into the following four sections:

- Firstly, it offers a brief summary of public sphere theory – digital and physical, followed by the Egyptian context.
- Secondly, it provides a historical analysis of the revolution in Egypt including how activist groups used social media to mobilize.
- Thirdly, it uses Actor Network Theory as a framework to explore how the relationship between the digital and physical public spheres was successfully cultivated and sustained via on-the-ground organizing and online coordination throughout the uprising.
- Finally, it builds upon Gurstein's (2011) analysis of lessons learned during the revolution as Egypt begins the process of moving toward a democracy.

Two Public Spheres

The most widely sited model of the "public sphere" was initially based on Jurgen Habermas's research on the emergence of the western European bourgeois public sphere as a counterpoint to state power (Benson, 2010); however, the model has since been applied to a variety of global political and civic contexts. "Public sphere" was a term used to describe a public social space where citizens gathered with the rights of assembly, association, and expression in order to form public opinion. The public sphere is the space that mediates between civil society and the state, with the expression of public opinion working to both legitimate and check the power of the state (Habermas, 1989). This interaction took the form of a rational democratic deliberation that was expected to fulfill three functions: "to mobilize and pool relevant issues and required information, to process such contributions discursively; and to generate rationally motivated yes and no attitudes that are expected to determine the outcome of procedurally correct decisions" (Habermas, 1989:24). Ideally, the public serves as a political force, influencing policy makers, holding political officials accountable, and ensuring that the actions of the state reflect the will of the citizenry.

In the Egyptian context, two public spheres will be discussed – the physical spaces occupied by thousands of people protesting the Egyptian government, and the digital public sphere – the spaces online where mass mobilization of the population and dissemination of news occurred. In 2009, the Arab region had 35,000 active blogs and 40,000 by late 2010 (Ghannan, 2011:5). Of the eighteen million people in Egypt, nearly five million, including journalists, political leaders, political opposition figures, human rights activists, social activists, entertainers, and royalty, use Facebook despite the fact that until the uprising, the government's interior ministry maintained a department of 45 people to monitor the site.

Physical public sphere

The physical public sphere was largely centered in Tahrir (Liberation) square, the site where thousands of people from many different backgrounds, ages, religions, and political parties came together for 18 days to first protest and ultimately bring down Mubarak's regime. In the years leading up to the uprising, this public sphere was often marked by the tension between the government's security apparatus that controlled and monitored the actions of the population, and by the strikes against the perceived corruption of the Mubarak regime, a consequence of which was rampant income inequality, high unemployment, and rising prices (Ghannan, 2011). The majority viewed the security apparatus in the public sphere as the protectors of the wealthy and the powerful, rather than enforcers of the law. Hamarneh (2011) notes, "Security services were everywhere, monitoring people and obstructing appointments to boards of major companies, as district governors and the higher levels of the bureaucracy were fully staffed with their people. The damage became more severe when appointment of university faculty was conditioned on security approval."

During 2009 and 2010, the physical public sphere was also the site of protests and demonstrations. Mass national strikes, nationwide sit-ins, and visible labor protests occurred in the same locations where the 2011 uprising took place. The rural areas were also rising up against the government's efforts to evict small farmers from their lands, opposing the regime's attempts to recreate the vast landowner fiefdoms that defined the countryside during the Ottoman and British Colonial periods (Amar, 2011). Thus, the physical public sphere functioned as both the site of the current uprising, and the space that was used over an extended period of time to create the conditions that made it possible.

The digital public sphere

The digital public sphere is the infrastructure through which a "new society ... where the key social structures and activities are organized around electronically processed" (Castells, 2007) digital information networks. The impact of the digital public sphere as the site of new forms of "citizen journalism" via user-generated content, weblogs, social networking sites like Facebook and Twitter have been debated for nearly two decades by scholars and activists, many of whom argue that the digital public sphere provides new opportunities to challenge traditional authority figures by offering on-the-ground perspectives while blurring the boundaries between news producers and news consumers (Bennett, 2003; DeLuca & Peeples, 2002; Eagleton-Pierce, 2001; Gurstein, 2011; Kahn, 2004). In the context of grassroots activism, the digital public sphere has been used as a space to promote activist organization with the use of videos and podcasts, which allows news to be posted globally in real time with an immediacy never possible before. Marginalized populations including underserved racial and ethnic minorities, undocumented laborers, gays and lesbians, human rights advocates and others who view themselves, and/or who can be viewed, as marginalized by dominant actors and discourses can, in theory, participate in this digital public sphere (Payne, 2006). Communities form in forums and chatrooms, and on social networking sites like Facebook, which create a new arena for public deliberation. Castells (2007) suggests that the development of "interactive, horizontal networks of communication" creates conditions for insurgent politics and social movements to be able to intervene more decisively. Along with a global reach and a decentralized structure that creates opportunities for increased participation, social activist movements may benefit from greater unity as they focus more on the cause and less on a prominent leader. Bennett (2003:147) notes, "Global activist networks have many centers or hubs, but *unlike* their predecessors, those hubs are less likely to be defined around prominent leaders ... the primary basis of movement integration and growth has shifted from ideology to more personal and fluid forms of association." In Egypt, this decentralization worked on behalf of the activists. The lack of a prominent leader kept the revolution from becoming an ideological one and paved the way for a wide coalition of various people to unite under the call for Mubarak's resignation. Indeed, Hamarneh (2011) suggests that while conditions for revolt are for the most part historically and culturally determined, the Egypt experience differs from other equally successful uprisings because of this very reason. "The mass events that led to what is now known as the January 25 'revolution' had no known leadership, no written manifesto or platform. And in a very early and crucial period of the transition, following Hosni Mubarak's resignation as president under popular pressure, the mass of demonstrators had no representatives in the military council or in the government."

The organizers of the uprising were a relatively young group of educated, tech-savvy, upper-middle class individuals, born around the same time Mubarak came to power – corporate executives, doctors, and lawyers, not the truly oppressed masses. They remained mostly faceless, a feat made possible by the anonymity online organizing provides, and thus were able to largely avoid arrest or abduction by the secret police (Kirkpatrick, 2011).

Certainly, not everybody agrees that the nonhierarchical, decentralization of online activism is a successful strategy. Gladwell (2010) argues that while this structure makes networks resilient and adaptable in low-risk situations, high-risk activism (and this chapter presumes that a national revolution that succeeds in overthrowing a government may be considered high risk) requires a hierarchy with an established authority figure. He suggests that a lack of a centralized leadership structure and clear lines of authority creates difficulty for a movement to reach consensus and set goals. "They can't think strategically; they are chronically prone to conflict and error ... But if you're taking on a powerful and organized establishment you have to be a hierarchy" (Gladwell, 2010).

Gladwell also theorizes that such high-risk activism depends on strong ties – people who are personally connected to and affected by the issue – and that social media sites like Facebook and Twitter can only support weak ties. "Twitter is a way of following (or being followed by) people you may never have met. Facebook is a tool for efficiently managing your acquaintances, for keeping up with the people you would not otherwise be able to stay in touch with. That's why you can have a thousand "friends" on Facebook, as you never could in real life ... But weak ties seldom lead to high-risk activism" (Gladwell, 2010).

In the context of Egypt, one might suggest that Gladwell's argument illustrates that indeed it was not social media that was responsible for the uprising in Egypt, but rather a very strategic group of activists with strong ties to the cause who knew how to organize successfully. I would argue, however, that Gladwell is perpetuating an irrelevant dichotomy by firstly arguing that there is a necessary correlation between strong ties and high-risk activism, and secondly, that these are the primary elements responsible for successful activist movements. Such dichotomies ignore, for example, that while news of the uprising reached a global audience via social networks – the majority of viewers arguably did not have strong ties to the cause. However, as a result of this reach, democratic governments around the world were obligated to speak out on behalf of democracy, ultimately putting pressure on Mubarak to resign (Butterworth, 2011). Gladwell's argument that social media platforms do not allow for the creation of strong ties may be valid in a general sense; however, this was not necessarily the case in Egypt, where many of the protesters, while active online, also had strong ties to the cause, and were personally affected by the current political situation. In short, people with weak ties and strong ties to the cause contributed to the revolt in Egypt, and arguably both contributions were made possible via coordination online and mobilization in the streets.

The revolt in Egypt: A case study

Although the revolt lasted for less than 3 weeks, tensions in Egypt had been building for years. One year before the protests began, police beat and tortured to death a young Egyptian businessman, Khaled Said. When Mohamed Bouazizi, a fruit seller in Tunisia, set himself on fire in protest of the humiliation inflicted upon him by a municipal official triggered an uprising in Tunisia, a group of young and educated activists were inspired to mobilize in Egypt. An Arabic version of the Facebook page "We Are All Khaled Said" was organized by Google executive Wael Ghonim, who at the time went by the pseudonym "El Shaheed," or The Martyr. After watching the fall of Tunisian President Ben Ali in Tunisia, Wael called for young Egyptians to take to the streets on the 25th of January, a day that Mubarak had declared as Police Day, and a public holiday. As video and pictures were posted online, the date became an online category for the protesters, immortalized in the Twitter hashtag #Jan25 (channel4.com, 2011). The #Jan25 tag became an effective way to group together online information about the protests. The use of a date stamp would later be used throughout different countries in the Middle East to signify individual unrest (channel4.com, 2011).

Phyllis Bennis, director of the New Internationalism Project at the Washington-based Institute for Policy Studies, suggests that the role of social media in the uprising is that of an instrument, not a strategy. "Just as the then-cutting edge fax machine played an unprecedented role in the Tiananmen Square protests (in China), cassette tapes in Iran's anti-Shah movement, and secretly printed and distributed nidat (leaflets) served to mobilise the activists of Palestine's first intifada, creative young activists took advantage of all the potential of cell phones, Facebook, Twitter accounts and more to build the Arab Spring" (Deen, 2011).

Amar (2011) notes that this instrument is being used to support three emerging trends in online-coordinated movements in Egypt. One trend is organized by and around international norms and organizations, and may tend toward a secular, globalizing set of perspectives and discourses. A second is organized through the active legal culture and independent judicial institutions. Amar notes that this strong legal culture is not a "Western human rights" import, but rather supported by lawyers, judges, and litigants – men and women, working-class, farmers, and elite – who have kept alive the judicial system and have a long unbroken history of resisting authoritarianism and staking rights claims of all sorts. A third group of new social movements represents the intersection of internationalist NGOs, judicial-rights groups and the new leftist, feminist, rural, and worker social movements. The latter group critiques the universalism of UN and NGO secular discourses, and draws upon the power of Egypt's legal and labor activism . . . (Amar, 2011).

While all three trends marked the events that unfolded in Egypt, it was arguably the latter that played a crucial role in the Egyptian uprising. Members of the activist group April 6th Youth Movement (which first formed on Facebook and Youtube in 2008 on behalf of textile workers seeking a raise in the minimum wage), had been building a movement online for three years (Frontline, 2011). The group used the Internet to study other movements, specifically the Serbian student movement. Using highly disciplined nonviolent tactics, Serbian students had played a crucial role in successfully tackling Slobodon Milosevic. Srdja Popovic, the leader of that movement shared his experience with the April 6th group, emphasizing the importance of nonviolent action while other members traveled to Serbia to learn the techniques of organizing peaceful demonstrations (Frontline, 2011). Thus, three years before the revolt, a relationship between the digital and physical public spheres was being cultivated by activists who were using the Internet to connect with and eventually meet others in person, in order to learn how to mobilize an actual demonstration in the streets.

On January 25, 2011, this group, and others who were active on Facebook and Twitter, took to the streets. Thousands flooded Egyptian's main thoroughfares on that first day of protest, standing strong against the regime's riot police. Subsequent demonstrations in Cairo and other cities including Alexandria and Suez were organized online. Rather than operate and counterattack within the digital public sphere, the government attempted to close down the channels of communication and organization. The regime, which thought it could achieve stability and secure its hold by tightening the public space and shutting down the Internet, was largely unsuccessful due to their lack of knowledge and experience with the digital public sphere (Morsi, 2011). Telephone, mobile, and Internet services were interrupted and curfews were imposed. Al Jazeera news network continued to broadcast information about planned demonstrations on the satellite station's news bar, but on January 25, Egypt began blocking Twitter and Facebook, in order to disrupt activists using the site to coordinate protests. On January 28, Mubarak cut nearly all Internet access in the country (Ghannan, 2011:17). It was a move that would fail. Morsi (2011) notes, "Faced with something they could not yet comprehend neither the workings nor the effects of, the best the regime could do was detain and intimidate, and ultimately completely shut down the medium when the revolution broke out (a move that only betrayed how weak they have become and added fuel to the fire)."

Throughout the following 18 days, protesters were joined by the country's opposition parties and popular reformist Mohamed ElBaradei, bringing together a new coalition of forces, uniting reconfigured elements of the security state with prominent business people, internationalist leaders, and relatively new (or newly reconfigured) mass movements of youth, labor, women's and religious groups (Amar, 2011). After 18 days of protest, Mubarak officially resigned, igniting celebrations across the entirety of Egypt.

Communication between the virtual and physical public spheres: Actor Network Theory and the revolt

Actor Network Theory (ANT) is a useful framework for exploring the relationship between the physical public sphere and the virtual public sphere in the context of the Egyptian revolution. Developed by Latour and inspired by Foucault and other poststructuralists, ANT is a social constructivist approach that emphasizes a material semiotic approach to understanding how people, ideas, and technologies are connected. It suggests that there is no reason to assume that either objects or people in general determine the character of social change or stability. Latour argues that the notion of networks points to a transformation in the way action is located and allocated ... (Latour, 2011:798). ANT takes any *substance* that had seemed at first self-contained ... and transforms it into what it needs to *subsist* through a complex ecology of tributaries, allies, accomplices, and helpers (Latour, 2011:799).

ANT explores the relationships between material and immaterial forces in order to better understand how they are connected and related in a network (Law, 1992). It insists that social agents are never located in bodies alone, but rather that an actor is a patterned network of heterogeneous relations, or an effect produced by such a network. According to ANT, such actor-networks are potentially transient, existing in a constant making and remaking. Relations need to be repeatedly "performed" or the network will dissolve. ANT contextually situates networks inside a relative space and time since the effects of power are generated in a relational and distributed manner, and always subject to change. An actor-network approach analyzes how actors and organizations mobilize, juxtapose, and hold together the bits and pieces out of which they are composed (Law, 1992). It is not only a material matter but also a matter of organizing and ordering those materials.

An ANT approach in the context of Egypt analyzes the role of social media in the uprising not as a singular phenomenon but rather in the context of how social media interacts with and relates to all of the other actors in the network that mobilized and coordinated the uprising. It recognizes that specific historically situated conditions made the revolutionary moment in Egypt possible.

The actors in the network that instigated the revolution constituted all of the material and immaterial conditions that made the uprising possible, including support from allies in Tunisia, an army that remained neutral, a nonideological mobilization that made it possible for liberals, socialists, Coptic Christians and members of the Muslim Brotherhood to protest together, a government that attempted to shut down online communication, rather than mobilize within the digital sphere, the organizers of the uprising, the hundreds of thousands of bodies that took to the street to protest, the public spaces where the action occurred and the online social media sites, particularly Facebook and Twitter where the coordination and mobilization occurred and where the details of the uprising were made public in real time. An ANT approach to the revolution seeks to understand the conditions that made it possible for all of the actors to organize into the network that produced the historical outcome, and specifically how the relationship between the digital public sphere and the physical public sphere was constructed and sustained.

Latour locates this relationship between the digital and physical public spheres in the inevitable materiality that is directly produced by and an effect of the digital network. He argues, for example, that there can be no GPS without three satellites; collective games without fast connections; drones in Pakistan without headquarters in Tampa, Florida; bank panic without Reuters screens; and so on (Latour, 2011:802). "When Proust could read a novel alone hidden in the shack of Combray, it was possible to say that his imaginary mental world was virtual, but we can't say that of our kids who have to hook up their modems, buy game stations, swap disks and pay their server for a faster connection, with our credit card…Go tell Google engineers that their vast arrays of servers are just virtual! ... It is fully dependent on its material condition. It cannot just expand everywhere for free ... Its universality is fully local." Latour's analysis is a useful framework for understanding the relationship between the digital and physical public spheres in the context of Egypt. In short, the success of the mobilization in the digital sphere was fully dependent on and arguably sustained by the materiality of real bodies in real time protesting in physical public spheres across the region. Without those bodies, there would be no pictures or videos of mass demonstrations to post online, and far less fuel for the momentum toward democracy.

Even though around twenty percent of Egypt has access to the Internet, (Ghannan, 2011), the "actor-network" first began to coalesce when the organizers started to mobilize in the digital public sphere. The digital sphere provided a necessary anonymity that eluded the secret police and kept the organizers relatively safe as well as a national and ultimately global reach (Kirkpatrick, 2011). But it also allowed people to communicate in a way that was not familiar to the older elites in the country, and their lack of understanding, along with their inability to instigate effective countermeasures inside that digital space may have contributed to the regime's downfall.

However, in a country where few have access to the Internet, organizers needed to find a way to negotiate a relationship between the general population, and the digital and physical public spheres. It is theoretically easier to post dissatisfaction with a regime on a blog, than it is to get out into the streets and risk physical bodily harm, and even more difficult to mobilize hundreds of thousands to follow suit. Locating the successful movement from the digital to the physical and the conditions that made it possible is useful for determining the trajectory of the uprising and its ultimate success.

The youth

The media has written much about the youth in Egypt. Sixty percent of the country's population is under 30, and many are unemployed, two facts that also arguably contributed to the uprising (Frontline, 2011). In the days leading up to the revolution, western and nonwestern media declared it to be a "Youth led uprising," referring often to "The Facebook generation." *Time* ran headlines such as "Egypt's Youthquake: At a Nerve Center of the Revolution" (Hauslohner, 2011). *The New York Times* ran similar headlines including "Wired and Shrewd, Young Egyptians Guide Revolt" (Kirkpatrick, 2011). Much of the media attributed the significant role of social media to the youth, who were the most adept at using the technology. Hamarneh (2011) notes, "This generation of Egyptians is exposed and rooted in the modern era. It was only natural that they would use cyberspace to plan and coordinate activities, cement their organization, and mobilize."

What has not yet been explored in depth, however, is that the youth organizers not only knew how to successfully mobilize online, but were also able to successfully mobilize in the streets. Activists were aware that those without access to the Internet would need to be mobilized in the physical space. Organizers were able to successfully maneuver between both spheres, and thus to gauge the level of willing participation and ensure that word would spread among those without access to the Internet. They did this strategically by encouraging online supporters to coordinate with friends and family by text and word-of-mouth as well as by putting up flyers and reaching out to people on the street (Giglio, 2011). Ghonim told *Newsweek* that organizing something significant would take more than just activism on the Web. "It's not just posting," he said. "To get people to the streets you need to rally. Rally very hard" (Giglio, 2011).

An important part of the on-the-ground organizing were the staged "field tests" in the poor neighborhoods of Cairo's slums. These occurred before the actual protest plans were posted online. Organizers divided up into two teams – one coaxing people in cafes to join them, the other chanting to the tenements above. They connected with the population by focusing on their immediate concerns. Instead of talking about democracy, they focused on minimum wage. "They are eating pigeon and chicken and we are eating beans all the time," they chanted. "Oh my, 10 pounds can only buy us cucumbers now, what a shame what a shame" (Kirkpatrick, 2011).

The group continued to remain active in the streets as they mobilized online, cultivating a thriving relationship between the digital and physical public spheres. The night before the "Friday of anger" demonstration planned for January 28, a small group of organizers walked the narrow alleys of a working-class neighborhood calling out for residents to protest, mainly to gauge the level of participation and measure the pace of a march through the streets. By going directly to the streets, organizers were able to ensure that the word would be spread word-of-mouth from neighbor to neighbor, community to community, making the lack of Internet access less of an issue. "Since everybody knows everybody on that organic level, [government] infiltration becomes difficult. Eventually, if the uprising continues, it will start trickling down into the neighborhoods; once that happens, the regime will have difficulties controlling the crowds" (Jahjah, 2011). Indeed, organizers had already developed a strategy for subverting government efforts at crowd control. Protesters would meet in three squares next to poorer areas throughout the city and converge from there on a preselected place. This gave more people an opportunity to join. Instructions were posted on Facebook. The Cairo protests began in Mostafa Mahmoud, Matraya, and Shubra squares, before the crowd met to occupy Tahrir Square, despite the reported presence of 20,000 police (Empire, 2011).

The movement inside the network flowed not just from the digital public sphere to the physical public sphere. In the same way, the activists moved from a presence online to a presence in the streets; they also moved from the streets to the Internet, posting photos of the protests, and videos of people being injured by the police. As violence flared in several Egyptian cities, pleas for medical aid were also circulated online, as well as tips on how to create home-made tear gas masks. Groups of demonstrators were pictured setting up communal "online hubs" near Tahrir Square, where information was filmed on the streets and then uploaded online. The latter is particularly indicative of the flow within the network

148

between both public spheres. The creation of "online hubs" was being documented in the physical public sphere, only to have those very photos uploaded online and flowed back into the digital public sphere. It is impossible to know the extent to which the speed of Mubarak's resignation was determined by the fact that the revolution was being posted online in real time and could thus be accessed by a global audience. Certainly, the uprising in Egypt was inspired by events in Tunisia – events made public immediately via the Internet, and subsequent uprisings in Syria and Bahrain were similarly inspired by watching the previous uprisings in neighboring countries.

Conclusion: What's next?

Sina Odugbemi, program head of the Communication for Governance & Accountability Program (CommGAP) at the World Bank, asks: "Is it possible to "technocratize" a revolution that is still roaring? The Arab Spring has been a spectacular surprise that so-called experts around the world failed to foresee, yet the same experts are now rushing to impose their favorite frameworks/paradigms on it. I call it the Explanation Olympics. There are experts who are tremendously certain the Arab Spring is all about social media. Others are quite sure it is all about the price of food. Still others say: it is the youth bulge, stupid" (Odugbemi, 2011).

As the Explanation Olympics undoubtedly continues, all of the actors inside the network that made the revolution possible will continue to operate and perform in new ways, shifting and evolving the network as Egypt begins the process of rebuilding itself. It is not yet possible to know whether the revolt and the uprisings that pre and proceeded it in the Middle East will lead to sustainable democratic social change. Yet, it is important to explore the relationship between the digital and physical public spheres – how it is cultivated, managed, and sustained, as the aspiration to democratic rule becomes more palpable around the world, and as more people use social media to communicate. The young activists who brought a diverse population together in Egypt in the name of dismantling a corrupt regime were able to do so by organizing online *and* in the streets, maneuvering between both the physical and digital public spheres in order to mobilize and coordinate a mass movement. Gurstein (2011) identifies several key lessons from the revolution that Egypt might use in the future as it, along with other countries in the Middle East, moves forward into the next phase of development. While his analysis is framed in terms of the value of social media during the revolution, I think it worth reframing to argue that the same points can be made for how a successful relationship between the physical and digital public spheres is created and sustained: First, *solidarity* was built online – as a combination of trust, ascribed legitimacy, and a sense of unity and common purpose (Gurstein, 2011). This solidarity flowed from the digital public sphere (where the activists were able to remain largely anonymous, preventing an ideological leader from taking over) to the physical public sphere where in true Habermasian form, the public was able to bracket their differences and come together in the name of democratic reform. Once this solidarity was cultivated it became possible to aggregate social action – organizers had to aggregate and consolidate the actions of multiple individuals and eventually, the actions of multiple groups with divergent interests toward a common purpose (Gurstein, 2011). Activists were diligent about doing this both online and on the ground, always acknowledging the importance of physical bodies demonstrating in the streets. Global communication was made possible by the digital public sphere – compared to earlier similar revolutions this one was wired not only internally but externally to the world (Gurstein, 2011). It is difficult to know how long Mubarak would have stayed in power had the entire world not had access to the images and video footage of hundreds of thousands of protesters calling for his resignation. However, if it were not for the successful flow of images in the physical public sphere in real time to the digital public sphere, governments around the world might not have pressured Mubarak to resign, and the revolution may have taken a more violent turn. Finally, social media makes possible a new level of transparency, and of decision-making from which new forms of accountability and democratic participation may be created. Operational flexibility and immediacy of response – the speed of communications and the facility in establishing and modifying communications avoided the tendencies toward authoritarianism, enabling decentralization and localized decision-making. The robustness, ubiquity, and flexibility of mobile communications enabled the movement to function effectively with tactical rather than institutional leadership. This inhibited the security forces from easily thwarting the movement by targeting individuals (Gurstein, 2011). The latter four – transparency, immediacy, flexibility, and decentralization – are all primary characteristics of social media and all played a role in the revolution. Without the actual bodies, however, sweating, screaming, chanting, praying, hoping, young and old, rich and poor bodies moving through the streets, risking sometimes their own lives for the dream of a better country – such characteristics of social media would remain free from an analysis contextualized by their relationship to the physical public sphere – an analysis necessary for increasing our understanding of how revolutions happen in the digital age.

References

Amar, P. (Feb. 1, 2011). Why Mubarak is Out. *Jadaliyya*. Retrieved March 20, 2011 from *http:// www.jadaliyya.com/pages/index/516/why-mubarak-is-out*.

Bennett, Lance. W. (2003). Communicating Global Activism. Strengths and Vulnerabilities of Networked Politics. *Information, Communication & Society*, 6(2), 143–168.

Benson, R. (2010). *Public Spheres, Fields, Networks: Conceptualizing Culture and Power in a Globalizing World*. Paper presented at Internationalizing International Communication Conference, City University of Hong Kong.

Butterworth, S. (Feb. 10, 2011). President Obama Increases Pressure on Mubarak's Government. *The Washington Post*. Retrieved on Feb. 15, 2011 *http://voices.washingtonpost.com/44/2011/02/ president-obama-increases pres.html*.

Castells. M. (2007). Communication, Power and Counter-power in the Network Society. *International Journal of Communication*. Retrieved January 11, 2011 from *http://ijoc.org/ojs/index.php/ijoc/article/view/46/35*.

Channel 4 News. (Feb. 25, 2011). Arab Revolt: Social Media and the People's Revolution. Retrieved March 1, 2011 from *http://www.channel4.com/news/arab-revolt-social-media-and-the-peoples-revolution*.

Deen, T. (May 13, 2011). World in the Throes of a Human Rights Revolution, Says Amnesty. *IPS News*. Retrieved on May 14, 2001 from *http://ipsnews.net/news.asp?idnews=55626*.

DeLuca, Kevin Michael & Peeples, Jennifer (2002). From Public Sphere to Public Screen: Democracy, Activism, and the 'Violence' of Seattle. *Critical Studies in Media Communication*, 19(2), 125–15.

Eagleton-Pierce, M. (2001). The Internet and the Seattle WTO Protests. *Peace Review*, 13(3), 331–337.

Empire. (2011). Social Networks, Social Revolution: Youtube, Facebook, and Twitter Have Become the New Weapons of Mass Mobilization. *Al Jazeera*. Retrieved on March 20, 2011 from *http://english.aljazeera.net/programmes/empire/2011/02/201121614532116986.html*.

Frontline. (Feb. 21, 2011). Revolution in Cairo: A Special Report from Frontline's Teams on the Ground. *PBS*. Retrieved on May 1, 2010 from *http://www.pbs.org/wgbh/pages/frontline/revolutionincairo/?utm_campaign=homepage&utm_medium=bigimage&utm_source=bigimage*.

Ghannan, J. (2011). Social Media in the Arab World: Leading up to the Uprisings of 2011. A Report to the *Center for International Media Assistance*.

Giglio, M. (2011). Egypt's Revolution by Facebook. *The Daily Beast*. Retrieved on March 20, 2011 from *http://www.thedailybeast.com/blogs-and-stories/2011-01-26/egypts-revolution-by-internet/#*.

Gladwell, M. (Oct. 4, 2010). Small Change: Why the Revolution Will not Be Tweeted. *The New Yorker*. Retrieved on March 2, 2011 *http://www.newyorker.com/reporting/2010/10/04/101004fa_fact_gladwell*.

Gurstein, M. (Feb. 23, 2011). Egypt: From the Iron Rule of Tyranny to the Iron Law of Oligarchy: Can ICT Change the Rules? *Gurstein's Community Informatics*, Retrieved on March 2, 2011 from http://gurstein.wordpress.com/2011/02/23/applying-the-ict-lessons-of-revolt-to-the-institutional-challenges-of-reconstruction-they-overthrew-hosni-mubarek-now-can-they-overthrow-robert-michels/.

Habermas, J. (1989). *The Structural Transformation of the Public Sphere: An Inquiry into a Category of Bourgeois Society* (trans. Burger, T. & Lawrence, E.). Cambridge, MA: MIT Press. (Original work published 1962).

Hamarneh, M. (March 12, 2011). Egypt 2011: From Movement to Revolution. *Ammon*. Retrieved May 1, 2011 from *http://en.ammonnews.net/article.aspx?articleNO=11683*.

Hauslohner, A. (Feb. 2, 2011). Egypt's Youthquake: At a Nerve Center of the Revolution. *Time*. Retrieved on May 2, 2011 from *http://www.time.com/time/world/article/0,8599,2045558,00.html#ixzz1NfI7PiLB*.

Jahjah, A. (Jan. 27, 2011). Egypt and Tunisia: How Do Revolutions Start and When Do They End? *Abou Jahjah Comments*, Retrieved on March 15, 2011 from *http://www.aboujahjah.com/?p=248#more-248*.

Kahn, R. (2004). New Media and Internet Activism: 'From the Battle in Seattle' to blogging. *New Media and Society*, 6(1), 87–95.

Kirkpatrick, J. (Feb. 9, 2011). Wired and Shrewd, Young Egyptians Guide Revolt. *New York Times*. Retrieved on Feb. 15, 2011 from *http://www.nytimes.com/2011/02/10/world/middleeast/10youth.html?_r=2&pagewanted=2&nl=todaysheadlines&emc=tha22*.

Latour, B. (2011). Networks, Societies, Spheres: Reflections of an Actor-Network Theorist. *International Journal of Communication*, 796–810.

Law, J. (1992). Notes on the Theory of the Actor-network: Ordering, Strategy, and Heterogeneity. *Systemic Practice and Action Research*, 5(4), 379–393.

Morsi, H. (Feb. 15, 2011a). The Virtualization of Dissent: Social Media as a Catalyst for Social Change (Part one: Why Gladwell is Wrong). *hanimorsi.com*. Retrieved May 12, 2011 from *http://www.hanimorsi.com/blog/index.php/archives/2011/02/15/the-virtualization-of-dissent-social-media-as-a-catalyst-for-social-change-part-one-why-gladwell-is-wrong/*.

——— (Feb. 22, 2011b). From clicktivism to activism: How shutting down the Internet helped fuel the Egyptian uprising. *hanimorsi.com*. Retrieved May 13, 2011 from *http://www.hanimorsi.com/blog/index.php/archives/2011/02/22/from-clicktivism-to-activism/*.

Odugbemi, S. (March 3, 2011). The Arab Spring: Welcome to the Explanation Olympics. *CommGAP: People, Spaces, Deliberation*. Retrieved on March 5, 2011 from blogs.worldbank.org *http://blogs.worldbank.org/publicsphere/arab-spring-welcome-explanation-olympics*.

Payne, Rodger (2006). Counterpublic Spheres and Emancipatory Change in World Politics. Paper presented at the annual meeting of the International Studies Association, Town & Country Resort and Convention Center, San Diego, California.

Chapter 8

Two Cases and Two Paradigms: Connecting Every Village Project and CSO Web2.0 Project in China

Song Shi

Introduction and theoretical frameworks

Since the 1980s, communication for development and social change has gained increasing significance in academic communities and among policy makers and development workers (Servaes, 1999). In this chapter, I will analyze two telecommunication and Internet development projects in China, Connecting Every Village Project and Civil Society Organization (CSO) Web2.0 Project, in the theoretical framework of communication for development and social change. I argue that Connecting Every Village Project is primarily a modernization paradigm and diffusion model project, whereas CSO Web2.0 Project is a more participatory model project. Besides, this chapter also addresses two theoretical issues. First, through the analysis of Connecting Every Village Project, I want to show that although the modernization theories were originally to analyze nations-state level development and the relation between developing countries and developed countries, they are also applicable in the study of regional development issues and, the relation between less-developed regions and relatively developed regions within one country. Second, by analyzing the relation between the two projects, I want to explore one facet of the relation between a participatory model project and modernization project in the specific context of Internet use and development in China, in the INEXSK (Infrastructure, Experience, Skills, Knowledge) model proposed by the United Nations Commission on Science and Technology for Development (UNCSTD) (Mansell & Wehn, 1998). I argue, although theoretically, participatory model emerged as a critic of modernization theories; in the INEXSK model, the two specific projects are reciprocal projects, which stress different factors in knowledge creation.

Most researchers agree that, in communication for development and social change studies, there were two dominant paradigms before the 1980s, modernization paradigm and dependency paradigm, and since the 1980s, the third paradigm, multiplicity paradigm, emerged as a critic of the first two paradigms (Servaes, 1999). The first two paradigms, modernization and dependency, shared the same view of communication. They embraced the same kind of communication model, the diffusion model, in which communication process was seen as the flow of message from a sender to a receiver, whereas the third paradigm, multiplicity paradigm, embraces a new model to look at communication and development issues, the participatory model (Servaes, 1999). Instead of passive receiver, in participatory model, the ordinary people is seen as the key participants for development and communication, and in communication and development project, the participatory model respects the value of local culture and indigenous knowledge (Servaes, 1999). In this chapter, I will situate my analysis and discussion in the three-paradigm two-model framework of communication for development and social change.

Connecting Every Village Project

My discussion on Connecting Every Village Project includes three sections. In the first section, I will review past research of China's telecommunication and Internet development. Because Connecting Every Village is an important part of China's national strategy to promote telecommunication development, this review will provide us good knowledge to begin our analysis. In the second section, I will make a brief introduction of Connecting Every Village Project. In the third section, I will analyze Connecting Every Village Project in the framework of modernization paradigm.

Literature review

China's development in telecommunication and the Internet has attracted increasing attention, but most of the past research focused on urban regions. Little research has addressed the telecommunication and the Internet development in rural or less-developed regions in China. This review will include both the literature focusing on rural China and the most relevant literature studying China's telecommunication and Internet development in general. Some of the past literature focused on the politics of telecommunication and Internet (e.g., Press et al., 1999; Guillén & Suárez, 2005). They addressed the regulatory and sociopolitical characteristics of China and their impacts on the development of telecommunication and the Internet as well as the control and governance issues. They argued Internet use increases with privatization, competition in the telecommunications sector, democracy, and cosmopolitanism (Guillén & Suárez, 2005).

Some other researchers looked at telecommunication and the Internet in China primarily as a development issue in a developing country (e.g., Mansell & Wehn, 1998; Press et al., 1999; Xue, 2003; Zhu & Wang, 2005). Press et al. (1999) focused on the advantages of China's model over Indian's. They argued that six factors were important to shape China's lead including "The pre-Internet Chinese decision to invest in telecommunication infrastructure and information technology industries provided complementary infrastructure and human resources for the Internet," and "able to create competition among government owned organizations without taking time for legislative change and the raising of private capital" (Press et al., 2003). UNCSTD's study proposed both the advantages and disadvantages of China in ICT use. They found that, on the one hand, by 1997, ICT use in China was characterized by rapid increases in the volume and range of ICT products, which triggered consumption. On the other hand, although the government has tried hard to push Chinese organizations to use ICT, the results were not promising. They argued that culture, technical skills, and management structure in Chinese organizations hindered the effective use of ICT (Mansell & Wehn, 1998).

As mentioned previously, little literature has addressed the telecommunication and the Internet development in rural or less-developed regions in China. Zhao's study on Internet adoption and usage among rural users in China fully embraced the theoretical framework of ICT for development (ICT4D) (Zhao, 2008). Through a qualitative approach, he studied the diffusion process of the Internet and its implications for rural development in two rural areas. He argued that society shapes the adoption of technology. The impacts of the Internet are primarily determined by the existing socio-economic contexts of the rural setting. Xia & Lu also addressed the telecommunication and the Internet development in rural China. Their study focused on Connecting Every Village Project. By analyzing the policy and the implementation of this project, they argued that this project is "neither explicit nor sustainable in terms of regulatory incentives and regulatory governance" (Xia & Lu, 2008). After reviewing the past literature, we can see little research has addressed either the telecommunication and Internet development in rural China or Connecting Every Village Project. Moreover, no research has situated Connecting Every Village Project in the theoretical framework of communication for development and social change.

Introduction of Connecting Every Village Project

Connecting Every Village Project is a nationwide project launched by the Ministry of Industry and Information Technology of China (MIIT) in 2004 to promote the universal access to basic telecommunication and Internet services in China's rural regions. By universal access, the policy makers in China embrace the definition proposed by International Telecommunication Union (ITU) in its World Telecommunication Development Report 1998. Universal access means "a telephone should be within a reasonable distance for everyone. The distance depends upon the coverage of the telephone network, the geography of the country, the density of the population and the spread of habitations in the urban or rural environment" (ITU, 1998). It was considered by ITU as a transitional goal to universal service for developing countries. ITU defined universal service as the composite of nationwide availability, nondiscriminatory access, and widespread affordability, a group of goals for developed countries. Although the policy makers of Connecting Every Village Project did not state that this project was guided by ITU's view of universal access and universal service, the project has been strongly influenced by the concepts ITU proposed. Also, in ITU's 1998 report, China's universal access policy was cited as "one family, one telephone in urban areas and telephone service to every administrative village in rural areas." The policy for rural areas, "telephone service to every administrative village," later became the official goal for Connecting Every Village Project.

In 2004, the MIIT announced that the goal for Connecting Every Village Project was "By 2007, every administrative village has access to telecommunication (cell phone or landline)," and then, in 2008, the goal was extended to "By 2010, every Xiang (a community of several villages) has access to the Internet" (MIIT, 2008). The policy of the MIIT regarding the operationalization of this project is that the six big state-owned companies, the main service providers of telecommunication service, and the Internet service in China conduct the project directly and almost independently around the country, and the provincial and local branches of the MIIT evaluate the progress of this project and the efficiency of the six companies in conducting this project (MIIT, 2004). Although the MIIT did not state it directly, it means that the six state-owned companies must build the infrastructure of telecommunication by themselves and provide financial support for this project. The result of this project is: according to the 2008's Report of Connecting Every Village Project (MIIT, 2009), "By 2008, the six companies have invested the 12.2 billion Yuan (on this project) ($1.79 billion). 99.7% of villages has access to phones … 98% of Xiang has access to the Internet and 95% of Xiang has broadband access. Moreover, 89% of villages have access to the Internet."

Connecting Every Village Project and the modernization paradigm

If we look at Connecting Every Village Project from the perspective of communication for development and social change, we can see in the three-paradigm and two-model framework, it is an example of modernization paradigm's development project in a subfield of communication (telecommunication and the Internet), conducted in underdeveloped regions. In this section, I will analyze the project on a socio-cultural layer, a technological layer, and a policy layer, respectively.

In his study of communication for development and social change, Servaes argued that on the socio-cultural layer, modernization paradigm has its root in a kind of dualism view, for example, traditional-modern dichotomy, developed-underdeveloped dichotomy. "The modernization paradigm supported the transfer of technology and sociopolitical culture of developed societies to 'underdeveloped' societies" (Servaes, 1999). In Connecting Every Village Project, we can see the same logic. In China's specific context, the rural is considered to be the traditional and the underdeveloped, whereas the urban is considered to be the modern and the developed. Thus, in this project, the rural-urban dichotomy replaced the traditional-modern dichotomy to be a core concept in the policy discourse, and the project's goal can be read as to transfer telecommunication technologies from the urban (the modern) to the rural (the traditional) regions. There is another key dichotomy in modernization paradigm, the Western (developed)-Third world (underdeveloped) dichotomy. Critics of the modernization paradigm argued that modernization is a veiled synonym for Westernization, copying Western mechanisms and institutions in a Third World context (Servaes, 1999). For Connecting Every Village Project, we can see that the development of rural regions is considered to be equal to urbanization. The current urban is considered to be the future of the rural. In its 2008 report on Connecting Every Village Project (MIIT, 2009), the MIIT highlighted its new experimental project, urban rural integration project at ChongQing (a city in central China), which aims to reduce the difference between rural regions and urban regions in telecommunication and Internet development. The current focus of this experimental project is to improve penetration rate of phone, the Internet, and broadband in rural regions so that it will reach the penetration rate in urban regions.

The modernization paradigm also considers development as endless growth in linear stages while "the criteria to identify different stages are a set of quantitative, predominantly economic, growth index" (Servaes, 1999). Almond's definition of "modern society" is a more obvious example of this kind of view: "A modern society is characterized ... by a comparatively high per capita income, extensive geographical and social mobility, a relatively high degree of commercialization and industrialization ..." (Servaes, 1999). ITU, which provided the basic concept of universal access for Connecting Every Village Project, looked at the development of communication in the same way. It used the GDP per capita and household telephone penetration rate as the criteria to identify universal access and universal service, two different stages in a linear growth. A figure from ITU's 1998 report gave us a more direct example (Figure 8.1).

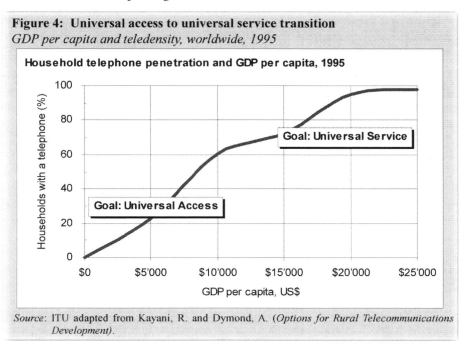

Figure 4: Universal access to universal service transition
GDP per capita and teledensity, worldwide, 1995

Household telephone penetration and GDP per capita, 1995

Source: ITU adapted from Kayani, R. and Dymond, A. (*Options for Rural Telecommunications Development*).

Figure 8.1: Universal access (Adapted from ITU's 1998 Report).

Also, in Connecting Every Village Project, the effectiveness of the communication development in rural region, a very complex issue for the local people and those who conducted the project, was evaluated only by one single quantitative measure, the percentage of the villages that have access to phone or the Internet. Here, we can also see the influence of modernization paradigm on this project.

On the technological layer, modernization paradigm has a strong belief in technological determinism. "It views technology as an inexorable force in development, an irresistible as well as an overwhelming force" (Servaes, 1999). This kind of belief can also be found in the passionate terms in ITU's World Telecommunication Development Report (ITU, 1998), a document that provided the definition and frame of universal access and universal service for the policy makers of Connecting Every Village Project. For example, "Now imagine how dramatically the lives of individuals or communities would be transformed by introducing communications access where previously there was none" (ITU, 1998). We can also see the same belief among policy makers of the Connecting Every Village Project in China. For example, Su jin Sheng, director of MIIT, in his 2005 report of Connecting Every Village Project stated that the universal access to phones will promote the economic development of rural regions, will promote the stability of rural society, will win the heart of the rural population, and will expand the market in rural regions (Su, 2006). This is very similar to the technologically deterministic view of modernization paradigm that adaptation of technologies can resolve almost all the problems of humankind, while the complexity of the changes brought by the technology in the local community has been ignored.

On the policy layer, the policy driven by the modernization theories is a top-down process. In Connecting Every Village Project, the policy and the implementation are also a top-down process. The central government office, MIIT, made the policy and the expected goals. The provincial and the local branches of the MIIT evaluate the progress. The six state-owned nationwide companies got the assignment from MIIT and the provincial and the local branches of the companies conducted the project directly. Moreover, the policy guided by the modernization paradigm assumes that development can be stimulated by external factors – the transfer of capital and technology, expertise and technique from industrialized nations (Servaes, 1999). The policy makers of Connecting Every Village Project also believe that the communication development of the rural regions can be stimulated by external factors although not from another more industrialized country but from more industrialized regions within one country. In this case, the more industrialized urban region plays the role of the developed western countries, whereas the rural region plays the role of developing countries. This opened up the door to introduce the modernization paradigm into the study of regional development issues, and the unbalanced development and relations among developed regions and underdeveloped regions in one country. In this project, the policy makers, the MIIT, and the six state-owned companies, who conduct the project directly, are all from the urban regions. They are the external factors for the rural regions and rural communities. Thus, this project can also be considered as that the external, the six state-owned companies, transferred capital, technology, expertise, and technique from the more-developed urban regions to the less-developed rural regions. The assumption of this project is that by so doing, the communication development of the rural regions can be achieved.

From what has been analyzed, we can see that Connecting Every Village Project is a modernization paradigm's communication for development project, and the modernization paradigm theories are also applicable in the study of regional development issues within one country.

CSO Web2.0 Project

In this part, I will analyze the second case in this study, CSO Web2.0[1] Project (an ICT training project for grassroots Chinese CSOs), in the theoretical framework of participatory model. This part also includes three sections: first, I will review past research of ICT usage among China's CSOs to provide context for further analysis; second, I will make a brief introduction of CSO Web2.0 Project; third, I will analyze this project in the framework of participatory model.

Literature review

In the past decade, with the increasing popularity of the Internet around the world, the study on the intersection of CSOs and the Internet has attracted growing interest. Specifically, for the use of the Internet among Chinese CSOs, the issue began to attract the attention of the academic community after 2003 (e.g., Yang, 2003; Tai, 2006; Yang, 2008). Through a qualitative approach, by exploring the specific cases and theoretical discussion, these researchers addressed the social and political influence of the use of the Internet among China's CSOs. They embraced an optimistic view regarding the Internet's impact on CSOs: they argued that, with the use of the Internet and other ICTs, CSOs can have more control of their communication, have their voices heard by the public and individuals at a very low cost, and facilitate the internal communication within the organizations (e.g., Yang, 2003).

Introduction of CSO Web2.0 Project

Before the introduction of the specific project, as important background knowledge, I will first briefly introduce the development of China's CSOs and the problem that hindered their development. Most researchers thought that, although facing political and regulation challenges, and difficulties in fundraising, China's CSOs have gained rapid development in the past two decades (e.g., Pei, 1998; Yu, 2002; Howell, 2007). The accurate number of Chinese CSOs is still open to discussion, but the number should be quite large, from the official reported 387 thousand (Ministry of Civil Affairs of the People's Republic of China, 2007) to the rough estimate of 3 million (Congressional Executive Commission on China, 2009). The political and regulation challenges are mainly about the registration regulation. Researchers argued that under the current regulation, most CSOs can hardly get themselves registered. In other words, they lack legal status in the current regulation system (e.g., Yu, 2002). Difficulties in fundraising are about the money a CSO can get to support its activity. According to the 2009 nationwide survey of 327 CSOs conducted by CSO Web2.0 Project, 38.23 percent (125 out of 327) responded that their annul financial support is less than 10,000Yuan ($1,493). Lack of legal status and lack of money are widely considered to be two main problems that hindered the development of Chinese CSOs (e.g., Zhu, 2004).

CSO Web2.0 Project is conducted by five partners [MIT New Media Action Lab at Massachusetts Institute of Technology, Institute of Knowledge Management at the University of Science and Technology of China, NGO Development & Communication Network (NGOCN.org), Institute of Civil Society at Sun Yat-sen University, and Friends of Nature (FON)] to enhance the capacity of grassroots CSOs in underdeveloped regions to use new ICTs such as Web2.0. The project thought that by adoption of Web2.0 technologies, grassroots CSOs can break the communication and development bottleneck they encountered. It is also a research project that wants to explore the ICT use among China's CSOs. The project began in January 2009. Its two years' goals include: First, hold four ICT and Web 2.0 training workshops for around 100 grassroots CSOs in west China. Second, design a set of open content-licensed social media and Web2.0 training materials for China's CSOs. By May 2009, a nationwide survey to explore the demand of China's CSO to ICT and related training has been done. According to the survey result and previous field research, the first version of training materials was designed. By 2011, four workshops have been done; three versions of materials have been developed.

CSO Web2.0 Project and participatory model

In this section, I will analyze CSO Web2.0 Project in the framework of communication for development and social change. I argue that this project is a more participatory model project as well as a participatory research. I will analyze the project on a socio-cultural layer, a communication layer, and a methodology layer, respectively.

Socio-cultural layer
On a socio-cultural layer, when discussing the multiplicity paradigm and participatory model, Servaes argued that the emergence of the two is related with the new social movements both in Western countries and in developing countries (Servaes, 1999). CSO

Web2.0 Project is congruent with participatory model in this respect. It is also related with new social movements, like environmental protection movement, driven by CSOs. It is widely agreed that China's CSOs played a significant role in new social movements such as environmental protection, community development, and women's rights (e.g., Yang, 2003; Zhu, 2004). The nationwide survey done by CSO Web2.0 project in 2009 also shows support to this argument. Regarding their field of activities, 24.5 percent (80 out of 327) of the CSOs chose environmental, 19.3 percent (63 out of 327) chose education, 15 percent chose community development, 4.9 percent (16 out of 327) chose women rights, and 3.4 percent (11 out of 327) chose poverty alleviation. More importantly, among the 33 percent (108 out of 327) of the CSOs who chose other, 21 (6.4 percent of the 327) focus on HIV/AIDS issue, 14 (4.3 percent of the 327) focus on Gay and Lesbian issue. Thus, we can say, by enhancing the ICT capacity of the CSOs, this project is related with the new social movements in China.

On a socio-cultural layer, Servaes argued that empowerment is a characteristic of multiplicity paradigm and participatory model (Servaes, 1999). From a communication studies' perspective, CSO Web2.0 Project can be read as a communication for empowerment project. By communication for empowerment, I use the definition from United Nations Development Program (UNDP): "Communication for Empowerment is an approach that puts the information and communication needs and interests of disempowered and marginalized groups at the centre of media support. The aim of Communication for Empowerment is to ensure that the media has the capacity to generate and provide the information that marginalized groups want and need and to provide a channel for marginalized groups to discuss and voice their perspectives on the issues that most concern them" (UNDP, 2006). As mentioned previously, lack of legal status and lack of money are widely considered to be two main challenges for Chinese CSOs. Because of lack of legal status, in the current social political context, mainstream media generally have concern to report information from CSOs. Moreover, because of lack of money, most CSOs cannot afford the cost to use mainstream media. Thus, CSOs, especially the grassroots CSOs who do not have legal status and CSOs in underdeveloped regions, become marginalized in the mainstream media. By enhancing CSOs' ICT capacity, CSO Web2.0 Project aims to help CSOs in underdeveloped regions take full advantage of new ICT such as Web2.0 to break the bottleneck in communication and have their voice heard by the public. Also, as mentioned in the last paragraph, many CSOs focus on disadvantaged or marginalized groups such as HIV/AIDS patients and their family. By empowering the CSOs, this project indirectly help those disadvantaged or marginalized groups to voice their needs and concerns.

Another question regarding empowerment I want to stress is why Web2.0 technologies, the focus of this project, can help CSOs break the bottleneck in communication. In other words, why could the adoption of Web2.0 technologies empower China's CSOs? A detailed discussion of this topic is beyond the scope of this chapter. In brief, it relates to two new characteristics of Web2.0. The first is Web-as-free-platform, which means Web2.0

platform is free and is open to anyone who has access to the Internet. In other words, it means anyone who has access to the Internet can read the web contents and generate his/her own contents on Web2.0 platforms without being charged. The second is that Web2.0 lowered the technical barrier for the end users or the common Internet users who do not have technical expertise in programming or coding to create web contents. These two new characteristics render the members of CSOs who generally do not have technical expertise the possibility to generate web contents for their CSOs with very low cost. This may largely lower the communication cost of the CSOs. Thus, by using Web2.0 platforms, lack of money is no longer a main obstacle for the CSOs to have their voice heard by the public. Also, because Web2.0 platform is open to anyone and CSOs can create contents by themselves, the gatekeepers' influence and effectiveness have been largely reduced. So lack of legal status is no longer a main obstacle either. From the discussion above, we can see that, because of its new characteristics, Web2.0 technologies can empower China's CSOs.

Besides empowerment, CSO Web2.0 Project is also about self-reliance, another key word in participatory model. Servaes argued, in multiplicity paradigm, self-reliance implies that each society or community relies on its own strength and resources in terms of its members' energies and its natural and cultural environment, and any development in multiplicity paradigm needs to be self-reliant (Servaes, 1999). By enhancing their capacity to use Web2.0, this project can improve the self-reliance of CSOs in their communication strategies. Because of the two characteristics of Web2.0 discussed previously, a CSO with Web2.0 capacity has the possibility to build their communication strategy that only relies on its own money and the skills of its own members. Although compared with mass media, which are carefully watched by gatekeepers, the Internet gives CSOs more control to their communications. But for a CSO without Web2.0 capacity, its communication is still not self-reliant. For example, when it wants to use the Internet to deliver its information to public, the general choice is to have a website. This means it has to rely on some outsider who has technical expertise such as website development and programming to develop and maintain its website. Also, because the cost to develop and maintain a website is generally very high, considering that most of China's CSOs are lack of money, they have to rely on other outside financial support. For a CSO with Web2.0 skills, instead of a website that requires heavy programming skills, it can choose any free Web2.0 service that does not require any technical skills, such as Blog or social networking websites and create Internet contents by its own members. Thus, its online communication strategy does not rely on any outside human resource or financial resource. From what we have discussed above, we can see that CSO Web2.0 Project can improve the self-reliance of CSOs in their communication.

Communication layer
On a communication layer, participatory model is more "receiver" oriented. Servaes argued: in the participatory model, "One is no longer to create a need for the information one is disseminating, but one is rather disseminating information for which there is a need." For

the role of experts and development workers, he thought experts and development workers respond rather than dictate; they choose what is relevant to the context. ... The emphasis is on information exchange rather than persuasion (Servaes, 1999). In the design and in the implementation process of the CSO Web2.0 Project, "receivers," the CSOs, also played a significant role. First, the creative use and the needs of ICTs and Web2.0 technologies first emerged among CSOs. Past research showed that, as early as 2002, grassroots CSOs who were not officially registered have emerged as virtual communities in cyberspace (Yang, 2003). Also, this project draws data and experience from past ICT training projects conducted by grassroots CSOs and for grassroots CSOs. One example is Green-web.org's 2 years' ICT training program for CSOs from 2004 to 2006. One experience the Green-web training program got is that traditional website, which required expertise such as coding and web server setup, is not sustainable for many CSOs who have participated into their training. To some extent, the focus on Web2.0, ICTs with lower technical barrier, is a response from the researchers of this project to the need of ICTs among CSOs and the experience of past projects.

Second, the training workshop can be viewed as the result of the interaction between the researchers and the participants (CSOs). Both quantitative approach and qualitative approach have been involved in the interaction. Before the first workshop, two field researches based on interview and participant observation have been done by the researcher of this project to look at the use of ICT among CSOs in west China. Also, the two CSO partners (NGOCN.org and FON) are deeply involved in the whole process to design the project and the training. From a quantitative perspective, the project conducted a nationwide survey of around 327 CSOs to explore the general ICT use and the ICT training demand among China's CSOs. Based on past research and the survey result, the first version training material was designed. After the first workshop, another survey was conducted to explore which parts of the workshop were most effective from the trainees' perspective. The training materials were updated according to the survey result. The most intensive interaction between experts and participants is the workshop. Participant observation, interview, and focus group have been conducted to explore the ICT needs of Chinese CSOs. Moreover, since the second workshop, the project opened part of the workshop time to the active ICT users among CSOs. Five CSOs were invited to introduce (to teach) one Web2.0 technology they think most helpful for their organizations to other CSOs. Through these interactions, experts and participants (CSOs) cooperated to build the ICT training workshop together.

In his analysis of participatory model, Servaes argued, "Listening to what the others say, respecting the counterpart's attitude, and having mutual trust are needed." Through the ways I have discussed in the last paragraph, this project listened to the voices from the CSOs, the "receivers." And they put the receivers' need into serious consideration. Servaes argued, "Participation supporters do not underestimate the ability of the masses (the receivers) to develop themselves and their environment" (Servaes, 1999). In this project, the receivers' voice and need including the voices from the minority of the potential participants influence not only the training workshop but also the design and the budget. One specific example is that, according to the previous study, the researchers in this project thought providing hardware to access the Internet is not a goal of this project. But the data from the nationwide survey of 327 CSOs show that 22.63 percent of the response chose donation of hardware and computer as the most effective way to help them better use the Internet. Also, 3.67 percent of the CSOs did not connect to the Internet, and the main reason is lack of hardware to access the Internet. Moreover, in the field research, grassroots NGOs in distant areas where Internet is not accessible at home expressed their difficulty to use the Internet: "Have to go to Internet cafes to access the Net. Affordability and time is a problem." These voices have been seriously considered by the researchers. The project adjusted its design to incorporate bridging the hardware donors from industry side with CSOs as one long-term goal. From the above discussion, we can see that receivers' voices and demands played a significant role in this project.

Unlike the diffusion model in which experts believed they have knowledge to disseminate to the receivers, the participatory model looks at knowledge from a new way. It thinks knowledge is constructed in the interaction and participation of all participants including "receivers," experts, and development workers. CSO Web2.0 Project is also congruent with participatory model in this respect. The indigenous knowledge regarding the use of ICT among receivers (CSOs) is highly valued by the researchers in this project. One example is, as mentioned previously, the project opened part of its workshop time to active ICT users among CSOs. For example, in the third workshop, a CSO was invited to introduce (teach) the use of Microblog (Twitter-like services) and now Microblog has become one of the most important tools in the training materials. By so doing, the indigenous ICT knowledge is incorporated into the workshop. The researchers help make these knowledge a shared knowledge of a bigger community.

Methodology layer

On a methodology layer, the participatory model embraces quantitative, qualitative, and participatory research methods (Servaes, 1999). In CSO Web2.0 Project, as mentioned previously, both quantitative and qualitative methods are used. Moreover, this project is also a participatory research. In his study of participatory model, Servaes proposed the principles of participatory research: first, "It is the research of involvement." (Servaes, 1999). By involvement, he means participatory research inherited the spirit of critical research, which actively pursues achieving real-world social changes to help the poor and the disadvantaged or marginalized. In this sense, CSO Web2.0 Project is also a research of involvement. In its two years' goals, the first, ICT workshop, the second, designing social media and Web2.0 training materials are all about empowering the marginalized grassroots CSOs or CSOs in underdeveloped regions. The second principle of participatory research is that the results must be shared (Servaes, 1999). CSO Web2.0 Project shared its research results with all participants. For example, after the result of the nationwide survey came out, it was sent to every participant of the survey. Also, as an important research result, the social media and

Web2.0 training materials were licensed under open content licenses, which grant everyone the right to share and reuse freely. The third and the most important one, "the inquiry must be of benefit to the community and not just a means to an end set by the researchers" (Servaes, 1999). In CSO Web2.0 Project, the inquiry, such as how China's CSOs use ICT and what technologies fit the needs of China's CSOs will benefit the CSOs. Also, the ICT workshop and the training materials will help the CSOs to enhance their ICT capacity and better their communication strategy. For example, according to the survey of the 25 participants of the first workshop, when asked "whether this workshop can enhance the Internet capacity of your organization," 36 percent chose "absolutely can"; 60 percent chose "can." From what we have discussed above, we can see that CSO Web2.0 Project is also a participatory research.

In sum, in this part, according to our analysis on a socio-cultural layer, a communication layer, and a methodology layer, we can see that CSO Web2.0 Project is a more participatory model project.

Connecting Every Village Project and CSO Web2.0 Project

In this part, I will analyze the relation between Connecting Every Village Project and CSO Web2.0 Project in the INEXSK frame proposed by UNCSTD (Mansell & Wehn, 1998). Moreover, by analyzing the relation between the two cases, I want to explore the relation between participatory model projects and modernization projects in the specific context of Internet use and development in China's less-developed regions.

Theoretical framework: INEXSK

In 1998, UNCSTD proposed the INEXSK (Infrastructure, Experience, Skills, Knowledge) framework to study the issue: information technology for sustainable development. The aim of this framework is to "provide insight into how infrastructure, experience, skills may contribute to knowledge-based economic growth and development" (Mansell & Wehn, 1998).

Figure 8.2 shows most of the key concepts in this framework. The first concept related with our analysis is infrastructure indicator. It is a means to assess how broad or narrow the foundation is for the development of experience and skills (Mansell & Wehn, 1998). The second concept is experience. It includes product experience and consumption experience. This framework thought the knowledge is accumulated through production or consumption experience. The third concept is skills. This framework thought "neither production nor consumption alone will bring infrastructure and experience into productive use in the creation of knowledge. This requires 'pull' influence" from the skills (production and consumption) (Mansell & Wehn, 1998).

The relation between Connecting Every Village Project and CSO Web2.0 Project

In the framework of INEXSK, Connecting Every Village Project can be read as a project to promote infrastructure development. In the INEXSK framework, the measure for infrastructure is the size and growth of the telecommunication network. They introduced this measure from ITU and thought "few other indicators are as comprehensive as those associated with telecommunications" (Mansell & Wehn, 1998). As we have discussed previously, Connecting Every Village Project's goal is to promote the telecommunication network development in rural region. Moreover, the measure that the MIIT used to evaluate the effectiveness of Connecting Every Village Project, the percentage of villages having access to phone or the Internet, is compatible with ITU's measures such as main lines/100 inhabitants. CSO Web2.0 Project, in the frame of INEXSK, can be read as a project to promote the consumption skills because CSOs can also be considered as consumers of ICTs and the Internet services. Thus, by examining the relation between infrastructure and consumption skills and their role in knowledge creation, we can explore the relation between the two projects.

As mentioned previously, the infrastructure development is about how broad or narrow the foundation is for the development of experience and skills. From 2004 to 2008, Connecting Every Village Project largely increased the percentage of villages having access to phone and the Internet. That is to say, it promoted the infrastructure development and broadened the foundation for development of skills and experience. But as stated previously, "neither production nor consumption alone will bring infrastructure and experience into productive use in the creation of knowledge" (Mansell & Wehn, 1998). As shown in Figure 8.2, the pull influence of consumption skills is a key factor for knowledge creation. UNCSTD argued, "much of the challenge in harnessing ICTs to development objectives lies in the problems of mobilizing tacit knowledge and organizational capabilities to effectively connect experience with skills in construction of knowledge based societies' (Mansell & Wehn, 1998). CSO Web2.0 Project targets this problem. It aims to mobilize the tacit knowledge and organizational capabilities in all participants including both the CSOs and researchers to enhance the CSOs' capacity to use ICT skills. Eventually, it helps to bring infrastructure assets (which is bettered by Connecting Every Village Project), and experience into the productive use in the creation of knowledge. From what we have discussed above, we can see, to some extent, Connecting Every Village Project broadened the infrastructure foundation for CSO Web2.0 Project. At the same time, CSO Web2.0 Project played a significant role to make the fruit of Connecting Every Village Project really useful for CSOs. From a theoretical perspective, in this specific context, the modernization paradigm project (Connecting Every Village Project) and the participatory model project (CSO Web2.0 Project) cooperate together to enhance the knowledge creation capacity of CSOs. They are reciprocal projects, which stress different factors in the creation of a knowledge society.

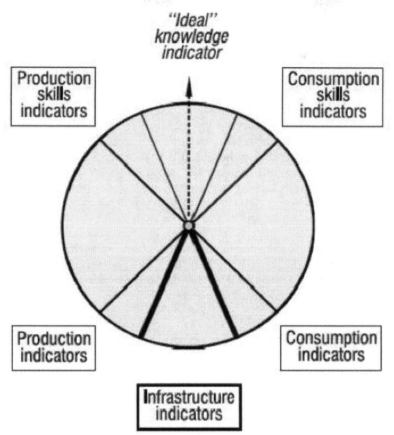

Figure 8.2: Dynamic processes in the INEXSK framework (Adapted from Mansell & Wehn, 1998).

Conclusions

In this chapter, I analyzed two ICT development projects, Connecting Every Village Project and CSO Web2.0 Project, in the theoretical framework of communication for development and social change. In the analysis of Connecting Every Village Project, I argued that it is primarily a modernization paradigm and diffusion model project. Also, from a theoretical perspective, I showed that although the modernization theories were originally to analyze the development issues of developing countries in an international context, they are also applicable in the study of regional development issues within one country. In the analysis of CSO Web2.0 Project, on a socio-cultural layer, a communication layer, and a methodology layer, I showed that it is a participatory model project. Finally, in the INEXSK framework,

I analyzed the relation between the two projects and explored the reciprocal relation between the participatory model project and modernization project in the specific context of Internet use and development.

References

Congressional Executive Commission on China. *Chinese civil society organizations.* Retrieved March 20, 2009 from *http://www.cecc.gov/pages/virtualAcad/rol/ngosumm.php.*

Guillén, M. F. & Suárez, S. L. (2005). Explaining the Global Digital Divide: Economic, Political and Sociological Drivers of Cross-national Nnternet Use. *Social Forces,* 84(2), 681–708.

Howell, J. (2007). Civil Society in China: Chipping away at the Edges. *Development,* 50(3), 17–27.

International Telecommunication Union (ITU). (1998). *World telecommunication development report 1998.* Retrieved September 28, 2012 from http://www.itu.int/ITU-D/ict/publications/wtdr_98/ index.html.

Jinsheng, S. (2006). *2005's report of connecting every village project.* Retrieved March 1, 2011 from *http://www.miit.gov.cn/n11293472/n11293877/n11302021/n13046758/13047478.html.*

Mansell, R., & Wehn, U. (Eds.). (1998). *Knowledge societies: Information technology for sustainable development.* Oxford; New York : Oxford University Press.

MIIT. (2004). *MIIT's policy regarding connecting every village project in 2004.* Retrieved March 2, 2011, from *http://www.miit.gov.cn/n11293472/n11293877/n11302021/n13046788/13047591.html*

—— (2008). *MIIT's policy in the 11th five year plan of china.* Retrieved March 1, 2011, from *http://www.miit.gov.cn/n11293472/n11293832/n11294072/n11302465/11641609.html.*

—— (2009). *2008's report of connecting every village project.* Retrieved March 3, 2011, from *http://www.miit.gov.cn/n11293472/n11293877/n11302021/n13046743/13047451.html.*

Ministry of Civil Affairs of the People's Republic of China. (2007). *2006's report of civil affairs.* Retrieved March 8, 2011 from *http://cws.mca.gov.cn/article/tjbg/200805/20080500015411. Shtml.*

Pei, M. (1998). Chinese Civic Associations: An Empirical Analysis. *Modern China,* 24(3), 285–318.

Press, L., Foster, W. A., & Goodman, S. E. (1999). *The Internet in India and China.* Retrieved May 13, 2009, from *http://www.isoc.org/inet99/proceedings/3a/3a_3.htm.*

Press, L., Foster, W., Wolcott, P., & McHenry, W. (2003). The Internet in India and China. *Inf. Technol.Int.Dev.,* 1(1), 41–60.

Servaes, J. (1999). *Communication for Development: One World, Multiple Cultures.* Cresskill, NJ: Hampton Press.

Tai, Z. (2006). *The Internet in China: Cyberspace and Civil Society.* New York: Routledge.

United Nations Development Programme. (2006). *Communication for Empowerment: Developing Media Strategies in Support of Vulnerable Groups (Practical Guidance Note).* Retrieved May 10, 2009 from *http://www.undp.org/oslocentre/docs06/Communicationforempowermentfinal.pdf.*

Xia, J. & Lu, T. (2008). Bridging the Digital Divide for Rural Communities: The Case of China. *Telecommunications Policy,* 32(9), 686–696.

Xue, S. (2005). Internet Policy and Diffusion in China, Malaysia and Singapore. *Journal of Information Science,* 31(3), 238–250.

Yang, B. (2008). NPOs in China: Some Issues Concerning Internet Communication. *Knowledge, Technology & Policy*, 21(1), 37–42.

Yang, G. (2003). The Co-evolution of the Internet and Civil Society in China. *Asian Survey*, 43(3), 405–422.

Yu, K. (ed.). (2002). *The Emerging of Civil Society and Its Significance to Governance in Reform China*. Beijing: Social Science Academic Press.

Zhao, J. (2008). ICT4D: Internet Adoption and Usage among Rural Users in China. *Knowledge, Technology & Policy*, 21(1), 9–18.

Zhu, J. (2004). The Grassroots NGO and the Development of Civil Society in China. *Open Times*, [Special Issue on NGO] 6, 36–47.

Zhu, J. J. H. & Wang, E. (2005). Diffusion, Use, and Effect of the Internet in China. *Communications of the ACM*, 48(4), 49–53.

Notes

1 The focus of the training workshop of this project is Web2.0 technologies. Although the accurate definition of Web2.0 is still open to discussion, some services or platforms have been widely accepted as typical Web2.0 technologies, including social-networking sites (Facebook for example), video sharing sites (Youtube for example), blogs (Blogger for example), wikis (wikipedia for example) and so on.

Chapter 9

From Liberation to Oppression: Exploring Activism through the Arts in an Authoritarian Zimbabwe

Verity Norman

An oppressed state of affairs

You park, carefully dodging the gaping potholes. Informal traders rush to your car to sell you eggs, milk, tomatoes, bananas, bread, stone carvings, and phonecards. All the things you can buy on the black market, but not in the supermarkets. Someone offers to change your forex (foreign currency) at a "good rate." Inside the OK Bazaar, once a bustling grocery store, you see shop tellers lounging over their inactive checkouts: no groceries on the shelves; no money in the tills. Above the OK Bazaar you hear cheers as a distorted microphone announces, "The Revolution is right here! The Revolution is right now!" Musical strains float behind the words, a drum thumps a hip-hop beat, and you realize the racket you hear is not the beginning of a new revolution to reclaim Zimbabwe's past glory, but rather an afternoon show of young poets and musicians at Harare's Book Café. [1]

For decades, Zimbabwean President Robert Mugabe has used all state instruments available to ensure his continued rule and control of Zimbabwe. He has jailed, beaten, or killed political opponents; restricted and banned expressions of opposition to his government; tightly controlled the military; continued strict state control of the media; given government authority to control commodity prices, and perform land seizures. By law, it is illegal to criticize the President. By law, it is illegal to distribute or broadcast material that may disapprove of the way government operates or of government policies. Harsh censorship laws restrict public performances, discussions, and even gatherings. It is illegal to meet in groups of more than fifteen people without police clearance. The list of oppressive policies goes on.

However, despite this authoritarian setting, with tight control of public expression and even stricter mass media regulations, Harare's Book Café continues to exist. The Book Café is an independently owned bookstore-cum-café-cum-performance space with a "no censorship" rule that has operated for more than a decade in central Harare, right in the heart of the "Avenues," an area infamous for prostitution and informal traders. In this space, poets, musicians, writers, artists, intellectuals, diplomats, and street-children mingle, and performers are welcomed into showcase their work, as well as participate in discussions or debates about anything, including politics. This is unusual in Zimbabwe, as usually discussions about politics, or the "*Zim situation*" (as is the term commonly used to describe Zimbabwe's deterioration), happen in private, behind closed doors. There is little public space for open discourse about government policy, let alone active organizing in opposition to government. But the Book Café boasts performances 6 nights a week and refuses to allow censorship to interfere with artistic expression (Ulman, 2007).

How did Zimbabwe get to this place where freedom of artistic expression is an anomaly, rather than the norm?

Zimbabwe's recent history is one of almost constant struggle. From the late 1800s onward, then-Rhodesia was occupied by British settlers, and became a self-governing British colony in the 1920s. The country was named after Cecil John Rhodes. When the rest of Africa was gaining independence from their colonial powers in the 1960s, and there were murmurings from Britain to grant Zimbabwe independence, the white minority in Zimbabwe declared "independence" from Britain with their 1965 Unilateral Declaration of Independence (UDI), which technically made Rhodesia "independent" but still under white minority rule. UDI helped ignite what was called the "Second Chimurenga," or Zimbabwe's liberation struggle, a guerilla war fought between Zanla (the military wing of ZANU, led by Robert Mugabe) and Zipra (the military wing of ZAPU, led by Joshua Nkomo) against the white Rhodesians. A short period of "internal settlement" in 1979 saw the police, security forces, civil services, and judiciary still controlled by white Rhodesians. This period preceded the negotiations that culminated in the signing of the "Lancaster House Agreement" by delegations from the British government, the Rhodesian government, and the Patriotic Front, in December 1979. The primary goal of the Lancaster House Agreement was to ensure a peaceful transition to majority rule and Zimbabwe's independence. One of the issues Robert Mugabe was coerced into agreeing to, the land redistribution policy, would cause problems later – Britain agreed to contribute funds toward redistributing land owned by white Zimbabweans to native Zimbabweans on a basis of "willing seller, willing buyer." This policy became highly controversial later on in Zimbabwe's history, when Mugabe started giving white-owned farms to his political supporters without adhering to the "willing seller" part of the agreement. This was after close to two decades during which few white farmers were "willing" to sell, and therefore little land had been redistributed. Britain subsequently stopped providing funding for land redistribution, which set off more than a decade of acrimony between Mugabe and the British government (Gascoigne, 2001).

Zimbabwe finally gained independence in 1980 and Robert Mugabe was elected Prime Minister. However, peace in Zimbabwe was fragile, and Ndebele uprisings against the Shona Zanu eventually led to the 1982–1985 government-instigated *Gukurahundi* massacres in Matabeleland, which saw thousands of Ndebele massacred by Mugabe's Zanu. When journalists reported on Gukurahundi, the government reacted by threatening to revoke journalists' accreditation, and made Bulawayo, the city where much of the violence occurred, almost inaccessible. Gukurahundi marked not only the first visible signs of the lengths to which Mugabe would go to cling to power, but was a precursor to what would take place in the future, most notably in terms of the government's clampdown on freedom of the press or freedom of expression (Meldrum, 2004).

Political grievances between ZANU and ZAPU simmered for several years until these two parties reached a unity agreement in 1988, with the formation of the Zanu-PF governing party, which Mugabe led. It was not until the late 1990s that things started to noticeably fall apart in Zimbabwe, when Mugabe effectively initiated and endorsed another campaign of violence, this time against the white farmers, which included occupation of and forced repossession of their land. As agriculture, the basis of Zimbabwe's economy, ground to a halt, so the economy started disintegrating, the country experienced economic inflation, a shortage of foreign currency, food, and fuel shortages. There was also a clampdown by government on any political opposition and Zimbabwe entered a period of massive human rights violations, which resulted in Zimbabwe's withdrawal from the Commonwealth, "smart sanctions" imposed by the EU against Mugabe and other Zimbabwean leaders, and sanctions imposed by the United States. Out of this period of unrest, a new political party emerged in the form of the Movement for Democratic Change (MDC) led by trade union leader, Morgan Tsvangirai.

While Mugabe always held a fairly firm grip on both the media and civil society, following a referendum in 2000, when Zimbabweans voted against the new constitution proposed by Zanu-PF, Mugabe and his Zanu-PF went into overdrive. Fearing defeat in the next polls, Mugabe passed the Public Order and Security Act (POSA), which effectively prevented political rallies or any public space for political debate by making public meetings illegal. The deterioration of Zimbabwe, from 2000 onward, needs little explanation here as it has been well documented in the international media. Violent measures were taken to contain or suppress any expressions of political opposition. Foreign journalists were systematically deported from the country, with the last one, Andrew Meldrum, being illegally expelled in 2003. The *Daily News* newspaper, the only independent newspaper in Zimbabwe, was first bombed and then banned, also in 2003. With a stranglehold on the mass media, and a ban on public gatherings, the Zimbabwean government and military maintained their grip of fear on the Zimbabwean people, for having dared oppose Mugabe. This included the devastating "Operation Murambatsvina" (interpreted as either "Operation Restore the Order" or "Operation Clear out the Rubbish") in 2005, which, according to a UN special report, left 700,000 people homeless and affected over two million Zimbabweans. This hurriedly planned and implemented operation effectively destroyed "illegal" informal housing and commercial structures, and left many without homes or places to conduct business. It was deemed "a disastrous venture based on a set of colonial-era laws and policies that were used as a tool of segregation and social exclusion" by the United Nations (Tibaijuka, 2005:7). "Operation Garikai" – the poorly planned and implemented "reconstruction" program that followed Operation Murambatsvina – failed to provide the housing needed by the hundreds of thousands of Zimbabweans left homeless and displaced by Murambatsvina (Sokwanale, 2006). These laws have still not been rectified and the people affected by the operation have had little or no aid in recovering from this devastating experience (Meldrum, 2004).

By December 2008, this country, whose people had fought for almost a decade for their "freedom" and "independence," was enmeshed in an economic crisis whose rate of hyperinflation ranked as the second worst ever in the world. Accoring to economist Steve Hanke's hyperinflation index, designed specifically for Zimbabwe, the inflation rate reached 80 billion percent a month, or 6.5 quindecillion novemdecillion percent per year. Another way to look at it is that inflation reached almost 100 percent per day. The Reserve Bank of Zimbabwe could not print money quickly enough to keep up with the levels of inflation. I lived and worked in Zimbabwe from 2006 to 2008 and witnessed and experienced the effects of Mugabe's draconian policies and actions in the preceding years: hyperinflation; constant food shortages; fuel and money shortages that resulted in queues that sometimes lasted days; government school and hospital closures. Hunger was something most people experienced daily. The only thing that appeared to be thriving was the artists' community, and the hub of this community seemed to be housed in Harare's Book Café (Hanke, 2008).

My questions continued to grow: in this kind of oppressive political environment, why was it that this artists' community was allowed to openly and publicly criticize the government? Why was the Book Café permitted to operate without interference from the police, the military, or the government, when most other channels or venues for voicing dissent had been violently shut down? Were the activities at Book Café playing a part in effecting positive social change on Zimbabwe?

Mugabe and the Zimbabwean government have systematically taken control of all means of independent expression, most importantly, but not exclusively, the mass media. The Zimbabwean national media policies clearly fall within the Authoritarian media theory, as defined by Siebert et al. (1963:10), which explains that "authoritarian theory of press control … is a theory under which the press, as an institution, is controlled in its functions and operation by organized society through another institution, government." Authoritarian control over the media gives the government total control over what is published or broadcast in public media. It also assumes that the state is essential to the survival of the individual, and that without the state the individual would not exist or would experience no level of development. This attitude is definitely true of Mugabe and his government: Mugabe has claimed that "only God will remove (him)" (Philp & Mahlangu, 2008). He portrays the people of Zimbabwe as children who are completely reliant on him for continued independence from Britain, and regularly spouts rhetoric implying that there is a British conspiracy to recolonize Zimbabwe, even 30 years after Zimbabwe gained independence.

The Zimbabwean laws that relate to media and freedom of speech or expression mirror this paternalistic and oppressive mode of control. Three laws in particular are worth noting: the POSA of 2000; the Broadcasting Services Act (BSA) of 2001; the Access to Information and Protection of Privacy Act (AIPPA) of 2002. All three of these laws put great restrictions on the Zimbabwean people's ability to access information, express themselves freely, or gather in public – all critical elements of a free and democratic society. It is worth noting the role of Jonathan Moyo, who was appointed Mugabe's Minister of Information in 2000, in relation to these laws. Moyo spearheaded the design of the POSA, BSA, and AIPPA, and oversaw the implementation of both BSA and AIPPA. He also engineered the "indigenization" of Zimbabwean media: for the years when Moyo was Minister of Information he banned any media content that was not Zimbabwean. Moyo became known as Mugabe's "spindoctor" or "Goebbels." In addition to implementing these highly oppressive media laws, he also cranked out propaganda in support of Mugabe and Zanu-PF, using the state radio, newspapers, and broadcasting services.

Siebert et al.'s "authoritarian" press theory explains that the authoritarian leader wants to achieve unity of thought among the population, in favor of the government and its policies. They go on to explain that the "realist" authoritarian recognizes that this unity of thought can usually be attained only "through constant surveillance and control" (Siebert et al., 1963:11). Zimbabwe's POSA, BSA, and AIPPA achieved almost exactly this: constant surveillance and control of not only the media, but also of the Zimbabwean people. POSA put a ban on all public gatherings of a "political" nature, and left the definition of "political" up to the government's regulating authority. Permission for public gatherings had to be requested and authorized at least four days before the gathering was planned, and the organizers had to prove they had taken necessary precautions to make the gatherings safe, peaceful, and without interference to traffic. While POSA's provision for public gatherings seemingly supports the democratic provisions articulated in the Zimbabwean Constitution, POSA also states that if the regulating authority has any reason to suspect that the gathering will lead to "public disorder he may … prohibit the meeting" (Matyszak, 2005:6). In practice, POSA has been enforced so as to close democratic space and prevent any political opposition to Mugabe and his government. Since POSA was enacted, no opposition rally has been approved or allowed to proceed without police interference. It is therefore not possible to gather publicly and voice dissent to anything that may be perceived as political in nature (Matyszak, 2005).

On the Media Institute of Southern Africa's website, there is a quote from author Mbana Kaitako that says, "If you cannot express yourself you are already behind bars." This is what has happened to Zimbabweans as a result of the enactment of both the BSA and AIPPA media and information laws. BSA gave the Broadcasting Authority of Zimbabwe and the Minister of Information complete control over all media and media licensing in Zimbabwe. This meant that not only was media licensing limited almost exclusively to state-run media outlets, but that under BSA, media sources were required to provide at least 75 percent local or African programming. There were also restrictions on language usage, as well as directives on how much content had to promote the government (MISA-Zimbabwe, 2007).

In true propagandist style, the AIPPA, which was enacted in 2002, had very little to do with ensuring access to information or protecting privacy. It had much more to do with the restricting of media freedom, and imposing laws that criminalize the publishing or broadcasting of information that may be unsupportive of the government. For example, AIPPA was designed to give the Media and Information Commission (MIC) substantial regulatory powers regarding journalists and media sources. The MIC was not an independent regulatory body, but one controlled by the government. In order to conduct business within Zimbabwean media, either as a media outlet or as a journalist, you had to acquire either a license or an accreditation from the MIC. The MIC also had the authority to revoke these licenses or accreditations (MISA-Zimbabwe, 2007).

One of the few independent newspapers in Zimbabwe, *The Daily News*, survived intense police and military intimidation, including two bombings of their premises after they launched their paper in 1999. When AIPPA was enacted in 2002, *The Daily News* owners, Associated Newspapers of Zimbabwe (ANZ), decided to challenge the constitutionality of AIPPA in Zimbabwe's Supreme Court, rather than register for accreditation through the MIC. The Supreme Court refused to hear the case, so ANZ subsequently applied for, and was denied, a license from MIC. Police seized the paper's equipment, but despite numerous court battles, some ruling in favor of and some ruling against *The Daily News*, the only independent newspaper in Zimbabwe still remains closed. *The Daily News* founding editor, journalist Geoffrey Nyarota, was arrested six times in connection with his work at the newspaper, and frequently received death threats. He even survived an assassination attempt in 2000. He published stories that uncovered widespread and large-scale government corruption, and was eventually forced into exile in South Africa in 2003, to escape government brutality. The closing down of *The Daily News* closed the door on privately owned and politically independent media in Zimbabwe (Nyarota, 2009).

There is one more law worth mentioning, as it relates not only to mass media, but also to monitoring of private information shared between individuals: the 2006 Interception of Communications Act (ICA). As it implies, this act legalizes the interception of any communication and allows the government to tap phones, intercept emails or web pages, or even censor or intercept hard copy mail. While this law is difficult to implement, especially in terms of intercepting emails, considering the government's low-tech knowledge-base, as with the other oppressive laws relating to sharing of information, it allows the government to apply the law sporadically and in a way that allows them to spy on individuals they suspect may be antigovernment. The combination of these oppressive laws – POSA, BSA, AIPPA, and ICT – means that there is almost no space for uninhibited sharing of information in ways that are in keeping with internationally agreed upon standards of freedom of speech; standards considered necessary basic to democracy and as articulated by the United Nations Declaration of Human Rights as well as the African Charter for Human and People's Rights (Crisis in Zimbabwe Coalition, 2007).

The Media Sustainability Index (MSI) of 2008 rates Zimbabwe as having one of the lowest levels of media freedom in the world. The MSI is an independent global media regulatory body that rates national media freedom based on indicators relating to free speech, professional journalism, plurality of news sources, business management, and supporting institutions. For all five categories, Zimbabwe scored either between 0 and 1 (Unsustainable, Anti-Free Press) or between 1 and 2 (Unsustainable Mixed System). On a scale of 0–5, Zimbabwe's overall Media Sustainability score was 1.15, lower than its score of 1.27 in 2007. Reporters Without Borders also indicated Zimbabwe's pitiful state of freedom in the media, and ranked Zimbabwe at number 151 in the world (out of 175) on their 2008 Press Freedom Index. The MSI 2008 report on Zimbabwe claims that not only are there no legal independent media sources or journalists in Zimbabwe, but that journalists suspected of being antigovernment are routinely beaten, disappear, abducted, and even murdered or die in mysterious circumstances. One of the MSI report panelists, Jestina Mukoko, a human rights activist and director of the Zimbabwe Peace Project, was abducted by Zimbabwean police in December, 2008, and held illegally for several months. During that time, she was severely beaten and tortured, while the police and government denied knowledge of her whereabouts. When her abduction was finally made public, she was formally charged with treason and made to go to trial. Although she was acquitted of the charges, her case became an example of what happens to Zimbabweans who publish or highlight information about human rights abuses. In early 2009, a Zimbabwean friend of mine was picked up by the police in a random and illegal sweep of Harare, and when she stated that what was being done to her was unconstitutional and violated her human rights, the police threatened her by saying "we made Jestina Mukoko disappear ... we can do the same to you and your friends" (Media Sustainability Index, 2009) (Reporters Without Borders, 2008).

Most Zimbabweans have stopped openly fighting for their freedom or right to democracy, as the perceived threat of violence is just too great a price. From a theoretical perspective, Zimbabweans are being controlled by what French social theorist, Michel Foucault, would describe as the "gaze." In his book *Discipline and Punish*, Michel Foucault (1982) describes the power of the "gaze" to control society, and uses the seemingly all-seeing panoptic prison structure as a metaphor for how an appearance of constant government surveillance controls society. His work on "power," "punishment," and "surveillance" explains how fascist forms of government use the apparatus of government, which have become acceptable in "normal" or democratic societies in order to achieve their destructive goals. He points out the danger of trying to deal with the excesses of power in a "rational" way, in other words by using seemingly rational tools or mechanisms to fight the irrationality or the "internal madness" (Foucault, 1982:779) of a fascist state. This danger has definitely been realized in Zimbabwe, where journalists, human rights activists, politicians, and everyday citizens have attempted to use the courts as a way to fight Mugabe's irrational, power-hungry machinery.

While many have fallen prey to this, Andrew Meldrum is an example of an independent journalist who followed the media laws to the letter, but still did not win in the struggle to publish the truth about what was happening in Zimbabwe. Meldrum relocated to Zimbabwe from Britain in 1980, following Zimbabwe's independence, and became a permanent resident several years later. In 2003, after being harassed and followed by Zimbabwean security police, Meldrum was accused of writing negative stories about Zimbabwe but the courts failed to convict him under BSA or AIPPA laws, as he was a legal permanent resident and had written stories for the British *Guardian* newspaper, not a Zimbabwean paper. It made no difference that Meldrum was found "not guilty" of these charges; following his acquittal he was issued orders to leave Zimbabwe within 24 hours. Despite legal protest, he was illegally expelled from Zimbabwe. Zimbabweans like Meldrum may have assumed that they were "safe" if they simply found ways to stay within the law. But this has not proved to be true (Meldrum, 2004).

To fully understand the state of communication in Zimbabwe, and therefore get a glimpse of the actual power relations at play in society, it is important to follow Foucault's advice not to study the power dynamics "from the point of view of its internal rationality." Why? Because there is no internal rationality. It is preferable to turn away from the supposed legal structures in place and examine the "struggle" movements that exist in Zimbabwe and to view the power dynamics in Zimbabwe through this lens, to truly get a view from within society (Foucault, 1982).

Whichever perspective you choose, independent media and freedom of speech in Zimbabwe are in tatters, and despite the 2008 power-sharing deal that saw Zanu-PF and MDC agree to partner in a "Government of National Unity" (GNU), there has been little substantial change to the oppressive environment in Zimbabwe, in which information is subdued, intercepted, and manipulated by the government and its apparatus, to serve the interests of Mugabe and his Zanu-PF. In order to better understand how Zimbabwe has gone from a state of liberation to one of oppression it is important we also look through the lens of the struggle. The lens of active grassroots activist communication movements may give us more insight into the struggle for freedom of speech in Zimbabwe.

Uncensored opposition or unimportant artists?

Despite the oppressive laws against verbalizing political dissent in Zimbabwe, there is a space in the capital Harare, the Book Café, where artists vigorously exercise their right to freedom of expression and use music, poetry, and discussion to speak out against the problems they see in their communities. Notably, there is a grassroots spoken word/hip hop for social change movement emerging, led by two of Zimbabwe's leading spoken-word artists, Comrade Fatso and Outspoken. Are these artists intentionally ignored by the Zimbabwean government? Do they pose no threat to the status quo? Or do they give an appearance of a tolerance for freedom of expression? I was curious to explore the work of these artists, the space in which they perform, and the reasons why they are largely left untouched in their performance of protest poetry. Here I attempt to situate this recent "rebel" arts movement in a more historical political movement within Zimbabwean literature and arts.

In his song "House of Hunger," self-professed "protest poet," Samm Monro (or "Comrade Fatso" as he prefers to be known) invites the listener into the house built with "walls of fear and anger," a place where "those with hope … are beaten, battered, left for dead." He welcomes the listener to Zimbabwe, sometimes referred to as the "House of Stone" after the Great Zimbabwe Monument. Comrade Fatso claims that Zimbabwe's problem is "not just the president" but is a system of corruption Zimbabweans inherited from the former colonial power, but which was endorsed and continues to be used by the current Zimbabwe government. He uses overtly political imagery, referring to graffiti, which can be found all over Harare, saying "Zwakwana" (Shona for "Enough!") or "WOZA" (the organization "Women of Zimbabwe Arise" or Ndebele for "Come forward") and urges listeners to stop supporting this corrupt system and to "stand tall" in support of a new Zimbabwe (Monro, 2008a).

Fatso's song and album, "House of Hunger," is named after the work of another literary artist who spoke out against oppression in Zimbabwe, Dambudzo Marechera. Although many would claim that Marechera was insane, he used his writing to confront oppression both during and after the colonial era. He wrote "House of Hunger" in 1979 while in self-imposed exile in Great Britain, and used his first novel to point out not only the contradictions of the colonial state, but also the need for the material, spiritual, and cultural "hunger" of Zimbabweans to be satisfied. He went on to write about the need for the freeing of the African mind so as to craft a new sense of identity, and following Zimbabwe's independence, refused to become a public supporter of Mugabe's regime of power. Rather, he continued to use his writing to rile against Mugabe and his government, and eventually left Zimbabwe to return to his homeless existence in Britain, where he died prematurely in 1987. Marechera has become something of a hero to cultural activists in Zimbabwe, which explains Comrade Fatso's homage to him in the form of his first CD release (Marechera Celebration, 2008).

Marechera's legacy also continues in the form of the "House of Hunger" poetry slams, monthly spoken-word poetry competitions hosted by the Book Café. At these poetry slams protest poets like Comrade Fatso and his performance partner and colleague, Outspoken, both frequent performers who made their way up through the ranks of poets, use this space as an opportunity not only to improve their poetry and performance, but also to voice their discontent about the society they see around them in Zimbabwe. These poetry slams started in 2005 in response to what artist-activists saw as a direct infringement on their freedom of expression. Independent media had collapsed, and the cost of publishing (or even purchasing) books was impossible, due to the free fall of the Zimbabwean economy. Performance became one of the only ways individuals could make their dissent heard, and the "House of Hunger" poetry slams provide an opportunity for just that. Right in the center of Harare, performing in front of a multiracial crowd, poets like Fatso perform poetry that directly addresses the issue of state domination of media and challenges the government by saying:

You wanna chain me, you wanna contain me
You wanna chop off my head and de-brain me
You want me to develop this "yes Comrade" mentality
All in the name of your supposed unity
Well, listen shamwari, my mind decides to be free
So though you control the police, the army, the TV and most society
You can't control the hearts of humanity
You can't control the desire for equality
Cos you can beat our bodies but our minds will be free
I said you can beat our bodies but our minds will be free

(Monro, MaStreets, 2008b)

Likewise, spoken-word poet, Outspoken, uses his poetry to highlight the fact that the so-called "liberation struggle" did not lead to freedom or true democracy. In his poetry, Outspoken contends with much of the social injustice in Zimbabwe, but focuses on this issue of freedom in his metaphorical poem called "Freedom Train," which tells listeners that:

> Everyday the death toll rises from the freedom trains wreckage
> That never saw democracy but destined us to heaven
> Through a passage of pain and tribulation attached
> That only seems to affect those of us stuck in economy class
> If only the inspector started checking on the drivers
> There wouldn't be this ugly scene of checking on survivors
> 18 April 1980 was the day we left the station
> Aboard the freedom train, but still haven't reached our destination

(Makawa, 2008)

Both of these poets, who use their words, poetry, and music as a form of protest against the lack of freedom in Zimbabwe, are regulars at the Book Café, and started their careers competing in the House of Hunger poetry slams. They are now cultural activists who help lead a movement of artist social activists through their nonprofit organization, the Magamba Cultural Activists Network, whose slogan is "The Word is our Weapon" and whose encouragement to their members is "Make Some Noise!" This fledgling organization, only in its third year, has a vision for "a free and just Zimbabwe where arts and culture is used as a tool for positive social change." Magamba is a youth-based organization, and its name means "Heroes" or "Freedom Fighters" and is intended to symbolize the role of youth today in the new fight for freedom in Zimbabwe. But this is a different type of struggle for freedom, from the liberation struggle leading up to Zimbabwe's independence. This is a struggle for freedom of the mind, for freedom of speech, for freedom of expression, even for freedom itself (Magamba Cultural Activists Network, 2009).

In an interview with Outspoken, he explained that the most vulnerable group of people in Zimbabwe are unemployed youth living in urban ghettos. This is due to the fact that the education system has effectively collapsed, as has the economy with unemployment levels anywhere between 60 and 90 percent, which leaves youth with little with which to occupy themselves. Zimbabwean youth are therefore susceptable to influence either by media sources like MTV, or to propaganda put out by the state. Magamba's vision is not to politicize youth, but to have them have a "conscious" mind of their own and to develop the critical thinking skills needed to analyze information in today's world. When they talk about "alternatives," they are not talking about the alternatives usually discussed in Zimbabwe: political alternatives. Rather, they are talking about an alternative state of mind that does not go along with the current societal framework. In this sense, Magamba and its poet organizers are suggesting a complete overhaul and redefinition of society, rather than simply continuing to work within the oppressive structure left by the colonial government, a structure that continues to be used to support the oppression exercized by Mugabe and Zanu-PF (Makawa, 2010).

Outspoken claims that Magamba has moved away from working with schools as they found the hierarchical infrastructure of the school interfered with their aim of enabling "the free expression of young people and to build a new generation of community activists who can heal and democratize their communities." The school structure was too hierarchical and similar in nature to society's hierarchy and this contradicted their goals of equality, free thought, and critical thinking. This rationale echoes the sentiments of another French social theorist, Pierre Bourdieu, whose theory of "symbolic power" considered the hierarchical structure of schools as a means to reproduce the hiearchical nature of capitalistic society. So, rather than partnering with schools, Outspoken describes Magamba's activities as an educational "de-schooling" program. By working with youth in the ghetto, in small poetry workshops and discussion groups, Outspoken and his colleagues have developed a grassroots communication movement that works in opposition to the oppressive state machinery, but which has developed without any obvious reaction or interference from the state. In fact, Outspoken talks more about the organizers' and participants' paranoia about state interference, rather than actual interference. He claims that part of Magamba's work is to help Zimbabwean youth break out of this mindstate that self-censors out of fear of actual state censorship (Swartz, 1997; Makawa, 2010).

The use of spoken word is another intentional tool with which Magamba hopes to engage youth, and the motivation is perhaps an obvious one, given the popularity of hip-hop and rap among young people around the world. Magamba's aim is to take this artistic form that has many negative connotations associated with it and to use it toward a more positive end, and to encourage not only engagement but also participation. Through Magamba's training, the youth become not only consumers of hip-hop and poetry, but creators of it, and in the work they have done thus far, Magamba organizers have already seen a change in the way the youth express themselves, and youth are becoming more politicized in their messages. While Magamba meetings and training sessions happen in the ghettos around Harare, the young poets are encouraged to take part in the House of Hunger poetry slams, as well as the monthly free "Mashoko!" ("Words") shows, which include poetry, music, dance, and more. The Mashoko! shows are held in another performance space, Mannenberg, which is also part of the Book Café complex and under the same ownership (Makawa, 2010).

In trying to understand whether or not there are truly pockets of free expression in Zimbabwe, it is important to examine the "safe" or open spaces in which artists feel able to express themselves freely. There are few of these spaces in Zimbabwe, but Book Café is an independent performance space that is heavily used by the hip-hop, music, and poetry community in Harare. The Book Café is a small café that opened over ten years ago as a small bookshop called Grassroots Books, and was founded by current Book Café owner, Paul Brickhill. It evolved into a café and independent performance space, and over the years the performance content has become increasingly political. Today, Book Café is famed because it is a "strictly no censorship" zone, and people from all walks of life seem to mingle freely, while sipping beers, and listening to performances by some of the best talent in Zimbabwe. Performances include live music, poetry, book launches and signings, discussions, and more. However, Book Café is not just a performance space. Since wireless Internet made its debut in Zimbabwe, artists, NGO workers, and other "hippies" gather at Book Café during the day to surf the Internet on their laptops. According to one journalist and photographer I interviewed, "there's no other place anywhere in Zim with the same sort of artistic vibe … artists walk in and out all the time, from Hope Masike, to Victor Kunonga, from Dudu Manhenga to Oliver Mtukudzi." While the artistic "vibe" holds a large part of the attraction, the fact that this is an open space makes it particularly desirable. As Brickhill said in a video interview with Al Jazeera, "It's not as though it has a political slant, it's just that it is open, you can say what you want" (Ulman, 2008a).

While Brickhill may claim Book Café does not have a "political slant," others may argue otherwise. Two of the people I interviewed claimed Book Café was the only space for open, public, political discussion in Harare, and both mentioned a recent booklaunch by the Crisis in Zimbabwe Coalition, which took place at Book Café in March 2010. The book was about the torture that occurred during the 2008 election, and the booklaunch was attended by a host of politically connected figures, including Prime Minister Morgan Tsvangirai. When issues around political violence are openly discussed, and the leader of the MDC attend events there, it is difficult to argue that Book Café is not a political space. Some may claim that events such as this are a reflection of how the new GNU is making Zimbabwe a more tolerant and "free" society. PM Tsvangirai himself claimed at the gathering that "the fact that we are here today is evidence that they failed to silence us." Although he also admitted that Zimbabwe has not reached its true democratic destination (The Zimbo Jam, 2010).

However, while events such as these, which are widely publicized and attended by those in Harare's middle-class, elite, and artistic communities, hint at a free and open society, the opposite still occurs in other artistic spaces in Zimbabwe. In the week following the Crisis in Zimbabwe Coalition event hosted at the Book Café, an art exhibition at the National Gallery in Bulawayo by artist Owen Maseko was shut down, and the artist and gallery curator were both arrested and detained. Maseko was held for a week before being released on US$100 bail. His exhibition depicted the violence experienced by the Ndebele people during the Gukurahundi massacres. As mentioned earlier in this chapter, these massacres occurred in 1983, but even today, any mention or depiction of them is shut down or destroyed by those in power. This was the second art exhibit to be shut down in the space of a week, with photos from a different exhibit at the Gallery Delta seized by police a few days before Maseko's arrest. These photos were also associated with politically motivated violence, but in this case the photos depicted violence around the 2008 elections (The Zimbo Jam, 2010).

So why do performers at Book Café go largely unhindered, while artists in other venues still get shut down by government authorities? Why has this overtly political space been allowed to operate and thrive during the ten years in Zimbabwe's history when freedom of every kind was disintegrating? There could be many reasons. One reason could be that owner Paul Brickhill, a white Zimbabwean, was involved in the liberation struggle and therefore still has connections to people in government. Another could be that the activists who go to the Book Café are simply not threatening enough to the power of the government. One interviewee described Book Café artists and patrons as "middle class, very small numbers, and probably (would) not start a demo on the streets. Most of the people who go (to Book Café) are not your typical hungry Zimbos and they would never go to a high-density suburb and be part of a protest." Another interviewee took this sentiment further and claimed that while poets like Fatso and Outspoken dominate the "alternative political voice" of Zimbabwe, they are educated, middle-class citizens who are not true representatives of the average Zimbabwean. Likewise, the same person claimed that the Book Café has become the only "alternative political and social space" in Harare and effectively crowds out other such spaces. The sentiment from several Book Café patrons is that its "hip" factor far outweighs the low threat level it may pose to the government.

Another reason suggested was that the Book Café, its shows and poetry slams, provides a form and level of entertainment unmatched by other Harare venues, and that the police and military personnel responsible for enforcing Zimbabwe's censorship laws actually frequent the venue as patrons. In a video produced by Al Jazeera, famed Zimbabwean singer-songwriter, Chiwoniso Maraire, describes how five policemen showed up at a Book Café show of hers dressed in full riot gear. She explains that one of the policemen encouraged her to "pretend we're not here" and to continue performing. She describes the dilemma faced by artists like herself, when confronted so directly by the enforcers of Zimbabwe's regime of oppression, while singing songs that question "Whose side is God on? They are killing me in this country of thieves" (Ulman, 2008b).

Lastly, the relationship between race and media is an important one to note in relation to Zimbabwe, and could play some role in why Book Café artists and performers are largely left alone, despite their sometimes overtly political message. Book Café is owned and run by white Zimbabweans, and some of the performers and patrons are also white. It is an unanswered question to what degree the Zimbabwean government would come under fire from the international media if they were to attempt to shut down a white-owned space such as Book Café.

Race and the international media have long played a large role in the observation, or lack thereof, of human rights in Zimbabwe. When Gukurahundi took place in Matabeleland and tens, perhaps hundreds of thousands of Ndebele were massacred, the international community continued to praise Mugabe, made an example of him as an African leader "success story," continued to shower him with honorary degrees. However, when white Zimbabwean farmers started getting forcibly evicted from their farms in the late 1990s, the international media went into overdrive and foreign governments rapidly slapped sanctions on Mugabe and his cronies. Likewise, whenever Mugabe's oppressive laws affect white Zimbabweans, there is an uproar in the international media, while similar experiences by black Zimbabweans go largely unnoticed. For example, the trials of former MP Roy Bennett or journalist Andrew Meldrum attracted worldwide coverage, while the 2009 abductions of activists Chris Dhlamini and Ghandi Mudzingwa went largely unnoticed.

I have personally experienced the "protection" a white skin affords you in Zimbabwe, as the police and military are acutely aware of the spotlight international media puts on abuse of white people by the Zimbabwean government. In early 2009, at a time when there was no legitimate government in Zimbabwe and the police and military were doing nightly sweeps of the city and unlawfully detaining people for no apparent wrongdoing, I drove some friends home and dropped them off in the "Avenues," close to where the Book Café is located. As we stepped out of the car, two truckloads of military and policemen swerved round the corner, grabbed my three friends, all of whom were black Zimbabweans, and forced them in the back of their truck. I was told to go back to my car and leave immediately. As the trucks drove away, the policemen commented to my friends that I was "lucky" I was white, implying they had been ordered to leave white people untouched. This unlawful detainment was simply an exercise in corruption, one that had become commonplace in Zimbabwe, and resulted in us paying a small bribe for my friends' release. However, it gave me a first-hand experience of how white and black people are treated differently in Zimbabwe. Corruption in the armed forces is tolerated, as long as it only affects black Zimbabweans. Why? The assumption is that the international media will not pay attention to the regular unlawful detainment of black Zimbabweans, and this assumption is largely true.

When it comes to measuring freedom and human rights, the UN's Universal Declaration of Human Rights (UDHR) has become the document we turn to for guidance. Among other things, the UDHR states that "no one shall be subjected to arbitrary interference with his privacy, family, home or correspondence" (Article 12), that "Everyone has the right to freedom of opinion and expression; this right includes freedom to hold opinions without interference and to seek, receive and impart information and ideas through any media and regardless of frontiers" (Article 19), and finally, that "Everyone has the right to freedom of peaceful assembly and association" (Article 20.1). However, Mugabe likes to argue that the UN represents western interests, so perhaps we should look at what the African Union states are requisites for basic human rights. The African Union Charter on Human and People's Rights (AUCHPR), of which Zimbabwe is a signatory, declares that "Every individual shall have the right to receive information," and that "Every individual shall have the right to express and disseminate his opinions within the law" (Article 9). This charter also declares "Every individual shall have the right to free association provided that he abides by the law" (Article 10) and that "Every individual shall have the right to assemble freely with others" (Article 11) (United Nations, 1948; African Union, 1981).

In conclusion

For decades, the UN and the AU have either ignored or failed to take action against the massive human rights violations perpetrated by Mugabe and Zanu-PF, while Zimbabwe experienced a free fall not only of its economy, but also from a state of alleged freedom or liberation, to one of hunger, suffering, tyranny, and oppression. A state where the freedoms articulated in the UDHR and the AUCHPR are far from being realized. Although there are possible signs of hope in the new Government of National Unity, and small, slow steps are being taken to attempt to open channels of communication and space for freedom of expression, artist activists fighting for this cause must be wary of not becoming actors for the same state apparatus they are opposed to. Mugabe has charmed and manipulated the people of Zimbabwe, as well as the international community, for three decades. We should not assume his reign of oppression is over yet.

There is no question that the Book Café, its poetry slams, and the rebel poets and musicians that frequent this space play a critical and significant role in the fight for justice in Zimbabwe. Artists raised their voices in a time and space where it was challenging and dangerous for individuals to do this. These performers articulated their opinions and dissent at great personal risk, but did this largely because they believe in the future of a free Zimbabwe; a Zimbabwe where everyone can express themselves freely. While it is important to acknowledge the role Book Café plays in the fight for freedom of expression in Zimbabwe, it is also important not to ignore the reasons why this space may not be interfered with by the usually rough-handed law enforcers of Zimbabwe. In so doing, artists and patrons alike can ensure they do not become a façade for the Zimbabwean state's lack of freedom of expression, and continue to play a significant role in the fight for justice. Programs that have grown out of Book Café, such as Magamba Cultural Activists Network, engage youth in arts-based social change work and continue Zimbabwe's rich history of using the arts to protest injustice. The struggle for freedom in Zimbabwe continues, but with artists like Outspoken, Comrade Fatso, spaces like the Book Café, organizations like Magamba, the flicker of hope burns strong and leaves the door open for a future where freedom of expression is the rule rather than exception.

References

African Union. (1981, June 27). *African (Banjul) Charter on Human and Peoples' Rights.* Retrieved May 5, 2010, from African Union: http://www.africa-union.org/official_documents/treaties_%20conventions_%20protocols/banjul%20charter.pdf.

Crisis in Zimbabwe Coalition. (2007, August 6). *Interception of Communication Act (ICA) a threat to democracy!* Retrieved May 3, 2010, from kubatana.net: http://www.kubatana.net/html/archive/inftec/070806ciz.asp?sector=LEGISL&year=0&range_start=1.

Daily News (Harare). (2010, April 8). In Wikipedia, The Free Encyclopedia. Retrieved 14:19, May 10, 2010, from http://en.wikipedia.org/w/index.php?title=Daily_News_(Harare)&oldid=354753642.

Foucault, M. (1982). The Subject and Power. *Critical Inquiry*, 8(4), 777–795.

Gascoigne, B. (2001). *History of Zimbabwe.* Retrieved May 5, 2010, from History World: http://www.historyworld.net/wrldhis/PlainTextHistories.asp?historyid=ad28.

Nyarota, Geoffrey. (2009, December 2). In Wikipedia, The Free Encyclopedia. Retrieved 14:59, May 10, 2010, from http://en.wikipedia.org/w/index.php?title=Geoffrey_Nyarota&oldid=329197818.

Hanke, Steve H. (2008, December 5). The Printing Press. Retrieved May 1, 2010, from The Cato Institute Web site: http://www.cato.org/pub_display.php?pub_id=9823.

Magamba Cultural Activists Network. (2009). About Us page. Retrieved from www.magambanetwork.com

Makawa, T. (Poet). (2008). Freedom Train. [T. Makawa aka "Outspoken", Performer] Harare, Zimbabwe.

——— (2010, March 27). (V. Norman, Interviewer).

Marechera Celebration. (2008). *About Dambudzo Marechera*. Retrieved May 4, 2010, from Dambudzo Marechera: A Celebration: http://www.marecheracelebration.org/about.html.

Matyszak, D. (2005, March 2). *Democratic space and state security: Zimbabwe's Public Order and Security Act (POSA)*. Retrieved May 3, 2010, from Kubatana: http://www.kubatana.net/html/archive/opin/050302dm.asp?sector=LEGISL.

Media Sustainability Index. (2009). *MSI-Zimbabwe, 2008*. The Development of Sustainable Independent Media in Africa. Washington, DC: IREX.

Meldrum, A. (2004). *Where We Have Hope: A Memoir of Zimbabwe*. London, UK: John Murray.

Monro, S. (Poet). (2008a). House of Hunger. [S.Monro aka "Comrade Fatso", Performer] Harare, Zimbabwe.

——— (2008b). MaStreets. [S.Monro aka "Comrade Fatso", Performer] Harare, Zimbabwe.

Philp, R. & Mahlangu, D. (2008, June 23). *'Only God will remove me!'*. Retrieved March 14, 2011, from Canada Free Press: http://www.canadafreepress.com/index.php/article/3612.

Reporters Without Borders. (2008). *2008 World Press Freedom Index*. Reporters Without Borders.

Siebert, F. S., Peterson, T., & Schramm, W. (1963). *Four Theories of the Press*. Urbana, Illinois, USA: University of Illinois Press.

Sokwanale. (2006, March 5). *How much longer will this defiance of the United Nations and violation of international law be tolerated?* Retrieved March 12, 2011, from Sokwanale: http://www.sokwanele.com/articles/sokwanele/howmuchlongerwillthisdefiance_5march2006.html.

Swartz, D. (1997). *Culture & Power: The Sociology of Pierre Bourdieu*. Chicago, Illinois, USA: University of Chicago Press.

The Zimbo Jam. (2010, March 12). *Book on Torture in Zimbabwe Launched*. Retrieved April 30, 2010, from The Zimbo Jam: http://zimbojam.com/culture/literary-news/1261-book-on-torture-in-zimbabwe-launched.html.

——— (2010, March 31). *Owen Maseko Released, Exhibition Closed*. Retrieved April 3, 2010, from The Zimbo Jam: http://www.zimbojam.com/culture/inside-art/1305-owen-maseko-released-exhibition-closed.html.

Tibaijuka, A. K. (2005). *Report of the Fact-Finding Mission to Zimbabwe to assess the Scope and Impact of Operation Murambatsvina*. United Nations, UN Special Envoy on Human Settlements Issues in Zimbabwe. United Nations.

Ulman, E. (2007, August 7). *Harare's Counter-Culture Cafe*. Retrieved April 27, 2010, from BBC 2: http://news.bbc.co.uk/2/hi/programmes/newsnight/6935608.stm.

——— (2008a, March 26). *Harare's Open Cafe Culture*. Retrieved April 3, 2010, from Al Jazeera English: http://english.aljazeera.net/programmes/peopleandpower/2008/03/200852519230810514.html.

——— (2008b, March 27). *Six Nights a Week at the Book Café – Part 2.* [Video file produced by Al Jazeera English]. Retrieved from http://www.youtube.com/watch?v=oo3JUXNkftQ.

United Nations. (1948, December 10). *Universal Declaration of Human Rights.* Retrieved May 5, 2010, from United Nations: http://www.un.org/en/documents/udhr/.

Note

1   Please note, the conditions described here are specific to Harare in 2007–2008, at the height of Zimbabwe's economic collapse. By 2012 conditions have changed substantially, specifically following the dollarization of the Zimbabwean economy and the formation of the Government of National Unity (GNU).

Chapter 10

Right to Communicate, Public Participation, and Democratic Development in Thailand

Boonlert Supadhiloke

Introduction

Problem and rationale

Since the adoption of the Universal Declaration of Human Rights (UDHR) in 1948, communication has been well recognized as a basic human right that is the right to communicate (RTC) for all. Sean MacBride (1980), former Nobel Peace Prize laureate, says that the right to communicate is a prerequisite for other human rights. The right to communicate involves other basic human rights, such as freedom of opinion, freedom of expression, freedom of the press, freedom of information, a right to privacy, a right to participation, and a right to equal access to information and knowledge.

The UDHR also demonstrates that the right to communicate involves the recognition of communication as a social process that has an impact on society's political, cultural, and economic life. Accordingly, democracy, peace, and development cannot be achieved unless the principles of communication as human rights, particularly public participation, have been guaranteed. It is, therefore, imperative to promote the analysis and formulation of communication strategies and policies to ensure that the resources be available to meet the communication needs of everyone, from the human rights perspective.

In Thailand, the concept of right to communicate as a human right has been obscure. Although communication has been well recognized as an integral part of the national development process, its linkage with the human right to communicate is missing and confusing. In the area of political democratic development, a long struggle for press freedom by the media did not recognize the people's right to participate and, consequently, failed to secure public participation. This situation resulted in a setback in Thai democracy.

Nowadays, Thailand has been increasingly confronted with a perplexing problem of political conflict, peace, and democracy. It is imperative to promote a better understanding of the right to communicate, which may be used as an alternative development paradigm for formulating communication policies and strategies to further develop a truly democratic system in Thailand.

Objective of the study

The objective of this study is twofold:

1. To describe the evolution of the right to communicate as a human right in Thailand, particularly its specific right to participate.
2. To analyze the application of the right to communicate and its specific right to participate in the process of democratic development in Thailand, especially the democratization of broadcasting and political system.

To fulfill the stated objectives, the study is divided in two parts.

The first part is a descriptive study designed to examine the emergence of the human rights and the right to communicate in Thailand within the global context and international community. This part is basically based on documentary analysis and personal interview with key informants. Historical and legal documents such as constitutions, laws, periodicals, official reports, and articles are major sources of data.

The second part is a case study designed to empirically examine the application of the communication rights, particularly the participation right, in the democratic development process in the country.

Two case studies have been used; one deals with the democratization of the broadcasting media, Thai Public Broadcasting Service (Thai PBS), which is the first public broadcasting system, and the other is concerned with analysis of the national referendum to adopt the 2007 Constitution on August 19, 2007 as an indicator of participatory democracy in Thailand. In both cases, the quantitative analyses were made, based on two sets of secondary data from individual and official sources. The author is greatly indebted to both Patrawadee Boontayapatana, a graduate student of Communication Arts at Bangkok University, and the National Election Commission for their permission to use the data. In addition, the author's personal observations during the referendum and related events had been noted to verify the data.

The results of the study are presented into three parts. Part one describes the explication of the concept: human rights and right to communicate in Thailand. Parts two and three present the two case studies relating to the Thai Public Broadcasting Service and the 2007 national referendum as an illustration of participatory democratic development, respectively.

Human rights and right to communicate in Thailand

The right to communicate website, officially launched on December 3, 2002, has established the following common understanding:

"Everyone has the right to communicate. This communication right allows the exercise of the other human rights" (The Right to Communicate, 2002).

Overview of human rights in Thailand

It is very difficult to define human rights. As the former Secretary General of the United Nations stated in 1998, they are probably "rights that any person has as a human being. They are what reason requires and what conscience commands" (as cited in AMIC, 2000:1).

It is commonly recognized that human rights are the foundations of human existence and coexistence and that human rights are universal, indivisible, and interdependent. It is also reaffirmed that all human rights are equally important, from civil and political to social, economic, and cultural rights and the right to development (Mizuta, 2000:1).

The adoption of the United Nations (UN) Charter in 1945 and the Universal Declaration of Human Rights (UDHR) in 1948 obliged all states to establish, enforce, and protect human rights at global, regional, national, and local levels.

In Thailand, human rights have presumably long existed; they were often linked to the precepts of Buddhism (Chamarik, 1983) or traced to the western world (Ditapichai, 2000). Whatever the case, the term human rights became known to the Thai people only after the 1932 democratic revolution when Thailand had been changed from an absolute monarchy to the constitutional monarchy (Ditapichai, 2000:77–86). During the first 40 years after the change of the administration, the country had been mainly under the military dictatorship in which top-ranking military officers took turn in taking over power. As a result, people were discouraged to engage in discussion about their "rights and freedom." After a military dictatorship in 1947, people were even barred from talking about "democracy" and their "human rights." As Ditapichai (2000:77) observed, "All people were able to do was to keep their lives safe and play 'Be Smart Play Safe' without offending anybody in power. Opposition politicians were murdered. Communism was always the charge imposed on people who had different ideas from the government and penalty was drastic. Members of the media were killed and disappeared. At that time, nobody talked or even thought about rights."

However, as democracy in Thailand has gradually emerged, the human rights concept has also developed. With the promulgation of the Constitution in 1968, the people were allowed more freedom to express their opinions about politics. The media also enjoyed more freedom to criticize the government and some injustices conducted against the alleged communists were uncovered.

Then came the student uprising on October 14, 1973, which ended the military dictatorship and marked the dawn of democracy. As Ditapichai (2000:78) remarked, "The 'October 14' event did not only restore a real democratic regime to Thailand and provide full freedom but also aroused the political and social consciousness of the people, which shook the administration violently and the public outcries had been heard. The Prime Minister and his associates were deposed and the public, for the first time, enjoyed their freedom and liberty. People became aware of their rights as the owners and citizens of the country. Also for the first time, workers had freedom to protest and demand what they were entitled to." It was also during this high tide of democracy that the concept of human rights was widely publicized by the mass media and mass struggles had taken place.

The human rights movement took shape as a result of the military coup d'état on October 6, 1976 in which more than 100 demonstrators were massacred and 3,000 students and lay people were arrested. Several nongovernment organizations and human rights organizations were established to protect and promote human rights.

Another major development took place as the aftermath of the coup d'état in February 1991 and the subsequent mass protest in May 1992 commonly known as the "Bloody May." In this crisis, hundreds of protesters were killed and some disappeared. People were dismayed and demanded justice and this time the term "human rights" was more openly and frequently discussed. Subsequently, a number of committees and organizations were set up in the country to deal with the growing issues of human rights.

Emergence of the right to communicate

The concept "right to communicate" (RTC) has emerged from the debate on the Universal Declaration of Human Rights, Article 19, stating that:

"Everyone has the right to freedom of opinion and expression; this right includes freedom to hold opinion without interference and to seek, receive and impart information and ideas through any media and regardless of frontiers" (United Nations, 1948).

The right to communicate was first proposed by a French public servant, Jean d'Arcy, in 1969. He wrote:

The time will come when the Universal Declaration of Human Rights will have to encompass a more extensive right than man's right to information, first laid down – in Article 19. This is the right of man to communicate. This is the angle from which the future development of communication will have to be considered to be understood (d'Arcy, 1969).

Later, Jean d'Arcy (1978) saw the Universal Declaration as encompassing several communication rights beyond those enshrined in Article 19 including assembly, participation, and privacy. Apart from Jean d'Arcy, a number of scholars have engaged in discussions of this new concept. One prominent figure, Professor L.S. Harms of Department of Communication at the University of Hawaii in Honolulu, has been well recognized worldwide as a dedicated leader who has made a significant contribution to the advancement of the right to communicate. Harms (2001) spearheaded the setting up of the original right to communicate group in 1974 with d'Arcy as chair and he himself as secretary. The group had accomplished numerous tasks, particularly publication and collection of the papers.

Before his death in 2004, Harms had initiated the setting up of the right to communicate website at www.righttocommunicate.org. Guided by the right to communicate group, the website was launched on December 3, 2002 to pursue four long-range goals:

1. Describe and define the human right to communicate;
2. Collect, organize, and expand the literature on the right to communicate;
3. Facilitate activities on the right to communicate in research and education; and
4. Advance the right to communicate – personal to universal – for everyone.

During a short period, the website has made several accomplishments. Noteworthy is the multilayer framework for the right to communicate, set forth as follows:

"Everyone has the right to communicate; this fundamental human right includes but is not limited to the following specific communication rights:

- a right to assemble, a right to speech, a right to participate and related association rights;
- a right to inform, a right to be informed, a right to inquire and related information rights;
- a right to privacy, a right to choose, a right to culture and related global rights.

As a standard for achievement, the full recognition of the right to communicate requires that the communication resources be available to meet the basic communication needs of everyone" (The Right to Communicate, 2002).

Insofar as Thailand is concerned, there has been a continuing effort by a member of the right to communicate group, Boonlert Supadhiloke, to explicate the concept. Supadhiloke (1984) argued that the right to communicate has long existed in Thailand. Conceptually, the right to communicate concept can be traced back to Buddhism, a national religion, being embedded in the very precept of the doctrine called Four Noble Truths or "Ariyasacca," which leads to the eradication of all sufferings in human life.

These truths consist of (1) suffering (Dukkha), (2) causes of suffering (Samudaya), (3) cessation of all sufferings (Nirodha) – "perpetual happiness" (Nibbana), and (4) the right path (Magga) leading to the cessation of all sufferings (see Ussivakul, 2003). Known as the Noble Eightfold Path (Ariyamagga), the right path starts with the right understanding (Sammaditthi), right thought (Sammasankappa), right speech (Sammavaca), and right action (Sammakammanta), which are closely related to the right to communicate or communication right. The others are: right livelihood (Sammaajiva), right effort (Sammavayama), right mindfulness (Sammasati), and right concentration (Sammasamadhi). It is noteworthy that the first four steps of the right path, closely associated with the right to communicate, provide a basis for the reach of the perpetual happiness, which may be interpreted as "knowledge" or wisdom (Panna) society.

Right to communicate, as Buddhism's ethical concept, can provide a conceptual framework for democratization of the mass media in Thailand and other countries in many ways. Of particular interest is the reconceptualization of the concept "freedom of information."

"Freedom of the Press," generally known as "freedom of information," has become a crucial controversial issue in Thailand as in many other countries around the world. The conflict between the government and the mass media originates mainly from how both perceive this core concept. Usually, the two parties tend to perceive freedom of information from their own perspectives, without much regard for the public interest, thus leading to a crisis threatening democratization in the country. Whereas the media claim that they are "free" to criticize the government to protect the people's right to know, the government usually reprimands the media for overexercising freedom of the press at the expense of social responsibility. The conflict has definitely jeopardized the public interest and the democratization process in the country (Supadhiloke, 2009).

The teachings of Lord Buddha, or "Dhamma," may be used to help redefine the concept "freedom of information." Of particular importance are the Four Noble Truths, or "Ariyasacca," which lead to the eradication of all sufferings in human life. Accordingly, Buddhism takes a significant departure from the Western tradition in defining the "freedom" of the press as "an individual's human right to be free from such defilement or "kilesa" as craving, anger, and illusion – all causes of mental suffering. With freedom from mental suffering, the mind will not be under the domination of one's lust, greed, and anger. Such press freedom should become a cornerstone for imposing self-regulation among media practitioners in Thailand and other countries.

In a sense, Buddhism views freedom as originating "inside" or "within" an individual, not "outside" or in "others" as viewed by a traditional school of thought. Thus, journalists should first look "inside" themselves and see "how far they have been mentally free from such defilement or "kilesa" as craving, anger and illusion" before they talk about or fight for press freedom.

As the late Prime Minister M.R. Kukrit Pramoj (1976) said, "Freedom of the Press exists inside oneself. If our inner part has been purified, freedom will naturally arise or be granted."

Thus, according to Buddhism, the struggle for freedom of the press should be the fight against oneself – how to free oneself from all defilement or "kilesa," not the fight against others or outsiders. This is indeed in line with the ideal of self-regulation and ethical standard of journalists.

Right to communicate and democracy in Thailand

As in the case of human rights, the right to communicate has gradually evolved along side with development of democracy in Thailand. It has been commonly known as freedom of the press, freedom of speech, and freedom of opinion. During the period of absolute monarchy, the term "communication right" had never been mentioned and only the jargon "freedom of the press" was used in reference to the publication of newspapers. Historically, the Thai press was started by an American missionary, Dr. Dan Beach Bradley in July 4, 1844, during the reign of King Rama III. The early press was restricted to the royal courts and run mainly by elites. It had most flourished during King Rama VI who himself issued his own newspapers and allowed commoners to express their opinions about concerned social issues. Thus, the reign of King Rama VI was considered the "golden age of press freedom" during the predemocracy period (Sirimanont, 1980). Although the term "right to communicate" was not explicitly mentioned, it was believed to have originated from the reign of King Rama V who was highly credited for having "freed" the Thai people from slavery.

After Thailand had been changed to the constitutional monarchy in 1932, the human right to communicate had emerged as a critical issue as part of mass struggle for full democracy. As earlier stated, after 1932, Thailand had been dominated by the military dictatorship for over 40 years, interrupted from time to time by elected civilian governments. So far, a number of seventeen coup d'états had been attempted out of which ten were successful. By average, there was one elected civilian government for every two coups. Altogether, eighteen constitutions had been promulgated in Thailand during a period of 67 years. It was interesting that all constitutions had guaranteed such communication rights as freedom of speech, freedom of opinion, freedom of the press, or freedom of information but such freedoms and rights were understood to be "subject to political interference and artificial censorship mainly for reason of national security" (Supadhiloke, 1984). Even worse, the dictatorial governments had imposed special decrees or "gag laws" to control the people's freedom of opinion and communication rights. During the first 40 years of the military dictatorship, the freedom of the press and freedom of expression had been severely curtailed. Noteworthy was the administration of Field Marshal Sarit Thanarat (1957–1963), which dealt a severe blow to the press freedom. Sarit's government issued the Revolutionary Announcement No. 17 in October 1958 to gag the press and other media. This gag law had been enforced for 17 years until 1975. During this period, at least fourteen newspapers were closed down for damaging "national security" while four newspapers were banned for leveling harsh criticism against the government (Sirimanont, 1980). Obviously, the people's communication rights had been severely affected.

The "golden era of the press freedom" came with the student uprising on October 14, 1973, which also marked the dawn of democracy in Thailand. This period was comparable to that of King Rama VI under the absolute monarchy (Sirimanont, 1980). Several newspapers had emerged and enjoyed a larger extent of freedom of expression. However, most newspapers were subject to criticism for lacking "social responsibility" and not responding to "public interest."

The golden era of the press did not last long. On October 6, 1976, the military staged another coup d'état to crush the student movement. The coup-backed civilian government had issued the Administrative Reform's Order No. 42 on October 21, 1976 to curb the press freedom and freedom of opinion. This new gag law proved to be more damaging to the press than the first one. It had been enforced for 13 years before it was scraped in 1986 by the elected government of General Chartchai Choonhawan. Altogether, the two gag laws had been enforced in Thailand for about 30 years, affecting the people's specific communication rights.

After 1976, the struggle for freedom of information by the press had intensified. Their demand for lifting the outdated Printing Act 1941 (with amendments in 1942 and 1945) did not materialize. It also suffered from another setback in 1991 as a result of the coup d'état and the subsequent mass protest in May 1992 known as "the Bloody May."

However, the milestone was set in 1997 when the people's Constitution was promulgated, aimed at reforming political democracy by means of people's rights and freedom of participation. Article 40 of the 1997 Constitution also set the goal for reform of broadcasting and telecommunication media to respond to public interest by allowing more freedom of information and rights of people's participation. The democratization of political system and the media should have been materialized if it was not for the unexpected coup d'état in 2006 that abrogated the participatory Constitution.

The 'participation' concept

As earlier stated, "participation" has been explicated as one of the nine specific communication rights. It is included in the multilayer framework, which reads:

> "a right to assemble, a right to speech, a right to participate and related association rights" (Harms, 2002:3).

More specifically the right to participate is included in Articles 21 and 27 of the Universal Declaration of Human Rights, which read:

> Article 21: Everyone has the right to take part in – and, Article 27: Everyone has the right to freely participate –

Numerous definitions of participation can be found. White et al. (1994:16) assert, "Participation is contextual, so local participation differs from nonlocal participation. And even at the local level, participation varies in type, level of intensity, extent and frequency. It is indeed kaleidoscopic; it changes its color and shape at the will of the hands in which it is held."

The euphoric word "participation" has become a part of development process and widely used in the field of communication for development and social change. Paulo Freire (1983), Brazilian educationist, has been credited for championing this concept, commonly known as "conscientization" in his popular book "Pedagogy of the Oppressed." Freire refers to it as the right of all people to individually and collectively speak their word.

"This is not the privilege of some few men, but the right of every (wo)man. Consequently, no one can say a true word alone – nor can he say it for another, in a prescriptive act which robs others of their words" (as cited in Servaes, 2003:11).

Similarly, the International Commission for the Study of Communication Problems, chaired by the late Sean MacBride, stressed the importance of public participation in a decision-making process for development. They said:

> The decision-making process has to involve social participation at all levels. This calls for a new attitude for overcoming stereotypical thinking and to promote more understanding of diversity and plurality, with full respect for the dignity and equality of people living in a different condition and acting in different ways (MacBride, 1980:254).

Recently, Servaes (1999, 2003) has put forth an emerging model of "participatory communication" within the cultural context. His multiplicity approach emphasizes the importance of cultural identity of local communities and of democratization and participation at all levels – international, national, local, and individual. It points to a strategy, not merely inclusive of, but largely emanating from, the traditional "receivers."

In Thailand, the term "participation" is still controversial. There is often disagreement over what "participation" means. For example, Suthawan Sathirathai, a leading environmentalist, argued, "It's a new concept. It's been imported from the West and even the translation (karn mee suan ruam) is clumsy. There's no tradition or culture of public participation in big decisions" (as cited in Lewis, 2003:63).

However, several Thai scholars argued that the concept "participation" originates in the traditional culture of Thai people, particularly in rural areas. It is clearly related to the term "wisdom of the people" or "folk wisdom" or in Thai word "Pumpanya." It is also linked to Buddhism belief, which reflects daily life of people in local communities. The folk wisdom or folk culture is important in Thailand because it provides a "cultural context" in which the participation process has taken place. Without common folk culture and wisdom, any form of participatory communication can hardly be achieved.

A good example of such folk wisdom is what has been commonly known as "karn long kaek" (a kind of collective activity): a rural tradition in which villagers or members of communities help one another in carrying out such collective activities as agricultural cultivation, merit making, and a way of daily life.

In a survey of over 50 communities in Thailand that have successfully implemented His Majesty the King's Sufficiency Economy projects, Seree Pongpis (2007) found that all the communities have one thing in common: a strongly unique folk culture or folk wisdom or "Pumpanya." He argued that such common folk wisdom provides a "cultural context" in which people's participation process has taken place to preserve their cultural heritages.

Democratization of communication media: The strange case of the Thai Public Broadcasting Service (Thai PBS)

This case is designed to illustrate how the specific communication right, i.e., the people's right to participate, has been used as a criterion to establish the first public service broadcasting named Thai Public Broadcasting Service (Thai PBS).

Democratization of communication

The call for democratization of communication was made by Sean MacBride, President of the UNESCO Commission for the Study of Communication Problems. In the book *Many Voices, One World* published in 1980 by UNESCO, MacBride (1980:166) says, "Because communication itself is going through an era of rapid change, any democratic relationship must be dynamic and evolutionary, not static. Democratization can be defined as the process whereby: the individual becomes an active partner and not a mere object of communication; the variety of messages exchanged increases; and, the extent and "quality of social representation or participation in communication are augmented."

To achieve democratization, MacBride (1980:169) proposed several approaches to break down numerous barriers including "participation of non-professionals in producing and broadcasting programs, which enables them to make active use of information sources, and is also an outlet for individual skill and sometimes for artistic creativity."

Clearly, MacBride has proposed "public participation" as an alternative approach to achieve democratization. MacBride (1980:173) finally concludes, "Without a two-way flow between participants in the process, without the existence of multiple information sources permitting wider selection, without more opportunity for each individual to reach decisions based on a broad awareness of divergent facts and viewpoints, without increased participation by readers, viewers and listeners in the decision-making and programming activities of the media – true democratization will not become a reality."

Recently, Splichal & Wasko (1993:5) drew attention to the linkage between democracy and communication based on the people's right to communicate. They argued that from the ancient Greek thought onward, the general conception of democracy was based on at least four assumptions related to the communication sphere, namely that:

1. Citizens are well informed.
2. Citizens are interested (as a consequence of socialization process) in general politics.
3. Citizens have equal rights to speak and participate in decision-making.
4. All decisions are submitted to public discussions.

Splichal & Wasko proposed that the generic concept of right to communicate, including the right to participate in the management of the mass media and communication organizations, lies at the heart of the democratization. As they put it:

> democratization implies primarily the development of conditions for active participation, that is, a direct and indirect incorporation of citizens into the production and exchange of messages in different forms of communication from interpersonal communication to the mass media in which the individual can realize his interests and meet his needs in a collaboration with others (Splichal & Wasko, 1993:12).

A strange case of Thai Public Broadcasting Service (Thai PBS)

In view of the earlier discussion of democratization of communication media, it can be seen that the broadcasting industry in Thailand is far from being "democratic." Based on the

Broadcasting Act 1955 (with fourth amendment in 1987), the whole broadcasting industry has been placed under the control of state agencies, notably the Defense Ministry, the Public Relations Department, the Mass Communication Organization of Thailand, the National Police Bureau, and so on. Consequently, there appeared a high concentration of radio frequencies and broadcasting ownership in Thailand (Supadhiloke, 2004:84). Given the fact that media ownership determines the type of programming, which in turn has effect on society, the broadcasting monopoly is more damaging to Thai society. It denies freedom of expressions, freedom of access and choice to audiences, and freedom of participation, which are of special importance to democratic societies (Supadhiloke, 2007).

Until now, the Broadcasting Act 1955 has been enforced for 53 years, even though it was considered obsolete and undesirable. The new Broadcasting Operation Act 2008 was enacted on February 26, 2008. However, it has not been enforced, pending the appointment of the National Broadcasting Commission (NBC), which has been dragging for over a decade.

There have been concerted efforts in the past to liberalize the broadcasting industry through "public participation" and decentralization processes. Noteworthy was the promulgation of the Constitution in 1997, which was considered the most popular people's charter, aimed at bringing about political reforms in the country. Insofar as communication is concerned, the 1997 Constitution guarantees press freedom and communication rights, promotes an ethical standard of media professionalism, and liberalizes a regulatory system of the broadcasting and telecommunication industry. Article 40 of the Constitution stipulates the establishment of an independent regulatory body to allocate the radio frequencies as well as to supervise the management of the broadcasting service to respond to "public interest" at both national and local levels. Article 40 also provides a legal framework for the establishment of both public service broadcasting and community broadcasting throughout the country by means of public participation. To fulfill these objectives, the organic law requires that "at least 20 percent of the radio frequencies be reserved for people's or public broadcasting at local levels, while the rest (80 percent) be shared between national public's service broadcasting and commercial broadcasting at national levels" (Supadhiloke, 2004:86).

If the 1997 Constitution and its organic laws had been duly enforced, the public service broadcasting and community broadcasting system should have already been put into operations in Thailand, thus involving public participation at all levels. It was, however, unfortunate that some unexpected events took place to prevent the enforcement of these laws. A major obstacle lies in the selection process of the seven members of the broadcasting regulator, NBC, which has become controversial and politically motivated. Finally, after more than five years of two rounds of selection processes, the newly established Administrative Court handed down the verdict striking down the final list of seven-member NBC, which has had already been reconfirmed by the House of Senate. The Supreme Court's final verdict came a few days after the last coup d'état on September 19, 2006, which also abrogated the 1997 participatory Constitution. These events have definitely foiled the people's dream to have "equal access and participation" in the public broadcasting system.

It is, however, ironic that the political change in Thailand in 2006 had led the coup-backed government to decide to turn one national TV network into the first public service broadcasting system in the country. This TV network, ITV, had come into being after the coup d'état in 1992 to provide an alternate channel for people who had been hitherto denied access to all existing TV networks during the political crisis, known as the Bloody May. ITV was originally known as an Independent TV network to disseminate 70 percent of public affairs information and 30 percent of entertainment to the audience. After the financial crisis in 1997, ITV had been purchased by Shin Corporation, which was owned by the former Prime Minister Thaksin Shinawatra. In the wake of the last coup d'état in September, 2006, ITV had become a controversial issue after its private owner failed to pay more than Bt 100 billion in concession fees and fines to its concession granter, the Prime Minister's Office. The concession was terminated in March 2007. Then in late April 2007, the coup-backed government under Prime Minister General Surayud Chulanont had reached the resolution to turn ITV into the first public broadcasting network in Thailand. Subsequently, the Thai Public Broadcasting Service Act 2008 was promulgated on January 5, 2008 to officially establish the first public broadcasting system in the country known as "Thai PBS" (Thai Public Broadcasting Service Act 2008). The new public broadcasting service is under the Board of Governors or Policy Committee composed of nine members and the Executive Board. According to Article 12 of the Act, Thai PBS will be financed mainly by tobacco and liquor revenues from the Excise Department under the Finance Ministry, estimated at about Bt 2 billion a year. One feature of the Thai PBS is to establish the Council of TV Audiences, which consists of 50 representatives throughout the country as a mechanism to encourage a wider participation from the people.

Thai PBS and right to participate

In view of the unexpected emergence of Thai PBS by political means, it is interesting to examine how this public broadcasting has served the public interest, based on the people's communication rights and responsibility, particularly a right to participate. More specifically, how far has Thai PBS, as a public broadcasting, been "accountable to" the Thai citizens as its active audiences so that they have "equal access to and participation in" the programming and management of the broadcasting? Based on the literature survey, a few empirical studies exist to provide an answer. Of particular significance is an independent study titled "Information Need and Viewing of Thai Public Broadcasting Service (Thai PBS) Among Bangkok's Audiences" by Patrawadee Boontayapatana (2008) at Bangkok University. Boontayapatana conducted a sample survey of 400 Thai PBS's audiences in Bangkok during May–August 2008 to find out about their information needs and viewing behaviors. The sample consists of adults, aged over 21 years old, both male and female, mostly educated and employed at private and public organizations. Only a brief account of the data analysis is presented here.

The result showed that Bangkok's audiences are very active to seek and receive information from Thai PBS. They are "highly motivated" to obtain relevant information and news to satisfy their needs. They also expect Thai PBS as an alternate public channel, to provide gratifications to Thai citizens. Asked why they watch Thai PBS, most Bangkokians cite the following reasons (in order):

1. To monitor news accuracy and reliability
2. To obtain up-to-date information and technology
3. To receive news feature and knowledge
4. To escape the everyday doldrums of life
5. To get objective and impartial news reports
6. To keep up with the current events and world affairs
7. To keep informed and entertaining
8. To relax and release tension
9. To communicate with other people, etc.

As for information needs, most of Bangkok's audiences cite the following items (see, Table 10.1):

Table 10.1: Information needs of Bangkok's respondents ($N = 400$).

List of Information Needs	Percentage
1. Education	72.0
2. News about public affairs (economics, business, and finance)	71.5
3. Politics	69.8
4. Public health	66.6
5. Information technology	65.0
6. Entertainment, tourism, and sport	62.6
7. Law	56.1
8. General knowledge	49.1
9. Foreign affairs	48.8
10. Environmental problems	48.1
11. Occupation	46.1
12. Society and culture	37.3

Note: A respondent can answer several items.

From the "functional" perspective, it can be said that Thai PBS is widely perceived by most Bangkokians to perform a "surveillance and cognitive" function with emphasis on education, information, and public affairs news. At the same time, it is also perceived to discharge a "diversion and social utility" function such as entertainment, escape, and keeping up with the world.

In line with these functions, the audiences have expressed their preferences for such programs as "news about public affairs, news analysis, feature and education-entertainment." The audience's participation program is also listed as their preference (see Table 10.2).

Further analysis of the data indicates that Bangkok's audiences have expressed "strong needs of information" as well as "high expectation of gratifications" from the first public broadcasting systems (see Tables 10.3 and 10.4). For example, about 70 percent or 283 respondents said they felt a "strong need" of public affairs information while 88 percent or 353 respondents indicated their "high expectation" for gratifications from Thai PBS.

However, when we consider the actual viewing behavior of Bangkok's audiences, a different picture has emerged. As shown in Tables 10.5 and 10.6, most Bangkokians had "low exposure" to and "minimal viewing" of Thai PBS's programs. In other words, Bangkok's audiences had only "limited access" to the first public broadcasting, as compared to other broadcasting systems. In terms of frequency of TV viewing, 54 percent or 217 respondents said they watched Thai PBS "less than 3 days a week." Only 33 percent or 131 persons said they watched Thai PBS "every day." As for "duration of time spent with TV per day," 70 percent or 279 persons said they "spent less than 3 hours a day viewing Thai PBS," which was below the national average index. According to the Bureau of National Statistics, the average of TV viewing nationwide was recorded at "3 hours a day." The findings clearly point to a "low level of public participation" in

Table 10.2: Program preferences among Bangkok's respondents ($N = 400$).

Program Preferences	Percentage
1. News about public affairs (economics, business, and finance)	88.8
2. News analysis	69.8
3. Education – entertainment	69.1
4. Feature	67.5
5. Audience's participation program	65.5
6. News feature	59.1
7. Commentary on social issues	55.6

Note: A respondent can answer several items.

Table 10.3: Levels of information needs among Bangkok's respondents ($N = 400$).

Information Needs	Number	Percentage
High	283	70.8
Medium	114	28.5
Low	3	0.7
Total	400	100

Table 10.4: Levels of expectations among Bangkok's respondents ($N = 400$).

Expectation of Gratifications	Number	Percentage
High	353	88.2
Medium	43	10.8
Low	4	1.0
Total	400	100

the first public broadcasting's programs, thus failing to meet the right to communicate standard.

Overall, the findings reflect the discrepancy or dissonance between the audience's needs and their actual viewing behaviors. While most Bangkokians expressed strong needs of information and high expectation from Thai PBS, they turned out to have a low level of exposure to the programs, below the national average of 3 hours a day. It would be difficult to conclude that Bangkok's audiences were gratified at their access to the first public broadcasting.

Table 10.5: Exposure to Thai PBS among Bangkok's respondents ($N = 400$).

Frequency of Viewing per Week	Number	Percentage
1–2 days a week	136	34.0
2–3 days a week	81	20.2
3–4 days a week	26	6.5
4–5 days a week	26	6.5
7 days a week	131	32.8
Total	400	100

Table 10.6: Viewing of Thai PBS among Bangkok's respondents ($N = 400$).

Duration of Time Spent per Day	Number	Percentage
Less than 3 hours	279	69.8
During 3–5 hours	90	22.5
During 5–8 hours	31	7.8
During 8–10 hours	0	0.0
Over 10 hours	0	0.0
Total	400	100

What accounted for such a low public participation? A number of factors were found in the study including:

1. Thai PBS was found lacking in creativity and credibility.
2. The principle of "editorial independence" was also found lacking. Owing to underrepresentation of citizens at the top management levels, Thai PBS was subject to interference from various interest groups. The Board of Governors or Policy Board had been dominated by representatives of NGOs, thus failing to respond to public interest and public accountability.

Had the people's right to communicate been enhanced, more public participation could have been achieved, leading to the effective management of the public broadcasting for public interest as originally envisioned by the Constitution.

Development of political democracy: The 2007 national referendum

This case is designed to illustrate how public opinion or the national referendum on August 19, 2007 had been manipulated through propaganda by state authorities to approve the Constitution.

Public opinion and democracy

Following a general description of democracy as a form of government of the people, by the people, and for the people, it is apparent that public opinion or vox populi is a foundation of true democracy. As Jean-Jacques Rousseau (1913) who explicated the notion of a "general will," a broad term of public opinion, said, all governments rest fundamentally on public opinion rather than on law or coercion. He also said that in social change, no government may be very far ahead of popular opinion. Of particular importance is the "effective public opinion," which requires a certain degree of "participation" among the individuals and groups who constitute the involved public on any particular issue (Hennessey, 1976:25).

The mass media serve as a mirror to reflect public opinion – a surveillance function. The mass media also serve as an agent to create and change the tide of public opinion. So, the mass media function to monitor, create, crystallize, maintain, and change the public process, the ebb and flow of public opinion tide. Granted freedom of information and expression, the media can convince the citizens to "participate in" the democratization process. However, if they are under control or censorship, the media are subject to loss of credibility and being a "propaganda" machine to change people's hearts and minds.

In the case of Thailand, given the fact that broadcasting has been under state control and print media under a few interest groups, it is interesting to see how the media are manipulated to create and change the tide of public opinion or more specifically, how far the media are used to convince the public to participate in the democratization process. Can public opinion be manipulated to achieve the established goal?

An illusion of the national referendum

The elected government of the former Prime Minister Thaksin Shinawatra had ruled the country from February 19, 2001 to September 19, 2006. Thaksin's popular Thai Rak Thai Party won the landslide victory in 2005 that secured his power for the second term. Then, on September 19, 2006, a coup d'état was staged by General Sondhi Boonyaratkalin, the Army Chief, to overthrow the democratic government and also the most participatory Constitution promulgated in 1997. The coup-backed government under Prime Minister General Surayud Chulanont vowed to hold the general election within one year. Accordingly, the new Constitution had been drafted by the National Assembly and was subject to approval by the people before being put into enforcement.

Historically, most constitutions have rarely been tested in the public opinion poll called national referendum. The new draft Constitution has some unique characteristics that require public approval. Firstly, it would like to be considered as a "democratic" charter, rather than a product of the dictatorial regime backed by the coup. Secondly, it may not be considered a "disguise" to get rid of the former Prime Minister Thaksin Shinawatra.

The national referendum was scheduled on August 19, 2007 for the Thai people to approve the draft Constitution. Indeed, the draft turned out to be very controversial and divisive. Heavy campaigns had been launched by various interest groups to back as well as to scrap the draft Constitution. The government and military group came out strongly to wage an offensive campaign in support of the draft using "green color" as their symbol. On the other hand, the defunct Thai Rak Thai Party's members and some liberal groups launched a proactive campaign to oppose the charter using "red color" as their symbol. The National

Election Commission, which was responsible for the national referendum, also made an all-out effort to appeal to the Thai people to participate in the poll.

Obviously, the national referendum campaign was tantamount to a "war of propaganda" or "psychological warfare" designed to swing the people's votes. The mass media were also polarized and manipulated by both pro- and con-groups to "frame" political issues for the people. A content analysis of four leading newspapers in the country before the referendum showed the negative and mixed coverage as a predominant frame (see Table 10.7). The three popular newspapers, Thai Rath, Daily News, and Kom Chad Luek, covered a wide range of negative and mixed frames around 33–40 percent each. Matichon devoted 65 percent of its coverage to a mixed frame. In contrast, the broadcast media, which were under control of the government, presented more coverage of positive frames in favor of the draft Constitution. (See, for details, studies by Pakpol Puengrasmee , 2007, and Alisa Lertsririvorakul , 2007).

Despite heavy media campaigns, the outcome of the national referendum came as a surprise. The data analysis provided by the National Election Commission (2007) showed that the overall vote turnout was quite low. As presented in Table 10.8, out of the total eligible voters of 45,092,955, only 57.61 percent or 25,978,954 persons went to the polls. The remaining 42.39 percent or 19,114,001 persons abstained from exercising their votes. These 42.39 percent nonvoters appeared to be a record high in Thai history. Across regions, the Northeastern region, which was a stronghold of the defunct Thai Rak Thai Party, recorded the highest nonvote with 45.61 percent or 7,001,296 persons. Thus, there exists a so-called "silent majority" in the Thai referendum, particularly in rural areas.

What accounted for such a low "public participation" in the crucial national referendum on August 19, 2007? In an independent study by Siritharakul (2007), the following factors were cited by academics, journalists, and civic leaders as causes of the low vote turnout:

1. political apathy
2. lack of knowledge and understanding of the draft Constitution

Table 10.7: News coverage of national referendum (August 1–18, 2007).

Newspapers	Positive Frame		Negative Frame		Mixed Frame		Total	
	Column Inch	Percentage	Column Inch	Percentage	Column Inch	Percentage		
Matichon	39	9.00	113	26.10	281	64.9	433	100
Thai Rath	94	24.80	151	40.00	133	35.2	378	100
Daily News	98	26.84	121	33.15	146	39.99	365	100
Kom Chad Luek	64	28.10	85	37.30	79	34.60	228	100

Table 10.8: Results of national referendum (August 19, 2007).

Regions	Voters		Nonvoters		Total Eligible Voters	
	Number	Percentage	Number	Percentage	Number	Percentage
Central	8,741,488	57.72	6,402,819	42.28	15,144,307	100
South	3,717,664	59.31	2,550,410	40.69	6,268,074	100
Northeast	8,350,677	54.39	7,001,296	45.61	15,351,973	100
North	5,169,125	62.06	3,159,476	37.94	8,328,601	100
Nationwide	25,978,954	57.61	19,114,001	42.39	45,092,955	100

Source: National Election Commission (2007).

3. credibility gap between government and citizens
4. mistrust of media credibility
5. lack of accurate information in order to make decisions
6. limited freedom of opinion and expression
7. limited access to information

A further analysis of the data indicated that, among those who cast their votes, 56.69 percent or 14,727,306 persons voted for the Constitution, whereas 41.37 percent or 10,747,441 persons voted against the charter (see Table 10.9). The number of the opposition group is still large, not much different from the pro-group. Across the regions, the Northeast recorded the highest proportion of "vote no" with 61.67 percent or 5,149,957 persons, followed by the North with 44.44 percent or 2,296,927 persons. On the other hand, the South recorded the highest proportion of "vote yes" with 86.47 percent or 3,214,506 persons followed by the Central with 65.38 percent or 5,714,973 persons. Apparently, the national referendum was polarized across regions. In addition, there existed numerous cases of invalid votes, that is, 1.94 percent or 504,207 persons.

In the final analysis, the "majority vote" of the public opinion amounts to 14,727,306 as compared to the "minority vote" of 10,747,441. However, if we combine the minority vote with the "non vote" or "abstention" of 19,114,001 and the "invalid vote" of 504,207, the total number amounts to 30,365,649, which is twice larger than the actual majority vote. Thus, the "majority rule" in this national referendum does not reflect the "true public opinion" of the Thai people. Had the "silent majority" been persuaded to participate in the poll, the outcome of the referendum could have been different.

The poor turnout of the national referendum augured ill for the subsequent general election scheduled on December 23, 2007. The National Election Commission reported that 74.49 percent of the total eligible voters or 32,775,868 persons turned out to cast their votes in the last general election. In view of the enactment of the Official Information

Table 10.9: Vote turnout of national referendum (August 19, 2007).

Regions	Vote For		Vote Against		Invalid Vote		Total	
	Number	Percentage	Number	Percentage	Number	Percentage	Number	Percentage
Central	5,714,973	65.38	2,874,674	32.89	151,841	1.73	8,741,488	100
South	3,214,506	86.47	425,883	11.46	77,275	2.07	3,717,664	100
Northeast	3,050,182	36.53	5,149,957	61.67	150,538	1.80	8,350,677	100
North	2,747,645	53.15	2,296,927	44.44	124,553	2.41	5,169,125	100
Nationwide	14,727,306	56.69	10,747,441	41.37	504,207	1.94	25,978,954	100

Source: National Election Commission (2007).

Act in 1997 to enhance the people's right to know and heavy election campaigns by the government, the election outcome was considered by many scholars as far from satisfactory.

It can go without saying that genuine public opinion can never be achieved without full participation of the people based on the right to communicate, which, in turn, leads to "true democracy." Time will come when this human right to communicate will be more recognized in Thailand as a basis for formulation of communication strategy and policy toward "true democracy."

Conclusion and discussion

This study seeks to describe the evolution of the right to communicate as a basic human right and its application in the democratization process in Thailand. The study was based on documentary analysis, personal interview and observation, case studies, and secondary data analysis. According to this study, the concept of human right to communicate can be traced back to Buddhism, a national religion, which takes a significant departure from the western traditions in defining the term "freedom" as "an individual's human right to be free from such defilement, known as "kilesa", as craving, anger and illusion – all causes of suffering." However, both concepts of human rights and right to communicate have become known to the public only after the 1932 democratic revolution when Thailand had been changed from an absolute monarchy to the constitutional monarchy. Henceforth, the right to communicate, commonly known as freedom of the press, freedom of speech, freedom of opinion, and right to know, has become part of the mass struggle for democracy in Thailand. Over a 80 year period, the democratic development in Thailand has been characterized by a long domination by military dictatorship, intervened from time to time by elected civilian government. During the dictatorial administration, the press freedom, freedom of speech, and other communication rights had been suppressed mainly by the two gag laws – the Revolutionary Announcement No. 17 and the Administrative Reform's Order No. 42. The communication rights flourished during the elected civilian administration. It was, however, unfortunate that, during the rise and fall of the press freedom, most Thai people were not provided with adequate information for making decisions to participate in the democratic process. Their communication right to participate was lacking.

With the promulgation of the Constitution and the Official Information Act in 1997, the people's right to know and right to participate had been well recognized. Subsequently, concerted efforts had been made to liberalize the broadcasting industry under the state monopoly in order to encourage citizens to participate in the national public service broadcasting and community broadcasting, but failed to materialize subject to the establishment of the national regulator. Although the first public broadcasting, Thai Public Broadcasting Service, had been finally set up by the government after the coup in 2006, it was found lacking in public participation and gratifications.

Similarly, the national referendum held on August 19, 2007 to approve the Constitution failed to produce "substantial" evidence to show that the "true majority" of people voted for the charter. Out of the total eligible voters of 45,092,955, only 57.61 percent cast their votes, whereas the remaining 42.39 percent abstained. Among the 25,978,954 voters, only 56.69 percent voted for, whereas 41.37 percent voted against. If one combines the nonvotes and the vote-no together, the total number amounts to 29,861,442, which is much larger than the actual "majority" vote. Thus, there exists a "silent majority" among Thai people who did not participate in the democratic process.

A lesson learned from these two cases indicates that the democratization of communication media, in this case broadcasting, is a precondition for the development of political democracy. It is, therefore, imperative to promote formulation of communication strategies and policies in Thailand from the human right to communicate perspective in order to democratize the communication media, which, in turn, may lead to a "true democracy" in the future.

References

Asian Media Information and Communication Centre (AMIC). (2000). *Media + Human Rights in Asia*. Singapore: Stamford Press.

Boontayapatana, P. (2008). *Information Need and Unpublished Viewing of Thai Public Broadcasting Service (Thai PBS) Among Bangkok's Audiences*. Unpublished Report, Bangkok University, Bangkok.

Chamarik, S. (1983). *Buddhism and Human Rights*. Bangkok: Thai Khadi Research Institute, Thammasat University.

d'Arcy, Jean. (1969). Direct Broadcast Satellites and the Right to Communicate. *EBU Review*, 118, 14–18.

—— (1978). *Right to Communicate*. Paper #36. Prepared for the MacBride Commission.

Ditapichai, J. (2000). *Human Rights in Thailand" in Asian Media Information and Communication Centre (AMIC). Media + Human Rights in Asia*. Singapore: Stamford Press.

Freire, P. (1983). *Pedagogy of the Oppressed*. New York: Continuum.

Harms, L. S. (2001). The Right to Communicate: Towards Explicit Recognition. *Intermedia*, 29, 32–35.

—— (2002). *Right to Communicate*. Retrieved December 24, 2008, from http://www. righttocommunicate.org/viewReference.atm?id=35.

Hennessey, C. (1976). *Public Opinion*. Belmont, CA: Duxbury Press.

Lertsririvorakul, A. (2007). *Influence of Opinion, Leaders in the National Referendum Campaigns 2007*. Unpublished report, Bangkok University, Bangkok.

Lewis, G. (2003). Television, Media Reform and Civil Society in 'Amazing Thailand', in Kitley, P. (ed.), *Television, Regulation and Civil Society in Asia*. New York: Routledge Curzon.

MacBride, S. (1980). *Many Voices, One World*. Paris: UNESCO.

Mizuta, K. (2000). Human Rights and the Media, in Asian Media Information and Communication Centre (AMIC). *Media + Human Rights in Asia*. Singapore: Stamford Press.

National Election Commission. (2007). *Official Statistics on Vote Turn-out of National Referendum August 19, 2007*. Bangkok: Office of National Election Commission.

Pongpis, S. (2007). *Sufficiency Economy: To Take Place If Desired*. Bangkok: Charoenwitya Press.

Pramoj, K. (1976). *Freedom of the Press in Thailand*. Unpublished paper, Department of Government Public Relations, Bangkok.

Puengrasmee, P. (2007). *The Agenda Setting of the Press in the National Referendum, August 19, 2007*. Unpublished report prepared for Graduate School, Bangkok University, Bangkok.

Rousseau, J. (1913). *"The Social Contract," The Social Contract and the Discourses* (trans. Cole, G. D. H.). New York: Dutton.

Servaes, J. (1999). *Communication for Development. One World, Multiple Cultures*. Cresskill: Hampton Press.

—— (ed.) (2003). *Approaches to Development: Studies on Communication for Development*. Paris: UNESCO.

Sirimanont, S. (1980). *Brief History of the Thai Press*. Unpublished paper, School of Journalism and Mass Communication, Thammasat University, Bangkok.

Siritharakul, W. (2007). *Analysis of Non-voters in the National Referendum August 19, 2007*. Unpublished report, Bangkok University. Bangkok.

Splichal, S. & Wasko, J. (eds.). (1993). *Communication and Democracy*. New Jersey: Alex Publishing Corporation.

Supadhiloke, B. (1984). *Right to Communicate in Thailand*. Bangkok: Thai Khadi Research Institute, Thammasat University.

—— (2004). Broadcasting Reform in Thailand, in Eashwar, S. (ed.), *Responses to Globalization and the Digital Divide in the Asia-Pacfic*. Kuala Lumpur: Asia-Pacific Institute for Broadcasting Development (AIBD).

—— (2007). *Media Ownership and Regulations: Some Reflections*. Paper prepared for Asia Media Summit organized by Asia-Pacific Institute for Broadcasting Development, Kuala Lumpur, Malaysia, May 28–June 1, 2007.

———— (2009). Right to Communicate, Media Reform and Civil Society in Thailand. *Communication for Development and Social Change*, 1(3), 323–338.

Ussivakul, V. (2003). *An Introduction to Buddhist Meditation for Results.* Bangkok: TIPITAKA Study Center.

Thai Public Broadcasting Service Act BE 2551. (2008). *Thai PBS: The First Public Broadcasting Service in Thailand.* Retrieved December 1, 2008, from: http://www2.thaipbs.or.th/about-history.php.

The Right to Communicate. (2002). Framework for the right to communicate. Retrieved January 3, 2009, from: http://www.righttocommunicate.org/.

United Nations. (1948, December 10). The Universal Declaration of Human Rights. Retrieved January 1, 2009, from: http://www.un.org/Overview/rights.html.

White, S. A. with others (eds.). (1994). *Participatory Communication.* Thousand Oaks, CA: SAGE Publications.

Chapter 11

The Child Reporters Initiative in India: A Culture-Centered Approach to Participation

Lalatendu Acharya and Mohan Jyoti Dutta

We are child reporters from Saralaguda village in Koraput, students of Tabhapadar Upper Primary School. We do not have electricity in our village and depend on Kerosene for lighting during our evening study. But we did not have the supply of Kerosene for the last three months and all of us in the village had been facing serious problems. So, we met the block officials at Kundra on a Saturday after our school hours. They assured us to look into the matter and then we also met the local media representative of a leading Oriya newspaper "The Samaj" and briefed about our problems. He visited our village with us and published a detailed report after interacting with the villagers. These combined efforts brought results and the dealer rushed to our village and supplied Kerosene helping our lives. The villagers congratulated us for our initiative (Saanta et al., Voice of the Child Reporters, 2011).

Increasingly, communication scholars have called for the examination of the role of participatory processes in the realm of development and social change (Storey & Jacobson, 2004; Diallo, 2007; Dutta, 2006; Acharya, 2009; Acharya & Dutta, 2011). Challenging the top-down conceptualizations of traditional development communication projects (Escobar, 1995; Servaes et al., 1996; Singhal & Rogers, 1999; Singhal, 2003; Chambers, 1984, 2008), these scholars have noted the importance of engaging with local communities in projects of development, eliciting genuine participation in the development of solutions (Chambers, 1984, 2008). In addition, the traditional argument underlying the work on participatory communication within the mainstream framework is drawn on the belief that engagement with local communities in participatory spaces creates more effective avenues for the diffusion of the innovation in the targeted communities (Storey & Jacobson, 2004). Critical engagement with the literature on participatory communication demonstrates multiple tensions that play out in the various commitments/agendas of the participating actors within the discursive space, particularly as it relates to the negotiations of relationships between the community and the outside actors (Acharya & Dutta, 2011; Dutta & Basnyat, 2006; Dutta, 2008a, 2008b;). Further, Dutta (2008a, 2008b), exploring the tensions that play out in participatory processes, articulates the notion of matching the rhetoric of participation with the actual practices of participatory communication, raising questions of authenticity and (im)possibilities of listening to community voices in the articulation of problem configurations. In questioning the location of power amidst dominant structures, they present the culture-centered approach (CCA) as a framework for understanding and interpreting participatory processes in underserved communities in the various sectors of the globe (Airhihenbuwa, 1995; Airhihenbuwa et al., 2000; Airhihenbuwa & Obregon, 2000; Dutta-Bergman, 2004a, 2004b; Dutta, 2007, 2008c). Child participation as a participatory process involving children is an interesting arena to engage with the politics of participation (Acharya, 2009).

This chapter builds on the literature on participatory communication and child participation and examines the tenets of participation through the CCA and how it might impact sustainable change through a case study of the child participation project "The child reporters" in Koraput, India. The CCA locates participatory processes at the intersections of structure, culture, and agency, examining the ways in which dominant structures erase the voices and agency of the subaltern sectors, thus creating points of entry for listening to the hidden voices (Dutta, 2008a, 2008b). Structures are systems of organizing that define the rules and roles that enable and/or constrain access to resources; culture refers to the dynamic and continually shifting contexts within which meanings are defined; and agency is constitutive of the meaning making capacity of local communities, which further underlies local participation in processes of change. Creating these spaces of listening is an important step in ultimately driving the processes of sustainable change through the participation of the local community by identifying the problem configurations and corresponding solutions (Dutta, 2007, 2008a, 2008b). This chapter starts with an introduction to child participation; a discussion on the culture-centered approach to participation and then presents the Koraput child reporters case in order to elucidate the tensions that play out in participatory processes at the intersections of culture, structure, and agency. Thereafter, we document some voices of the child reporters and engage critically with the notion of child participation within the framework of the CCA.

Child participation

Child participation construes one of the fundamental rights of the child to have a voice (UNCRC, 1989). Children's rights have been documented by social reformers with different and ever-changing visions from the early 1990s till present (Woodhead, 2009). Through this, the primary concern of policy-makers and agencies engaged with children has been to improve the health and well-being of all children and provide them a nurturing environment to grow and become responsible members of society by creating opportunities of participation for them. The importance of child participation was underscored in 1989 when the United Nations Convention on the Rights of the Child (UNCRC) redefined the status of children and young people and a majority of world's countries became signatories to the document. Article 12 of the convention said that,

(1) State Parties shall assure to the child who is capable of forming his or her own views the right to express those views freely in all matters affecting the child, the views of the child being given due weight in accordance with the age and maturity of the child and

(2) For this purpose the child shall in particular be provided the opportunity to be heard in any judicial and administrative proceedings affecting the child, either directly, or through a representative or appropriate body, in a manner consistent with the procedural rules of national law (UNCRC, 1989).

Since then, there has been an increase in academic and community initiatives about engaging children and focusing on their participation, the foundational principles being drawn from the UNCRC. Participation is a human rights principle and as such, it is not a gift or privilege bestowed by adults on children but the right of every child capable of "expressing a view" (Lansdown, 2001, 2009; UNCRC, 1989). In other words, child participation is a right for all children – especially the most marginalized and vulnerable children in society who do not figure in discursive spaces and have minimal opportunities of articulating their voices (Acharya, 2009).

Experiences and case studies have shown that in many cases child participation efforts turn out to be a patchy implementation, frequently tokenistic, and with variations between different institutional settings, government and private sectors, and in different political and cultural contexts (Woodhead, 2009). In 1992, Roger Hart theorized and wrote, "Children's participation: The theory and practice of involving young citizens in community development and environmental care" for UNICEF. Hart (1992) developed an excellent tool called the "Ladder of Children's Participation" to serve as a benchmark for engaging in child participation efforts. The ladder lists eight degrees of participation from manipulation and tokenism to the ultimate step of "young people initiated shared decision with adults" and is widely engaged and debated as a tool of child participation (see Malone & Hartung, 2009). A similar framework was proposed by Francis & Lorenzo (2002) called "The seven realms of child participation." They developed seven theoretical categories under which they claimed that most child participation efforts can be categorized, viz., "romantic," "advocacy," "needs," "learning," "rights," "institutionalization," and "proactive." These participation frameworks, when applied to different programs and initiatives, serve as an indicator of child participation and provide direction to move from a lower level to a more engaged scenario of active children participants.

The realization of children's rights involves the transition of children from passive recipients of education passed down from adults to active participants in different programs implemented for their benefit (Lansdown, 2001). However, this continues to be an elusive goal for most children and child participation initiatives. Scholars note that there is an increasing need to face the challenges in realizing children's right to participation (Acharya, 2009). There is a lack of recognition of children's right to be heard and that they possess capacities to contribute to decision-making. Further, as Lansdown (2009) notes, our knowledge and understanding of children's capacity for informed and rational decision-making remain limited. Research into children's perspectives and experiences indicates that adults consistently undermine children's capacity for decision-making and this failure takes different forms in different cultural contexts and geographies (Lansdown, 2009).

Further, children are physically and mentally vulnerable and need guidance from adults in their childhood and this fact impacts the nature of their participation. A study of child participation in South Asia indicated the need of continued support for children from adults with respect to information access, administrative help, additional skills training, access to policy-makers, and the larger society (UNICEF ROSA, 2004; Lansdown, 2009). Of particular relevance in the realm of child participation are evaluations of the agency and capacity of children to participate in decision-making and the ways in which these evaluations shape the various tensions in the participatory processes. It is in this backdrop of the tensions and paradoxes in the relational spaces of participatory processes that we introduce the CCA as a theoretical framework for conceptualizing, evaluating, and applying culture-centered processes to child participation for social change (Dutta, 2007, 2008a, 2008b; Acharya & Dutta, 2011).

Culture-centered approach to participation

Founded on the principles of Subaltern Studies that attends to the continual erasure of the subaltern sectors of the globe (Guha, 1988), the CCA is concerned with the voices of those communities and groups that have traditionally been displaced from dominant discursive structures and spaces, with the goal of examining and transforming those relationships of power that silence local communities (Basu & Dutta, 2009; Dutta, 2008c; Dutta-Bergman, 2004a, 2004b). The CCA questions the constructions of culture in traditional communication theories and applications, and examines the ways in which these traditional communication theories and applications have systematically erased the participation of the cultural voices of marginalized communities by interpreting local culture as a pathological collective of backward or primitive behaviors (Dutta-Bergman, 2004a, 2004b). The CCA further builds dialogical participatory spaces for engaging with the cultural voices that have historically been placed at the margins of discursive processes (Dutta, 2006, 2007, 2008c; Dutta-Bergman, 2004a, 2004b). The focus therefore is on a continual critique of the positions of power that get written into structures of communication, participatory communication, and the ways in which communication then carries out the agendas of those in positions of power (Dutta, 2008a, 2008b; Acharya & Dutta, 2011). With its emphasis on interrogating the participatory erasures in communication discourse and applications, the CCA primarily focuses on understanding meanings and experiences in marginalized, vulnerable settings and thus is aligned with the goals of participatory communication, especially in the context of child participation where implementation and evaluations of participatory capacity and processes are continually made by adult program planners, policy makers, field workers, and evaluators. In the case study of child participation in Koraput, the tribal children of Koraput constitute the vulnerable group in a marginalized setting whose voices need to be listened to and views respected, in order to create spaces for justice, equity, and dignity (Acharya, 2009). As noted in the articles of the UNCRC, all children are capable of expressing a view, have the right to express their views freely, have the right to be heard in all matters affecting them, and have the right to have their views taken seriously and in accordance with their age and maturity (UNCRC, 1989). What the CCA critically notes in the context of this logic is that the locus of decision-making is always in the hands of top-down policy planners, especially in terms of dictating and determining the parameters and scope of participation, situating participatory discourses amidst negotiations of power, control, and agency (Dutta, 2008a, 2008b, 2008c).

Attending to the paradoxes of participation and the dialectical tensions in participatory processes, the CCA is built upon three key concepts of structure, culture, and agency, and their mutual interactions (Dutta, 2008a, 2008b, 2008c; Dutta & Basnyat, 2006). The intersections of structure, culture, and agency create openings for listening to the voices rendered silent through mainstream platforms of society, thus creating discursive spaces that interrogate these erasures and offer opportunities for co-constructing culture-centered narratives by engaging subaltern communities in dialogue. The articulations of dialogue in the CCA are built upon the very recognition of the limits of dialogue as framed within the structures of the emancipator rhetoric of enlightenment that continue to be carried out in much of development communication work (Dutta & Pal, 2010).

Culture

The concept of culture, in the CCA, refers to the local contexts within which meanings are constituted and negotiated, attending to the dynamic and constitutive processes in local cultures through which meanings are continually set in motion, are contingent, incomplete, and therefore, open to multiple interpretive frames (Dutta, 2008c). The emphasis here is on looking at the constitutive and dynamic nature of culture, situated amidst the discursive terrains of power. Culture provides the communicative framework for meanings such that the ways in which community members come to understand that their lived experiences are embedded within cultural beliefs, values, and practices (Dutta, 2008c). These beliefs, values, and practices are contextual and the meanings can be understood located within these contexts. It is this contextual nature of meanings that contributes to the dynamic nature of culture, which continually shift as the context is negotiated through interactions and locations shift. Furthermore, cultural meanings provide the locally situated scripts through which structures influence the communicative choices of cultural participants (Dutta, 2008c). The context of the child reporters' initiative was the tribal district of Koraput in Eastern India. A predominantly tribal and rural district that is contiguous to the tribal district areas in adjoining states, Koraput is noted to be home to 25 different types of tribes and subtribes (Mahapatra, 2009) who have their own unique cultures, beliefs, and practices. Furthermore, the cultures that define the contexts within which the children live are negotiated amidst a wide variety of structural relationships and processes.

Structure

Structure, in this context, refers to those aspects of social organization that both constrain and enable the capacity of cultural participants to participate in communicative platforms and in utilizing the fundamental resources of mainstream societies (Dutta-Bergman, 2004a). The emphasis on structure particularly lends the CCA to the development of communication theories and applications that engage communities in marginalized settings through the explorations of the structural barriers and structural factors that impact on the agency and communicative practices of locals (Dutta, 2008c; Dutta & Pal, 2010). Attention to structure creates entry points for reflecting about the fundamental elements of dominant structures and discourses that limit the possibilities for participation, thus also creating entry points for continually challenging these structures (Dutta, 2008c). The tribal children in Koraput live within several social structures that influence their lives. The various structures such as school, village, local clubs, government structures, and so on regulate their activities and their participation. As child participation scholars note, the key to sustainable child participation is the creation of structures that empower children within their families and communities (Lansdown, 2001). Furthermore, the CCA underlines the importance of continually interrogating the monolithic narratives of empowerment as constituted in enlightenment discourses of rights that assume that outside agencies and structures can create spaces of emancipation and thus liberate local communities from local structures (Dutta, 2008a, 2008b, 2008c). Culture-centered interrogations of structures will depend on the contexts in which the children live and the type of participation used within the framework of local, federal, and global spaces of organizing.

Agency

Agency refers to the capacity of cultural members to enact their choices and to actively participate in negotiating the structures within which they find themselves (Dutta, 2008a, 2008b, 2008c; Dutta-Bergman, 2004a, 2004b). The concept of agency reflects the active processes through which individuals, groups, and communities participate in a variety of actions that directly challenge the constraining structures and simultaneously work with them in finding communicative avenues for expressing their needs and desires. Agency is both dynamic and constitutive and is negotiated through various forms of communicative processes that continually engage with the structures and attending to the paradoxes and tensions that emerge in the processes of power negotiations. From a participatory communication standpoint, agency taps into the ability of communities to be active participants in determining the agendas on participatory platforms and formulating solutions to problems as perceived by the community (Dutta, 2008c). The emphasis, therefore, shifts to the community as an entry point for the articulation of local knowledge.

An opportunity for the communication scholars and practitioners to engage with the agency of cultural participants, not from the standpoint of an outside expert empowering the community, but from that of the privileged coconstructor of narratives who works through her privileges in order to continually explore possibilities for listening to these ignored voices and creating spaces of transformative politics (Dutta, 2008c; Dutta & Pal, 2010). This is a key point for child participation, which encourages child participation practitioners to engage with the key question that "what is the agency of children and how agency is built or may be built for them," pitting it against the traditional social answers that are available to practitioners in dominant discursive spaces. So we should look at what kinds of structural and cultural resources children draw on in expressing their agency, and how these shape their participation in different ways as they negotiate different sites of power (White & Choudhury, 2007).

Interactions among structure, culture, and agency

The three concepts of structure, culture, and agency are intertwined (Dutta, 2008c). Structures within social systems are played out through the culturally situated contexts in local communities. Structural features gain meaning through the contexts of the local culture, thus creating a site for the articulation and sharing of meanings. Structural constraints become meaningful through the lived experiences of cultural members and through the sharing of these lived experiences. Simultaneously, culture offers the substratum for structure, such that structures are both reified and challenged through the cultural meaning systems that are in circulation within the culture. It is through the articulation of new meanings that cultures create points of social change and structural transformations. For instance, it is when cultural members in a marginalized context start sharing about their stories of deprivation that greater awareness is created and opportunities are introduced for changes in the dominant healthcare infrastructures (Dutta-Bergman, 2004a, 2004b; Wang & Burris, 1994) as we will see with the reports/voices of child reporters.

Agency offers an opportunity to situate the lives of marginalized individuals, groups, and communities in the realm of their active engagement in challenging and participating in the structures that constrain their lives (Dutta-Bergman, 2004a, 2004b; Dutta & Basu, 2008; Acharya & Dutta, 2011). It is in the realm of culturally situated meanings and actions that individuals enact their agency and participate in processes of social change. Culture provides the conduit through which agency and participation are realized and the culturally situated symbols constitute the communicative practices, the community's participation in the social structures, and collective organization to address constraints. Now that we have discussed the CCA and its basic configuration, in the next section we will discuss the child reporters' project and demonstrate the ways in which it embodies the principles of culture, structure, and agency.

The child reporters initiative: Children as agents of change

The story of child reporters of Dangarpaunsi

Dangarpaunsi is a small tribal village in Koraput district. The children from Dangarpaunsi had visited Koraput to attend a child reporters' workshop and had interacted with children from a school for the visually impaired and blind. The child reporters discussed amongst them and met with the teachers and authorities from the school and learnt about the admittance process. Upon returning home, they met the parents of a blind child in their village. They narrated the facilities available at the school for visually impaired at Koraput and urged them to admit the child after which the parents visited the facility and admitted their child. This is a great example of the participation of the child reporters in processes of change played out in the form of the aligning of agency, culture, and context. Through their participation, the child reporters participated as agents of change in connecting individual community members with structural resources.

The story of child reporters of Sunki

Sunki is a small village on the Koraput–Andhra Pradesh border and children from the Sunki primary school are child reporters (Andhra Pradesh is a southern state in India). After discussions at the child reporters' meetings that all children should go to school and no child should be left behind, the children noticed that they are missing one of their classmates "Pollama" since some months. They went to her house and asked that why she was not coming to school anymore. Pollama said that her single mother is struggling to make ends meet and so has to double her work outside. So, she was staying home to take care of the cooking and house needs. Moreover, having missed school, she was feeling shy and ashamed to resume. The child reporters noted this and had discussions with their school teacher and then Pollama's mother. After some convincing and engagement, Pollama was back in school. Once again, it is through the enactment of their agency as a collective that the child reporters drew attention to structural resources, and worked together with various stakeholders to develop solutions.

The story of child reporters of Kundra

The child reporters from Katriguda upper primary school in Kundra had only one teacher in their entire school with six grades. The children faced the need for more number of teachers since long and wrote this in their published reports. They also spoke to their parents and other influential villagers repeatedly and persuaded them to talk with the senior officials of the government administration and education department. This resulted in the posting of one more teacher in their school.

In the above experiences, the participation of the child reporters in constructing an issue and in mobilizing resources around the issue demonstrates the intersections of culture, structure, and agency as the child reporters enact their agency in influencing the structures to achieve a social goal. In the enactment of agency is the collective mobilization of structures and in the identification of structural resources toward solving problems identified through participation. Their initiative emerged through their thinking and articulation of the problem and they found a local culturally acceptable solution by working through various stakeholders located at various structural entry points. Furthermore, the participation of child reporters is contextually situated in the realm of the structures that constitute their education and development. They function as agents of change, negotiating with the meanings of development as constituted in the local realm of the dominant structures.

The context

The Child Reporters project was conceived in the context of children in Odisha. The leading concern while framing was ensuring meaningful participation of children (Acharya, 2009). There have been numerous projects involving children across the spectrum of developmental activities and programs in different regions around the world with varying degrees of participation and engagement. Children and women form the most vulnerable section of the society and are invariably in the weaker end of the power equation. Children come out getting the worst treatments amidst the politics of power structures, as physically and mentally they are less equipped in negotiating a favorable situation. Here, the participatory goals of the Child Reporters project are aligned with the basic emphasis of the CCA on creating spaces for listening to the children's voices that do not find space in mainstream structures (Acharya, 2009).

The child reporters' effort involved training groups of children from different schools on fundamental news reporting skills, involving them in discussions regarding development, and inspiring their thoughts on development issues. The child reporters initiative started in a small way with five schools in 2004 (Acharya, 2009). The children as a part of the initiative reported on development issues before the leaders of the local government and voiced their concerns. The participatory avenues articulated in the realm of the project engaged with dominant structures by creating opportunities for dialogues with powerful institutional actors and key agents within the social structures (Dutta, 2008c). Furthermore, the project demonstrated the intersections of agency and structure as children enacted their agency in the choice of topics, in their reports on these topics, and in their engagement with key institutional actors. In 2005, the initiative shifted to the tribal district of Koraput to work with children from a marginalized and disadvantaged context.

Koraput district and its deprivation

Koraput is one of the 30 districts of Odisha. Koraput, with 5.38 percent of Odisha's area, has a population of 1.18 million mostly rural with more than 50 percent of the population tribal (Census GoI, 2001). Koraput was amongst the poorest districts of Odisha and had some of the lowest development indicators in Odisha (Planning Commission of India, 2003). According to the Government of India Census 2001 (Census GoI, 2001), Koraput literacy rate was found to be 36.20 percent as against 63.61 percent in Odisha with a low female literacy rate of 24.81 percent. Another significant area of concern relates to children's education where figures indicated that of the total number of children enrolled at the primary level in the district, nearly 88.27 percent do not reach the upper primary stage with the situation more alarming in the case of tribal children. In health, Koraput had a low percentage of institutional deliveries (11 percent), a high proportion of deliveries conducted by untrained personnel (79 percent), poor newborn care practices, and a high infant mortality rate (UNICEF Multiple Indicators Cluster Survey, 2001) . The district also suffered from many endemic diseases like Malaria, Tuberculosis, Anthrax, Diarrhea, and Sickle cell anemia and was also vulnerable to disasters like droughts; it was a part of the severely drought-affected belt of Odisha (Planning Commission of India, 2003). These health and socioeconomic deprivations of Koraput place it at the margins of the margins, at the peripheries of the mainstream social configuration in Odisha. The situation becomes more acute for the more vulnerable sections of the tribes and castes of Koraput. It is also this existence of Koraput at the margins that lends it to the participatory processes in the CCA as these processes offer opportunities for bringing the voices from margins into the mainstream social structures (Dutta, 2008a; Acharya, 2009).

The child reporters' process

The child reporters' initiative in Koraput started with the selection of 100 child reporters from ten schools, chosen from a representative two blocks of Koraput. The selection was made after detailed consultation and discussions with the district education department officials, nongovernment organizations (NGOs), civil society representatives, and teachers and parent-teacher associations of the respective schools who desired to be part of the project and children themselves. Local NGOs facilitated the entire process. All child reporters were in the age group of 8 to 14 years of age studying in Grades 3rd to 7th. The children were oriented on the broad issues of development in Odisha, their district, their village, and issues surrounding their individual lives. They were also oriented on media journalism and reporting. Further, the children were exposed to discussions and field visits where local communication experts, media reporters, facilitated the children with necessary skills of observation and reporting. The children were given an identifying badge and access to all government service providers and other stakeholders in the course of their reporting assignment, thus creating communicative entry points for access to structures. Each child reporter was provided with a diary to note her thoughts and reports down. The dairies were collected every month and the best writings were put together in the form of a monthly newsletter called "Ankurodgam," 1000 copies of which were circulated to the top decision-makers of the state and district, media, and people from key nongovernmental organizations. The writings were selected by the local facilitating group who ensured that most children's voices found a representation in the newsletter. The new reports, their content, quality, and process of selection were discussed with the children during the facilitator visits to their schools and child reporter meetings in the district headquarters. In 2005, a group of child reporters participated in a filmmaking workshop and they made their own documentary films using technical help. These films were subsequently shown to larger audiences of decision-makers. The child reporters have grown across the years and now in 2011–12, seven years into the participatory process, number a total of 6000 child reporters across 600 schools from all fourteen blocks of Koraput district. They have formed child reporter clubs in those schools and present their findings at the school level in the child reporters' corner, in the block level newsletter and the state-level publication "Ankurodgam." In 2005, the child reporters' newsletter was being distributed by the local facilitating NGO but now it figures as a supplement in a popular regional daily "Anupam Bharat" with a high circulation. In the years since 2004, the child reporters of Koraput have presented their reports, voices at their village, school, block, district, state, national, and international levels in numerous forums. The child reporters of Koraput have traveled to different places in the country and shared their experiences and understandings. They have interacted with local political representative, government officials, and state-level decision-makers. They are regular participants and presenters at all the state-level children conferences in Odisha. The process has gained support, appreciation, and gradual involvement from many stakeholders, notably the media and the government functionaries.

One imperative since beginning was getting the support of more and more stakeholders in the process of listening to children and child participation and move on the ladder of participation from tokenism toward real participation (Acharya, 2009). The other imperative was to create a framework in Koraput where the ownership of the process rests with multiple stakeholders and the children themselves so that the process is sustainable.

A UNICEF supported evaluation (UNICEF, 2010) reported in its key findings that the children have been able to discover a unique voice through the child reporter initiative. The children have raised important and pertinent issues from their experience and observation like the problem of teachers' absenteeism, corruption in mid-day meal schemes, girl-child education, child marriage, health and environment problems, condition of public roads, cleanliness in their village, and so on. More importantly, the child reporter initiative has also created scope for the articulation of problems plaguing their communities like that of caste discrimination, health and hygiene, malpractices in government schemes, or poor development infrastructure in their villages (UNICEF, 2010). Since the process is facilitated by local media, they have picked up on the children's reports and have brought these concerns to the fore in their media outlets. The children across time have also honed their skills of observation and expression with increases in self-confidence, access to information/ knowledge, and initiative. The evaluation report cites the convergence created among the child reporters, the media, the government and nongovernment implementing agencies, and local communities as one of the strongest points of achievement (UNICEF, 2010). Further the task of being reporters has contributed to the children's creativity and exposed them to developmental issues as they observe and report on their own and communities' experiences. This reporting has enriched the children and increased their confidence and has also got recognition and adulation from their peers and adults, especially their family members and teachers. The UNICEF evaluation report goes on to mention that many of the adults have discerned improvement in language and articulation, enhanced analytical abilities and reinforcement of positive values among the child reporters. Most importantly, the child reporters' process has created avenues for the children's voices to be heard, brought them into a dialogic space with adults, and instilled them with a value system of critical reflection and questioning their milieu (UNICEF, 2010). In the context of the CCA (Dutta-Bergman, 2004a, 2004b), the articulation of the participatory spaces is situated at entry points for creating spaces for listening to the subaltern voices; here the voices of the children who are traditionally unheard; and for shaping policy agendas based on the foregrounding of these voices. In the next section, aligned with the goals of the CCA, we co-construct the narratives of the child reporters.

Voices of the children (Source: Child Reporters newsletter #3, 2008–9)

The voices of the children draw attention to the structural locations of community problems, and foreground the structural locus of development and social change initiatives. "It would be nice if we had a hospital in our village. Due to lack of money, people cannot go to other village hospitals for treatment," wrote, Hemabati Pandu, Dumadangara village. Here is the articulation of local community need in the context of a structural problem and the foregrounding of structural solutions to local community needs. Similarly, note the following articulation:

> In our school we have nine teachers. We have no problems in learning from them. But it would be better if we had interesting reading materials too. There is another problem. Some children are having problems with studying because of lack of pens, pencils and books.

This was reported by another school student Prashant Kumar Dhalai, Kanimusa village. Once again, the emphasis of the narrative here is on the absence of structural resources in local schools. The community-based articulation of solution through the voice of the child reporter attends to the need for building resources such as reading materials, and supplies of pens, pencils, and books. Here's another report from a child reporter:

In our village there is a pond. But since we do not have toilets, people use the pond for answering the call of nature. During rainy days the pond becomes much polluted. We are suffering from scabies and skin infections by bathing in the pond. It is important to have toilets in our village.

This report by Shantimani Nayak, Bhaluguda village draws attention to the necessity for building structures such as toilets in the village that are responsive to the everyday problems of the community. In another narrative, Minarao Melka of Kumbhariput village wrote:

Our village Kumbhariput is surrounded by mountains. The people of our village fall prey to various diseases like Malaria. Even though there is a doctor in our village, we are facing a problem because there is a shortage of health workers.

The emphasis here is placed on securing access to health resources such as health workers and the problem is framed in terms of the shortage of health workers in the Kumbhariput village. Here is yet another narrative that frames local community problems in the realm of structures:

People of my village regularly suffer from Malaria, Scabies and other diseases. People use water from the river and suffer from Diarrhea. It is difficult to travel to and from our village as the road is in a bad state.

This was written by Senkarao Huluka from Garidi village. In each of these instances, the articulation of local agency among the children creates avenues for the framing of local problems, and drawing attention to the problems of everyday living as understood by the children. These interpretive frames constituted around the local problems of the communities are framed within the broader domain of the need for creating structural resources for the community. Culture-centered processes of participation in the child reporters' project create entry points for local articulations that situate development efforts in terms of structural transformations and the creation of structural capacities at the local level.

Culture-centered approach to participation: Lessons from the project

The Child Reporters project brings forth the ways in which participation in subaltern contexts is articulated at the intersections of culture, structure, and agency (Dutta, 2008; Acharya, 2009). The Child Reporters project demonstrates that a culture-centered participatory project begins with its commitment to listening to subaltern voices; in this case the children whose voices do not always find a space in adult dominated discussions are seen as enactors of agency. Therefore, the emphasis of the project was on creating open-ended spaces that fostered communicative capacities in local contexts for listening to the voices of the child reporters. Worth reiterating here is the emphasis of local communicative processes in fostering open communicative spaces for dialogue and listening, where the content and frameworks of dialogue are not limited to predetermined frames imposed by outside agencies (Dutta, 2008a, 2008b). Instead, the emphasis is on simply creating spaces for listening to local communities, attending to the ways in which the children understood their problems at the community level, and respecting the solutions they framed as ways for entering into the practice of development for social change (Dutta, 2008a, 2008b, 2008c). In this direction, the goal of the project is to disrupt the dominant discursive structures by interrogating the silences in these structures, and by creating spaces for listening by continuously interrogating the silences written into these structures. Participatory platforms such as the newsletters and the diaries of the child reporters, their presentations at different forums, and their public interactions create opportunities for change in the dominant structures through the co-creation of locally situated narratives of social change. As noted in the CCA (Dutta, 2008a, 2008b), culture-centered participation is directed at fostering communicative openings precisely for the purposes of disrupting structurally perpetuated silences, and not under the framing of enlisting participation toward serving the top-down preconfigured goals of funding agencies and program planners. The emphasis is on opening up spaces to seeing what are the narratives that emerge locally, and how can these narratives provide entry points for social change and structural transformation, rather than utilizing participatory platforms as channels for disseminating top-down messages. Participation is an end in itself rather than being conceptualized as a co-optive tool that is directed toward serving the agendas of dominant structural actors. The locally centered narratives of participation for social change point toward the possibilities of transformative politics as co-constructed through the sharing of local narratives and local voices.

The participatory frameworks brought forth by the project created opportunities for the enactment of agency in the locally situated cultural contexts, and in dialogue with the structures within which this agency was constituted. The enactment of agency in the participatory platforms created openings for listening to the voices of children in the dominant discursive spaces, and foregrounding the rationality of the children in terms of how they saw the problems that were most meaningful to them. These voices of the children from Koraput sought to disrupt the communicative hegemony in the dominant discursive structures and create points of listening to local narratives in the context of the broader structures. These points of listening also opened up the local structures to possibilities of change. It is important to note here the culturally constituted nature of participation. Participatory processes become meaningful only in the realm of the local cultures through the involvement of local participants, and framed in the context of the everyday lives' experiences of local communities. The voices of the child reporters in mainstream mediated spheres and public discursive spaces of policy stood to challenge the dominant framings of these policies. As a result, they created alternative frameworks for understanding the logics of these policies, for questioning these policies, and for creating avenues for transformation.

In this case study, participatory opportunities are mobilized in order to disrupt the silences in mainstream public spheres. The goal of the Child Reporters project was to create avenues for the children to articulate and foreground whatever issues they considered important, and to work toward solving these problems through their own participation (Acharya, 2009). As opposed to dominant frameworks that utilize participation to fulfill the interests of the stakeholders at the center, the Child Reporters project opened up opportunities for engaging with subaltern publics and for listening to their voices with the goal of bringing about structural changes through these articulations of voices.

It is in this realm of the structurally situated nature of participation that the Child Reporters project creates alternative entry points. Not only does the project commit itself to the simple representations of messages, but also toward the utilization of available resources to address the problems articulated in the participatory platforms through the foregrounding of local frames. The project also builds agency in the participants, the children by bringing them into the participatory process of questioning and engagement. Further, the project engages the participatory platforms with structurally situated practices that are directed toward mobilizing resources in addressing the broader structures and structural disparities from the perspectives of local communities. Finally, the project demonstrates the ways in which participation as constituted in the realm of CCA is committed to the voices of local communities, embedded and situated within the local contexts of these communities. The Child Reporters project creates a space for the local culture and for the voices of the children who have otherwise been marginalized in mainstream public spheres. In doing so, the child reporters project directs us toward the possibilities of participation that resist the dominant structures in their very goals of creating spaces for listening to subaltern voices.

Challenges and lessons for the future

A number of challenges still remain and encourage us as communication professionals to devise new ways to address them. A key challenge is ensuring that the child reporters' initiative has some direct or indirect impact on the socioeconomic indicators of the Koraput district in the long term, especially because many of the children's narratives drew attention to these structural disparities. One could argue here that within the child reporters' process, we are contributing in building confident, analytical and knowledgeable citizens of the society, and creating participatory spaces where the children feel that they can have a voice. This is true and it also is reflected in the UNICEF process evaluation (UNICEF, 2010), but another immediate result of the child reporters' process could be that the reports worked as a monitoring tool for the government and nongovernment functionaries. So, the challenge is to position the initiative as a support to many behavioral change programs implemented by UNICEF and other developmental agencies. The creation of the space to listening to children's voices could also provide us with opportunities to build healthier and responsible citizens.

The other challenges relate to the dilemma of agency as outlined by White and Choudhury (2007), that is, with the adult facilitated child participation process, how do we ensure that children's participation and agency are not co-opted by the structures around them? As they further write, "children who were posed as subjects in giving voice to their experiences simultaneously became objects of the gaze of others." A further challenge is ensuring security and safety of the child reporters. A child is physically and mentally vulnerable compared with the adult, and when she is reporting on an issue that is detrimental to an adult's interest, she is at risk. What ways could be devised to ensure that the right to safety and security of the child along with the right to participation are juxtaposed in complementary spaces? As the ongoing experience with the child reporters' process in Koraput underlines, there is a long way to traverse in child participation and a sustainable social change needs time and constant innovation.

References

Acharya, L (2009). Child Reporters as Agents of Change, in Barry Percy-Smith & Nigel Thomas (eds.), *A Handbook of Children and Young People's Participation Perspectives from Theory and Practice*. London: Routledge, pp. 204–215.

Acharya, L. & Dutta, M. J. (2011). Deconstructing the Portrayals of HIV/AIDS Among Campaign Planners Targeting Tribal Populations in Koraput, India: A Culture-Centered Interrogation, Health Communication, DOI:10.1080/10410236.2011.622738.

Airhihenbuwa, C. (1995). *Health and Culture: Beyond the Western Paradigm*. Thousand Oaks, CA: SAGE.

Airhihenbuwa, C. O. & Obregon, R. (2000). A Critical Assessment of Theories/Models Used in Health Communication for AIDS. *Journal of Health Communication*, 5(Suppl.), 5–15.

Airhihenbuwa, C. O., Makinwa, B., & Obregon, R. (2000). Toward a New Communication Framework for HIV/AIDS. *Journal of Health Communication*, 5(Suppl.), 101–111.

Basu, A., & Dutta, M. (2009). Sex workers and HIV/AIDS: Analyzing participatory culture-centered health communication strategies. Human Communication Research, 35, 86–114.

Census of India. (2001). *States at a Glance*. Retrieved on October 1, 2010 from http://www.censusindia.gov.in/Census_Data_2001/ /States_at_glance/State_Links /21_ori.pdf

Chambers, R. (1984). *Rural Development: Putting the Last First*. New York: Longman.

———— (2008). *Revolutions in Development Inquiry*. London: Earthscan.

Diallo, Y. (2009). *Genuine Participation in Social Change Programs: The Experiences of Benefactors and Beneficiaries in Guinea*. Saarbucken: VDM Verlag

Dutta, M. (2007). Communicating about Culture and Health: Theorizing Culture-Centered and Cultural-Sensitivity Approaches. *Communication Theory*, 17, 304–328.

———— (2008a). Participatory Communication in Entertainment Education: A Critical Analysis. *Communication for Development and Social Change: A Global Journal*, 2, 53–72.

———— (2008b). A Critical Response to Storey and Jacobson: The Co-optive Possibilities of Participatory Discourse. *Communication for Development and Social Change: A Global Journal*, 2, 81–90.

———— (2008c). *Communicating Health: A Culture-Centered Approach.* Cambridge: Polity.

Dutta, M. & Basnyat, I. (2008). The Radio Communication Project in Nepal: A Critical Analysis. *Health Education and Behavior,* 35(6), 459–460

Dutta, M. J. & Pal, M. (2010). Dialog Theory in Marginalized Settings: A Culture-Centered Approach. *Communication Theory,* 20(4), 363–386

Dutta-Bergman, M. (2004a). The Unheard Voices of Santalis: Communicating about Health from the Margins of India. *Communication Theory,* 14, 237–263.

———— (2004b). Poverty, Structural Barriers and Health: A Santali Narrative of Health Communication. *Qualitative Health Research,* 14, 1–16.

Escobar, A. (1995). *Encountering Development: The Making and Unmaking of the Third World.* Princeton, NJ: Princeton University Press.

Francis, M. & Lorenzo, R. (2002). Seven Realms of Children's Participation. *Journal of Environmental Psychology,* 22: 157–169.

Guha, R (1988). The prose of counter-insurgency. In R. Guha & G. Spivak (Eds), Subaltern studies (pp. 37-44). Delhi: Oxford University Press.

Hart, R. (1992). *Children's Participation: From Tokenism to Citizenship.* Florence: UNICEF.

Jacobson, T. L. (2003). Participatory Communication for Social Change: The Relevance of the Theory of Communicative Action, in Kalbfleisch, P. (ed.), *Communication Yearbook 27.* Mahwah, NJ: Erlbaum, pp. 87–124.

Landsdown, G. (2001). *Promoting Children's Participation in Democratic Decision Making.* UNICEF Italy: UNICEF Innocenti Insight.

———— (2009). The Realization of Children's Participation Rights, in Barry Percy-Smith & Nigel Thomas (eds.), *A Handbook of Children and Young People's Participation Perspectives from Theory and Practice.* London: Routledge, pp. 1–23.

Malone, K. & Hartung, C. (2009). Challenges of Participatory Practice, in Barry Percy-Smith & Nigel Thomas (eds.), *A Handbook of Children and Young People's Participation Perspectives from Theory and Practice.* London: Routledge, pp. 24–38.

Mohapatra A. K. (2009). Theory of Feminism and Tribal Women: An Empirical Study of Koraput, *Mens Sana Monographs.*7 (1), 80–92.

Planning Commission of India. (2003). An overview of the Scheduled Tribes of Orissa. Retrieved on 1st October 2010 from http://planningcommission.nic.in/plans/stateplan/sdr_orissa/sdr_orich15.pdf Delhi: Planning Commission of India.

Saanta, Sanjay, Saanta, Bhima, Saanta, Dasrath, Saanta, Sada, Saanta, Shyamsunder, Saanta, Dilip, & Saanta, Madhab (2011). Voice of the Child Reporters in Saralaguda village in Bagderi panchayat of Kundra block, Koraput.

Servaes, J., Jacobson, T., & White, S. (1996). *Participatory Communication for Social Change.* New Delhi: SAGE.

Singhal, A (2003). Focussing on the forest , not just the tree. Cultural strategies for combating HIV/AIDS. MICA Communications Review, 1(1): 21–28

Singhal, A. & Rogers, E. (1999). *Entertainment-Education: A Communication Strategy for Social Change.* Mahwah, NJ: Lawrence Erlbaum Associates.

Storey, D. & Jacobson, T. (2004). Entertainment-Education and Participation: Applying Habermas to a Population Program in Nepal, in Singhal, A., Cody, M., Rogers, E., & Sabido,

M. (eds.), *Entertainment Education and Social Change*. Mahwah, NJ: Lawrence Erlbaum, pp. 377–397.

UNCRC. (1989). *United Nations Convention on the Rights of the Child*.

UNICEF. (2010). *Evaluation of the Child Reporters Initiative*. New Delhi: UNICEF.

UNICEF MICS. (2001). *Multiple Indicator Cluster Survey*. New Delhi: UNICEF.

UNICEF ROSA (Regional Office of South Asia). (2004). *Wheel of Change: Children and Young People's Participation in South Asia*. Kathmandu: UNICEF ROSA.

Wang, C. & Burris, M. (1994). Empowerment through Photo Novella: Portraits of Participation. *Health Education Quarterly*, 21, 171–186.

White, S. C. & Choudhury, S. A. (2007). The Politics of Child Participation in International Development: The Dilemma of Agency. *The European Journal of Development Research*, 19(4), 529–550.

Woodhead, M.(2009). Foreword, in Barry Percy-Smith & Nigel Thomas (eds.), *A Handbook of Children and Young People's Participation Perspectives from Theory and Practice*. London: Routledge.

Chapter 12

Advancing a Pedagogy of Social Change in Post-Katrina New Orleans: Participatory Communication in a Time of Crisis

David J. Park and Leslie Richardson

Introduction

This chapter explores a social justice-oriented participatory model of communications pedagogy, through a case study focusing on a series of courses at a private New Orleans (US) university that were transformed into community-led partnerships after Hurricane Katrina. The courses were adapted to respond directly to the needs of marginalized people in the immediate and extended aftermath of the hurricane. This community-oriented educational approach involved three and a half years of campaigns to rebuild lower socioeconomic neighborhoods in New Orleans. Under the direction of the community, often through a local nonprofit group, students conducted national and international media campaigns to bring in volunteers to remove debris and gut houses in mostly African-American neighborhoods. They also worked with media to generate publicity for the cause and to bring in much-needed building supplies and professional workers. When entire neighborhoods were displaced, with residents unable to return to their ruined homes, these community-led campaigns generated over $1,250,000 worth of building supplies and pro-bono labor (through over 5,000 volunteers) for predominantly lower socioeconomic status African-American households, community centers, and other public goods.

The purpose of this chapter is to describe a re-envisioning of the communication field building upon this New Orleans experience, which offers an effective case study of a project that addresses community needs while enhancing student learning. The chapter begins by discussing the theoretical framework to this project, then describes the mechanisms of the case, firmly grounded in a context of social justice. The role of the university course as change-agent is contextualized within various power relations, which hobbled the courses from continuing to address community needs over the long term. If there is a lesson to be learned from this case study, the logical outcome is to present alternative ideas about the present state of communications pedagogy, participatory communication, and the communication field in general. Perhaps educators and communication programs could experiment with responding not only to disasters, but also to other social, cultural, political, and economic issues. If they choose to do so, it is hoped that this chapter will inspire future scholars while warning them of the possible trials and tribulations of community-oriented social justice work within university settings.

Social justice-oriented pedagogy

Although it seems important to define social justice if we choose to work toward it, and if we hope to convince others of its value, "people have been arguing about what social justice is for millennia" (Pollock et al., 1996:144). Instead of arguing for one precise meaning of social justice, as many others have already done (Artz, 2006; Pearce, 1998), this chapter hopes to offer some examples of what can be accomplished in the communication field. What will be described here resonates with Pollock et al.'s (1996: 143) conceptual framework of a communication approach to social justice, which:

> (1) foregrounds ethical concerns; (2) analyzes the structural dimensions of inequity and injustice; (3) insists on transforming those social structures that restrict or deny access to recourses; and (4) identifies with and advocates the interests of the economically, socially, politically, and culturally underresourced, the subordinate, and/or the oppressed.

Fortunately some university communication programs do support and incorporate varied concepts of social justice into their curricula. For example, Loyola University in Chicago ultimately supported communication scholars' efforts to create a social justice concentration in the department (Pearce, 1998), although there is little uniformity among universities concerning commitments to social justice. Other private and religious universities may have "social justice" in their mission statements, but academics should not assume this means there is a green light to address injustice and oppression through the institutions. Indeed, some religious institutions still carry vestiges of their original conceptualization of "social justice," which was often defined through principles of proselytizing, unlike Pollock et al.'s (1996) conceptualization.

Harnessing higher education and social justice implies a certain understanding of learning. The important trends in pedagogical theory over the last few decades have all advocated engaged learning: active learning rather than passive reception, learning through problem solving, through service, through dialogue, and so on. One point where engaged learning can potentially further social justice is in Service Learning. Service Learning can be defined as an experience where students "participate in an organized service activity that meets identified community needs and reflect on the service activity in such a way as to gain further understanding of course content, a broader appreciation of the discipline, and an enhanced sense of civic responsibility" (Bringle & Hatcher, 1996:222). Effective Service Learning can "create positive change in communities and organizations, while allowing students to increase academic comprehension, civic involvement, and career-related skills" (Gibson et al., 2001:199). Service Learning projects can ultimately defend the status quo, or can work for social justice and liberation (Artz, 2001). If one decides to work for social justice by addressing oppression through Service Learning, these choices are likely to lead to unexpected challenges and implications, some of which will be described within this chapter. Many scholars have noted that participatory communication projects in general face a lack of institutional support (Huesca, 2008).

Educators from the past few decades have addressed both the trials and the possibilities of social justice–oriented pedagogy for student learning as well as for community development. Important writers on education since John Dewey (1936) have emphasized the liberatory function of learning, but in the past generation community engagement and the fostering of student learning communities have become increasingly influential strategies and goals (Boyer, 1990, 1994; Palmer 1998; Damon, 1998; Barber, 1998). In this environment, educators are all invested in the process of offering students deep, transformative learning, guiding them in their journey toward becoming responsible citizens and leaders for a better world. Many in the academy also advocate Paulo Freire's (1970) call for education as democracy: "Liberating education consists in acts of cognition, not transferrals of information" (p. 67). Or as bell hooks (1994) puts it, we must recognize the fundamental "difference between education as the practice of freedom and education that merely strives to reinforce domination" (p. 4). Learning can be empowering only when it is "owned" by the learners; simply demanding that students regurgitate received academic wisdom inhibits rather than nurtures critical thought. Empowering education actually transforms the learner, allowing him or her to grow and develop personally as she develops her cognitive abilities (Barnett, 2007; Bain, 2004). If educators wish to train graduates habituated to independent, critical thought, they must find ways to harness student caring along with curiosity. That is what the post-Katrina communication courses accomplished.

Students in college classrooms can rediscover the excitement of learning (an excitement that can be so hammered out of them in elementary and secondary schools) when they are assisted to see themselves as members of a community, treated as adults, and allowed to understand their role as potential agents of social change (Bain, 2004l Barber, 1998; Boyer, 1994). When the skills and masteries students need to acquire for an academic class can be exercised for the tangible benefit of a community in need, learning is intensified in every way: acquisition is swifter, mastery more complete, and retention more secure (Stage et al., 1998).

This project and the analysis of it both draw upon the ideas of Freire (1970, 1985, 1993) in approaching education as a democratic process. Returning to a city in crisis, some faculty enacted Freire's call for educators to teach empowerment, highlighting sources of oppression while cultivating agency in marginalized groups. Freire insisted that marginalized groups be actively involved in education processes, and in shaping their own path to freedom: this project was carefully crafted to maintain this focus on the autonomy of those it served.

Role of community participation in the aftermath of Hurricane Katrina

As Freire repeatedly insisted, there is a profound difference between charity and work done *with* the oppressed (1970, 1983). Even though the students involved in this case study were not necessarily oppressed, many of them were homeless or traumatized as a result of the levee breach and the lack of government response to the crisis. For the students and the community, the success of this project, among others, is largely owing to its responsiveness to community needs. Here, community concerns created and guided the objectives of the communication courses, which espoused action-oriented praxis through strategic media production skills. Because the majority of community members were homeless, few residents were able to directly participate in the student media campaigns. Indeed, because the community was largely dispersed, and its residents spread across countless sites of "relocation," community organizing was extremely difficult. Across the board, however, displaced residents avowed their wishes to return home so that they could begin the task of rebuilding their community. Within this context, community participation directed the goals of the courses. In this respect, Freire's concept of committed involvement (1970:56) by the oppressed was operationalized through the community's articulation of their basic needs. Pedagogy and community participation became united here, showing that the roles of activist and educator can be mutually enhancing, rather than mutually exclusive (Kezar et al., 2005). The project strove to enact "critical teaching," as propounded Stephen Brookfield: "developing people's powers of critical thinking so that they can critique the interlocking systems of oppression embedded in contemporary society" (2006:57). In crisis situations, such teaching becomes relevant, necessary and a stepping stone for addressing forms of oppression.

Case study: New Orleans post-Katrina

Although people around the world saw the aftermath of Katrina on TV, with startling poverty and the absence of US government response on display, a brief description of New Orleans in the fall of 2005 is useful to contextualize the environment in which this project developed. The disaster was not a direct result of the hurricane, but of the failure of the man-made levees. Roughly 80 percent of New Orleans flooded when the levees breached, and putrid standing water was not pumped from the lower neighborhoods for over a month. Basic services such as garbage pick-up, water, electricity, medical, emergency, and others were not restored to most of the city for several months; in the hardest-hit and poorest areas, such services were not restored for close to a year, if at all. In many ways, Hurricane Katrina exposed the reality of poverty in the United States (Thomas, 2008). In the most vulnerable (economically as well as geographically) areas, there was a complete collapse of any kind of government and infrastructure. At no level, whether local, state, or federal, did government mobilize to rebuild these areas or return residents to their homes.

According to Amnesty International, the human rights of hurricane victims were consistently violated by the US government and Gulf Coast states. With communities dispersed, government policies in health care, housing, and policing prevented poor minority residents from rebuilding and returning to their homes (Associated Press, 2010). As has happened in many other disaster situations, vital public services, such as public housing,

Figure 12.1: The devastation caused by Hurricane Katrina.

public health care, and public schools, were quickly either eliminated or privatized while many residents were still evacuated (Klein, 2007). Universities throughout New Orleans also used the levee breaches as a means to cleanse universities of faculty and programs, using claims of financial exigency to dispose of nontenured and tenured faculty alike. Disaster situations like Katrina enable businesses to expand by privatizing defunct public goods resulting from the disappearance of public infrastructure, and this practice was rampant in New Orleans. For concerned citizens/residents attempting to return home and in need of public assistance, volunteers were the main source of hope for progress.

Nonprofit connection

The US military did not allow citizens to enter the lower Ninth Ward for several months after the levee failure, but the upper Ninth Ward, which was less profoundly damaged, was open a little over a month after Hurricane Katrina hit.[1] When one of the authors returned to the city and explored the flooded neighborhoods, he found no government or organizational relief presence anywhere in many of the hardest-hit areas. All civil services were notably absent, and they remained so for many months to follow. Apart from the military, the only organizational presence in the Ninth Ward was the nonprofit group Common Ground Relief (henceforth CGR, for brevity), which at its start consisted of a few people who came to respond to the disaster. They acquired a small house and converted it into a "communications center." After making introductions, the question then became "what can a communication professor do to help?" Together CGR and one of the authors developed a plan to bring in what residents wanted the most: volunteers to help gut houses and remove debris. This work was to continue for several years, often battling to rebuild New Orleans' neighborhoods, community centers, churches, schools, houses, and other public treasures. While the accomplishments of the partnership discussed here were significant for some communities, they were minimal in terms of CGR's overall impact for New Orleans, which brought in several million dollars in pro-bono labor and services.

CGR was born when activist and former Black Panther Malik Rahim sent out a national call to action in the immediate aftermath of Hurricane Katrina. His strategy was twofold: to provide short-term relief for victims and long-term support for rebuilding the communities affected by disasters in just and sustainable ways (Hilderbrand et al., 2007). CGR was essentially a response to the lack of an effective emergency strategy by the local, state, and federal governments. They eventually evolved to offer basic services for people returning to their shattered neighborhoods.

The philosophical orientation of the nonprofit group may be one of the most important determinants of an effective relief group. It will establish the character and define the agenda for most outcomes resulting from university course collaborations. CGR's key philosophical pillars, at its inception, were self-determination and political activism. They

Figure 12.2: Common Ground Relief's House of Excellence.

embraced vestiges of Black Panther as well as Zapatista philosophy in "leading by obeying," in other words by asking questions rather than attempting to force their own answers. CGR simply asked what residents needed, and often each neighborhood had different needs. For example, older residents on the West Bank of New Orleans needed medical care, while those in the lower Ninth Ward needed their houses gutted. In this way, CGR differed substantially from the Red Cross, which embraced a one-plan-fits-all needs approach (Hilderbrand et al., 2007). CGR's philosophy resonated with Freirean pedagogy (1970), and the organization was structured to eventually be taken over by residents. "Solidarity, not Charity" was their slogan, and the organization did not assume it knew what was best for a particular community. Thus, while CGR was not the only group the authors' classes worked with, it was one of the most effective partnerships, both in terms of practical results for the community and in terms of student learning outcomes. This is why it is described in detail.

While each disaster is different, it quickly became apparent in New Orleans that there must be an effective infrastructure set-up to receive volunteers, donations, tools, and other needs. In order to be effective, this infrastructure cannot take a large percentage of financial donations for overhead costs, and it needs to be located within the neighborhoods where the disaster took place. It also should only act on local needs, with community members participating in and directing these objectives. In addition, the organization must be efficiently and intelligently run and motivated, and it must accept the pedagogical goals of the classes. It is a fundamental principle of Service Learning that both partners benefit from the partnership: student learning must be enhanced while the goals of the community organization are measurably advanced. CGR met all of these requirements.

The first discussions with the group of key CGR organizers led to an overhaul of the course curriculum to focus on ways in which students could help the needs of lower socioeconomic neighborhoods. Immediately after Katrina, the goal was to bring in volunteers to gut houses and remove debris, but how could this be combined with effective instruction and appropriate learning objectives in the field of mass communication? In addition, after the first year post-Katrina, community needs evolved, shifting the focus toward retaining public infrastructure or community centers where people could organize and/or share resources. Years after Katrina, neighborhoods were still in major need of public schools, health care, after-school programs, and other services. This rapidly evolving environment required faculty and curricula to be adaptable, but as we will explain, the results on student learning and community rebuilding were well worth the investment.

Courses, learning objectives, and beneficiaries

Students began responding to community needs once the semester restarted roughly five months after the hurricane hit. They created databases with national and international media (print, online, radio, etc.) contact information, web pages discussing volunteer processes, and radio public service announcements (PSAs); they packaged DVDs about

CGR, emailed contacts, and wrote numerous on- and offline news articles and releases. They put together "good-bye thank you" packets for volunteers, containing directions and samples of news releases, so the volunteers could contact their local media upon returning home, hopefully to spark additional interest in volunteering, as well as receive recognition for their efforts. Success was to be measured by the generation of volunteers, as well as through the value of donated building supplies and monetary donations.

The hands-on work allowed students to put the strategic communication skills they were learning to use immediately: not only did they study practical media skills and persuasive writing strategies, but they ultimately learned how to organize national and international media campaigns to improve living conditions for thousands of people. They learned through first-hand experience how the media work and are organized, and they discovered how to communicate with and through the media. Allowing students to *do* rather than just listen ensured that their learning was engaged and thorough, the sort of deep learning that many faculty strive to foster. And because they could see that their work had important real-world consequences, the students were more powerfully inspired to be attentive to detail and precision than they could possibly have been when motivated solely by grades. Perhaps most importantly, the students developed a sense of empowerment as change-agents once they saw the fruits of their labor. When the initial results of their campaigns began to come in, first in the hundreds then in the thousands of volunteers, the students felt more confident and accomplished. The experience allowed students to see that their actions and education could positively affect the world. The local campus newspaper interviewed the participating students and lauded their accomplishments, citing one student as saying something similar to "we are always told that students are the future, but now I feel as if I am actually directing it." For our field, the implications are vital: students began to believe that communication could solve problems and that they had agency to positively affect their communities.

The process was not simple, of course. Students were also living through a disaster. Some students from local families had lost their own homes and were dealing with this emotional trauma, whereas many others had not been exposed to the flooded neighborhoods. Bringing the students to see the affected areas at the beginning of the classes helped motivate them, lending them a sense of community and solidarity with those who had lost their homes and way of life. Having the students meet and discuss problems with neighborhood residents also enabled the students to gain a concrete view of the challenges faced by the community, and allowed them to view themselves in "leadership" positions. Ultimately, the students were learning skills that many of the neighborhood residents did not yet have, but in putting these skills to work for the community, they were guided by the expressed needs of the community, and did not presume to tell the displaced and returning residents what they needed. It is also important to remember that many of the students were community members themselves and that they also wanted their neighborhoods to return. Nonetheless, the participation of the community directed the campaigns toward gutting houses and removing debris, then toward rebuilding social, cultural, and political infrastructures in hopes of reestablishing a public sphere. The communication students

Figure 12.3: Some of the communication student volunteers.

became the "SOS" of the community, working directly but behind the scenes with the media by networking and generating publicity. They provided infrastructure that residents were otherwise unable to access.

It is important to stress that the traditional curriculum for the courses was not diluted by the service work, but instead greatly enhanced. Even though the communication field is often viewed as a practical one (Craig, 1989), for faculty who have little choice to but to teach "skills courses," there is a way to incorporate social justice and community participation into the curriculum. Indeed, many students may have been socialized into a system that inhibits questioning or resistance, and that expends enormous energy in obscuring its own workings from its citizens. If educators can provide the conditions that wrest students from complacency to conscientization, they can not only foster the attainment of educational thresholds but also empower students as agents of social change. Requiring them to use their skills and privileges in the interests of less fortunate neighbors benefits both parties. Thus, students in their liminal situation can serve as intermediaries between the university and the community, achieving a "big-picture" grasp of social systems as they come to perceive their own complicity and responsibility. Along these lines, Brookfield (2006) notes, "a critical adult … is one who can discern how the ethic of capitalism, and the logic of bureaucratic rationality, pushes people into ways of living that perpetuate economic, racial, and gender oppression. … a critical adult [is] one who takes action to create more democratic, collectivist economic and social forms" (p. 56).

Students involved in the post-Katrina project attained what Freire called "conscientization": they came to experience the workings of social, cultural, and economic systems in ways that might otherwise have remained abstract and distant. They learned about social systems, oppression, discrimination and inequity, community problems, local politics, how nonprofits operate, and they gained a sense of purpose, along with the strategic media skills to achieve public goals. They gained a commitment to analyzing and criticizing these systems, and they earned a sense of agency in attempting to alter them. They also did important work in rebuilding a disadvantaged and devastated community by assisting many displaced New Orleanians to return home. After participating in the recovery, many students continued being active in other projects benefiting various public goods. This was exciting and encouraging to witness.

The nonprofit groups gained in their volunteer workload: they also gained time and publicity, in the form of articles, news releases, and so on. They gained postage, equipment, paper, and CDs, but the labor was by far the most important benefit. For the community, one of the only means by which neighborhoods could benefit was through the influx of volunteers, who gutted houses free of charge to the former residents. Because contractors were in short supply in proportion to the thousands of flooded homes, they could command enormous fees, and citizens who were already being stalled and even cheated by insurance companies and neglected by their officials could not have mustered the funds to pay for this first step toward returning home. Not only did the work save them each thousands of dollars, it often spared them the emotional trauma of digging through the rotting, mold-encased relics of their former lives. Even with all of the much-valued volunteer relief efforts, given the immensity of the disaster, tens of thousands of New Orleanians were still unable to return to their homes and neighborhoods.

Importance of power relations

While there were many successes and victories for disadvantaged populations in New Orleans post-Katrina, existing power structures will always threaten the efficacy of participatory social change projects. Sustaining such a relationship with the community is often difficult, mired in politics at many levels. Emergency relief situations, in particular, are "often among the most politicized in the world" (Anderson & Woodrow, 1989:39).

University, departmental, city, state, and even federal politics will inevitably affect short- and long-term outcomes of any project that addresses social justice. In general, scholarship examining social justice projects in the communication field adopts a supportive, yet cautionary stance, largely because concepts of social justice as well as projects that address inequities can be deeply unpopular with elites (Servaes & Malikhao, 2008). Once a university Service Learning project crosses the line and works for social justice through participatory communication, problems are likely to arise. Indeed, as this article will demonstrate, a course that successfully addresses structural inequities is likely to attract attention, because universities often function to perpetuate dominant social relations, ideologies, and practices (Apple, 1982; Giroux, 1981). Indeed, in discussing Lozare (1989), Servaes & Malikhao (2008) note that authentic participatory communication projects that empower communities should expect resistance from those who favor the status quo. Resistance can occur when participatory projects transfer control from officials to beneficiaries (Huesca, 2008). In discussing how this process works through a model of participatory communication, Servaes (2008: 202) notes:

> Participation involves the redistribution of power. Participation aims at redistributing the elites' power so that a community can become a full-fledged democratic one. As such, it directly threatens those whose position and/or very existence depends upon power and its exercise over others. Reactions to such threats are sometimes overt, but most often are manifested as less visible, yet steady and continuous resistance.

Palmeri (2006) and Pearce (2006) make it quite clear that resistance to participatory communication projects is not limited to influences outside the university. It is not uncommon, and probably more the norm, that faculty in the communication field resist and oppose efforts to embrace social justice.

The rebuilding of New Orleans became politicized quite rapidly after the failure of the levees. On one side, business groups and some politicians wanted a smaller city footprint, while displaced residents naturally wanted to return home and rebuild. Many of those being denied the right to return to their neighborhoods were lower-income African-Americans. This was duly noted by the United Nations Human Rights Committee, which cited the poor response by the United States to disadvantaged citizens during Katrina and its aftermath. It noted, "the Committee ... remains concerned about information that poor people, and in particular African-Americans, were disadvantaged by the rescue and evacuation plans implemented when Hurricane Katrina hit the United States of America, and continue to be disadvantaged under the reconstruction plans" (Perlstein, 2006:1).

Each side of the rebuilding efforts had various supporters. Local and federal government officials, university administrators, and senior faculty were not united in terms of support for social justice-oriented projects. Each group overtly and/or covertly resisted efforts to rebuild poorer areas of the city, which eventually led to the cessation of the community-engaged relief efforts described in this chapter.[2] Indeed, universities located in flooded areas also saw opportunities to expand if fewer residents returned to the neighborhoods bordering the institutions. At this time in New Orleans, it was not in the best interest of any university to be affiliated with a community-directed faculty member's participatory relief project that directly questioned and challenged the interests of local elites and the business class. Faculty participating in these kinds of responses to disaster situations will need to thoughtfully consider the ramifications of their projects beforehand. However, for educators who find themselves in similar situations and choose to organize and participate in similar projects, they will likely find these experiences to be the most rewarding and exciting of their teaching careers.

Role of communication as change-agent

Advocating this type of project and pedagogy has obvious implications for the way educators view the communication field. Communication programs, like higher education in general, can be seen as in crisis. Market forces are pressuring institutions to remake themselves as preprofessional training grounds, whereas some educators in traditional higher education may still aspire to cultivate intellectual curiosity and critical inquiry. On the one hand, faculty are often expected to offer professional skills training for a media-related workforce, where instruction focuses primarily on providing hands-on skills like newspaper layout and the creation of news releases. On the other hand, many programs see themselves as providing social science courses based on mass communication theory and research. Most programs endeavor to combine the two to some degree. Unfortunately, few of them manage to address the problems facing many populations – hunger, food crises, homelessness, energy crises, deepening economic inequities, and an expanding global economic system that is exacerbating these issues around the world (Klein, 2007). Educators need to ask whose interests are served by the content and structure of public and private communication programs alike. Communication faculty and programs also need to ask how they can respond to the changes and disasters in the United States and around the world.

This chapter suggests that faculty can provide highly effective instruction of practical skills without sacrificing the rigor of sociological and critical analysis, and that working with a community-directed nonprofit can address some forms of oppression or injustice. Communication faculty members are uniquely poised to respond to crisis situations, harnessing student energy and passion to important social causes while enhancing learning. There is indeed a way to bridge academia with the public interest at the classroom level.

In the case of this project in New Orleans, the role of the educator was first as a teacher and second as a participatory change-agent. Using this university/nonprofit/community partnership as a case study, then, we argue that communication departments can and should embrace roles as potential community change-agents. We argue that active education based on community needs can directly affect social inequities. Extending knowledge and resources during crisis situations is a great place to start, but this approach can be expanded to address local needs during "noncrisis" situations through experiential and community-led pedagogies. A re-envisioning of the nature of the communication field toward understanding itself as a potential change-agent for community needs can positively impact crises and noncrisis community needs.

Along these lines, one of our most important goals as educators is to enable students to achieve critical consciousness, an awareness of their sociocultural existences as constructed and ideological – and hence subject to improvement. To this end, educators must be willing to relinquish their central places in the classroom, surrendering control so that students have the liberty to build a sense of empowerment, which shows them their own right, responsibility, and capacity to change the world around them. Teaching in "a structuralized worldview that analyzes private experiences and personal dilemmas as structurally produced" cannot be accomplished solely with books or with abstractions (Brookfield, 2006:58). The post-Katrina projects did precisely this. Perhaps the most valuable aspect of the students' learning as a result of this project was their progress toward Freire's (1970, 1995) "conscientization."

There is no doubt a need to address critical justice and equity issues facing communities through communication strategies (Thomas, 2008). Fixing the world's problems is a grandiose goal, but a modest place to start is having a class "adopt-a-non-profit." There are thousands of them in the United States and around the world. Find one in New Orleans, in a local community or country, study it, and try to partner with it. Closely examine the organization to see where its money goes, how closely it incorporates community participation, what students can contribute and learn from it, and study the backgrounds and philosophies of its members. Work with local papers to raise awareness about the issue, start student projects to create news releases and letters to editors, create Internet pages where people can donate money, or film promotional videos for PR purposes for the nonprofits. Interested faculty need to create and share templates to address situations of crisis like what New Orleans experienced: maybe campaign templates, templates for Internet pages, for videos, and so on, that students can use and transfer to nonprofits around the world. Maybe someday soon someone will establish a pedagogy center, where educators can share syllabi, assignments, and case studies with each other, as well as other interested parties. This university course-non-profit partnership, focusing on social justice and community participatory communication, came to an end like many projects before it. It was severed as a result of the power relations described in this chapter, yet the idea, outcome, participants, and proponents live on better prepared for the next crisis. All signs point to more crises if our global political and economic culture does not change. We urge academics to consider partnering with community or nonprofit groups that help address some of the problems facing the world.

References

Anderson, M. B. & Woodrow, P. J. (1989). *Rising from the Ashes: Development Strategies in Times of Disaster*. Boulder, CO: Westview Press.

Apple, M. (1982). *Cultural and Economic Reproduction in Education*. London: Routledge.

Artz, L. (2001). Critical Ethnography for Communication Studies: Dialogue and Social Justice in Service-Learning. *Southern Communication Journal*, 66, 239–250.

——— (2006). Conclusion: On the Consequence of Defining Social Justice, in Swartz, O. (ed.), *Social Justice and Communication Scholarship*. Mahwah, NJ: Lawrence Erlbaum, pp. 239–248.

Associated Press. (2010, April 09). Amnesty International Accuses Federal, State Governments of Katrina-Related Abuses. *Associated Press*. Retrieved June 9, 2010 from *http://www.nola.com/politics/index.ssf/2010/04/amnesty_international_accuses.html*.

Bain, K. (2004). *What the Best College Teachers Do*. Cambridge: Harvard University Press.

Barber, B. R. (1998). *A Place for Us: How to Make Society Civil and Democracy Strong.* New York: Hill and Wang.

Barnett, R. (2007). *A Will to Learn: Being a Student in an Age of Uncertainty.* New York: Open University Press (McGraw-Hill).

Boyer, E. (1990). *Scholarship Reconsidered: Priorities of the Professorate.* Princeton, NJ: The Carnegie Foundation for the Advancement of Teaching.

——— (1994, March 9). Creating the New American College. *The Chronicle of Higher Education,* A48.

Bringle, R. G. & Hatcher, J. A. (1996). Implementing Service-Learning in Higher Education. *Journal of Higher Education,* 67, 221–239.

Brookfield, S. D. (2006). A Critical Theory Perspective on Faculty Development, in Robertson, D. R. & Nilson, L. B. (eds.), *To Improve the Academy.* San Francisco: Jossey-Bass, pp. 55–69.

Craig, R. T. (1989). Communication as a Practical Discipline, in Dervin, B., Grossberg, L., O'Keefe, B. J., & Wartella, E. (eds.), *Rethinking Communication: Vol. 1. Paradigm Issues.* Newbury Park, CA: SAGE, pp. 97–122.

Damon, W. (1998, October 16). The Path to a Civil Society Goes through the University. *The Chronicle of Higher Education,* B4–B5.

Dewey, J. (1936). *Democracy and Education: An Introduction to the Philosophy.* New York: Macmillan.

Eggler, B. (2005, October 29). City Planners Want Role in Rebuilding; Some Felt Bypassed by Mayor's Panel. *Times-Picayune,* 3.

Freire, Paulo. (1970). *A Pedagogy of the Oppressed* (Rev. ed.) (trans. Ramos, M. B.). New York: Continuum International Publishing Group.

——— (1985). *The Politics of Education: Culture, Power and Liberation* (D. Macedo, Trans.). South Hadley: Bergin and Garvey.

——— (1993). *Education for Critical Consciousness.* New York: Continuum International Publishing Group.

——— (2005). *Education for Critical Consciousness.* New York: Continuum International Publishing Group.

Gibson, M. K., Kostecki, E. M., & Lucas, M. K. (2001). Instituting Principles of Best Practice for Service-Learning in the Communication Curriculum. *Southern Communication Journal,* 66(3), 187–200.

Giroux, H. (1981). *Ideology, Culture and the Process of Schooling.* Philadelphia, PA: Temple University Press.

Hilderbrand, S., Crow, S., & Fithian, L. (2007). Common Ground Relief, in The South End Press Collective (ed.), *What Lies Beneath: Katrina, Race, and the State of the Nation.* Cambridge, MA: South End Press, pp. 80–98.

Hooks, Bell (Gloria Watkins). (1994). *Teaching to Transgress: Education as the Practice of Freedom.* New York: Routledge.

Huesca, R. (2008). Tracing the History of Communication Approaches to Development: A Critical Appraisal, in Servaes, J. (ed.), *Communication for Development and Social Change.* Thousand Oaks, CA: SAGE Publications Inc., pp. 180–198.

Kezar, A. J., Chambers, T. C., Burkhardt, J. C., & Associates (eds.). (2005). *Higher Education for the Public Good: Emerging Voices from a National Movement*. San Francisco: Jossey-Bass.

Klein, N. (2007). *The Shock Doctrine: The Rise of Disaster Capitalism*. New York: Metropolitan Books.

Lozare, B. (1989, February). Power and conflict: Hidden dimensions of communication, participative planning and action. Paper presented at Participation: A key concept in communication for change and development. University of Poona, Pune.

Moller, J. (2007, May 18). LRA Members Defend Their Performance to Senate Panel; Bill to Dissolve Agency Is Shelved for Now. *Times-Picayune*, 2.

Palmer, P. (1997). *The Courage to Teach: Exploring the Inner Landscape of a Teacher's Life*. San Francisco: Jossey-Bass.

Palmeri, T. (2006). Media Activism in a "Conservative" City: Modeling Citizenship, in Swartz, O. (ed.), *Social Justice and Communication Scholarship*. Mahwah, NJ: Lawrence Erlbaum, pp. 149–173.

Pearce, W. B. (1998). On Putting Social Justice in the Discipline of Communication and Putting Enriched Concepts of Communication in Social Justice Research and Practice. *Journal of Applied Communication Research*, 26, 272–278.

———— (2006). Reflections on a Project to Promote Social Justice in Communication Education and Research, in Swartz, O. (ed.), *Social Justice and Communication Scholarship*. Mahwah, NJ: Lawrence Erlbaum, pp. 215–238.

Perlstein, M. (2006, July 29). Panel Blasts Katrina Response; N.O. Activists Hail U.N. Announcement. *Times-Picayune*, 1, Metro Section.

Pollock, M. A., Artz, L., Frey, L. R., Pearce, W. B., & Murphy, B. A. O. (1996). Navigating between Scylla and Charybdis: Continuing the Dialogue on Communication and Social Justice. *Communication Studies*, 47, 142–151.

Russell, G. (2006, February 12). Race Could Define Mayor Election; Nagin Already Facing Roster of White Rivals. *Times-Picayune*, 1.

Servaes, J. (2008). Communication for Development Approaches of Some Governmental and Non-governmental Agencies, in Servaes, J. (ed.), *Communication for Development and Social Change*. Thousand Oaks, CA: SAGE Publications Inc., pp. 201–218.

Servaes, J. & Malikhao, P. (2008). Development Communication Approaches in an International Perspective, in Servaes, J. (ed.), *Communication for Development and Social Change*. Thousand Oaks, CA: SAGE Publications Inc., pp. 158–179.

Stage, F., Muller, P., Kinzie, J., & Simmons, A. (1998). *Creating Learning Centered Classrooms. What Does Learning Theory Have to Say?* Washington, DC: George Washington University, Graduate School of Education and Human Development.

Swartz, O. (2006). *Social Justice and Communication Scholarship*. Mahwah, NJ: Lawrence Erlbaum.

Thomas, P. (2008). Communication and the Persistence of Poverty: The Need for a Return to Basics, in Servaes, J. (ed.), *Communication for Development and Social Change*. Thousand Oaks, CA: SAGE Publications Inc., pp. 31–44.

Winkler-Schmit, D. (2009, January 26). Brandon Darby- FBI Informant & Common Ground Co-founder. *The Gambit Weekly*. Retrieved June 9, 2010 from *http://bestofneworleans.com/gyrobase/Content?oid=oid%3A49882*.

Notes

1   Despite this prohibition, in the months immediately following Katrina, some volunteers borrowed military uniforms to sneak past the military checkpoints into the lower Ninth Ward to surreptitiously rebuild and paint a house. The goal was to inspire returning residents not to give up, that it was possible to rebuild and that there was help (Sakura Kone of *http://www.savewesleyunited.org*, personal communication, June 17, 2009).

2   The lack of federal government response suggested that the government did not see rebuilding sections of New Orleans as a priority. The Federal Bureau of Investigation eventually infiltrated CGR through at least one informant who mismanaged the organization by pitting people against each other, verbally abusing others, and by purging volunteers who did not agree with various methods, ultimately making the organization ineffective by disenfranchising volunteers (Winkler-Schmit, 2009). The origins of these tactics likely stem from similar techniques used by the US government on various activist groups during the civil rights movement. Ultimately CGR became too influential and powerful for governing elites.

At the local level, the business class clearly conveyed to the Mayor that it wanted a smaller city by keeping some areas while eliminating other neighborhoods. The Mayor's "Bring New Orleans Back Commission" consisted primarily of business leaders (Eggler, 2005) whose official recovery plan called to reduce the city's footprint (Russell, 2006). Indeed, this was a concern because poorer (predominantly African-American) sections of New Orleans were more likely to flood than white sections (Russell, 2006). In order to have a city with a smaller footprint, many leaders advocated rebuilding only some (less damaged, more prosperous) neighborhoods. In these circumstances, work toward returning homeowners to the Ninth Ward and other disadvantaged areas was seen by some as subversive.

At the university level, the university president was the chairman of a state Recovery Authority, which was critiqued for the slow pace of recovery after the hurricane (Moller, 2007). The university did not invest in its Service Learning program, but the institution did allow the program on campus if it ran on grant money. However, when CGR volunteers and community members came to classes on campus to work directly with the students, they were on occasion harassed by police for their appearance. To some of the employees at this small, Southern, and conservative religious institution, the volunteers and community members did not conform to their perceptions of appropriate dress or way of thinking.

Support for this kind of community engagement at the departmental level was not strong among senior faculty members. The chair was reluctant to support an application for a grant to work with the recovery and was unable to comprehend the connections between the field of mass communication, service learning, and recovery work. Once the grant was funded and course releases were issued, this created tension, jealously, and outright anger on behalf of the senior colleagues. While resources and volunteers began arriving as a direct result of the student campaigns, the grant recipient was still pressured to limit or stop working with the community. With the classes eventually generating over 5,000 volunteers, a million dollars in pro-bono labor to the community and a national award, one influential senior faculty member still asked "What have the mass communication faculty done anyway?" Although perhaps harmful to disadvantaged communities in New Orleans or beneficial to those who are threatened by empowerment of the disadvantaged, these kinds of attitudes eventually led to an environment where it was best to part ways.

Chapter 13

Gender as a Variable in the Framing of Homelessness

Solina Richter, Katharina Kovacs Burns, Ramadimetja Shirley Mogale, and Jean Chaw-Kant

The media is a powerful communication tool, and the journalists are influential in creating cultural awareness, or an "awareness culture" concerning broad and specific societal issues or needs. The public, who include citizens, health and social service providers, governments, and decision-makers, are not only made aware of these issues and needs, but are also provided with verbal and/or pictorial context surrounding the issues, which society should address through social change. Homelessness in our society is one of those areas fraught with images, values, and emotion, which the media can frame and position to influence the public's views and actions to either support the status quo or to advocate for changes that impact on those who are homeless as well as society as a whole. The media plays an important role in setting the public agenda, mobilizing public opinions (framing), and swaying decision-makers to offer possible solutions around gender and racial, disparity, health, and other social issues experienced by people who are homeless. Many factors influence how this type of social issue is communicated or framed by the media, for example the social-cultural and political context. The newspapers' ownership and their historical context can also influence the amount and type or emphasis of coverage of this specific social issue. A factor less studied is the gender of the journalists and whether this is a variable in the framing of societal issues such as homelessness. In this chapter we investigated whether the gender of the journalists influenced agenda setting or framing of disparity, health, and other social issues faced by individuals or families who are homeless.

The chapter starts with a background overview of the key concepts of the media's framing of homelessness as a social or societal issue, and the arguments that arise around the gender of the journalist and how this might influence the outcomes of homelessness communications to the public. The focus of this chapter is the description, analysis, and discussion of the results of a case study based in Alberta, Canada. In this case, gender is investigated as a variable in the media's framing and influence concerning homelessness as a social issue and as part of cultural awareness or an "awareness culture."

Background

The media characterizes homelessness through specific words, images, and values, which shape the portrayal of people who are homeless and the related range of inequity and inequality issues and challenges they experience. Without the media to describe the circumstances of those who are homeless, the majority of the public would construct their own reference of homeless people in a number of ways. Some would form their perceptions based on their occasional personal experiences with panhandlers on street corners or from sidewalk squatters. Others, who do not spend any time in the inner city centers or locations where the people who are homeless most often frequent, may not know about them and their issues except from the newspapers or telecasted news.

Kinder (2007) explained ways in which the news media influenced how the public made sense of social issues such as homelessness (framing), how the public decided on what was important about homelessness (agenda setting), and how the public evaluated existing policies regarding the management of homeless people and their situation that politicians placed before them (priming). A process model of framing described the interconnectedness between frame building, frame setting, individual-level effects of framing, and journalists as audiences. Frame building refers to structural factors of the media system, or individual characteristics of journalists, such as gender, that impact the framing of news content, whereas frame setting is concerned with the importance of issue attributes. Individual-level effects of framing focus on the impact of thematic media framing of issues on attributions of personal and or societal responsibility (Scheufele, 1999).

The writing of human-interest stories is influenced by different humanistic and environmental factors and contexts of the journalist, including personal experiences or relationships, gender, economics, politics, societal views, and community cultural expressions of interest. Most of these factors are acknowledged as influencers of the journalists in their portrayal of homelessness, but what do we know or understand about the gender of journalists and its possible importance in media framing of homelessness as a societal issue? Differences between men and women in many contexts have been well studied from two contrasting arguments – that there are gender differences in physical, mental, cognitive, psychological, and communication characteristics (difference hypothesis), versus the gender similarities hypothesis stating that these differences are very minor or the evidence does not exist to clearly show that there are many gender differences (Hyde, 2005). A differences hypothesis on gender has been made popular through mass media and in popular books such as *Men are from Mars and Women are from Venus* by John Gray (1992). Hyde (2005) moved toward a different view – a similarity hypothesis that argued that there are more similarities than differences between males and females. Males and females are similar on most, but a few psychological as well as physical variables. Hyde warns against an exaggeration of the differences between males and females that could lead to stereotyping of females as caring and nurturing and males as lacking these characteristics. This latter stereotyping has been culturally accepted and has a large cost implication in various areas including work, parenting, and relationships. These arguments are important to study and understand, especially for their implications concerning how men and women communicate issues and facts in the media. How does this relate to the journalists' framing of homelessness as a societal issue? Why do we need to know if there are potential differences of male/female journalist and their stories?

In the news media, the gender of journalists has been linked to gender representation in news stories that can lead to biases; for example, male journalists tend to quote male subjects. Armstrong (2004) noted, "if men are continually used as knowledgeable sources and women are repeatedly underrepresented or misrepresented in news coverage, an inaccurate reflection of society will be presented" (p. 140). In contrast, female journalists are more likely to advocate for women and address issues specifically affecting women. Len-Rios et al. (2008) noted that female reporters are more likely to use female sources, thus gender does matter in story sourcing. Although the media professionals are key players in "framing" the homeless and their situation, decision-makers, researchers, and others also have a role in creating a social constructionist frame of homelessness. How are our beliefs and construction of social issues caused? Boghossian (as cited in Anderson, 2008) argued, "we are not actually moved to belief by things that justify: we are only moved by our own social interests" (p. 62). With this view, the gender of the journalists might influence how we frame a social issue such as homelessness, which in turn can either be supportive or nonsupportive of the homeless. Effective policies are based not only on evidence, but also on media experiences and perceptions that support the resulting social constructionist frame of the homeless and their situation. We note that this is a perception that not all journalists agree with, particularly if they believe they have a social responsibility to objectively report the "real world" experiences of homeless people.

Case study of gender as a variable in the media's framing of homelessness

This case study, situated in Alberta, Canada, focused on the media's portrayal of homelessness in two key newspapers in Edmonton and Calgary. The information gained from this case study will be a significant reference for other similar media studies. The purpose of our study was to explore the content of newspaper coverage of homelessness and homeless people and determine whether gender differences existed in how male and female journalists report on homelessness. In order to identify how the various issues and challenges were portrayed, we examined the content of the media coverage and the corresponding gender of the journalists reporting on these stories.

A descriptive, cross-sectional design was followed in this study. A purposive sampling technique was used to obtain articles. The basic methodology for this research was content analysis (Krippendorff, 1980). Content analysis has previously been used in both print and electronic media and has been used with social topics such as violence against women and children (Oxman-Martinez et al., 2009; Sims, 2008), crime reporting (Taylor, 2009; Yanich, 2004), homelessness (Buck et al., 2004) and urban health (Berry et al., 2007; Campbell & Gibbs, 2008; Piaseu et al., 2004). The unit of analysis was newspaper articles. Based on circulation, readership popularity, and online accessibility, two local newspapers were chosen for analysis, one from each major city in Alberta: *The Edmonton Journal* and *The Calgary Herald*. The daily circulation rates of these two newspapers were identified to be at least 100,000 on an average day as per the Canadian Newspaper Association (Daily Newspaper Circulation Report, 2011).

The online database Canadian Newsstand, which searches articles in all Canadian news media, was used to search for newspaper articles over a 5-year period (July 2000–June 2005). This period marked a change in the economic development and "boom" in Alberta and resulted in increasing numbers of identified people living with low income or poverty, or who were counted as homeless in both Edmonton and Calgary. The increased cost of housing (rented or ownership) combined with the high cost of utilities made it difficult for many families in the low-income group to afford housing (The City of Calgary, 2006; Edmonton Joint Planning Committee on Housing, 2004).

Search terms for newspaper articles included "homeless" and "homelessness." A modified rating scale for article selection was adapted from Buck et al. (2004). The articles were rated on a 4-point scale: 1 = low intensity/little relevance, 2 = moderate intensity/some relevance, 3 = high intensity/theme, and 4 = very high intensity/major theme. One team member rated each article and two other investigators independently rated a subset (20 percent) of the same articles. Discrepancies were resolved by consensus. Statistical analysis of the data was performed using the Statistical Package for Social Science Research (SPSS 11.5). Descriptive information on the content of the articles and gender of the journalist was extracted using an extraction form. Evaluation of the relationship between the content themes and gender was analyzed using chi square.

Results and analysis

Identifying major themes in media coverage

A total of 4,167 articles contained the words "homeless" or "homelessness" for the period July 2000–June 2005; 1,887 from *The Edmonton Journal* and 2,280 from *The Calgary Herald*. All articles with a rating of 3 (high intensity/theme) and 4 (very high intensity/major theme) were included for the content analysis. Thirteen percent ($n = 545$) were ranked 3 or 4 and subsequently analyzed.

The research team identified three themes with associated subthemes from the content analysis. Under the theme of "Personal economics," housing and related issues had the most articles (29 percent), followed by "Community aid and support" with 23 percent of articles. For the theme of "Profiling of homelessness or people who are homeless," about 26 percent of articles focused on "Family and socio-economic aspects." The third theme was "Causes of homelessness" with significantly less articles. Table 13.1 provides the details of thematic analysis results and the frequencies of these articles for both *Edmonton* and *Calgary* combined.

For the gender analysis we removed all articles that were anonymous and the articles for which the gender of the journalist was unsure and unknown. Seventy-four articles were written anonymously ($n = 67$) or the gender of the authors was uncertain ($n = 7$, authors only used initials). The 67 anonymously written articles were analyzed as to the themes and subthemes. Table 13.2 provides this analysis. There was more diversity of articles by themes

Table 13.1: Major homelessness themes and coverage in newspaper articles within *The Edmonton Journal* and *The Calgary Herald* (2000–2005).

Major themes and subthemes		
Personal economics	**Personal economics**	**Frequency of articles (%)**
Housing-related issues	- Emergency shelters, neighborhood - Complaints/protests/NIMBY's - Tent cities - River valley camps - Eviction from city parks - Weather related (cold or heat spell) - Seeking shelter (church, parkades, train station) - Affordable housing	29.4
Community aid and support	- Food and clothing - Support programs and fundraising - Charity - Helping the homeless	23.2
Illegal activities	- Begging/panhandling - Bottle picking - Illegal activities/crime related - Victims of crime/abuse/child abuse in past	4.8
		Total: 57.4
Profiling of homelessness or homeless people		
Family and socioeconomic aspects	- Family demographics (family/single parent/women, children, seniors, youth, second-generation homeless, visible minority/aboriginal) - Profiling character traits of the homeless or a day in the life of a homeless person - Discrimination - The rights of homeless people - The homeless person's escape from the street or how homelessness was overcome	26.1
Health-related issues	- Mental illness - Alcoholism - Drug abuse - Susceptibility to diseases/lack of hygiene/sanitation	3.4
		Total: 29.5
Causes of homelessness		
Social factors as cause	- Family break-up - Lack of support from family and friends	2.2
Government reduction of social assistance	- Government cutbacks - Government spending/aid - Economic factors as cause (minimum wage/economic boom/jobs)	10.9
		Total: 13.1

Table 13.2: Types of articles (news, opinion, column, and profile) broken down by themes and subthemes, as written by anonymous journalists ($n = 67$).

Type of articles	Personal economics		Illegal activities	Profiling of homelessness or homeless people		Causes of homelessness		
	Housing-related issues	Community aid and support		Family and socioeconomic aspects	Health-related issues	Social factors as cause	Government reduction of social assistance	
News	8 (12%)	9 (13.4%)	11 (16.4%)	11 (16.4%)	3 (4.4%)	0 0%	10 (14.9%)	52 77.5%
Opinion	1 (1.5%)	1 (1.5%)	0	0	0	0	1 (1.5%)	3 4.5%
Column	5 (7.5%)	2 (3%)	0	1 (1.5%)	0	1 (1.5%)	2 (3%)	11 16.5%
Profile	0	1 (1.5%)	0	0	0	0	0	1 1.5%
Total	14 21%	13 19.4%	11 16.4%	12 17.9%	3 4.4%	1 1.5%	13 19.4%	67 100%

and subthemes in this anonymous group of writers. In addition to similar ones mentioned generally in Table 13.1, this group also had more articles on "Illegal activities" under the theme "Personal economics," and on "government reduction of social assistance" under the theme "Causes of homelessness."

Our assumption was that authors would keep their name anonymous only when they were writing about more sensitive issues. News articles are generally written by newspaper journalists and the other categories are written by freelance journalists and/or the public. Freelance journalists and columnists are allowed more subjective views and opinions. Most (77.5 percent) of the anonymous articles were published as news articles and 21 percent as opinions and column articles.

Table 13.3 shows the findings of the gender of journalists as aligned by the subtheme of their articles. Generally, there were 31 more articles written by female journalists (251 compared with 220). A chi-square analysis determined that there were no significant differences between the subthemes addressed and the gender of the journalist. Although we found no significant difference between the gender of the journalist and the themes of news articles, our findings revealed some noteworthy trends. More female journalists reported housing-related issues (emergency shelters, neighborhood, complaints/protests/NIMBY's, tent cities, river valley camps, eviction from city parks, weather related, seeking shelter, and affordable housing) and family and socioeconomic aspects (family demographics, profiling character traits of the homeless or a day in the life of a homeless person, discrimination, the

Table 13.3: Number of articles identified by gender differences and themes/subthemes ($N = 471$).

Personal economics		
Themes	**Male**	**Female**
1. Housing-related issues	62 (13.1%)	77 (16.3%)
2. Community aid and support	56 (11.9%)	53 (11.3%)
3. Illegal activities	11 (2.3%)	12 (2.5%)
Profiling of homelessness or homeless people		
4. Family and socioeconomic aspects	51 (10.8%)	72 (15.3%)
5. Health-related issues	7 (1.5%)	9 (1.9%)
Causes of homelessness		
6. Social factors as cause	4 (0.9%)	6 (1.3%)
7. Government reduction and social assistance	29 (6.2%)	22 (4.7%)
Total	220	251

Results of chi-square test between the subthemes addressed and the gender of the journalist

	Value	Asymp. Sig. (2 sided)
Pearson Chi-Square	1.554[a]	.460
Likelihood ratio	1.556	.459
Linear-by-linear	.006	.937
Association number of valid cases	472	

[a]Four cells (19.0 percent) have expected count less than 5. The minimum expected count is 27.41.

rights of homeless people, the homeless person's escape from the street or how homelessness was overcome). Male journalists tended to report on government reduction and social assistance.

A more specific comparative analysis of the type of article written (news, letter to the editor, opinion, column, and profile) and the gender of the journalist is provided in Table 13.4. No statistically significant difference was found between the gender of the journalist and the type of article written, but again trends were identified. More news articles and letters to the editor were written by female journalists.

Discussion

Gender issues in newspaper coverage have previously been researched on topics such as the framing of violence and crimes committed against women (Oxman-Martinez et al., 2009; Sims, 2008), the political election (Liebler & Smith, 1997), people with disabilities (Gold & Auslander, 1999), and coverage of cancer (Len-Rios et al., 2008), but according to our search,

Table 13.4: Gender distribution for different types of articles (news, letter to editor, opinion, column, and profile) (*n* = 471).

Type of article	Gender	
	Male	Female
News	161 (34.1%)	186 (39.5%)
Letter to editor	26 (5.5%)	37 (7.9%)
Opinion	6 (1.3%)	5 (1.1%)
Column	26 (5.5%)	23 (4.9%)
Profile	1 (0.2%)	0
Total	220 (46.6%)	251 (3.4%)

the media's framing of homelessness with gender of the journalists is a new investigation that has not been researched and/or published.

Journalism has historically been recognized as a predominantly male occupation. The involvement of women in journalism has changed significantly in some countries over the last decade (Cann & Mohr, 2001), although Galagher (2001) argued that women still have little decision-making power inside the media organizations and in political and economic organizations with which the media interface. Today, women are the majority within the journalism profession; however, they still remain highly vulnerable to being stereotyped (Galagher, 2001). For example, in a study conducted by Zeldes et al. (2007) on the 2002 Michigan gubernatorial campaign in the United States, it was found that male reporters outnumbered female reporters although at that time women made up more than half of the journalist population. They also proved that female reporters were more likely to use different sources than their male counterparts. Female reporters were much more likely than male reporters to use female sources and provide them with more airtime. In another study, 56 percent of the journalists that participated in a survey conducted in ten European countries indicated their belief that women were:

> still directed towards topics which traditionally have had less status (human interest, social affairs and culture), rather than being steered towards the 'high status' topics such as business, economics or foreign news. Men were thought to be more convergent, more dispassionate, and more analytical than women. Women have been assumed to be better at writing the empathetic, people-oriented stories (Gallagher, 2001:64).

Soderlund et al. (1989 as cited in Cann & Mohr, 2001) also emphasized that women were more likely to report stories of a more general nature. The difference in the writing style between male and female authors was found in a study conducted by Siebel (2008) where she reported on how the gender of the authors played a role in how arguments were constructed around tobacco control. In their study, males and females differed in their persuasive appeals. The men defended their arguments "by writing in an accusatory, resolute and directive manner, pointed fingers, made judgment-laden statements about others, and directed action through powerful language" (Siebel, 2008:419). The differences hypothesis reiterated this statement by arguing that "women speak in a moral voice of caring, whereas men speak in a voice of justice" (Gilligan, 1982 as cited in Hyde, 2005:589). Regardless of evidence that contradicts this statement, the differences hypothesis has a strong influence in western culture. Female reporters are often assigned to health, education, and social issues, while men reporters are given the political and economic assignments, which are seen as part of the career path to senior editorial and media management positions. We found this to be aligned with our study, as topics such as housing-related issues and family and socioeconomic aspects were generally covered by female journalists, and topics such as government spending covered by male journalists.

Ziegler & White (1990) suggested that gender-role typing continues to exist in the field of journalism, but Sebba (1994) argued that the way men and women report news were similar and that the differences detected can be attributed to personality rather than gender. Empirical indications show that there were mixed results on how the reporters framed news. However, Craft & Wanta (2004) argued that reporting is based on gender, race, or ideology. More politically conservative newspapers and those that hold more traditional gender-role beliefs attributed gender differences more to biological factors than liberal newspapers (Brescoll & LaFrance, 2004). Our findings are in line with those of Liebler & Smith (1997) in that we postulate that journalist attributes such as individual experience and background, knowledge and personal association, or contact with homeless people might influence what is written irrespective of gender. In a recent qualitative study, Richter et al. (2010) interviewed journalists who said that personal interests and contact with the homeless population have motivated them to write a story about homelessness. Five of the journalists that were interviewed in this study reflected their personal experiences with homelessness as either someone they loved or an experience they briefly had. A particular journalist shared that his own brief personal experience of living on the street was negative but it allowed him to gain an appreciation for the reality of homelessness. He suggested that education along with knowing how to access critical resources was essential for knowing how to escape homelessness. This is further supported by Armstrong & Nelson (2005) who stated, "gender differences may exist with respect to cognitive processing based on different world views and ways of thinking" (p. 823).

Differences in reporting that are normally attributed to gender may not be gender based but instead based on worldviews. Experiences of the various media professionals are said to have a positive impact on their ability to write about homelessness and provide insight and character to their articles. Liebler & Smith (1997) supported this argument by saying: "Journalists are more likely to report facts that are congruent with their own world view; journalists' own frames of references may be reflected in news content; and stronger feelings are most likely to be manifested in story content" (pp. 58–59). On the other hand, if individual experience and background, knowledge, and personal association influence the construction of news content, men and women may report differently on issues. Socialization to different gender roles may contribute to communication differences.

Other factors such as women in managerial positions in journalism can lead to better coverage of issues related to women. Research has proven that there is a significant difference between male and female reporters in their selection of male and female information or story sources. Female journalists report more often on female news subjects, use more personal assertions in their stories, and put emphasis on social and humanitarian issues (Armstrong, 2004; Craft & Wanta, 2004). Deciding who makes news, when and why, is influenced by the subjective choices made by journalists and editors. These choices are influenced by principles such as prominence, proximity, major disasters, war and conflict, timeliness (pressing issues of the day), crime, corruption, and an act or event that is out of the norm. Individual assignments are often made on the basis of the editor's knowledge of the type of reporter that would match the type of assignment the best, and not necessarily on the basis of the gender of the reporter (Ericson et al., 1987). Zeldes et al. (2007) stated, "a 'critical mass' of women in management and reporter level may alter reporter socialization" (p. 350). Our findings show that gender may not have significantly impacted what was written about the homeless in the media but gender cannot be ignored as a variable in setting the public agenda or mobilizing public opinions. Limitations to our study include a small timeframe of 5 years and local content limited to a small geographical area. Future research direction could include national newspaper coverage over a wider time span.

Conclusion

For the media to truthfully portray our society and to produce reporting that is complete and diverse, it is important that the news reflects the world as seen by women and men in an equal and equitable manner. This is how we construct our notion of reality of today's homelessness issues. Homelessness crosses over all gender, age, and other demographic and social boundaries. We note the social constructionist frame of the homeless is fluid and dynamic and the framing of homelessness might shift with changes in not only the environmental context, but also with the changes in employment in the media profession where more women may accept positions traditionally given to men. As more women become involved in all levels of media organization as reporters, senior editors, and media decision-makers, the stories will reflect these changing roles and experiences. Homelessness is a problem with societal, community, family, and individual roots. The media and the journalists, regardless of gender, can frame stories in a positive or negative light, thus promoting debate regarding social issues and influencing or supporting existing public perceptions. This traditional media practice is culturally acceptable, and gender may not enter into the public's analysis of the article written. The nature of how a social issue is framed in the media and how the public interprets the issue based on the gender of the author requires further study. More gender-based research is also needed to examine individual-level and societal perceptions of the framing of social issues such as homelessness.

References

Anderson, K. (2008). *Social Constructionism and Belief Causation.* New York University. Retrieved from http://philosophy.stanford.edu/apps/stanfordphilosophy/files/wysiwyg_images/anderson.pdf

Armstrong, C. L., (2004). The Influence of Reporter Gender on Source Selection in Newspaper Stories. *Journalism & Mass Communication Quarterly,* 81(1), 139–154. Retrieved from http://aejmc.org/_scholarship/_publications/_journals/_jmcq/index.php.

Armstrong, C. L. & Nelson, M. R. (2005). How Newspaper Sources Trigger Gender Stereotyping. *Journalism & Mass Communication Quarterly,* 82(4), 820–837. Retrieved from http://aejmc.org/_scholarship/_publications/_journals/_jmcq/index.php.

Berry, T. R., Wharf-Higgins, J., & Naylor, P. J. (2007). SARS Wars: An Examination of the Quantity and Construction of Health Information in the News Media. *Health Communication,* 21(1), 35–44. Retrieved from http://www.informaworld.com/smpp/content~db=all~content=a788021026.

Brescoll, V. & LaFrance, M. (2004). The Correlates and Consequences of Newspaper Reports of Research on Sex Differences. *Newspaper Reports of Research,* 15(8), 515–520. Retrieved from http://www.psychologicalscience.org/pdf/ps/media_gender.pdf.

Buck, P. O., Toro, P. A., & Ramos, M. A. (2004). Media and Professional Interest in Homelessness over 30 Years (1974–2003). *Analyses of Social Issues & Public Policy,* 4(1), 151–171.

Cann, J. & Mohr, P. B. (2001). Journalist and Source Gender in Australia Television News. *Journal of Broadcasting & Electronic Media,* 45(1), 162–174.

Campbell, C. & Gibbs, A. (2008). Representations of HIV/AIDS Management in South African Newspapers. *African Journal of AIDS Research,* 7(2), 195–208.

Craft, S. & Wanta, W. (2004). Women in the Newsroom: Influences of Female Editors and Reporters on the News Agenda. *Journalism & Mass Communication Quarterly,* 89(1), 124–138. Retrieved from http://www.aejmc.org/_scholarship/research_use/jmcq/04spring/craft.pdf.

Daily Newspaper Circulation Data (2011). Retrieved from http://www.newspaperscanada.ca/daily-newspaper-paid-circulation-data.

Edmonton Joint Planning on Housing. (2004). *A Count of Homeless People in Edmonton.* Retrieved from http://intraspec.ca/HTE_homeless_count_2004_report.pdf.

Ericson, R. V., Baranek, P. M., & Chan, J. L. (1987). *Visualizing: A Study of News Organization.* Milton Keynes: Open University Press.

Gallagher, M., (2001). Reporting on Gender in Journalism: Why Do So Few Women Reach the Top? *Women International,* Winter, 63–65. Retrieved from http://www.nieman.harvard.edu/reports/article/101542/Reporting-on-Gender-in-Journalism.aspx.

Gold, N. & Auslander, G. (1999). Gender Issues in Newspaper Coverage of People with Disabilities: A Canada-Israel Comparison. *Women & Health*, 29(4), 75–95.

Gray, J. (1992). *Men Are from Mars, Women Are from Venus: A Practical Guide for Improving Communication and Getting What You Want in Your Relationships*. New York: HarperCollins.

Hyde, J. S. (2005). The Gender Similarities Hypothesis. *American Psychologist*, 60(6), 581–592.

Kinder, D. R. (2007). Curmudgeonly Advice. *Journal of Communication*, 57, 155–162.

Krippendorff, K. (1980). *Content Analysis*. Beverley Hills: SAGE.

Len-Rios, M. E., Park, S. A., Cameron, D. L., Duke, D. L., & Kreuter, M. (2008). Study Asks If Reporter's Gender or Audience Predict Paper's Cancer Coverage. *Newspaper Research Journal*, 29(2), 91–99. Retrieved from http://hcrc.missouri.edu/PDF_articles/Reporter%20 gender_LR.pdf.

Liebler, C. M. & Smith, S. J. (1997). Tracking Gender Differences: A Comparative Analysis of Network Correspondents and Their Sources. *Journal of Broadcasting & Media*, 41(1), 58–69.

Oxman-Martinez, J., Marinescu, V., & Bohard, I. (2009). Shades of Violence: The Media Role. *Women's Studies International Forum*, 32(4), 296–304. .

Piaseu, N., Belza, B., & Shell-Duncan, B. (2004). Less Money Less Food: Voices from Women in Urban Poor Families in Thailand. *Health Care for Women International*, 25(7), 604–619. DOI: 10.1080/07399330490458141.

Richter, M. S., Kovacs Burns, K., & Chaw-Kant, J. (2010). Analysis of Newspaper Journalists' Portrayal of the Homeless and Homelessness in Alberta, Canada. *International Journal of Child Health & Human Development*, 3(1), 125–136 Retrieved from https://www.novapublishers. com/catalog/product_info.php?products_id=24419.

Sebba, A. (1994). *Battling for News: The Rise of the Female Reporter*. London: Hodder & Stoughton.

Scheufele, D. T. (1999). Framing as a Theory of Media Effects. *Journal of Communication*, 49(1), 103–122.

Siebel, C. (2008). Letters to the Editor and the Tobacco Debate. *Feminist Media Studies*, 8(4), 407–422.

Sims, C. L. (2008). Invisible Wounds, Invisible Abuse: The Exclusion of Emotional Abuse in Newspaper Articles. *Journal of Emotional Abuse*, 8(4), 375–402.

Taylor, R. (2009). Slain and Slandered: A Content Analysis of the Portrayal of Femicide in Crime News. *Homicide Studies: An Interdisciplinary & International Journal*, 13(1), 21–49.

The City of Calgary. Biennial count of homeless persons (2006). Retrieved from http://www. calgaryhomeless.com.

Yanich, D. (2004). Crime Creep: Urban and Suburban Crime on Local TV News. *Journal of Urban Affairs*, 26(5), 535–563.

Zeldes, G. A., Fico, F., & Diddi, A. (2007). Race and Gender: An Analysis of the Source and Reporters in Local Television Coverage of the 2002 Michigan Gubernatorial Campaign. *Mass Communication & Society*, 10(3), 345–363.

Ziegler, D. & White, A. (1990). Women and Minorities on Network Television News: An Examination of Correspondents and Newsmakers. *Journal of Broadcasting and Electronic Media*, 34(2), 215–223.

Chapter 14

Understanding the Spread of HIV/AIDS in Thailand

Patchanee Malikhao

Introduction

HIV and AIDS are like both ends of a string but they do not necessarily have a causal relationship. In principle, a person can have HIV viral loads in the body but does not develop AIDS, thanks to many preventive measures advocated by the Joint United Nations Programme on HIV/AIDS (UNAIDS). I still would like to put HIV and AIDS together, but like to remind the reader that these two terms are not synonymous. However, HIV most often causes AIDS in many unfortunate socioeconomic and political contexts.

To elaborate, not everyone has an equal chance to access the antiretroviral therapy due to many factors: HIV prevention policy of one's country; national and personal religious worldviews; budgeting priorities; stigma and discrimination created by a society that prevents the person to disclose his/her HIV positive status; lack of counseling and testing service facilities, marginalization, human rights abuses, and more. In the UNAIDS & WHO report of 2007, many causes of HIV/AIDS, such as poverty, gender inequality, lack of (sex) education, religious constraint, and so on, were mentioned.

HIV/AIDS is thus not just a biomedical issue. Sociocultural and socioeconomic contexts are also responsible for the cause of HIV/AIDS. It is not exaggerated to state that, in fact, the HIV/AIDS epidemic is a symbolic representation of unequal development. Economically speaking, by looking at different countries that have people living with HIV or AIDS, one notices that the percentage of people living with HIV in a rich country is less than that of the people living with HIV in a poor country. And also, the causal relationship of HIV and AIDS is stronger in a poorer country than in a rich country. Money plays an important role in providing the antiretroviral therapy to the citizens who live with HIV and in providing the counseling and testing services to all needed citizens. From this epidemic, we can conceptualize not only the social injustice at the world level but also at a nation-state level. HIV/AIDS prevention involves risk management between the self and the state policy/politics and the emergence of iatro-globalization, a process that describes how new medical innovations, skilled personnel, and biomedical trades are being exchanged at a global scale (Turner, 2004:244).

Globalization is not just what is happening in this century, that is, the reduction of barriers physically, legally, linguistically, culturally, and psychologically, so people can engage with one another no matter where they are (Scholte, 2005:59). In fact, many history scholars reveal that globalization has occurred since the sixteenth century, in the forms of cultural exchanges via bilateral and later transnational connections. With the help of modern communication technology, the transfer of cultural products via the mass media has been more pronounced and one can see the fluidity of the localized culture aided by communication.

Changes in sexuality have been documented in different phases of globalization, as I will elaborate later. Sexuality, according to Hollander et al. (2011:20), refers to a group of concepts, such as eroticism, sexual behavior, sexual orientation, and desire to engage in sexual activity, which is closely related to gender. A local culture has had an enormous impact on the regulations and expressions of an individual sexuality. Not only has a local culture evolved through phases of globalization, but sexuality also has. Part of the factors that help spread HIV is the hybridized sexual culture as influenced by the pop culture.

In this chapter, I will explain first what globalization is as interpreted by many scholars. I, then, will move on to the interrelationship between the mass media, sexual culture, and globalization. Next, I will discuss Thai sexuality in relation to globalization. Finally, I will use the HIV/AIDS issue in Thailand as a sociological case in point affected by sexuality and globalization.

Understanding globalization

Globalization involves many aspects and layers of areas such as communications, travel, production, market, finance, organizations, military, ecology, health, law, and consciousness, fostering physical and virtual interactions of people across state boundaries (for more details, see Scholte, 2005:49–84). From this definition, it seems as if globalization is related to only the modern and postmodern era. To the contrary, some history scholars argue that the globalization process can be traced back to the sixteenth century with the start of trading between Europe and Asia (see Held & McGrew, 2007; Hopkins, 2002; Hopper, 2006; Edelman & Haugerud, 2005; Leimgruber, 2004; Wallerstein, 1979, 1983, 1990, 1997). The process can be called transnationalization in the old globality. Contemporary globalization, as the nonhistorians refer to, emerged as a process from the 1970s onward. [Hopkins (2002) suggests the starting point as after the Second World War, in the 1950s; Berger (2004:19) suggests it to start after the cold war in the 1970s.] Leimgruber (2004:19) states that the concept of globalization must not be reserved only for phenomena in the twentieth and twenty-first centuries. According to Hopkins (2002:1–10), globalization is a new terminology that denotes the following ongoing historical process: first, archaic globalization; second, proto-globalization; third, globalization; and fourth, postcolonial globalization.

Hopkins explains further that archaic globalization occurred from Byzantium and Tang to the renewed expansionism of Islamic and Christian power after the 1500s. He identified proto-globalization with the political and economic developments that became especially prominent between about 1600 and 1800 in Europe, Asia, and parts of Africa. The third historical process, globalization, he refers to as the colonial period from the 1760s onward. Globalization that can be related to modernity started from 1800, according to Hopkins. It refers to the rise of the nation-state and the spread of industrialization. The last process, postcolonial globalization, refers to the contemporary form that can be dated approximately from the 1950s.

Globalization has brought changes in the way people think, behave, and pass on to later generations, in other words: culture. A controversial debate over the global versus the local has been noted: whether one culture should trade its identity, good old values, traditional customs – or in other words, local culture – with the so-called, "popular culture" or not; and if so, to what extent?

Many people see globalization as a scapegoat for whatever that has gone wrong with their cultures and identities. Is that so? Let me explain how globalization has been considered as a mindset. Giddens (1990:64) defines globalization as "the intensification of worldwide social relations which link distant localities in such a way that local happenings are shaped by events occurring many miles away and vice versa." According to him, globalization is seen as the widening, deepening, and speeding up of worldwide interconnectedness in all aspects of contemporary social life. Globalization seems to be a driven force to the change of values, practices, and norms. According to Appadurai (2001:17), globalization is an interactive process in which "locality" and 'globality" interact via the shrinking of space-time in the world system due to communication technology.

Cohen (2006:165) views globalization as the continuation of Westernization that creates virtual interconnectedness but with physical disparities. Tomlinson (2001:176) equates the process to Americanization. Dicken (2004:17), however, disagrees with equating globalization to modernization[1] or a veiled form of Westernization, and argues that globalization is "neither inevitable, all-pervasive, homogenizing end-state nor is it unidirectional and irreversible. It is certainly not deterministic." Dicken's view supports Chen's view in Chen & Starosta (2004:10) that Westernization is an outdated cultural imperialistic view existed in the debates in the 1960s and 1970s. Westernization assumes that the ultimate goal of development must and should be the way the Western Worlds organize their societies. But globalization is not planned and flows happen in many directions and with different degrees. Moreover, a globalized locality is not necessarily a Westernized (or Americanized) society. It can lead to some other form of hybridized society (Dicken, 2004). Therefore, one area can be more globalized than the other and some areas can manifest different degrees of hybridization depending on what Starosta referred to as "the level of reinstitution of differences a the level of community or of nation" (Chen & Starosta, 2004:10).

Globalization goes hand in hand with intercultural communication

The term "Culture" has a wide scope and invites different definitions. Crothers (2007:14) states that culture is the result of socialization. Huntington (2000:XV) perceives culture:

> … in purely subjective terms as the values, attitudes, beliefs, orientations, and underlying assumptions prevalent among people in a society.

Brown (1995:8–9) explains that culture comprises different elements: artifacts; language; behavior patterns in the form of rites, rituals, ceremonies, and celebrations; norms of behavior; heroes; symbols and symbolic action; beliefs, values, and attitudes; ethical codes; basic assumptions; and history. There are interactions between three levels of culture, from a superficial level to the deepest level. The shallowest level of culture is artifacts. The form of artifacts can be stories, myths, jokes, metaphors, rites, rituals, and ceremonies; heroes; and symbols. Beliefs, values, and attitudes are grouped at the second level of culture. The deepest level of culture is basic assumptions that concern the environment, reality, human nature, human activity, and human relationship.

Culture can also be described as a framework with four distinguishable but interrelated analytical components: a worldview (*Weltanschauung*), a value system, a system of symbolic representations, and a social organizational system (Servaes, 1999:12). The worldview component is more or less equivalent to the third level of culture as defined by Brown. The value system can possibly be overlapping with Brown's first and second levels, that is, beliefs, values, myths, and metaphors. The social organizational system would be the first tangible level of culture that represents the value and the worldview of a particular culture.

From these definitions, it is valid to state that culture is socially constructed and subjective. The concept "cultural relativity" was introduced by Edward Hall (1959). It is based on the assumption that there are no superior cultures, and culture, though it has its own strengths and weaknesses, should not be compared in terms of values or merits (Hall, 1959). Not only does intercultural communication concern national cultures, it also concerns the studies of the subcultures classified by tribes, communities, classes, and ethnic groups (Geertz, 1995).

Servaes' (1999) definition – that culture is a dynamic factor that can condition change in society and a way to assess the change in worldview and cultural values is through the investigation of the symbolic interactions and representations, and the social organization system – fits in the multiplicity paradigm he proposed in 1989. In a nutshell, the multiplicity paradigm calls for the interpretive or critical approach of Social Science, together with an interdisciplinary approach, to study the holistic influences of development, culture, social change, and participatory communication. In considering globalization and the emergence of global messages at a local level, Lie (2003:109) also emphasizes an interdisciplinary approach (Geertz, 1983; Giddens, 1990), in which culture plays an important part (Geertz, 1988; Robertson, 1992), and in which the global is linked to the local (Sztompka, 1993). The interpretive approach of the Social Science framework for intercultural communication studies can be summarized from Yashitake's (2004:34) description as the understanding of the lifeworld through dialogue and that requires intersubjective relations between the observed and the observer. For the critical approach of this Social Science framework, Yashitake (2004:34) sees it as "a defense against the invasion of system into the lifeworld and/or as empowerment of the oppressed." The critical approach seems to be an antidote for the interpretive approach in which any intrusion in the systemization and rationalization of a particular culture is being investigated and interpreted. It implies the realization of power embedded in the interrelations among race, gender, class, and sexuality in the construction of culture.

What constitutes the construction of culture?

First of all, I would like to discuss the differences between sex and gender. Sex and gender are related but denote different meanings. Sex means biological differences between a man and a woman. Gender is socially constructed. It depends on a social system to justify and allocate rewards and resources to sort women and men into females and males; and social expectation of what constitutes the characteristics of masculinity and femineity (Hollander et al., 2011:14). A concept like marriage has something to do with social construction as a marriage partner depends on individual attributes as well as social ones. Race is also a socially constructed component of culture. It is based on visible physical characteristics, such as skin color, stature, and facial features (Rothman, 1993:6). Racial identity varies on both a societal and an individual level. Hollander et al. (2011:25) describe that on an individual level a light-skinned Middle Eastern person can pass for white in certain situations and a Jewish person might consider himself white compared to black people, but as Jewish to white people. The concept "social class" influences prestige, power, and authority over resources and possibilities for advancement; class position is related to race and gender (Hollander et al., 2011:27–28).

Worldview is also a part of the construction of culture. It is directly influenced from beliefs and religion. Berger & Luckmann (1996) discuss in *The Social Construction of Reality* the interaction between thinking and action. Socialization within a tradition and culture shapes an individual's thinking, and at the same time, this internalized form is reflected in the manifestation of culture (Holm, 1997:75). This model stresses the importance of religion, as it provides a symbolic universe that explains birth, life, and death, as well as providing the individual with an identity. Religion explains the world through myths and legends and also through rational discourses. Therefore, Robertson (1972:47) defines *religious culture* as: "… a set of beliefs and symbols (and values deriving there from) pertaining to a distinction between an empirical and a super-empirical, transcendent reality; the affair of the empirical being subordinated in significance to the non-empirical."

Interrelationship among the mass media, sexual culture, and globalization

Without the mass media as weaving threads in the globalization process, the differences between the global and the locals would not have been very prominent. Martin & Nakayama (2004:6) describe five aspects of the influence of communication technology on cultures: increase of general information about the citizens of the world and the cultures; increase contact with peoples who possess "the otherness"; increase contact with people within the same culture for support; redefine one's own identity and think of identity management; and the gap of access to communication technology, or the so-called digital divide. These aspects together with the changing of immigration patterns and demographics result in a culturally diverse society across the globe. The mass media (and communication in general) help define and redefine the local cultures and identities by helping create a global consciousness, by which people can compare how others live to their own locality (Nash, 2000:53). Most often mass media diffuse their messages globally but the consumers of the mass media consume the messages locally, the process of which is called *the axis of globalized diffusion and localized appropriation* (Thompson, 1995).

The mass media audience tends to follow the notion that Festinger (1957) proposed about cognitive dissonance, that people tend to avoid adopting messages and information that are not congruent to their existing worldview. Sets of cultural products shared among many localities are what constitute "popular culture" (which were in the past labelled as "low culture" – as an opposite to "high culture" shared by the elites such as classical music, opera, and ballets). The concept popular culture has been discussed by scholars such as Burke, Evans-Prichard, and Geertz (http://www.answers.com/topic/popular-culture, accessed January 25, 2012). Nacbar et al. (1978:6–8) explain that examples of popular mythologies are beliefs, values, superstitions, and actual myths; popular artifacts are, for example, product packaging, architecture, toys, and icons and logos; popular arts and performing arts such as rock and roll, and films; and popular rituals such as the Olympics, concerts, holidays, and festivals. Therefore, Holmberg summarizes popular culture as follows:

> … popular culture includes the human activities, languages, and artefacts that grow and nourish people in communities and that generate observable, describable interest about its events and artefacts, within a community and between communities. (Holmberg, 1998:15)

The production and distribution of communication controlled by the communication industry promotes popular culture. The industry, according to Macbride et al. (1980:96–97), consists of printed media enterprises, radio and television companies, news and features agencies, advertising and public relations firms, syndicates and independent companies producing and distributing print, visual and recorded material for print and broadcasting conglomerates, public or private information offices, data banks, software production, manufactures of technological equipment, and so on. Productions from the communication industry are also known as the cultural industry because they record and reproduce cornucopia of social interactions, representations and organization systems in diverse media forms such as books, arts, films, recordings, television, radio, the Internet, plays, concerts, and music. With the breakthrough of the new media as a consequence of the digitization revolution, the symbolic representations of popular culture rapidly transmitted by the information super highway create diverse interpretations of self and identity, sex, gender, and sexuality, as Thompson puts it:

While communication and information are increasingly diffused on a global scale, these symbolic materials are always received by individuals who are situated in specific spatial-temporal locales. The appropriation of media products is always a localized phenomenon, in the sense that it always involves specific individuals who are situated in particular social-historical contexts, and who draw on the resources available to them in order to make sense of media messages and incorporate them into their lives. And messages are often transformed in the process of appropriation as individuals adapt them to the practical contexts of everyday life. The globalization of communication has not eliminated the localized character of appropriation but rather has created a new kind of symbolic axis in the modern world. (Thompson, 1995:174)

Thus, domains of sexuality such as eroticism, sexual behavior, social power, and gender roles in one culture may have certain degrees of impact on the worldview of the audience in the other culture. Elliot & Lemert (2006:4–5) support this idea by revealing that there is also evidence that increasing globalization within media systems in the United States, among American youth culture, has shaped the degree of individualism in society, which in turn could alter attitudes toward sex, sexuality, and individual identity. From a more critical and general perspective, Elliott & Lemert (2006) propose that globalization has a profound impact on the individual level, and that causes a new kind of individualism. They define this *new individualism* as a highly risk-taking, experimenting, and self-expressing individual underpinned by new forms of apprehension, anguish, and anxiety. As each individual has become a consumer of the media conglomerate in a capitalistic society, the impact on each person's experiences of gender identity, sexuality, and family life is the topic discussed by many scholars.

Sex, sexual behavior, and sexuality have been major components in most media contents in popular culture because of their power of attraction to the mass consumerism. Sex sells. Therefore, Holmberg (1998:16) reports that phenomena, artifacts, events, language, images, sounds, music, gesture, fashion rituals public and private, daily habits, and more can be sexualized, gendered, and oriented in the process of globalization.

Elliot & Lemert (2006:114) note that sexuality in the United States is currently framed and regulated through mass media, advertising, and information culture as a consequence of globalization and that various forms of sexuality can be called *discursive sexuality* among the new generation.

Thai culture, sexuality, and globalization

In 2004–2008, Patchanee Malikhao (2007) studied the influences of globalization periods on the sexuality of Thai people. She defined globalization as a flow of ideas, services, cultural products, and technology that includes the global diffusion and local consumption of culture, values, social, political, and economic concepts (Appadurai, 2001). These factors have had an impact, via different communication modes, on a different locality in a different way at a different speed from the archaic past to the present. The periods of globalization, as distinguished by Hopkins (2002), can be used to explain the dynamic interaction between Thai culture and globalization: (a) archaic globalization, starting from the ancient time to the 1500s during the pre-Siam (Siam is the former name of Thailand) period and the beginning of the Siam period when Ayutthaya was the capital city; (b) proto-globalization starting from 1600 to 1768, with the end of the Ayutthaya period; (c) globalization starting from 1769, when Bangkok became the capital of Siam to 1946, after Siam changed its name to Thailand in 1939 and turned from absolute monarchy to institutional monarchy shortly before the assassination of King Rama VIII; and (d) contemporary globalization starting from 1947, when Thailand has been under institutional monarchy and the monarch has been King Rama IX or King Bhumibol to the present. I prefer the term contemporary globalization to postcolonial globalization, to avoid any confusion, as Thailand was never physically colonized by European imperialists. The demarcation year of the globalization period from proto to globalization is based on the shift of the old capital, Ayutthaya, to Bangkok while the globalization period to the contemporary globalization period started with the ascent to the throne of King Bhumibol, the present King.

Thai culture as a result of different phases of globalization periods

Thai culture has its distinguished features: Patriarchy and the Thai Buddhist worldview as a consequence of its dyanmic interaction with different globalization periods, from the archaic to the contemporary. Each phase of globalization is discussed in detail in Malikhao (2007). A summary is presented here.

During the archaic and proto-globalization, animistic Thai culture was infused with Brahmanism and Buddhism via cultural exchanges with Sri Lankan and ancient Cambodian or Khmer cultures. Thai culture incorporated hierarchical order in social status and patriarchal values from Cambodian civilization. The social stratification had impact on its sexual culture. Evidence of polygamy and female subordination was already found in those periods. Also in those periods, premarital sex was tolerated. During the global colonization period, though Thailand has never been colonized by the Western power, Thai culture was infused with Western culture via globalization. Economic and political transform occurred in this period for fear of being colonized by the Western world. This resulted in the adoption of premarital sex and monogamy from the Victorian culture in the Thai sexual culture. Monogamy was not adhered to by many males but keeping virginity till marriage was imposed on the females as patriarchy prevails. In this globalization phase, prostitution emerged from the abolishment of slavery as former slave wives needed to survive. Sex workers thus played an important role to keep the notion of premarital abstinence among unmarried Thai females alive because traditionally Thai males are allowed to have sexual experience but Thai females are not. During the contemporary globalization period, Thailand entered modernization by way of economic development. The introduction of capitalism, neoliberalism, tourism, and the Vietnam War in the beginning of this globalization period helped spur the commodification of sex in Thailand. As communication technology, such as the Internet and satellite and cable TV, became popular in this contemporary globalization period, different forms of sexuality can be observed, namely the traditional, the convergent as influenced by the pop culture, and the hybridized forms. First, the traditional forms of sexuality include extramartial sex with either casual partner or mistresses for married males and sex with sex workers or casual sex workers among married and single males. Second, sexuality as part of the popular culture (convergence or globalized sex) can be described as premarital sex among the single, homosexuality and transgender, and exporting of Thai sex workers abroad. Last, hybridized forms of sexuality can be explained as first sexual encounters of adolescents on Valentine's day, selling sex among female teenagers supported by their boyfriends to help the boyfriends buy luxurious accessories for their motorcycles, trading sex among female teenagers for luxurious items such as handbags or cell phones, phone sex, webcam sex, nudity for the public, and sex races (for more details, see Malikhao, 2007).

HIV/AIDS and diversified sexuality in the contemporary globalization period

From the latest data presented by the Asian Epidemic Model (AEM) Projection for HIV/AIDS in Thailand: 2005–2025 (FHI & Bureau of AIDS, TB, and STIs, Department of Disease Control, Ministry of Public Health, Thailand 2008, p. 31), the state of the Thai HIV epidemic in 2008 is as follows:

"1,115,000 adults have been infected with HIV in Thailand since the start of the epidemic.
585,800 of these people have subsequently died of AIDS.
532,500 people are currently living with HIV.
12,800 new infections occur this year.
48,000 people have serious illness by the end of the year."

According to Mr. Mechai Viravaidya, founder and chairperson of the Population and Community Development Association of Thailand (PDA) and a leading Thai activist on the issue of HIV/AIDS, the impact of HIV/AIDS in Thailand can be described as: loss of foregone earnings from the death of adults in working age groups; loss of home care and public health care cost such as antiviral drugs and treatments of opportunistic diseases; and macroeconomic cost, including tourism, the export of labor, and the loss of prospective foreign investment (Viravaidya interviewed by Techawongtham, 1995:104–105). I would like to broaden the third aspect to include politico-cultural and social costs in addition to the mentioned economic cost, because HIV/AIDS has raised global attention on good governance and human rights advocacy to deal with marginalized groups who are subject to stigmatization and discrimination of PLWHA, sex workers, migrated laborers, men who have sex with men, homeless children, and drug users (Poolcharoen et al., 1999:24). Larson & Narain (2001:24–25) explained the economic impact at the level of the family and community, especially among poor and marginalized groups, by referring to a research result in Thailand that

> half of the households surveyed had reduced their consumption to more than 50 percent to care for a family member with HIV/AIDS, 60 percent had used all their savings for medical costs, 19 percent had sold property such as land, animals or vehicles, 15 percent had pulled their children out of school to help at home and 11 percent had borrowed money to pay for medical costs and help maintain household needs. Overall, poor families became even poorer and lower middle-income households became poor ones.

HIV/AIDS in Thailand is still a health-threat issue after the Thai government, under the responsibility of the Ministry of Public Health, has introduced a number of interventions: behavioral change, social marketing, school-based interventions, and multisectoral approach since the 1980s (Malikhao, 2012).

One variable that has changed overtime is the sexuality of Thais that has affected the mode of HIV transmission. The first case of AIDS in Thailand was reported in 1984 when a foreigner brought the HIV virus into the country (UNDP, 2004:7). According to Punpanich et al. (2004), it was a homosexual man who had returned from overseas and was receiving treatment in Bangkok. Since then HIV spread to diverse groups in the Thai society. This can be explained alongside with the change of Thai sexuality and sexual behavior from the 1980s to the 2010s. How HIV spread to diverse groups in Thailand can be seen in Table 14.1 and be explained next.

HIV spread from the male who have sex with male group in the early 1980s to the injecting drug user group in 1988. From Table 14.1, new infection rate among IDUs in 1988 was high (61 percent), but this mode of transmission has become less and less prevalent during the past decades. HIV then spread among immates via sharing needles. Boonmongkol et al. (1998:32) reported that IDU users exchanged syringes, did not know the correct way of sterilizing the syringes, and had more than one sexual partners, and 70 percent of them did not use condoms on a regular basis. Later with prevention campaigns focused on IDU risks together with counseling and testing during the past decades, the rate of new HIV infection dropped dramatically but not to the unnoticeable level.

In contrast, the rate of new HIV infection of males who have sex with males increased during the past decades. Though the males who have sex with male group, later expanded to be an LGBT group known then as the Rainbow Sky group, which started to campaign on HIV/AIDS prevention in 1999, (http://www.rsat.info/about.html, accessed March 3, 2012), the rate of new infection among males who have sex with males is still high. From comparative research on Asian (especially Thai) and Western homosexuality and

Table 14.1: Percentage of new adult infections by modes of transmission from 1988 to current date and project the data up to the year 2025.

% new infections from each transmission route	1988	1990	1995	2000	2005	2010	2015	2020	2025
Wife from husband	2	8	43	48	39	28	22	21	20
Husband from wife	0	0	4	8	10	10	8	6	5
Male sex with male	2	5	8	12	22	33	43	49	52
Drug injection	61	5	9	11	6	9	11	12	12
Client from sex worker	30	73	27	12	11	10	8	6	4
Sex worker from client	4	9	7	5	4	4	3	2	2
Casual sex	0	0	1	4	7	7	6	5	4
Total from all modes of transmissions	100	100	100	100	100	100	100	100	100

Source: The Asian Epidemic Model (AEM) Projection for HIV/AIDS in Thailand: 2005–2025 (FHI & Bureau of AIDS, TB, and STIs, Department of Disease Control, Ministry of Public Health, Thailand 2008, p. 33).

HIV done by scholars such as Peter A. Jackson, Malcolm McCamish, Graeme Storer, Gerard Sullivan, and Susan Kippax, it is very important to report that (1) Western homosexuality is quite different from the traditional Thai definitions of homosexuality (kathoey, tom, dee, etc.), (2) one should pay attention to the context of homosexuality rather than counting on the frequency of homosexual intercourse and HIV prevention, and (3) globalization in the dimension of modernization and urbanization does have an impact on the homosexuality of Thais. Murray (1992) defined four types of homosexual expression:

1. age-structured homosexuality, when a person expresses his homosexuality exclusively during adolescence but later bisexauality or heterosexuality in adulthood.
2. profession-defined homosexuality, when some male sex workers are, in fact, heterosexuals but sell sex for a living to male-who-have-sex-with-male customers.
3. transgender homosexuality, which involves cross-dressing and same sex sexuality, and typically redesignates the gender of one partner.
4. egalitarian homosexuality whereby the people establish their own cultural patterns and institutions.

The first three types are prevalent in pre-industrial societies while the fourth type is only in industrialized societies. However, for the Thai case, the establishment of the Rainbow Sky Association of Thailand in 2001 confirmed that Thai sexuality has crossed the boundaries of the pre-industrial society types to the industriaized type but is not mutually exclusive. To elaborate, Jackson (2001) and McCamish et al. (2000) reported of the fluidity between heterosexuality and homosexuality among Thai males who have sex with males. Jackson (2001) noticed that the Asians selectively and strategically used foreign forms to create a form that I would call a hybridized form of Western homosexuality, although nowadays, the terms lesbians, gays, bisexauls, and transgenders (LGBT)[2] are not uncommon for Thais due to the mass media and the Internet.

The not-mutually-exclusive heterosexuality and homosexuality among Thai males who have sex with males explains how HIV spread from males who have sex with male group to the heterosexual groups while HIV in the Western countries is more prevalent within the males who have sex with male group and among IDU users.

In 1988, hereosexual males contracted HIV mainly from sex workers. In 1990, the new infection rate of (male) clients from sex workers was high. As many Thai single males and married males frequent sex workers. Estimates suggest that between 12 percent and 31 percent of married men have sex outside marriage (Ghosh, 2002:31). Research results confirmed by Boonmongkol et al. (1998), Gunpai (1998), and Saengtienchai et al. (1999) that one of the reasons HIV/AIDS was spurred among heterosexuals was because of the Thai sexual culture: for the males, for example, it is culturally acceptable that they have their sexual experience before marriage and that they may continue to buy commercial sex after marriage. Klausner (1997) and Sermsri (1999:8) explain that the customary *rite de passage* of a young Thai male was to have his sexual debut with a sex worker. It was also quite common for husbands to use the services of sex workers when they were on upcountry trips. The male machismo leads to HIV high-risk behaviors such as alcohol consumption followed by sexual activity (and they tend not to use condoms when drunk, see also Malikhao, 2007). Peer groups influence males to have sex with different women as extramarital sex is allowed for men, but not for women. For females, "good" girls should not know much about sex, nor negotiate for safer sex, nor request the use of a condom. They should be chaste before marriage, and practice monogamy with their partners/spouses after marriage. In 1998, Boonmongkol et al. reported that many adult females were ignorant about their own husband's risk behavior. They lack knowledge on safe sex, birth control, and the bargaining power for safe sex. Condoms are considered the symbol of distrust and anti-intimacy; it is difficult for those who practice premarital and extramarital sex with friends or those who are regular customers of sex workers to use condoms. For those who admitted having extramarital sex, the rate of condom use is below 30 percent (http://www.aidsthai.org, accessed November 20, 2009).

Before 1997, the Thai government launched massive mass media campaigns against HIV/AIDS. A massive television campaign nationwide "100% Condom Program" started in 1992, when the Minister of Public Health gave away 60 million free condoms (UNDP, 2004:17–18). The Thai government was then complimented worldwide for its successful campaign. The government provided condoms in brothels and imposed that the sex clients use a condom every time they had sex (http://www3.niaid.nih.gov/news/ newsreleases/1996/campaign.htm, accessed April 16, 2008). The "100 %condom program" was later eliminated due to the lack of budget. However, this major change in Thai sexuality resulted in the disappearance of "formal" brothels. It turned into a plualism of sexual venues and made the 100 percent condom use control impossible. Diverse sexualities are reported to be sex in karaoke bars, in womens' dormitories, in massage parlors, phone sex, selling one's own nude photos, and so on (Malikhao, 2012:60). When brothels were closed down, it became more difficult to control the use of condoms.

It is worth noticing that HIV/AIDS prevalence is found in major cities in Thailand as a result of urbanization and sex toursim. Ghosh (2002:31) reports that extramarital sexual affairs in the urban areas is three times higher than in the rural areas. Those who can afford to go to karaoke bars, restaurants, massage parlors, and so on are the Thai middle class men. Malikhao (2007) studied the localized meaning of Abstinence, Be faithful and use Condom (ABC) in a Buddhist and a Christian community in the North of Thailand and found that the respondents did not think that abstinence would work as urbanization and modernization creep into their communities. Be faithful, as known in lessons from Africa, does not work because the majority of Thai men are not faithful, according to the respondents. Condom use works the best according to the respondents, but the rate of condom use is low.

From Table 14.1, the rise of new HIV infection rate among those who practice casual sex since 1995 confirms that premarital sex among single males and females is gaining more acceptance. A Department of Mental Health, Ministry of Public Health's report (2004:7) reveals that around eighteen percent of female university students in Bangkok had premarital sex in 2000; around 6 percent of high school female students in year 11 already had premarital sex in 2003; and half of the female adolescents who work in factories reported to have had premarital sex in 2003. This supports Boonmongkol et al.'s (1998:54), Plipat's (2005), and Malikhao's (2012) report that there is an increasing trend for adolescent males to have their first sexual encounters with nonsex workers. Casual sex was uncommon, what was apparent was a regular pattern of both genders having multiple partners at the same time, not serial monogamy (interview with Mr. Viravaidya on April 11, 2007).

News about low condom use among adolescents was alarming in the 2000s despite the teaching of abstaining from premarital sex, be faithful, and use condom in sex education curricula (Smith et al., 2000). According to Chinnawornsophak (2004), sex education in Thailand was not available before 2000. It was taught under sections of family planning, reproduction organs, and disease prevention in the subjects of Health Education and Biology. In 2000, the Ministry of Education launched "Life and Family Education" to include human sexual development, relationships, sexual behavior, sexual health life-skills, and society and culture (Chinnawornsophak, 2004). Malikhao (2012) reports of sex education that was launched officially in Thailand in 2007 that most students interviewed were aware of condom use, thanks to the social marketing campaign, "yeud ok pok thung" (carry condoms with pride). However, gender equality is not well promoted as textbooks still warn females that wearing too sexy clothes may cause harm of raping to them.

Conclusion

HIV/AIDS has spread from men who had sex with men in the early 1980s, to injecting drug users, to sex workers, to the male population at large, and finally to the partners of the males and their children. This chapter explains this fact by analyzing Thai sexuality. It is evident that political ideology and religious culture in each period of globalization has affected Thai sexuality and sexual practices. Traditionally, Thais tolerated polygamy since the archaic globalization period. Later in the modernization period, sex work was reported to be an occupation, which needs to pay tax. During the contemporary globalization period, Thais have witnessed the commercialization of sex work as a consequence of capitalism and modernization. Many Thais still tolerate polygamy even though Thailand, or Siam in those days, issued the monogamy act in 1935. During this period, Thailand experienced all kinds of hybridization in sexuality as a result of the Thai ways of localizing Western sexuality and practices. These new sexuality practices made it harder for public health policy makers in Thailand to cope with HIV prevention. In the 1990s, it was possible to target 100 percent condom use of sex worker customers, but at present sex work comes in diverse, not easy to police, forms. In combination with injecting drugs, HIV spread via mateship of sharing syringes and unsafe sex practices. From IDU users and men who have sex with men, HIV transmission moved to the heterosexual group due to the fluidity of homosexuality-heterosexuality of Thais. Currently there is more evidence of premarital sex among teens, or among both male teens and sex workers, instead of only among male teens and sex workers.

HIV/AIDS is still a problem and will continue to be a problem in Thailand if researchers go on counting the numbers of safe sex practices without looking at the context of sexuality (Jackson, 2001). Using Western sexuality definitions and purely quantitative research methods won't work because Thai sexuality is hybridized and that needs specific qualitative research strategies developed by competent Social Science researchers who are aware of current days' diverse sexuality.

References

Answers.com http://www.answers.com/topic/popular-culture. Retrieved on January 25, 2012

Appadurai, A. (2001). Grassroots Globalization and the Research Imagination, in Appadurai, A. (ed.), *Globalization*. Durham and London: Duke University Press, p. 21.

Berger, M. T. (2004). *The Battle for Asia, from Decolonization to Globalization*. London: Routledge Curzon.

Berger, P. L. & Luckmann, T. (1966). *The Social Construction of Reality: A Treatise in the Sociology of Knowledge*. New York: Doubleday & Co.

Boonmongkol, P., Pradupmuk, P., & Raungsaun, S. (1998). *State of the Art Review in Socio-economic and Behaviour Research on AIDS, Mahidol University*. Bangkok: Roongsaeng Press.

Brown, A. (1995). *Organisational Culture*. London: Pitman Publishing.

Bureau of AIDS, TB and STIs, Ministry of Public Health http://www3.niaid.nih.gov/news/ newsreleases/1996/campaign.htm. Retrieved on April 16, 2008. http://www.aidsthai.org, retrieved on November 20, 2009.

Chen, G.-M. & Starosta, W. J. (2004). Communication among Cultural Diversities, in Chen, G. M. & Starosta, W. J. (eds.), *Dialogue among Diversities*. Washington D.C.: National Communication Association, pp. 3–15.

Chinnawornsophak, W. (2004). Phed Sueksa: Krabuan Karn Rian Roo Pue Damrong Withee Cheewit Tang Phed Yang Mee Khunnaphab (Sex Education: the Learning Process for Sustaining Quality Sex Life). *S-exchange*, 1, 1.

Cohen, D. (2006). *Globalization and Its Enemies* (trans. Baker, J. B.). Cambridge, MA: Massachusetts Institute of Technology Press.

Crothers, L. (2007). *Globalization & American Popular Culture*. Lanham-Boulder-New York-Toronto-Plymouth, UK: Rowman & Littlefield Publishers, Inc.

Department of Mental Health. (2004). *Review of Sexual Behaviour in Adolescents, Life Skill Development and Counselling*. Nonthaburi: Ministry of Public Health, Thailand.

Dicken, P. (2004). Globalization, Production and the (Im)morality of Uneven Development, in Lee, R. & Smith, D. M. (eds.), *Geographies and Moralities: International Perspectives on Development Justice and Peace*. Malden, MA and Oxford, UK: Blackwell Publishing Ltd., p. 312.

Edelman, M. & Haugerud, A. (2005). Introduction: The Anthropology of Development and Globalization, in Edelman, M. & Hougerud, A. (eds.), *The Anthropology of Development and Globalization from Classical Political Economy to Contemporary Neoliberalism*. Malden, MA: Blackwell Publishing Ltd., p. 488.

Elliot, A. & Lemert, C. (2006). *The New Individualism: The Emotional Costs of Globalization*. London and New York: Routledge.

Family Health International (FHI) and Bureau of AIDS, TB and STIs, Department of Disease Control, Ministry of Public Health, Thailand. (2008). The Asian Epidemic Model (AEM) Projections for HIV/AIDS in Thailand 2005–2025. Report. Ministry of Public Health, Thailand: Nonthaburi.

Festinger, L. (1957). *A Theory of Cognitive Dissonance*. Stanford, CA: Stanford University Press.

Geertz, C. (1983). *Local Knowledge*. New York: Basic Books, Inc.

——— (1988). *Works and Lives: The Anthropologist as Author*. Stanford, CA: Stanford University Press.

——— (1995). *After the Fact: Two Countries, Four Decades, One Anthropologist*. Cambridge, MA: Harvard University Press.

Ghosh, L. (2002). *Prostitution in Thailand: Myth and Reality*. New Delhi: Munshiram Manoharlal Publishers Pvt. Ltd.

Giddens, A. (1990). *The Consequence of Modernity*. Cambridge: Polity Press.

Gunpai, K. (1998). *An Analytical Approach to HIV/AIDS Prevention Communication Campaigns in Thailand*. PhD thesis, University of Essen, Essen.

Hall, E. T. (1959). *The Silent Language*. New York: Doubleday.

Held, D. & McGrew, A. (2007). *Globalization/Anti-globalization*. Cambridge-Malden, MA: Polity Press.

Hollander, J. A., Renfrow, D. G., & Howard, J. A. (2011). *Gendered Situations, Gendered Selves*. New York: Rowman & Littlefield Publishers, Inc.

Holm, N. (1997). An Integrated Role Theory for the Psychology of Religion: Concepts and Perspectives, in Spilka, B. & McIntosh, D. (eds.), *The Psychology of Religion*. Oxford: Westview Press, pp. 73–94.

Holmberg, C. B. (1998). *Sexualities and Popular Culture*. Thousand Oaks, CA: SAGE Publications.

Hopkins, A. G. (2002). Introduction: Globalization – An Agenda for Historians, in Hopkins, A. G. (ed.), *Globalization in World History*. London: Pimlico, pp. 1–10.

Hopper, P. (2006). *Living with Globalization*. Oxford, New York: BERG.

Huntington, S. (2000). Foreword: Cultures Count, in Harrison, L. E. & Huntington, S. P. (eds.), *Culture Matters*. New York: Basic Books.

Jackson, P. A. (2001). Pre-Gay, Post-Queer. *Journal of Homosexuality*, 40(3–4), 1–25.

Klausner, W. (1997). *Thai Culture in Transition*. Bangkok: The Siam Society.

Larson, H. J. & Narain, J. P. (2001). *Beyond 2000: Responding to HIV/AIDS in the New Millenium*. New Delhi: World Health Organization Regional Office for South-East Asia.

Leimgruber, W. (2004). *Between Global and Local: Marginality and Marginal Regions in the Context of Globalization and Deregulation*. Hants, England and Burlington, USA: Ashgate Publishing Limited.

Lie, R. (2003). *Spaces of Intercultural Communication: An Interdisciplinary Introduction to Communication, Culture, and Globalizing/Localizing Identities*. New Jersey: Hampton Press, Inc.

Macbride, S., Abel, E., Beuve-Mery, H., Ekonzo, et al. (1980). *Many Voices, One World*. Paris: UNESCO.

McCamish, M., Storer, G., & Carl, G. (2000). Refocusing HIV/AIDS Intervention in Thailand: The Case for Male Sex Workers and Other Homosexuality Active Men. *Culture, Health & Sexuality*, 2(2), 167–182.

Malikhao, P. (2007). HIV/AIDS Strategies in Two Thai Communities: Buddhist and Christian. Ph.D. thesis: the University of Queensland.

—— (2012). *Sex in the Village. Culture, Religion and HIV/AIDS in Thailand*. Southbound: Penang & Silkworm Books: Chiang Mai.

Martin, J. N. & Nakayama, T. K. (2004). *Intercultural Communication in Contexts*. Boston: McGraw Hill.

Murray, S. O. (1992). Introduction: Homosexuality in Cross-Cultural Perspective. *Oceanic Homosexualities*. New York: Garland.

Nachbar, J., Weiser, D., & Wright, J. L. (1978). *The Popular Culture Reader*. Bowling Green, OH: Bowling Green University Popular Press.

Nash, K. (2000). *Contemporary Political Sociology*. London: Blackwell Publishers.

Plipat, T. (2005). HIV-Related Behavior among General Population, Thailand. *AIDS Journal*, 17(4), 175–183.

Poolcharoen, W., Chandaratatna Ayutthaya, P., Bhavanaporn, V., Teokul, V., & Tantinimitkul, C. (1999). *Evolution of AIDS Prevention in Thailand: A Model of Health Development Concept*. Nonthaburi: The Public Health System Research Institute Publishing.

Prachatai http://prachatai.com/journal/2010/12/32460. Retrieved on March 2, 2012.

Punpanich, W., Ungchusak, K., & Detels, R. (2004). Thailand's Response to the HIV Epidemic: Yesterday, Today, and Tomorrow. *AIDS Education and Prevention*, 16(Suppl A), 119–136.

Rainbow Sky Association of Thailand http://www.rsat.info/about.html. Retrieved on March 3, 2012 .

Robertson, R. (1972). *The Sociological Interpretation of Religion*. Oxford: Basil Blackwell.

Robertson, R. (1992). *Globalization: Social Theory and Global Culture*. London, Newbury Park and New Delhi: SAGE Publications.

Rostow, W. W. (1953). *The Process of Economic Growth*. Oxford: Clarendon Press.

Rothman, R. A. (1993). *Inequality and Stratification: Class, Color, and Gender*. Englewood Cliffs. NJ: Prentice-Hall.

Saengtienchai, C., Knodel, J., Vanlandingham, M., & Pramualtratana, A. (1999). Prostitutes Are Better Than Lovers: Wives' Views on the Extramarital Behavior of Thai Men, in Jackson, P. & Cook, N. (eds.), *Genders & Sexualities in Modern Thailand*. Chiang Mai: Silkworm Book, pp. 78–92.

Scholte, J. A. (2005). *Globalization: A Critical Introduction*. Basingstoke: Palgrave Macmillan.

Schramm, W. (1964). *Mass Media and National Development: The Role of Information in the Developing Countries*. Stanford: Stanford University Press.

Sermsri, S. (1999). *Socio-Cutural Perspectives in Health*. Bangkok: Sam Charoen Panich Printing Co. Ltd.

Servaes, J. (1999). *Communication for Development: One World, Multiple Cultures* (1st ed.). Cresskill, New Jersey: Hampton Press, Inc.

Smith, G., Kippax, S., & Aggleton, P. (2000). *HIV and Sexual Health Education in Primary and Secondary Schools*. Sydney: National Centre in HIV Social Research (NCHSR), Faculty of Arts and Social Sciences, the University of New South Wales.

Sztompka, P. (1993). *The Sociology of Social Change*. Cambridge, USA: Basil Blackwell Inc.

Techawongtham, W. (1995). Heading off a Catastrophe, in Reid, E. (ed.), *HIV/AIDS: The Global Inter-Connection*. Hartford: Kumarian Press Inc.

The Guardian http://www.guardian.co.uk/world/2010/dec/21/gay-rights-row-un-resolution. Retrieved on March 2, 2012.

Thompson, J. (1995). *The Media and Modernity. A Social Theory of the Media*. Cambridge: Polity Press.

Tomlinson, J. (2001). Cultural Globalization and Cultural Imperialism, in Schuurman, F. J. (ed.), *Globalization and Development Studies: Challenges for the 21st Century*. London, Thousand Oaks and New Delhi: SAGE Publications.

Turner, B. (2004). The New Medical Sociology, in Alexander, J. C. (series ed.), *Contemporary Societies*. New York & London: WW. Norton & Company.

UNAIDS & WHO. (2007). *AIDS Epidemic Update*. Geneva: UNAIDS.

UNDP (2004). *Thailand's Response to HIV/AIDS: Progress and Challenges*. Bangkok: United Nations Development Program.

Viravaidya, M. (2007). Interview, Bangkok, Thailand on 11th April.

Wallerstein, I. (1979). *The Capitalist World Economy*. Cambridge: Cambridge University Press.

——— (1983). *Historical Capitalism*. London: Verso.

——— (1990). Culture as the Ideological Battleground of the Modern World-system, in Featherstone, M. (ed.), *Global Culture*. London: SAGE.

——— (1997). The Nation and the Universal: Can There Be Such a Thing as World Culture?, in King, A. D. (ed.), *Culture, Globalization and the World-System*. Minneapolis: University of Minnesota, pp. 91–105.

Yoshitake, M. (2004). Research Paradigm for Dialogue among Diversities. Refinement of Methodological Pluralism, in Chen, G.-M. & Starosta, W. J. (eds.), *Dialogue among Diversities*. Washington D.C.: National Communication Association.

Notes

1 Servaes (1999:17–23) explains modernization as the unilinear and evolutionary perspective of seeing development in the West as an ultimate goal for the rest of the world. By catching up with the West in terms of transferring Western technology, building up communication networks, adopting to a capitalistic economy and Western forms of democracy, et cetera, the assumption of modernization is that the developing world will become a developed one (Rostow, 1953; Schramm, 1964).

2 It is worth noticing that on December 21, 2010, the Thai government abstained from voting in the UN general assembly to renew its routine condemnation of the justified killing of various categories of vulnerable people including gays, lesbians, bisexuals, and transgenders (The Guardian December 20, 2010 http://www.guardian.co.uk/world/2010/dec/21/gay-rights-row-un-resolution, accessed on March 2, 2012 and Prachatai http://prachatai.com/journal/2010/12/32460, accessed on March 2, 2012).

Chapter 15

Framing Illness and Health on the USAID Website for Senegal

Joelle Cruz

Introduction

As we consider sustainability and culture in communication, it is particularly important to be critical of hegemonic discourses deployed by transnational development agencies. These institutions have gained prominence in a global context characterized by the contraction of national borders and the subsequent erosion of the nation-state. In Africa in particular, institutions such as the World Bank, the IMF, and USAID have an overt social change goal and significantly shape education and health. In the latter area, development agencies edict public health policies and allocate significant resources to infrastructures and equipment. This increasing role deserves attention from scholars because such interventions are far from being innocuous. Development organizations often prioritize certain items on a political and economic agenda. Their framing of illness and health is connected to larger ideological, cultural, and socioeconomic dimensions.

This chapter examines USAID health success stories for Senegal, a West African country with a total population of 12,171,265 (http://www.gouv.sn). This country was selected for this study because of the vested interests of the American government in this part of sub-Saharan Africa. Hills (2007) contends that USAID and other types of American aid serve as "Trojan horses" (p. 627) in a post 9/11 context characterized by heightened concerns about terrorism. In this perspective, countries such as Senegal, Tanzania, and Kenya fulfill a counterterrorist agenda (Hills, 2007). The stories that are featured on the website for Senegal celebrate the accomplishments of the agency in the realm of health. They cover topics as various as HIV/AIDS, malaria, malnutrition, mutual health organizing, and reproductive and women's health. USAID success stories are a prime public relations' tool written in accessible and nontechnical language and targeted at a general audience. They are often accompanied by photographs capturing the changes brought about by USAID. In addition, the stories rely on personal testimonies of aid beneficiaries, who are quoted verbatim. The first objective of this chapter is to grasp systemwide oppression, which is often masked by a generic social change agenda. If USAID programs make health improvements in the lives of Senegalese people, they also have structural consequences. Not only does aid affect local economies, but also cultures and traditions. In the latter realm, it can disrupt community and kinship ties by changing how individuals relate to one another. Of interest here is the fact that USAID success stories are oblivious to these implications. The stories weave a common narrative of triumph over illness and dire health conditions and overlook the economic and political gains of USAID in the process.

The second objective of the chapter is to document the use of a negative historical trope in order to further a social change agenda. This is visible in the framing of illness and health. The success stories deploy images of Africa as an uncivilized continent stricken by disease. In doing so, they play on negative stereotypes originating from the European colonization of Africa. In such a perspective, USAID health accomplishments are presented as a departure from archaism and a move toward progress. Finally, this chapter questions a participatory approach to social change, which has emerged as a dominant paradigm in development praxis in recent years. USAID success stories emphasize the involvement of local communities in its health programs. This is a welcome change from previous top-down approaches focusing on expert voices. However, the emphasis on participation overlooks problematic aspects of collaboration between USAID and locals. As much as community members provide feedback on the type of health assistance and support needed, the primary decision-maker remains USAID. In this vein, the idea that all stakeholders are equal is illusory. In what follows, I first present a review of literature, followed by an analysis and a discussion sections.

Review of literature

Communication and the discourse of development

Scholars have given increasing attention to discursive approaches to development since the end of the eighties (Escobar, 1995). Critical and deconstructionist perspectives (Escobar, 1995) in particular suggest the existence of a dominant discourse of development defined as "a specific and historically produced way of looking at the world [...] embedded within wider relations of power-power that is manifest in the scientific 'expertise' of development economists" (Ebrahim, 2001:80). This idea has emerged as an explanatory framework for asymmetrical transactions between developed and developing countries on a macrolevel, and unequal relationships between development institutions and aid recipients at a micro scale. The discourse of development is characterized by "the construction of the poor and underdeveloped as universal, preconstituted subjects, based on the privilege of the representers; [and] the exercise of power over the Third World made possible by this discursive homogeinization" (Escobar, 1995:53). This meta discourse includes a set of "interconnected discourses in which these development experts and organizations might be located: development discourse, environmental discourse, human rights discourse" (Ebrahim, 2001:80).

Analyses of development discourse have invested talk and written text (Ebrahim, 2001). While much research that stems from development anthropology has emphasized ethnographic approaches (Kaufmann, 1997), a second trend has been the analysis of institutional artifacts like reports, meeting minutes, and memos (Escobar, 1995; Rew, 1997; Sridhar, 2008). For instance, Ebrahim (2001) explored the impact of development discourses on Indian NGOs by using archival and project documents. Similarly, Ferguson (1990) conducted extensive work on development discourse in Lesotho by examining among other texts a World Bank report on the country. The focus on organizational documents is also shared in development communication (Wilkins, 1999). Over the years, the analysis of organizational texts has gained prominence in a field concerned with "strategic intervention toward social change initiated by institutions and communities" (Wilkins & Mody, 2001:385). For example, Rodríguez (2001) conducted a case study on an agrarian reform project funded by the World Bank in Columbia. She (2001) analyzed several project documents as well as a field diary written by a member of the project management team. Results reveal the exclusion of women from the World Bank's project documents. This absence corroborates the predominance of a male-dominated focus in the field of development. Rodríguez (2001) specifies that this emphasis is supported by local articulations of women's roles.

Like Rodríguez (2001), Wilkins (1999) researched institutional documents, studying more specifically texts originating from USAID as well as NGOs, multilateral, and bilateral organizations. Her goal was to uncover the importance of gender in the framing of project recipients as well as communication as it related to social change. She found that a majority of the projects sought to "persuade audiences to change their behavior" (p. 55). They also used a "social-marketing model," which emphasizes the private sector (p. 56). Existing literature demonstrates that organizational artifacts like project documents and mission statements are rich texts, which inform us on the discourse of development. Success stories constitute an unexplored media that may add to our understanding of knowledge and power. In the following section, I explain the importance of the social construction of disease in Africa.

Africa and the social construction of disease

But before going any further, it is necessary to define social constructionism and to connect it to meanings of health and illness. Social constructionism focuses on the arbitrariness of collective meanings and the notion that there is no tangible reality (Miller, 2005). Rather, individuals co-construct their world through interaction with others. These interactions, which contribute to shape our beliefs on health and illness, also inform our behaviors. In a contemporary world characterized by large-scale information diffusion, the social construction of health and illness is also fostered by the mass media.

Scholars in the humanities (Young, 2009; Arrington, 2008; Williams et al., 2008) and social sciences (Dowbigin, 2009; Sember, 2008) have shown how various illnesses and health conditions are framed in particular ways. Social construction of illness and health is particularly relevant for critical research on Africa. Perhaps more than anywhere else is the framing of disease connected to larger historical, ideological, political, and socioeconomic dynamics. The continued exploitation and marginalization of the African continent as well as the permanence of stereotypical images has durably shaped representations of disease. As we examine the topic of health and Africa, a first observation pertains to the most commonly studied illnesses. A significant strand of research has focused on HIV / AIDS (Chepngeno-Langat et al., 2010: Collins et al., 2009; Dlamini et al., 2009; Lynch et al., 2010; Veenstra

& Oyier, 2006; Uys, 2003). While HIV/AIDS rightfully constitutes a health crisis (Brijnath, 2007; Yeboah, 2006), which deserves our full attention, the constant scrutiny exerted by Western scholars and practitioners points to the existence of deeper systemic bias.

Brijnath (2007) uncovers this dimension in a study on the coverage of HIV/AIDS by *TIME Magazine*. Using content analysis, she (2007) argues that the depiction of the HIV/AIDS crisis fits into a larger narrative, which paints Africa in a negative light. Brijnath (2007:376) states, "Africa is portrayed as the epicenter of the world's human crises – AIDS, overpopulation, poverty, illiteracy and malnutrition". This vision dates back to the colonial era, where both science and literature saw Africa as a disease-ridden site (Brijnath, 2007). Brijnath's (2007) study is interesting because it deconstructs contemporary representations of HIV/AIDS and shows their connections with a wider system of oppression. In the same vein, Jones (2004:391) contends that the construction of Africa as the "Dark Continent" during colonialism informs donor discourses on HIV/AIDS in contemporary times. In such a perspective, "not only has Africa been represented as the cradle of HIV/AIDS, it is also depicted by academics through the lens of sexual practices which are seen as abnormal, untamed, and dangerous" (Jones, 2004:391). Jones (2004:392–393) argues that:

> The spatial tropes [...] have provided the most enduring metaphors for Western misrepresentation of the Other. These metaphors have also provided the intellectual foundations for the tutelage (previously the "civilising mission"), management and intervention upon which modern development is premised.

This argument sheds light on the significance of power in discourses of health and illness. It encourages scholars studying health and Africa to question their ideological tenets and to give attention to macro meanings. Because much research on social construction of disease in Africa has been conducted on HIV/AIDS, this study takes a more general stance by examining various illnesses and conditions. The intent here is to gain a broader understanding of framings of health and illness in Africa.

Research questions

How does USAID construct illness and health in its health success stories for Senegal?
In what ways does this framing fit into larger ideological, cultural, and political considerations of development?

USAID

This section provides background information on USAID and its work in Africa. The American agency was formally instituted at the beginning of the sixties and draws its origins from the Marshall Plan, which provided recovery assistance to Post World War II

Europe (Lancaster, 2007; *About USAID*, 2009). USAID fulfilled a "dual purpose of diplomacy and development" from its inception (Lancaster, 2007:72). In Africa in particular, diplomatic goals of the agency often hindered its development agenda. This was particularly relevant during the Cold War era, when USAID continuously supported the Democratic Republic of the Congo, despite misuse of aid and rampant corruption (Lancaster, 2007). Over the decades, USAID has expanded its economic mission to include issues pertaining to human rights, security, and peace operations (Lancaster, 2007). The agency faced criticism in the nineties with "a growing sense that aid had not been as effective as hoped, especially in Africa" (Lancaster, 2007:86). This period was marked by a decrease in aid (Lancaster, 2007). At the beginning of the twenty-first century, assistance to developing countries was part of a larger strategy, adopted by the Bush administration after the September 11th attacks. Emphasis was put on the fight against HIV/AIDS as a conservative Christian lobby influenced foreign affairs (Lancaster, 2007).

Method: Critical discourse analysis

Critical discourse analysis, often referred to as CDA, is used as a method for the study. Scholars across disciplines have declined this approach in various ways, but I use Fairclough's (1989, 1995) perspective here. In his pioneering work, he (1989, 1995) contends that CDA emphasizes context and power. This means that language doesn't exist in a vacuum. Rather, it is part of our social word and "is conditioned by other, non-linguistic, parts of society" (1989:24). This idea differentiates critical discourse analysis from other approaches like linguistics and sociolinguistics, which have often conceptualized language as abstraction and focused on surface features of texts (Fairclough, 1989). On the contrary, CDA regards discourse as "process" (1989:24). What the term suggests is constant change and fluidity in a discursive space characterized by the reciprocal influence between language and its users. A second important idea is the relation of discourse to power.

At a microlevel, language and its uses shed light on the nature of daily interactions suffused with rapports of authority and obedience. At a macrolevel, discourse is connected to relations of power in a capitalist system (Fairclough, 1989). In this perspective, the powerful group attempts to maintain its position by achieving a "maximization of its exploitation and domination of another" (Fairclough, 1989:35). Discourse ultimately constitutes the locus of a struggle, shaped by class interests under capitalism. CDA as a method is suited for this study because it connects local dimensions of texts to macro phenomena. It can thus account for the intricacy of transactions in the development sphere. On the one hand, these exchanges are mundane and characteristic of everyday life in the development world. On the other hand, meanings of illness and health can't be detached from larger economic, political, and ideological considerations.

Texts

I examined fifteen health success stories featured on the USAID website for Senegal. Stories that were one to two pages long covered the topics of HIV/AIDS, malaria, malnutrition, mutual health organizing, and reproductive and women's health. When analyzing the stories, I followed the three steps outlined by Fairclough (1989, 1995), which move us from microlevel to macrostructure. First is description where critical discourse analysts focus on lexicon and grammar. Specific attention was given to key words and to descriptions here. Second is interpretation that connects linguistic characteristics of texts to "common-sense assumptions" (Fairclough, 1989:140). During this stage, individuals typically use previous knowledge to make sense of texts. This often involves drawing on "a repertoire of schemata" (1989:144). Finally, it is explanation that constitutes the macrolevel part of critical discourse analysis. This step shows how discourse is "part of a social process, as a social practice, showing how it is determined by social structures, and what reproductive effects discourses can cumulatively have on those structures, sustaining them or changing them" (1989:163).

Analysis

There are two overarching themes for this analysis: illness and health. Four major pairs fit under these themes. First is inevitability and control. Second is archaism and modernity. Third is disconnection and organizing. Fourth is underdevelopment and development.

Inevitability and control

Inevitability pertains to illness as opposed to control, which is connected to health. As we consider inevitability, it is essential to note that it is a key characteristic of illness in Senegal prior to intervention by USAID. It can be defined as the permanence of rampant disease, which is a daily occurrence. It is also framed as dangerous and pervasive. This idea is illustrated by the following quote:

> Senegal's annual rainy season brings both a blessing and a curse. While every drop is precious to the country's farmers, rains also create a breeding ground for malaria-laden mosquitoes. Thousands of Senegalese die every year from the disease, and children and pregnant women are particularly vulnerable. In the immense collective of Dialocoto in southeastern Senegal, Malaria hits hard. (Story 8)

Present in this excerpt is fatalism. This is apparent through the reference to death, which often strikes individuals of all age groups. The idea conveyed in this passage is that nothing can be done to stop the loss of human lives. There is a notion of permanence visible through the mention of the "rainy season," which irremediably brings malaria. This is framed in such a way that it overlooks temporality. Rather, the immemorial dominates as malaria seems to go back far in time. A strong impression is the lack of control and agency of individuals, who are subjected to a hostile environment. This idea is representative of a common trope, which depicts the African continent as a space governed by environmental forces. In such a configuration, natural elements are unleashed and bring devastation and disease. In addition to environmental factors, human vulnerability is accentuated by conditions of poverty. For instance, one story offers the testimony of a woman who became a sex worker because of a life of scarcity. It reads:

> I quit school in the 11th grade. My parents were poor. At a young age, I was confronted with the hardships of life and started going out with boys to earn money to meet my needs. I was caught in a trap that cost me the best years of my life. (Story 2)

As shown by this quote, risky sexual behavior that can lead to illness is connected to destitution and misery. These two factors increase the likelihood for individuals to contract illnesses. By focusing on a hostile environment and on poverty, the stories create a common narrative of inescapability. Individuals are caught in a vicious circle from birth and can't change their lives. A last idea featured is the human, material, and economic cost engendered by the inevitability of disease. As indicated previously, illnesses cause many deaths. For example, one story mentions "For every 100 Senegalese babies born, six die before their first birthday. Although this rate is an improvement over the past, it is still too high" (Story 4). By shedding light on the human drama of infant death, USAID adds a dramatic element to the success stories. It also frames Africans of all age categories as victims. Other consequences of illness are of a material and economic nature. For instance, a story reads that women have "spent scarce resources, and missed work to care for others" in times of illness (Story 1).

The opposite of inevitability is control. This dimension comes with USAID intervention and is associated with health. Control encompasses the close circumscription and monitoring of disease as well as means deployed to tackle it. This process is often framed using strong and vivid terminology. One story in particular employs the metaphor of war to describe USAID efforts to fight malaria. This is apparent in the following quote:

> Masked assailants moved swiftly from hut to hut, sweeping through entire villages and spraying lethal doses in a search-and-destroy mission. But there was no cause for fear – among humans, that is. The welcomed intruders blasted long-lasting insecticides on walls and ceilings to terminate the real killers in Senegal: mosquitoes. (Story 3)

This quotation conveys a vision of extreme technology, deployed aggressively to tackle malaria and its vectors. When considering illness monitoring, the notion of measurement is an important one. USAID emphasizes the use of rigorous methods, which document the extent of illness. The organization also associates success with quantifiable results. For example, one story states that "nearly 700,000 Senegalese were less likely to contract malaria during the rainy season" after a USAID spraying campaign (Story 3). Another story indicates that a local radio "reached 7,550 Senegalese with life-saving sexual health messages" (Story 2).

As shown by these two exemplars, it is important that the effects of health campaigns be assessed by numerical data. Lacking here is a more systematic use of in-depth qualitative account of results, despite a few testimonies of locals who report that their lives have improved. Not only are measurement methods rigorous, but also means used in the field to respond to epidemics. USAID often employs multilayered strategies and plans, which consider alternatives in case of failure. In the stories, control serves to change the narrative of inevitability by inverting the negative consequences associated with it. It reduces numbers of infections and deaths, and allows individuals to garner more savings, and to use their time productively by working. Control is more generally linked with notions of progress, as defined by the West. In this vein, being able to predict environmental changes and disease is often associated with civilization. These meanings that suffuse the success stories take us back to the traditional dichotomies of barbarism/civilization and Africa/the West.

Archaism and modernity

A second pair is that of archaism and modernity. These dimensions apply both to the individual and structural levels. First is archaism, which translates to beliefs and behaviors. Beliefs pertain to a set of convictions, whereas behaviors encompass actions taken by individuals to enact change. Health success stories for Senegal implicitly connect beliefs and behaviors of aid beneficiaries to ignorance. Locals are presented as being uninformed and unaware of vital health information. For instance, one story reports the testimony of a taxi driver who states about sexual activity: "At the station, they say 'a virile man must enjoy sex flesh-to-flesh without any barrier in between'" (Story 12). In a similar story, an individual working in the transport industry reports: "many believed that AIDS was a myth, a white man's disease, and that condoms were a ploy to slow down procreation and take the pleasure out of sex" (Story 11). He adds: "at the station, sexual banter passes easily between men and women, youth, and adults. It's a market governed by supply and demand" (Story 11). These two stories, which play on the ignorance of the locals, also convey a strong subtext of morality. Senegalese men are featured as promiscuous individuals who have numerous sexual partners and are irresponsible. This notion can be traced back to colonialism (Jones, 2004) where African sexuality was depicted as animal-like and practices like polygamy were cut out from the cultural and social contexts of their emergence and reduced to perversion.

In many stories, ignorance is often conflated with superstition and nonscientific assumptions. For instance, one story features a HIV positive woman who lived in isolation, because she feared stigma from a community misinformed about HIV/AIDS (Story 15). This ignorance is remedied through knowledge, which allows individuals to make the transition from archaism to modernity. This move made possible thanks to USAID training, impacts beliefs and behaviors positively. For instance, in terms of beliefs, one individual mentions that "This program has triggered something in myself personally and for the whole radio station. It has really changed us" (Story 10). In another story, a man states: "My friends are getting tested for STIs and HIV and we are all more willing to use condoms now that we know how to protect our own health" (Story 9). By focusing on change in beliefs and behaviors, USAID frames itself as an agent of transformation, thus justifying its organizational mission. Not only do dimensions of archaism and modernity apply to the individual level, but also to the structural one. In terms of archaism, success stories emphasize the absence or inadequacy of health equipment, personnel, and infrastructures in Senegal. As an illustration, one story indicates: "Dialocoto has only one health worker, a nurse, to serve the needs of 14,000 people spread among 50 villages in a space larger than Delaware. For many patients, a trip to the nurse is an exhausting and expensive ordeal" (Story 8).

This passage sheds light on the lack of medical personnel and the negative consequences resulting from it. It is also a general commentary on the inadequacy of the Senegalese healthcare system. When stories acknowledge the existence of equipment, personnel, or infrastructures, they are presented as unfit. Rudimentary tools are used by workers who lack essential training tenets and treat patients in underequipped facilities. This situation improves after USAID involvement. The organization focuses on its contribution to systemic change by training health personnel, providing equipment, and creating medical accommodations. For example, one story credits USAID for the introduction and diffusion of newborn warming tables in a rural health center (Story 4). In addition, the story mentions that the health center "is starting to train all its nurses in essential newborn care techniques" thanks to USAID (Story 4). Evident here is an emphasis on technology brought about by USAID. Emphasizing the role of USAID as an organization aiming for structural and individual change calls for several remarks.

First, it frames it as an institution concerned by humanitarian dimensions of development. As stated in the stories, the material support brought by USAID is needed and sometimes contributes to saving lives. For instance, many stories show how healthcare provided in rural areas allows for the alleviation of chronic diseases, which were previously endemic. This emphasis on the humanitarian constructs the organization as altruistic while disguising other dimensions like economic control and demands, which USAID imposes on aid recipients.

Disconnection and organizing

A third pair is disconnection and organizing. Disconnection is related to the atomization of community members, who fail to organize and generate change in the area of health. Of interest in the success stories, is the notion that individual attempts to organize are doomed to fail. For instance, one story relates the efforts deployed by women to create a mutual health organization (MHO) by stating: "They realized their need for an MHO, and even studied the possibilities, with the first attempt failing in 2005. A second feasibility study led to an activity that rattled and crumbled over a leadership crisis" (Story 6).

Highlighted in this excerpt, is the inability of the women to organize efficiently and to create an MHO. This obstacle is overcome thanks to USAID, which "stepped in to help resolve the conflicts by convening several meetings to set up a 32-member steering committee from community-based organizations" (Story 6). This quote emphasizes the role of USAID as an organizing force. The agency focuses on the importance of this dimension in all the stories studied. Salient here is a specific organizational model connected to the notion of participatory development. The latter is an approach that stresses involvement of all societal actors as a way to foster economic and social development. This perspective attempts to encourage collaboration between local communities, state agents, and USAID. This is visible through the following statement: "USAID, the Government of Senegal, and local communities are working together to change that" (Story 4). Of interest in the stories, is the representation of local communities as heterogeneous. They typically include various actors with divergent interests. In this perspective, USAID frames itself as a facilitator making individuals realize the importance of unity. For instance, one story emphasizes the involvement of religious leaders by focusing on an imam: "In fact, ever since his exposure last November to what Islam has to say about birth spacing and discussions of related health issues, he takes every occasion to talk about them: weddings, funerals, baptisms, prayers, religious holidays" (Story 14).

This quotation underlines the centrality of imams in local communities. USAID reports that it is essential to involve them in a conversation on health because of their significance. The story attempts to demonstrate that contrary to dominant beliefs in local communities, Islam is not opposed to contraception. As a conclusion, the participatory approach to health is seen here as the best way to involve local communities in health matters. It replaces a perspective that privileged the discourse of experts and imposed itself on aid beneficiaries. In this regard, it seems promising as it focuses on social change from the ground up (Cooke & Kothari, 2004). However, a strand of development research has criticized this perspective, deemed as a "tyranny" by some (Cooke & Kothari, 2004:3). I argue that this dominance serves to mask certain problematic aspects of collaboration between USAID and locals. First, as much as community members provide feedback on the type of health assistance and support that they need, the sole decision-maker remains USAID. This comment encourages us to remain cautionary as participatory approaches convey the flawed assumption that participants are equal.

In the specific case of USAID, aid beneficiaries often take part in predesigned programs with set aid packages, which provides them with little leeway to give input. It appears that their impact on shaping development projects is less important than what USAID indicates. This dimension is absent in the stories, which often accentuate the adhesion of aid recipients. Of importance here, is the use of individuals' voices, which serve as a testimony of success. There is no space for dissent in the stories as a majority of locals who are helped by USAID appear satisfied. While it is clear that individuals benefit from programs, which can have life-changing effects, the systematic focus on success is problematic. This extreme vision conveyed thanks to the instrumentalization of the disenfranchised masks the possible shortcomings of development projects.

Underdevelopment and development

Illness and health framed in USAID success stories for Senegal ultimately help articulate underdevelopment and development. As defined in the stories, underdevelopment constitutes a mythical site circumscribed in space and time and governed by a set of norms. Underdevelopment stands as the opposite of contemporary understandings of development. If the latter is defined by the existence of infrastructures and the access of individuals to basic life necessities and to a relative comfort, underdevelopment is marked by absence and destitution. In the success stories, the space of underdevelopment is remote and inaccessible. In this space, change is inexistent and living conditions have remained identical since immemorial times. Not only are space and time framed in a specific manner but also norms, which are of a political, social, and religious nature. These norms constitute hampers to USAID's mission of development. Stories report political disorganization and unruliness and archaic beliefs. For example, one story about a woman who sells condoms reports:

> At times, she faces obstacles in her work. People sometimes tell her that Islam forbids the use of condoms because it entices young men and women to have "bad behavior" and encourages sexual relations. Others believe that condoms prevent pregnancy, and many traditional Senegalese still prefer large families. (Story 13)

Religious and individual beliefs constitute obstacles to the use of condoms, thus encouraging the spread of illness. The latter is inescapable and dominant in underdevelopment. It governs the lives of individuals, who have to organize their lives around disease. The framing of underdevelopment as it relates to space, time, and individuals is not novel. In reality, USAID employs an existing trope, which can be traced back to the colonization of West Africa by European countries in the nineteenth and twentieth centuries. As Europe established itself as the center of the enlightened world, it depicted Africa as its uncivilized other. The latter was set in another space and time, and governed by practices and customs, deemed barbarian. This vision justified a project of civilization, which to some extent is rearticulated in contemporary times through the mission of development agencies. If underdevelopment is a disease-stricken space, development allows for its tight circumscription. In this regard, illness relegated to marginal spaces is not endemic. Rather, it is rigorously controlled by individuals, who use technology to measure it. USAID ultimately traces a progression from illness to health in the success stories, by framing the two notions in broader texts of underdevelopment and development. The following chart summarizes findings for the study:

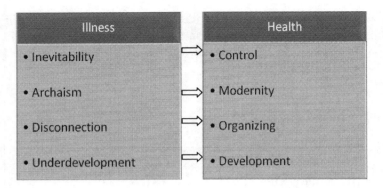

Conclusion and discussion

This study sheds light on the importance of USAID success stories for Senegal, which constitute an important medium to understand how the organization frames illness and health. First is the pair of inevitability and control, which respectively fit under illness and health. Inevitability is characterized by the endemic nature of diseases, which are inescapable and have serious human, economic, and social consequences. On the other hand, the dimension of control is defined by the tackling of illness through rigorous methods and means, which include technology. The second pair is that of archaism and modernity, which apply to both individual and structural levels. On an individual level, archaism is connected to ignorant beliefs and behaviors perpetuated by misinformed locals. On the structural level, it applies to the lack of medical supplies, equipment, and infrastructures. Modernity is achieved through knowledge, which helps individuals change negative beliefs and behaviors. It also translates to macrolevel transformation through the development of health structures by USAID. A third pair is that of disconnection and organizing. In terms of disconnection, individual efforts are inefficient prior to USAID intervention because of poor organizing. This is resolved by the organization, which serves as a facilitator. It connects communities and enables them to be united through a participatory development approach. Ultimately, understandings of illness and health feed into larger ideological, economic, and political considerations of development. They contribute more specifically to shape underdevelopment as a disease-ridden space and development as a site where illness is systematically controlled by individuals, who regain agency of their settings.

As we consider theoretical implications, the study sheds light on the importance of power, which shapes texts as innocuous as success stories. On the one hand, we gain much information on the micro nature of situated health transactions between local communities and USAID in Senegal. On the other hand, the stories are rich in ideological meanings as they reflect the unequal power balance between the United States and countries of the South. One way of expanding, this study would be to include more success stories and to possibly compare different West African countries. A second idea would be to explore the space between underdevelopment and development, which as now is absent of the success stories.

In terms of practical implications, this study encourages us to reexamine the paradigm of participatory development, which has become a dominant perspective and is widely used in health. As highlighted previously, this approach presents improvements from a first perspective, which didn't give voice to the locals. However, it is important that participatory development be examined in a more critical light. The tendency to view it as a cure-all is problematic because it masks the fact that this model still operates on a given ideology. In addition, it can be instrumentalized to serve the political and economic interests of aid agencies. Secondly, the framing of health and illness by USAID is important because it feeds into praxis. Aid programs are developed based on the ideological assumptions that are present in the stories. Until these change, transformation toward more positive ways of developing won't occur.

References

About USAID. (2009). USAID website.

Arrington, M. (2008). Prostate Cancer and the Social Construction of Masculine Sexual Identity. *International Journal of Men's Health, 7*(3), 299–306.

Brijnath, B. (2007). It's about TIME: Engendering AIDS in Africa. *Culture, Health & Sexuality, 9*(4), 371–386.

Chepngeno-Langat, G., Falkingham, J., Madise, N., & Evandrou, M. (2010). Socioeconomic Differentials between HIV Caregivers and Noncaregivers: Is There a Selection Effect? A Case of Older People Living in Nairobi City Slums. *Research on Aging, 32*(1), 67–96.

Cooke, B., & Kothari, U. (2004). *Participation: The New Tyranny?* New York, NY: Zeb Books.

Collins, P., Berkman, A., Mestry, K., & Pillai, A. (2009). HIV Prevalence among Men and Women Admitted to a South African Public Psychiatric Hospital. *AIDS Care, 21*(7), 863–867.

Dlamini, P., Wantland, D., Makoae, L., et al. (2009). HIV Stigma and Missed Medications in HIV-positive People in Five African Countries. *AIDS Patient Care & STDs, 23*(5), 377–387.

Dowbiggin, I. (2009). High Anxieties: The Social Construction of Anxiety Disorders. *Canadian Journal of Psychiatry, 54*(7), 429–436.

Ebrahim, A. (2001). NGO Behavior and Development Discourse: Cases from Western India. *Voluntas: International Journal of Voluntary and Nonprofit Organizations, 12*, 79–101.

Escobar, A. (1995). *Encountering Development: The Making and Unmaking of the Third World.* Princeton, NJ: Princeton University Press.

Fairclough, N. (1989). *Language and Power.* New York: Longman.

——— (1995). *Critical Discourse Analysis: The Critical Study of Language.* New York: Longman.

Ferguson, J. (1990). *The Anti-politics Machine: "Development," Depoliticization, and Bureaucratic Power in Lesotho.* Cambridge: Cambridge University Press.

Hills, A. (2006). Trojan Horses? USAID, Counter-terrorism and Africa's Police. *Third World Quarterly, 27*(4), 629–643.

Jones, P. S. (2004). When 'Development' Devastates: Donor Discourses, Access to HIV/AIDS Treatment in Africa and Rethinking the Landscape of Development. *Third World Quarterly*, 25, 385–404.

Kaufmann, G. (1997). Watching the Developers: A Partial Ethnography, in Grillo, R. D. & Stirrat, R. L. (eds.), *Discourses of Development: Anthropological Perspectives*. New York: Berg Publishers, pp. 107–133.

Lancaster, C. (2007). *Foreign Aid*. Chicago: The University of Chicago Press.

Lynch, I., Brouard, P., & Visser, M. (2010). Constructions of Masculinity among a Group of South African Men Living with HIV/AIDS: Reflections on Resistance and Change. *Culture, Health & Sexuality*, 12(1), 15–27.

Miller, K. (2005). *Communication Theories: Perspectives, Processes, and Contexts*. New York: McGraw-Hill.

Rew, A. (1997). The Donor's Discourse: Official Social Development Knowledge in the 1980s, in Grillo, R. D. & Stirrat, R. L. (eds.), *Discourses of Development: Anthropological Perspectives*. New York: Berg Publishers, pp. 81–106.

Rodríguez, C. (2001). Shattering Butterflies and Amazons: Women and Gender in a Colombian Wilkins, K. 1999. Development Discourse on Gender and Communication in Strategies for Social Change. *Journal of Communication*, 49, 44–64.

Sember, R. (2008). The Social Construction of ARVs in South Africa. *Global Public Health*, 3, 58–75.

Sridhar, D. (2008). Hungry for Change: The Worldbank in India. *South Asia Research*, 28 (2), 147–168.

Uys, L. (2003). Aspects of the Care of People with HIV/AIDS in South Africa. *Public Health Nursing*, 20(4), 271–280.

Veenstra, N. & Oyier, A. (2006). The Burden of HIV-related Illness on Outpatient Health Services in KwaZulu-Natal, South Africa. *AIDS Care*, 18(3), 262–268.

Wilkins, K. 1999. Development Discourse on Gender and Communication in Strategies for Social Change. *Journal of Communication*, 49, 44–64.

Wilkins, K. & Mody, B. (eds.). 2001. Communication, Development, Social Change, and Global Disparity. *Communication Theory Special Issue*, 11(4).

Williams, S., Seasle, C., Boden, S., Lowe, P., & Steinberg, D. (2008). Medicalization and Beyond: The Social Construction of Insomnia and Snoring in the News. *Health: An Interdisciplinary Journal for the Social Study of Health, Illness & Medicine*, 12(2), 251–268.

Yeboah, I. (2007). HIV/AIDS and the Construction of Sub-Saharan Africa: Heuristic Lessons from the Social Sciences for Policy. *Social Science & Medicine*, 64(5), 1128–1150.

Young, E. (2009). Memoirs: Rewriting the Social Construction of Mental Illness. *Narrative Inquiry*, 19(1), 52–68.

Chapter 16

Communication for Social Change in Kenya: Using DVD-led Discussion to Challenge HIV/AIDS Stigma among Health Workers

Katrina Phillips and Betty Chirchir

Introduction

Communication for social change involves a range of programs and materials addressing the health needs of the public. Far less attention has been focused on the needs of health workers. However, as health workers are also members of the public, their dual cultural reference is an important point to consider in the broader process of communication for social change. Professionally speaking, health workers may be well-armed with information on health, prevention, diagnosis, and treatments. But as individuals, their own health behaviors and attitudes and subsequent social impact are often overlooked.

Health workers are in the frontline position of interpersonal communicator, encouraging people to change widely held attitudes and behaviors for their own health and well-being. As such, they are in a significant position of influence. Nevertheless, health workers may lack the self-awareness and self-confidence that their professional role assumes they possess.

This chapter describes an integrated communication approach that was developed with and used by health workers in Kenya, challenging stigma among health professionals. The overall objective was to improve the delivery and uptake of TB and HIV health services, specifically through the participation of those tasked to bring about change: the health workers.

Developed from a paper presented to the Communication and HIV/AIDS Working Group at the IAMCR Conference 2010 in Portugal, this chapter focuses on using DVD-led awareness sessions featuring personal testimonies and drama clips. At closed group sessions held in health facilities, the DVD aims to serve as a catalyst to open discussion, reflection, and ultimately social change as determined by the participants. The design process of the DVD content and its use was closely guided by a core group of HIV/TB specialist health workers. The DVD awareness sessions provided the space and opportunity for interpersonal communication within the broader public health communication project to address TB and HIV stigma using a multimedia strategy.

In a bid to support the sustainability of change, this chapter closes with a plea for funders to pay more attention to the value of longer-term evaluations of communication for social change projects.

The project context

TB or tuberculosis is the most common opportunistic infection among people living with HIV and AIDS. Close to 48 percent of new TB patients in Kenya are co-infected with HIV (UNAIDS, 2010). Within the Ministry of Public Health and Sanitation in Kenya, the national HIV/AIDS program (NASCOP) and the division dedicated to TB control (DLTLD) work with a national policy to cross-test and treat for TB and HIV whenever a customer needs either.

In 2006, the United States Centers for Disease Control, Global AIDS Program Kenya awarded Danya International the contract to manage a communication program promoting the public uptake of cross-testing for TB and HIV, funded by PEPFAR. Mediae, a production and development company based in Kenya, was contracted to design and deliver the communication strategy and materials. The co-authors participated as Project Manager for Mediae (Katrina Phillips) and Lead Facilitator of the Awareness Sessions for HLSP (Betty Chirchir).

Designing a strategy

Denise Gray-Felder of the Communication for Social Change Consortium describes Communication for Social Change as "a process of public and private dialogue through which people themselves define who they are, what they want and how they can act collectively to get what they want and need in order to improve their lives" (UNAIDS, 2007). As a first step toward developing the project, the issues around and barriers to testing for HIV and TB were explored with representatives of the multiple stakeholders at individual, environmental, and policy levels. Research included holding nine Focus Group Discussions (FGDs) in three different provincial locations and among three different groups: TB Patients, Health workers, and Community members. Further interviews were held with thirteen key informants working with TB and HIV programs in Kenya, ranging from those working on the health delivery frontline to decision-makers at policy level. A literature review was also carried out. The findings of the background research were then presented to and explored at a two-day stakeholder meeting attended by 45 stakeholders. The goal of the meeting was to define the focus of the activities, to identify the core objective, message, and channels of communication of the campaign.

Situation analysis

The FGDs and interviews revealed that there is a relationship between TB and HIV. As an interviewee put it: "They are friends, those two" (FGD, Nairobi). This perception of a co-relationship led to a widespread reluctance to test for either and a fear of being seen seeking treatment for either. At the heart of these findings was stigma. Not only among and between patients but often directed at patients by health workers themselves. Wider literature research supports these findings. "Stigma and discrimination by health workers compromises their provision of quality care, which is critical for helping patients adhere to medications and maintain their overall health and wellbeing. Stigma also acts as a barrier to accessing services both for the general population, as well as health providers themselves" (Nyblade et al., 2009).

Within the FGDs, health workers expressed their own reluctance to test for HIV, disclose their status to family and colleagues and their fear of being seen accessing treatment by patients or colleagues. In a work environment where health workers who were responsible for counseling patients to cross-test for HIV and TB themselves conveyed high levels of stigma and discrimination, many were finding their task difficult. They were reporting poor uptake for cross-testing among their clients.

Yet conversely, where health workers and counselors had tested and were confident of their own status (be it negative or positive), they reported better uptake among clients offered cross-testing, better adherence to treatment, and greater recognition of the need for patients' family members to come in for testing, counseling, and possibly treatment. In short, health workers who know, and are comfortable with their own TB and HIV status, appear to be more confident and successful communicators when counseling patients.

The communication strategy

Having discussed and reflected upon the research findings and key presentations, the stakeholder meeting agreed that the primary audience for the communication strategy would be health workers and the secondary audience of TB clients and their families. The objectives were to reduce HIV/TB stigma among health workers and to empower them to be effective communicators, with a positive impact on their own lives, the lives of their patients and families, and through the process to improve their skills and lessen their workload. The secondary audience representing members of the public were identified as having specific needs and would benefit from cross-testing.

The core message of the overall program was "to know your status is good for your health, your family's health and your professional skills" alongside the message "everybody can be cured of TB and treated for HIV."

Working within the budget, access to the mass-media component was national. Interactive and interpersonal communication campaigns were designed to be conducted in two provinces with the highest HIV prevalence rates in the country: 8.5 percent in Nairobi and 14.5 percent in Nyanza (NASCOP, 2009). In addition, a stigma index study reported that all forms of stigma and discrimination among the general community range from high to very high in Nyanza and Western Provinces. Stigma index indicators are (1) people expressing fear of contracting HIV from noninvasive contact with people living with HIV (PLHIV);

(2) those who judge or blame PLHIV for their illness; (3) those who have experienced with enacted stigma; (4) those who fear and express concern disclosing their status; and (5) those who note impacts of stigma on the individual, family, and community (Action Aid, 2010).

Channels of communication selected were the mass media and interpersonal communication. They reach the different levels of the social context: individual, workplace, and wider community; and reach both primary and secondary audiences. This also created opportunities for adaptable material that could work across all media and communication contexts, such as using some clips from the TV drama in the DVD as catalysts for group discussion. Sharing content and materials took a limited budget further and was also based on lessons learnt from previous programs. "Successful programs have the capacity to blend participatory methods of community dialogue and empowerment with mass media approaches and other forms of informational and motivational communication and advocacy" (UNAIDS, 2007). This approach also built on earlier Mediae experience of developing video-led discussion training, mixing drama and documentary for participatory learning through discussion among a group (http://www.mediae.org).

Mass-media approaches were focused on two storylines featured throughout six episodes of *Makutano Junction* (Campbell, 2008), a weekly television drama produced by Mediae and watched by nearly seven million Kenyans. The scriptwriters drew on the research findings and all scripts were then reviewed by Kenyan public health professionals and behavioral scientists within CDC Kenya. Plots were designed to appeal to health workers, TB patients, and their families as well as members of the wider public. At the end of each episode broadcast, a dedicated SMS number was trailed on the bottom of the screen and in voice-over, for those who wanted information leaflets in comic format, print, and further sources of information. SMSs received were logged and mapped for monitoring and response purposes.

Alongside the television programs, twelve weeks of call-in radio programs were held in local languages in Western and Nairobi Provinces. Each week covered different myths and facts around TB and HIV/AIDS with studio experts responding to SMS questions and call-ins from listeners, encouraging informed dialogue in the mass media.

The interpersonal communication method selected was to use DVD-led awareness sessions to spark discussion among health workers. The DVD featured four types of content: clips from the edutainment TV series; additional tailor-made drama scenes; interviews with professional health workers; and text leaders into a discussion break. It was designed to work as a catalyst, to illustrate behaviors and attitudes that will provoke discussion, to raise questions among the group, and to encourage the participants to determine a shift in knowledge and self-awareness, and to lead, ultimately to a call for a commitment to change. The drama clips recreated familiar scenarios, often using humor to help make initial responses and discussion more relaxed. Interviews with health workers broke the ice in opening what could be a difficult discussion of personal experiences among fellow professionals. Evidence and learning in HIV and AIDS communication more generally have highlighted the importance of interpersonal dialogue to promote reflection and change, and this interpersonal dimension has been key to the effectiveness of a range of different peer-to-peer interventions (Singhal and Rogers, 2003).

Designing the DVD

The one on one interviews featured in the DVD were filmed by health professionals, some of whom had participated in the initial stakeholder workshop, the development of the strategy, and content of the different materials. The interviewees were working in government-funded, faith-based, or privately funded health clinics, covering a range of personal experiences as health professionals to reflect different realities and possible better practices. The DVD drama content was developed from the storylines in the TV series *Makutano Junction*, featuring familiar characters who are celebrities in the Kenyan media, with specific additional scenes scripted and shot for the DVD to illustrate specific issues health workers had raised. The scripts drew on the situation analysis research and in some cases the phraseology from the FGDs and were further reviewed by CDC's Kenya team to ensure technical accuracy. These were then edited into three sections, with on-screen questions in text where the DVD would be paused to provide space for open group discussion after each scenario.

Each stage of the DVD development was reviewed by the members of the CDC team and key informants who had participated in the stakeholder meeting.

The first of three segments on stigma and discrimination gave health workers an opportunity to explore their own actions and attitudes toward TB-HIV patients and the impact of these on their work and their own health. The second segment on testing and disclosure raised different experiences and fears of health workers around knowing one's HIV status and telling others. The last segment on good communication skills helped health workers recognize the critical importance of these skills and the benefits of knowing one's own status when counseling others.

The DVD was then tested in two settings. First, with health workers attending a counseling skills course run by a team from the Eastern Deanery AIDS Relief Program in Nairobi. It was then screened and discussed by participants at a government-run health clinic in a densely populated low-income area of Nairobi, Kangemi. The DVD was well received and its comments and suggestions were included.

A training manual was developed, for use by the facilitators at the awareness sessions. Stills from the DVD were edited into a take-home handbook for participants to refer to at the end of the session, for personal notes and so they could share the program with family, friends, and colleagues. A final test of all materials was carried out by the facilitators with 25 participants from Mbagathi Hospital, Nairobi. Before screening the DVD, during a warming-up session, participants explored the relationship of TB and HIV, diagnosis, and treatment, and understandings of stigma and discrimination as approved by the Ministry of Public Health.

Extracts from the session handbook are included here to give readers a sense of the style and content of the DVD and the questions featured on the screen at the end of each part to open the group discussion. In the handbook there are stills from the *Makutano Junction* clips, specifically scripted scenarios, and interviews with professional health workers.

How does Stigma and Discrimination affect Health Workers?
Despite being able to access treatment and support, some health workers are dying silently, rather than testing and seeking treatment. Why?
(Drama Clip)

Discussion Question:
What fears prevent health workers from knowing their HIV status?
Should all health workers know their HIV status?
Possible points to discuss include
- Fear of how colleagues and patients may treat an HIV-positive staff member.
- Fear of the unknown – ignorance of one's HIV status.
- Everyone is at risk of contracting HIV, including health workers.
- Health workers will understand patients better if they know their own HIV status

How Do Health Workers Approach Testing?
(Interview clips with health professionals)
"I would prefer to be tested at any other site for VCT other than where I work"
"I've tested like three times. First and foremost I told my wife, but so far she hasn't tested. She's also hospital staff. I think it is the fear, as you could have pricked yourself"
"I went all the way to Kenyatta VCT. I introduced myself as a student. The reason I didn't say I was a health worker was so as to be able to listen to the information the counsellor was to give me"

Discussion Question:
Are these experiences familiar?
How can we make it easier?
- The importance of confidentiality.
- However you test, tell someone you trust so that you can be supported

How Do Health Workers Approach Disclosure?
(Interview clips with health professionals)
"Being open about my status has made it easy for me to talk to patients. Most colleagues look at me as an honest person by disclosing my status. It has earned me more respect"
"I formed a support group for staff who are living with HIV. And it's working ...The management is encouraging staff to know their status. You know attending to clients will be very easy if you know your own HIV status"

"Health providers need to show a lot of confidentiality, for people to come and approach you. This will only come after seeing you as a good example"

Discussion Question:
Are these experiences familiar?
How can we make it easier for health workers to disclose their status?
Are there private and accessible options for testing at your workplace?

Session participants

Thirty one awareness sessions were held in two provinces (Nyanza and Nairobi), reaching 790 health workers. The Ministry of Health (MOH) selected the clinics, at each of which a cross section of all staff was encouraged to attend. Each of the three-hour sessions had between 20 and 30 participants who were clinical and administrative members of staff including counselors, lab technicians, doctors, nurses, auxiliaries, nutritionists, and records officers. The sessions were led by two facilitators with four assistants. Eight representatives from the head office of the MOH took part in each session, providing answers to medical and policy questions in the discussions.

The range of participants throughout the design and implementation of the DVD addressed different levels of context and society. Individual health workers formed a social network of colleagues and were encouraged to reach them and the wider environment by sharing their experience of the session when using the take-home handbook. The sessions reached the workplace management who participated as individuals and as experts representing the MOH. While this project aimed to foster understanding and change attitudes, it also required action at the level of institutional policy and workplace management to support and maintain social change. "In conjunction with changing attitudes, such attention to policies in institutions such as workplaces, schools and health clinics, and wider laws and policies that challenge discriminatory practices is vital" (Panos and Healthlink Worldwide, 2007). One of the regular points raised in the discussions was the need to provide regular, confidential testing facilities for staff, although many still felt this would not be perceived as discreet and confidential enough and that self-testing was the only real option.

Evaluation

Various tools were used to evaluate the awareness-raising sessions, including pre- and posttests, end-of-session evaluations, and self-reported personal action steps. The evaluation tools were designed by Danya International to meet a project requirement for findings to be included immediately in the end-of-project report and so relied upon

Table 16.1: Average scores from participants' end-of-day evaluations.

	Score (1–5)	
Item	Nairobi	Nyanza
The level to which the objectives were achieved	4.3	4.4
Rank relevance of content covered to achieve the workshop objective	4.4	4.5
Rank the effectiveness of the learning methods used in the sessions	4.6	4.6
Rate your participation in today's session	4.1	4.1
Rate the participation of the other course participants in today's session	4.2	4.1
Rate the performance of the main facilitators	4.6	4.7

Source: Danya International (2008) *Kenya TB-HIV Communication Campaign*, Evaluation Report.

questionnaires completed on the session day. These alone may not have drawn the most informative feedback considering the context and subject matter. Further observations from the facilitators are included in this chapter to try to expand the feedback available. The findings from the tests (Table 16.1) were, however, very positive.

Perhaps more interesting from the point of view of social change was the facilitators' feedback from the open discussions participants held among themselves as a group in the DVD Awareness sessions. It appeared that many health workers felt that they were not at risk of HIV infection as were the general population. When asked for their personal experiences with testing, the health workers were initially hesitant to discuss it. The health workers who spoke about their own experiences of testing on the DVD created an opportunity for session participants to begin to share their own experiences. This led to revelations that many went to great lengths to avoid other healthcare workers or their spouse knowing their HIV positive status. Many regularly tested themselves for HIV and others would only consider knowing their status by self-testing. It was clearly a difficult experience and making HIV testing easier for health workers is needed.

Participants' exploration of fears about what others may think or do if they thought they were HIV positive or had AIDS is a very significant segment of the training. For many, as had come out when the DVD was in development and being tested, this was the first time they had spoken with colleagues about their personal attitudes to knowing their own HIV status, accessing treatment and how they reacted to HIV-positive colleagues. Many healthcare workers felt that colleagues would gossip and discriminate against them if they were HIV positive, including not wanting to use the same cups, spoons, or plates. If they were positive, the health workers were encouraged by the character in the drama Kate who received support from her spouse and reported that the same could apply to them.

During the discussions it was agreed that stigma would be reduced if more people felt free to test, free to disclose that they had gone for the test and even to disclose their status.

Disclosure of HIV-positive status was still difficult among healthcare workers. Most said that they would disclose their status to their partner, colleagues, and even the person in charge of the health facility. Many felt that it was unprofessional to disclose their status to patients, although several indicated that they had done so during counseling sessions. It was felt that disclosure of one's status and history of testing was a useful method in convincing clients to test.

"I learned the importance of confidentiality and that stigma is very high among health workers."

"If I'm going to help TB and HIV patients I have to empathize with them and learn a more positive attitude towards colleagues who are infected with TB and HIV." (Evaluation questionnaire)

However, they were clear that willingness to be tested had to begin with health workers. "If you know your TB and HIV status, it makes you more effective." (Evaluation questionnaire)

The sessions provided a unique opportunity for the health workers to reflect upon their personal risk to HIV and TB infection among colleagues. Many of the participants felt the DVD clip was a great idea and that the sessions were interactive and so enabled learning to take place. They particularly liked the link between the DVD and the TV drama series.

At the end of each session, the participants were asked what personal action they would take. Their plans varied:

"I and my family (wife) will visit a VCT within a week's time"

"Disclose my status to my husband to facilitate him to be tested and my teenage girl and boy"

"lobby for support for HIV positive workers"

"I have learned a lot and have no fear about my status"

Overall, participants came to the realization that it was their individual and group responsibility to resolve issues relating to stigma and discrimination including improving confidentiality (identified as a high priority), change of attitudes, increased openness, and disclosure.

Evaluating the DVD and session structure

As a training material, the facilitators felt the use of the DVD was innovative, effective, and captured the audience's attention. Participants were thoroughly engaged in discussions around stigma and discrimination in a structured yet flexible manner. The facilitator felt confident that the tool worked as a catalyst for the group. The questions following each clip were effective in achieving the objectives of participants holding their own discussions and reaching their own conclusions at every one of the 31 sessions.

The DVD was used in conjunction with flip charts to record the discussions and an LCD projector for power point slides for the MOH introduction on TB and HIV. The districts where the awareness sessions were held were all in rural areas with poor infrastructure. The difficulties encountered in organizing logistics for using a DVD in rural health facilities cannot be underestimated. Despite the assumption that electricity is universally available in health facilities, this was not always the case and the team of six facilitators went around with a generator and two vehicles. It thus possibly made the activity relatively expensive. Nonetheless, participants thoroughly enjoyed the sessions, which made it a worthwhile activity. They made many suggestions including that in future the DVD could be used during a health day, where voluntary counseling and testing (VCT) could also be made available on site.

The participation of the MOH participants was very beneficial. They were able to provide new information on the results of the recently conducted Kenya AIDS Indicator survey (NASCOP, 2007). They were available to answer questions related to their work and workplace policy. Coming from the central level, the MOH representatives were also familiar with programs at the national level and were able to share new insights on HIV and TB. There was no apparent shyness in front of higher authority at all and official representation should be encouraged in any future events.

Evaluating social change

A medium-term outcome evaluation was planned as part of the communication strategy, for 3 to 6 months after the end of the campaign. Ultimately, however, the short-term outcome survey that immediately followed the awareness-raising sessions was the only evaluation funded. Unfortunately this is a regular challenge to evaluating communication and social change programs. It would have been extremely valuable to explore the level of commitment to the personal and workplace action plans stated at the end of sessions from a more long-term perspective. On-the-spot training evaluation in this context may provide immediate feedback of the session but any insight into impact on social change is severely limited.

While this project lost the planned evaluation six months after the end of the project, there are practitioners presenting strong arguments for even longer-term evaluations. "Assessing the impact of communication has been made even more difficult by the current practice of donors, who require evaluation to be carried out before the end of projects, when the effects of communication activities might only have begun to produce results. Donors want visible results within the relatively short timeframe (3 to 5 years) of programs, while communication processes take much longer to achieve. Long-term outcomes would require long-term studies that focus on processes of change. But donors and program managers rarely have the time and resources for such in-depth analysis" (Balit, 2010).

The DVDs and handbooks used in the sessions were given to each of the health clinics visited. In some of the larger hospitals, several copies were requested and received. As a format, DVD-led discussion is easily replicable for other groups as the key segments and discussion question guides are on the DVD. With a facilitators' handbook, the session could be closely duplicated numerous times among staff, led by staff themselves (a key element of the participatory design). While there was no longer-term evaluation, a chance encounter with a member of management staff from one of the main Nairobi hospitals provided anecdotal evidence of the uptake and longevity of the awareness tool. She reported that following the visit, over the next 6 months, hospital staff had used the DVD within a regular monthly training slot for up to twenty different staff each time. It was a popular and much-valued tool.

Conclusion and recommendation

Developing a participatory communication tool that can spark dialogue, reflection, and change around stigma and discrimination is a considerable challenge. The time and work spent on research and development of materials for this program were extremely important. The most cost-effective stage of the communication strategy would be to extend access to the materials to as wide a reach as possible. DVDs and handbooks are relatively inexpensive to produce; the greater expense is in agreeing, developing, testing, and producing the content. "The availability of tested stigma-reduction tools and approaches has moved the field forward. What is needed now is the political will and resources to support and scale up stigma reduction activities throughout health care settings globally" (Nyblade et al., 2009).

In 2009, the HIV Prevention Response and Modes of Transmission Analysis in Kenya found that "the largest new infections (44 percent) occur among men and women who are in a union or in regular partnerships" (UNGASS, 2010). These are infections in apparently stable but concurrent relationships. In such a context, it is critical to combat stigma and discrimination toward and among those who deeply fear that they will be judged as "immoral" if they are seen to be having an HIV test or seeking treatment. Health workers in Kenya live and work within a context of stigma. They are working with the additional challenges of providing healthcare in a limited resource setting with high HIV prevalence. The discussion that the DVD session led to was a new experience for many, and one that could have been an anxious and frightening situation. Yet it was very positively received. A participatory tool such as this DVD provided extra support and confidence, breaking down stigma and hopefully, building much needed personal and professional skills among health workers. Whether it led to a process of social change and whether it is or could be sustainable will require knowledge gained through long-term evaluation.

References

Action Aid International Kenya (2010). *Towards Social Mobilization to End AIDS: Learning from the HIV Stigma Index Study: Extent and Impact of HIV and AIDS Related Stigma and Discrimination of Women and Children.*

Balit, S. (2010). Some Challenges in Measuring Impact: Communicating with Decision Makers. Glocal Times May 2010 http://www.glocaltimes.k3.mah.se/viewarticle. aspx?articleID=183&issueID=21.

Campbell, D. (Executive Producer). (2008). *Makutano Junction.* Kenya, Citizen TV. http://www. makutanojunction.org.uk/ and http://www.mediae.org.

Danya International (2008). *Kenya TB-HIV Communication Campaign.* Evaluation Report.

National AIDS/STI Control Programme (NASCOP), Kenya (2009). *2007 Kenya AIDS Indicator Survey*, September 2009.

Nyblade, L., Stangl, A., Weiss, E., & Ashburn, K. (2009). Combating HIV Stigma in Health Care Settings: What Works? *Journal of the International AIDS Society*, 12(15).

Panos and Healthlink Worldwide Background Briefing: How Can We Tackle Stigma and Discrimination through Effective Communication? *SPARK*, 2007 Retrieved May 17 2010 from http://www.panos.org.uk/download.php?id=55.

Singhal, A. & Rogers, M. Everett (2003). *Combating AIDS, Communication Strategies in Action.*, London: SAGE.

UNAIDS website, retrieved 18 May 2010 http://www.usaid.gov/our_work/global_health/id/ tuberculosis/countries/africa/kenya_profile.html.

UNAIDS, Report of the Technical Consultation on Social Change Communication 2–3 August 2007 UNAIDS, Geneva.

National AIDS Control Council, Kenya (2010). United Nations General Assembly Special Session on HIV and AIDS, Country Report – Kenya.

Chapter 17

Effect of a Public Service Announcement on Couple Testing for HIV in Uganda on Beliefs and Intent to Act

Jyotika Ramaprasad

Introduction

This chapter discusses the results of a prepost experiment conducted in a slum in Kampala, Uganda, to test the effectiveness of a video public service announcement (PSA) to encourage couple testing for HIV status. Effectiveness was measured in terms of positive changes in beliefs, knowledge, and intent to act. The beliefs examined were largely about HIV, disclosure, discordancy, couple testing, confidence to persuade partner to test together, intent to test as a couple, and the benefits of couple testing.

The PSA was produced with the intent to distribute it to nongovernment organizations (NGOs) in Kampala for their use in community meetings for HIV education. The PSA focused on prevention rather than care and support. Prevention continues to be important in the context of continuing new infections (UNAIDS, 2008). Prevention fatigue cannot be allowed to set in if the gains made in the fight against the disease are to be maintained and increased. While the prevention message needs to be kept alive for each new generation of young people, UNAIDS suggests that prevention efforts be strategically focused on sexual partnerships, especially those that increase the risk of HIV exposure; these include serodiscordant relationships and multiple concurrent partners (UNAIDS, 2008).

Disclosure

For prevention of the disease, disclosure of HIV status is critical. In *Sizwe's Test* (Steinberg, 2008), a story about a charismatic young man, Sizwe (disguised name), living in South Africa, Dr. Hermann Reuter, head of the Doctors Without Borders project in Lusikisiki, says, "… unless people disclose they are not going to deal with AIDS" (p. 88). But disclosure has serious consequences including violence (Collini & Obasi, 2006; Greeff et al., 2008; Van der Straten et al., 1998) and loss of economic support (Collini & Obasi, 2006; Greeff et al., 2008) particularly in long-standing relationships. At the same time, disclosure can also be beneficial, opening the door to support (Collini & Obasi, 2006; Greeff et al., 2008; Were et al., 2006).

HIV testing

For disclosure to happen, first a person must know her/his HIV status. Couples often enter relationships and marriage without knowledge of their or their partner's status. Testing for HIV status is critical for couples because marriage has become a risk factor for HIV transmission (Freeman et al., 2004; Mubangizi et al., 2000). According to the Uganda AIDS Commission (2007), "up to 65% of new HIV infections are occurring among married people" (p. 9) and "HIV transmission is the highest during marital sex (42%)" (p. 13).

Fear of testing is one reason for the lack of knowledge about one's status. Steinberg (2008) brings home the real fear of testing: "the pairs of eyes that note who goes into the makeshift testing center and how long their post-test counseling lasts; the whispering and the silent scorn" (p. 88). Thus, testing needs to be done sensitively, particularly for couples in long-standing relationships, and couple testing is suggested as the answer (Malamba et al., 2005; Were et al., 2006).

Couple testing is critical to knowledge of partner status. But ">70% of VCT clients present as individuals, and most of these do not know the HIV status of their partners" (Malamba et al., 2005:580), and while the figure has been increasing (Malamba et al., 2005), "only 10–30% of persons in Africa … come as a couple… [partly] due to the reluctance of men to be tested … coupled with the assumption that their partner's HIV-1 status is the same as theirs" (Lingappa et al., 2008:3), a phenomenon known as "testing by proxy" (Morrill & Noland, 2006).

Couple testing

Not all couples, however, share the same HIV status. Couple discordancy refers to the fact that one member in the couple is HIV positive and the other is HIV negative, making it imperative to try and keep the uninfected partner HIV negative. Couple testing can identify discordant partners, and do much more because of the counseling that precedes and follows HIV tests. By channeling discordant couples into relevant services and through her or his own counseling, the counselor can repel discordancy-related myths (Bunnell et al., 2005; Lingappa et al., 2008), can help the couple deal with emotional and sexual issues including reproductive decisions, and can help the family plan for the future (Carpenter et al., 1999; Collini & Obasi, 2006; Tangmunkongvorakul et al., 1999; Van der Straten et al., 1998; Van Devanter et al., 1999).

HIV/AIDS and discordancy in East Africa and Uganda

It is estimated that of the approximately 33 million people (adults and children) living with HIV, 22 million are in sub-Saharan Africa and about a million of these are in Uganda (UNAIDS, 2008). The HIV prevalence rate in Uganda, which has been one of the most successful countries in reducing prevalence, appears to have stabilized around 5.4 percent (this is a 2007 figure) (prevalence is measured for adults 15–49 to allow comparisons across countries), but sexual risk taking appears to be increasing (UNAIDS, 2007) and with it the possibility of an increase in prevalence.

Specifically, with regard to discordancy, a 2000 study (Mubangizi et al., 2000) indicated that 18 percent of married couples visiting the AIDS Information Centre in Kampala, Uganda, were discordant. According to Wawer et al. (2005), the uninfected partner in a heterosexual discordant relationship has an estimated 8 percent annual chance of contracting HIV.

The public service announcement

The topic for the PSA—couple testing benefits—emerged from a focus group (translation was used when necessary) on disclosure with discordant couples and from several in-depth interviews with staff of an HIV/AIDS NGO and members of the community it served. The in-depth interviewees and focus group participants prioritized a couple testing message because of the need for disclosure of HIV status between partners to prevent infection of a negative partner. Such problem definition is in keeping with the tenets of participatory communication for social change (Diaz-Bordenave, 1989).

The video public service announcement is roughly one-minute long. It presents on-screen text about the benefits of couple testing, reinforced by a voice-over (by an East African female volunteer), which is in places a little more elaborate than the text. The PSA benefits were taken from the focus groups and in-depth interviews as well as the literature. The background is brownish-yellow on which text is laid using a thick white, slightly back-shadowed font giving it a three-dimensional embossed effect and leading to good legibility. The text appears on the screen point-by-point as the narrator voices it. The language is English. Uganda was a British colony and English is commonly used in Uganda. The script for the PSA is presented below (words in parentheses represent major additional voice-over).

Couple testing benefits:

1. Makes disclosure easier.
2. Reduces the fear of disclosure.
3. Helps you to support your positive partner.
4. Allows your partner to accept your positive status.
5. Increases the chances of keeping a negative partner negative.
6. Reduces domestic violence.

If the results indicate discordancy, the counselor gives you the options you have…

For seeking help to keep the negative partner negative.
To be supportive of each other.

Other benefits of couple testing:

1. Allows you to take your medicine regularly (because you do not have to hide your medicines from your partner).
2. Helps to reduce mother-to-child transmission of HIV (because you can seek medical help during pregnancy and birth, and not be forced to breastfeed your baby for the sake of appearance. All of these help to keep HIV from being transmitted to your baby).
3. Allows you to plan for the future of your family and particularly for your children.

Effectiveness of interventions

Evaluations of the effectiveness of various interventions have been conducted. These interventions may relate to nonhealth and health/HIV topics, may use nonmediated program such as voluntary counseling and testing for HIV or mass media campaigns, enter-education programs, and such. They may be focused on individuals or couples and specifically on discordant couples, though not many interventions of this type are available or evaluated. The effects expected could be increase in condom use, partner reduction, discussion with others, negotiation skills, and so on, though the most commonly evaluated interventions are ones that look for increase in condom use.

Meta-studies of these intervention evaluations have found increased condom use and testing and increased discussion (Kincaid, n.d.; Vidanapathirana et al., 2005). Other studies specifically focused on communication interventions have found, for example, increased HIV knowledge and increased testing (Kuhlmann et al., 2008; McCombie et al., 2002; Vaughan et al., 2000). More specifically, an analysis of effects of behavioral interventions specifically targeted for couples such as counseling revealed effects in terms of reducing unprotected sexual intercourse and increased condom use (Burton et al., 2010). In a meta-study of campaign effects, Noar et al. (2009) found that "the vast majority of recent well-controlled HIV/AIDS campaign studies have demonstrated effects on behavior or behavioral intentions" (pp. 34–35). Another meta-study, however, found medium to small effects and in some cases no effects (Bertrand et al., 2006).

One study looked particularly at the effect of radio PSAs on HIV dealing with topics such as risk perception, benefits of testing, condom use, and so on, in Nigeria, Kenya and Tanzania (Mundy & Wyman, 2006). It found a relationship between exposure level and respondents' attitudes and knowledge of benefits of HIV testing. Jansen and Janssen (2010) found that for cryptic billboards on HIV/AIDS, comprehension was related to inclination to dialogue about HIV.

For an intervention that encouraged couple counseling at antenatal clinics, Farquhar et al. (2004) found greater uptake of nevirapine and decreased breast feeding of babies by HIV positive mothers. The authors believe couple counseling is very beneficial, and they encourage more promotion of the same. A few interventions specifically focused on discordant couples also had positive results (Allen et al., 2003; Roth et al., 2001). McGrath et al. (2007) found that an intervention that used study activities to increase communication and negotiation skills about sex resulted in a reported increase in comfort discussing sex and condoms with partner and use of learned skills with partner.

Sufficient evidence of the effectiveness of interventions is available. Thus, the main research question of this study was:

How effective was the PSA depicting the benefits of couple testing in:

- Changing beliefs about the disease, and about disclosure, discordancy, and couple testing,
- Changing subject confidence in ability to persuade partner to test together, and in intent to test together, and
- Changing beliefs about the benefits of couple testing?

Method

The research was approved by an Institutional Review Board in the United States and a Ugandan government agency with oversight of research, and study subjects were consented. A US university–linked organization in Uganda assisted with getting the Ugandan permission and in recruiting and training research assistants. A staff member from the NGO that had been the site of the initial research assisted in recruiting study participants.

The site selected for evaluating the video was a slum in Kampala, where English is commonly used. A staff member from the NGO and the head research assistant went to the slum before the arrival of the researcher and trained local community mobilizers to recruit subjects for the study. The mobilizers were provided a small remuneration for their effort, and subjects were provided a small transportation allowance. Because experiments are more concerned with internal validity (controlling rival explanations so that the effect of the PSA, if any effect is found, is attributable to the PSA and not to other variables) than with external validity (generalizability), subjects are recruited rather than selected by probability sampling.

The mobilizers screened participants for age, for their status as member of a couple by marriage or by cohabitation but not having tested together, and their background in health-related work. Those under the age of 18, not in couple relationships, and having a work background that was related to health were excluded. Because the evaluation was done in an open shed in the center of the slum, the possibility of infiltration by community members attracted by the transport allowance existed. So, all subjects were rescreened before being allowed to participate, but the definition of couples used ultimately was based within the Ugandan context such that those who had more or less permanent sexual partners as represented in boyfriend/girlfriend relationships were also included.

The method was quasi-experiment and the design was prepost providing greater power than a between-subjects design. Altogether, 38 subjects participated in the experiment. Research assistants administered the pretest questionnaire individually to each subject.

When about three to five subjects had taken the pretest, they were taken to an adjoining room and shown the PSA on a computer screen. They were then led to the open area of the shed and asked not to discuss the PSA with anyone. When all subjects had completed the pretest, the research assistants began to administer the posttest to those who had watched the PSA. Essentially, a rotation system was set up. While this may violate the strict control required in experiments, where all subjects ideally should receive the treatment at the same time, the reality of data collection in a slum in Kampala does not allow this and such control is more essential in a between-subjects design where the control and experimental group need to experience the intervention at the same time. A control group was not used here because the open shed would make it impossible to keep the two groups separate. At the same time, there is an advantage to the system used in this study. The conditions under which the subjects participated in the experiment, within their own community, in the field (generally, TV sets are not present in the slum), with the only foreigner present being the researcher, approximated a more realistic viewing situation lending greater validity to any effects that may be found. All the data were collected within a few hours on one morning.

Upon her return from Uganda, the researcher went through each questionnaire carefully. Because the questionnaires were administered by research assistants, very few questionnaires had (a very few) missing values and hence only one questionnaire had to be discarded because of a missing value on age, leaving 37 subjects. Data were entered into an SPSS file and analyzed using descriptive statistics and paired sample t-tests.

Before the experiment was conducted, the questionnaire had been pilot tested with twelve volunteers and the feedback had been used to adjust the English to fit its use in Uganda. The questionnaire first gathered demographic information. It then asked subjects whether they had been tested for HIV and counseled, but specifically told them that they should not disclose their HIV status.

The questionnaire then went on to list ten statements/questions each followed by a five-point Likert scale for agreement, or likelihood or confidence, as relevant. The ten items were about subjects' HIV risk perception (Witte, 1992), beliefs about discordancy and testing by proxy, perceived importance of disclosure and couple testing, likelihood of trying to convince their partner to go for couple testing and actually going for couple testing in the near future, and confidence about convincing their partner and convincing a friend to go with his/her spouse for HIV couple testing. These statements were not directly derived from the text of the PSA but were related to the script by inference and by reference in the script to discordancy. It was expected that the means for these statements would change in the direction of greater alignment with the beliefs of experts and interviewees for this project and greater intent to test as a couple.

If subjects indicated that they were unlikely to try to convince their partners to go for HIV testing, unlikely to go for couple testing in the next three months, or not confident they could convince their partners to go to test together, another set of statements corresponding to these three conditions provided respondents with reasons with which they could indicate their agreement level.

The next set of statements (nine) asked subjects to rate the benefits of couple testing using a five-point strongly agree to strongly disagree Likert scale; these items matched the script of the PSA citing such benefits as couple testing eases disclosure and enables couples to plan for the future including children. It was expected that subjects' mean responses to these items would change in the direction of increased belief in the benefits of couple testing.

The final set of four statements asked subjects to what extent they had discussed couple testing with their partners, extended family, friends, and community. Possible responses ranged on a five-point scale from "A Lot" to "Not at all."

Findings

Demographics and discussion of couple testing

The posttest repeated all questions from the pretest including those on subjects' demographics, experience with HIV testing and counseling, and discussion of couple testing with friends, and so on. These answers were not expected to change between pre- and posttest because they were not related to the intervention. Some changes were found and, where major, they are reported.

Mean age of the subjects was 25 years (Table 17.1). About 58 percent of the respondents were male, and 81 percent had a secondary 1 or higher education. Occupations were varied but bead making was a common business for women, and the subjects included several

Table 17.1: Distribution of subjects and mean scores from pretest.

Variable	N = (37)	(%)	Mean*
Gender			
Male	22	57.9	
Female	16	42.1	
Education (1 missing value)			
Primary 7 or below	7	18.9	
Secondary 1 or higher	30	81.1	
Have you ever been tested for HIV?			
Yes	18	47.4	
No	20	52.6	
Mean Age		25.24 years	
To what extent have you discussed couple testing with your (= mean discussion level):			
Partner?			3.18
Family?			1.84
Friends?			2.66
Community?			1.89

*Higher scores equal greater agreement/likelihood/confidence. Scale ranges from 1 to 5.

students. About 47 percent of the subjects had been tested for HIV, and they had all received their results. Almost all of these subjects had received counseling before and after the test.

Subjects were asked about the extent to which they had discussed couple testing with others. The results for the pretest were as follows. Subjects said they had engaged in some discussion of couple testing with their partner (mean = 3.18 on a five-point scale, where 5 represented "a lot" and 1 "not at all") and friends (mean = 2.66), and less discussion with community (mean = 1.89) and extended family (mean = 1.84). They changed their answers in the posttest for friends from 2.66 to 2.95 ($t = -2.73$; $p = .01$) and community from 1.89 to 2.11 ($t = -2.25$; $p = .031$). Given that there was no time for actual change to happen between pre- and posttest, this is hard to explain. Possibly respondents discussed couple testing in the short time they had between pre- and posttest with the friends and community members present for the experiment despite the fact they were asked not to discuss the PSA. If in fact this happened, it still would point to the effectiveness of the PSA in leading to discussion, which in turn could lead to a positive change in beliefs.

Disease risk, discordancy, disclosure, and likelihood of testing together

Two sets of statements were expected to demonstrate a change in means. For the first set that dealt with disease seriousness and risk, testing by proxy, discordancy, disclosure, and confidence/likelihood of testing together, all means changed significantly but one of the changes was not in the expected direction (Table 17.2).

The PSA effected change in perception of the seriousness of HIV and personal risk of infection, of the possibility of discordancy existing as a phenomenon, and of the importance of disclosure and of testing together as a couple. It also increased subjects' perception of their likelihood of trying to convince partners to couple test and of couple testing within the next 3 months, and increased subjects' confidence in being able to convince partners to test with them and convince friends to test with her/his partner.

Among the significant results, with one exception, none of the pretest means were lower than the midpoint of three, but the PSA did increase the means. For example, awareness of the seriousness of HIV was high (4.03) but it still went up in the posttest (4.71), within the range of agree to strongly agree. Similarly, awareness of importance to test together was high (4.16) but went up to (4.46). Critically, the mean awareness of the phenomenon of discordancy went up from 3.08 (close to neutral) to 4.05 (above agree). Means of importance of disclosing went up from 3.81 to 4.24. Thus, the PSA was successful in making an effective impact on beliefs about disclosure, discordancy, and testing together, key variables in this study.

The statement that changed its mean significantly but not in the expected direction was: "You believe that your partner's HIV status is the same as yours." While this finding appears contradictory to the finding that indicated respondents understood discordancy better as a result of the PSA, the means provide a clearer picture. Both the pretest mean (2.44) and the posttest mean (2.81) are below the midpoint of three, so the respondents went from more

Table 17.2: Differences in mean knowledge, understanding, and intent of action.

	Pretest mean*	Posttest mean*	t-value	p-value
HIV/AIDS is a serious disease	4.03	4.71	−8.03	.000
You are at high risk for getting HIV/AIDS	3.32	3.92	−3.54	.001
You believe that your partner's HIV status is the same as yours	2.44	2.81	−2.19	.035
It is possible for a person to have HIV/AIDS and for his/her sexual partner to be negative	3.08	4.05	−3.67	.001
It is important to disclose one's HIV status to one's partner	3.81	4.24	−2.93	.006
It is important for a couple to go and test together for HIV status	4.16	4.46	−2.06	.047
How likely is it that you will try to convince your partner to go with you for couple testing?	3.84	4.11	−2.70	.010
How likely is it that you and your spouse will go for an HIV test together in the next 3 months?	3.45	3.79	−3.36	.002
How confident do you feel that you can convince your partner to test for HIV together with you?	3.82	4.16	−3.36	.002
How confident do you feel that you can convince a friend to go with his/her spouse to test for HIV?	3.13	3.66	−3.64	.001
Couple Testing:				
It makes disclosure easier	3.92	4.66	−7.05	.000
It reduces the fear of disclose	3.76	4.21	−3.81	.001
It helps partners to support each other	3.95	4.18	−2.16	.037
It allows partners to more easily accept the other partner's positive or negative status if their status is different from their partner's	3.54	4.08	−3.33	.002
It increases the chances of keeping the negative partner negative	3.51	4.08	−3.40	.002
It reduces domestic violence	2.97	3.29	−1.23	.227
It allows a partner to take medicine regularly because the partner does not have to hide it	3.87	4.21	−2.40	.022
It helps to reduce the chances of an HIV+ mother transmitting HIV to her child	4.16	4.55	−2.75	.009
It allows couples to plan for the future, including for children, if any	4.11	4.53	−3.42	.002

*Higher scores equal greater agreement/likelihood/confidence. Scale ranges from 1 to 5.

to less disagreement with the statement, but they still disagreed with the phenomenon of testing by proxy.

Reasons for diffidence about convincing partner

From those who indicated lack of likelihood to try and convince partner to test together or go for a test in the next 3 months, or lack of confidence to convince partner to couple test, the questionnaire listed reasons for respondents to evaluate. Very few respondents fell in the group that had to evaluate the reasons. Still these results are discussed for the benefit of future researchers and in the interest of providing complete results.

Only one subject indicated s/he was unlikely to try to convince the partner to test as a couple both in the pre- and posttest; the reasons were that s/he did not know how to bring it up and fear of results rather than reasons such as believing it is not useful to know one's status, worry about stigma or a negative reaction from partner, and fear of results.

Three subjects indicated in the pretest that they were not confident about convincing the partner to test together. One of these respondents attributed this diffidence in the pretest to the fact that the partner thinks it is not useful to know one's HIV status; this respondent and the others did not attribute their lack of confidence to the other reasons listed in the questionnaire such as lack of communication with partner, partner does not believe you need to test, and partner is afraid of results or worried about stigma. Interestingly, one of the three respondents attributed lack of confidence in the posttest to partner does not believe you need to test. The number of subjects indicating diffidence went down to two in the posttest possibly indicating that the PSA may have increased the confidence of at least one of the respondents.

Three respondents said that it was unlikely they would go with their spouse for an HIV test in 3 months. Two of these said in the pretest that it would take longer than 3 months to convince the partner. None believed that lack of time in the next 3 months was a reason for not going to test. Interestingly, one of two persons who felt it would take longer than 3 months to convince partner changed her/his mind in the posttest to likelihood of going to test in the next 3 months again possibly indicating the influence of the PSA.

Benefits of couple testing

The PSA also effected change in beliefs about all but one (reduction in domestic violence) of the benefits of couple testing. Subjects' beliefs aligned more with those depicted in the PSA. Thus, they believed to a greater degree that couple testing would reduce the fear of disclosure, would make partners more supportive and accepting of the other's positive status, would increase the chance of keeping the negative partner negative, would allow positive partners to take their medicine openly and increase the chance of positive mothers not transmitting HIV to their babies, and would allow couples to better plan for their future including for children.

Pretest means were above the midpoint of three for all except the domestic violence statement, indicating that benefits of couple testing were known somewhat, but the PSA increased this knowledge significantly. For mother to child transmission reduction and for allowing couples to plan for the future, the respective pretest means of 4.16 and 4.11 increased to 4.55 and 4.53 moving from closer to agree to closer to strongly agree. Means for making disclosure easier and reducing the fear of disclosure increased from 3.92 to 4.66 and 3.76 to 4.21 respectively, indicating stronger agreement than before viewing the PSA.

But subjects were not convinced that couple testing reduces domestic violence. Their pretest mean was 2.97 (close to neutral), the lowest of all means and did not change significantly even after viewing the PSA. Subjects did not believe that disclosure within a couple testing situation with a counselor would reduce violence. Possibly, they believed that this violence could occur later once the couple had left the counseling setting. Thus, subjects' beliefs did not align with beliefs of the NGO staffers and community members with regard to this benefit of couple testing. Staffers believed couple testing would reduce domestic violence because of the counseling that accompanies couple testing. Community members had told stories of abandonment and physical violence upon disclosure outside a counseling setting and believed that reduced domestic violence is a benefit of couple testing.

Conclusions

HIV discordancy between members of a couple is an important area deserving of greater attention. Few interventions, particularly mediated ones, are available for discordant couples to prevent infection of the negative partner. The PSA evaluated in this study is an attempt to fill this gap.

The PSA was found to be effective in creating change, with one exception, at the individual level in beliefs and intent to act. Because it has demonstrated its effectiveness in communicating the benefits of couple testing, the PSA will be made available in Uganda for use in community groups for HIV education. It will be recommended that the viewing be accompanied by discussion sessions to enhance the PSA's effectiveness by generating family and community dialogue about couple testing. It will also be recommended that particular attention be paid in the discussion to address the testing by proxy belief.

The PSA is an individual level prevention effort. Individual level change theories, approaches, and practice have come under considerable criticism, but the development of this PSA tried to overcome some of the criticisms of this approach and was conducted with the belief based on experience that the individual level change approach is effective as one among many strategies for change. A brief review of the history of the field is in place to situate the project (the PSA development) given the effectiveness findings and the subsequent likelihood of use of the PSA by NGOs in Uganda.

The proponents of the first (also called "dominant") paradigm of development conceived of development in economic (wealth), political (democracy), and psychological ("rational" individual) terms, and development communication in top-down (elite external expert), mediated (mostly mass media or interpersonally through opinion leaders), and technological (the then new media) terms (Lerner, 1958; McClelland, 1964; Rogers, 1976; Rostow, 1990; Schramm, 1964). Thus, both the end and the means were modeled, ethnocentrically, after the West.

Challengers of the paradigm, mostly nonwestern scholars, argued that this model did not take into account power relations and cultural practice, and further did not dignify indigenous knowledge and communication modes (Beltran, 1976). They called for a different kind of development, one that did not create dependency and was participatory and inclusive at every stage, one that focused on empowering communities to make their own change, to better their lives holistically (Servaes & Malikhao, 2008). Freire's dialogic approach to raise the consciousness of the oppressed and thus ignite self-initiated iterative change is often included in this alternative approach (Freire, 1970). In time, these theories also came under criticism: dependency theory for not offering an alternative and being too focused on economic determinism of power and therefore of life conditions, and participatory theory for lack of specificity, consistency, and comprehensiveness in the operationalization of participation, among other reasons (Huesca, 2008; Jacobson, 2004; Servaes & Malikhao, 2008).

These two theoretical models of development communication and their various applied manifestations (Waisbord, 2001) – for example, respectively, social marketing, behavior change communication (BCC) and enter-education; or media advocacy, social mobilization, and communication for social change – continue to populate development discourse and practice (http://www.comminit.com/). The more vertical, diffusionist strategies look for social change through individual change, but are becoming increasingly multidimensional adding policy and institutional change and sometimes change in social norms as well. The alternative horizontal approach looks for social change through societal change, using communities as its starting point, but has not made any allowance for individual level change. Thus, the diffusion approach has recognized its limitations, and the horizontal approach, particularly its Freirian dimension, continues to hold the status of the ideal.

The diffusion approach is more able to measure outcomes but is faulted for the narrow scope of these outcomes. The participatory approach describes larger outcomes such as empowerment but these are difficult to measure. As ethically appealing as participation theory is, it provides little practical guidance for use in the field beyond applications that are criticized as a continuation of the dominant paradigm and power dynamics (Huesca, 2008; Kothari, 2006, as excerpted in Gumucio-Dagron & Tufte, 2006). On the whole, actuation of intervention and evaluation may be easier in the diffusion approach and this might partly explain its popularity particularly among donors for whom accountability is critical. But explication of the participatory approach is continuing, with scholars and practitioners attempting to implement practical interpretations of these theories; this may continue to increase the use of this approach (Jacobson, 2004).

At the same time, mutual borrowing and adjustment are taking place in both the theory and practice of these paradigms, and an understanding may be developing that there can be no grand theory of communication development, only integrative theories and practices that most suit the development communication problem at hand. "Participatorians" are borrowing from the "diffusionists" particularly in operationalizing outcomes (Morris, 2003), but the single largest modification appears to be the acceptance by followers of the dominant paradigm of exchange, and thus of community involvement, as integral to success. Today, most models include participation (see, for example, UNAIDS, 2005). Waisbord (2001) suggests that the starting point for this integration is "The realization that communities should be the main actors of development communication" (p. 37).

The PSA evaluated in this study had its genesis in community priorities about the HIV/ AIDS issue that needed attention. It involved the community in problem definition and in the content of the PSA by asking the community to define the benefits of couple testing. Granted this community included the staffers of an NGO, but many of these staff members were deeply engaged in addressing HIV at the grassroots level and some even belonged to the community. The evaluation of the intervention was conducted within the community and its subjects were drawn from the community.

Community focus also places high value on community discussion and dialogue. The PSA that was the subject of this evaluation is meant to be used in community settings where HIV-related education is provided. The evaluation found that discussion with friends and community increased between pre- and posttest. This was not expected because subjects were told not to discuss the PSA. This could be an indication of an unreliable result but there is another possibility. If in fact subjects discussed the PSA in between the pre- and posttest, it is an indication that the PSA could lead to discussion, which could add to an increase in positive beliefs. In view of the emergence, in more recent discussions of communication for social change, of societal discussion and consequent societal level acceptance of a belief set as critical to sustaining change, this finding adds value to the PSA. Figueroa et al. (2002 as excerpted in Gumucio-Dagron & Tufte, 2006) suggest communities rarely initiate dialogue spontaneously; rather a catalyst (such as the PSA) triggers dialogue.

Jansen & Janssen (2010) found that dialogue played a role in comprehension of cryptic commercials. The plan is for this PSA to be used in community meetings on HIV prevention for couples as a starting point to generate discussion and dialogue in the meeting and later in the community.

The buzz these days is around social change communication, which "involves the strategic use of advocacy, communication, and social mobilization strategies to facilitate or accelerate social change. In the context of HIV, social change communication strategies can help to change underlying social attitudes and behaviors that contribute to HIV risk and vulnerability. Successful communication programs blend mass media approaches, community engagement strategies, and empowerment strategies with other forms of informational and motivational communication and advocacy. The goal of social change communication is to act as a catalyst for action at the individual, community, and policy levels" (UNAIDS, 2008:91).

Social change communication does not divide the field of communication for social change into binaries. Thus, theories, approaches, and practices are not held in opposition to each other. So, while the participatory/dialogic, community change model holds sway today as the ideal, and for very good reasons, social change communication finds use in individual level change too, suggesting a combined approach. This is slightly different from the hybrid models discussed above wherein diffusion models add participatory elements and are still subject to criticism for not being truly participatory. Rather the social change communication model has a place for each – individual level behavior change, community engagement and empowerment, and policy advocacy and change.

Thus, mediated communication aimed at individuals, with the objective of knowledge, attitude, and intent to act (and actually act) such as the PSA developed in this project, fits in the newer realm of thinking about communication for social change. Communication interventions of the type evaluated in this study will continue to be useful within the context of holistic approaches. Each approach will have a part to play in solving the problems of social justice and change because: Are knowledge, attitude, and behavior gains at the individual level not empowering? Should outside involvement be completely ruled out for true participation to happen? Are large-scale, nonlocal projects, and the mass media inherently nonparticipatory? Jacobson & Storey (2004) particularly address the last question in relation to the definition of participation, suggesting it can be multiscale. Figueroa et al. (2002 as excerpted in Gumucio-Dagron & Tufte, 2006) also suggest a variety of change processes from individual behavior to collective action, and a number of catalysts for change from an internal stimulus to an external change agent. Specifically, they suggest that the catalyst is missing from the literature on development communication and that communities rarely take action without an external stimulus.

This study also demonstrates the conditions under which research has to sometimes be conducted in a different cultural and economic setting. The task was demanding, particularly in terms of obtaining permission and keeping control at the site of data collection, but the engagement of local partners considerably aided the process. Future researchers must be prepared to expect the unexpected, to be prepared for delays and for not very congenial field conditions for data collection, to plan an adequate number of days for data collection, to screen subjects for a comprehensive list of relevant variables just before administration of the questionnaire, and to train research assistants intensively and take them through pilot data collection to identify common errors.

The different cultural and economic setting also created the limitations of this study. Managing the study site was important but also demanding. A control group would have added to the validity of the study in theory but given the field conditions for data collection (an open shed with two small rooms on one side), the groups would have had to come at separate times leading to possible contamination due to communication among the experimental and control group subjects in the community. The same type of contamination could occur if the groups were brought to the open shed at the same time. This would have also made the group that did not get to see the PSA feel deprived, and created a rather difficult management situation in terms of keeping track of the different rotating groups.

References

Allen, S., Meinzen-Derr, J., Kautzman, M., et al. (2003). Sexual Behavior of HIV Discordant Couples after HIV Counseling and Testing. *AIDS*, 17(5), 733–740.

Beltran, L. R. (1976). Alien Premises, Objects, and Methods in Latin American Communication Research, in Rogers, E. M. (ed.), *Communication and Development: Critical Perspectives*. Beverly Hills, CA: SAGE, pp. 15–42.

Bertrand, J. T., O'Reilly, K., Denison, J., Anhang, R., & Sweat, M. (2006). Systematic Review of the Effectiveness of Mass Communication Programs to Change HIV/AIDS-Related Behaviors in Developing Countries. *Health Education Research*, 21(4), 567–597.

Bunnell, R. E., Nassozi, J., Marum, E., et al. (2005). Living with Discordance: Knowledge, Challenges, and Prevention Strategies of HIV-Discordant Couples in Uganda. *AIDS Care*, 17(8), 999–1012.

Burton, J., Darbes, L. A., & Operario, D. (2010). Couples-Focused Behavioral Interventions for Prevention of HIV: Systematic Review of the State of Evidence. *AIDS and Behavior*, 14(1), 1–10.

Carpenter, L. M., Kamali, A., Ruberantwari, A., Malamba, S. S., & Whitworth, J. A. G. (1999). Rates of HIV-1 Transmission within Marriage in Rural Uganda in Relation to the HIV Sero-Status of the Partners. *AIDS*, 13(9), 1083–1089.

Collini, P. & Obasi, A. (2006). *Interventions to Reduce HIV Sexual Transmission within Discordant Couples*. BMJ Publishing Group. Retrieved September 30, 2012, from http://www.scribd.com/doc/78829447/9-Interventions-to-Reduce-HIV-Sexual-Transmission-Within-Discordant-Couples.

Diaz-Bordenave, J. (1989). *Participative Communication as a Part of the Building of a Participative Society*. Paper presented at the seminar Participation: A Key Concept in Communication and Change, University of Poona, Pune, India.

Farquhar, C., Kiarie, J. N., Richardson, B. A., et al. (2004). Antenatal Couple Counseling Increases Uptake of Interventions to Prevent HIV-1 Transmission. *Journal of Acquired Immune Deficiency Syndromes*, 37(5), 1620–1626.

Figueroa, M. E., Kincaid, D. L., Rani, M., & Lewis, G. (2006), Communication for Social Change: An Integrated Model for Measuring the Process and Its Outcomes (excerpted from same title, 2002), in Gumucio-Dagron, A. & Tufte, T. (eds.), *Communication for Social Change Anthology: Historical and Contemporary Readings*. South Orange, NJ: Communication for Social Change Consortium, pp. 589–591.

Freeman, E. E. & Glynn, J. R.; for the Study Group on Heterogeneity of HIV Epidemics in African Cities. (2004). Factors Affecting HIV Concordancy in Married Couples in four African Cities. *AIDS*, 18(12), 1715–1721.

Freire, P. (1970). *Pedagogy of the Oppressed*. New York, NY: The Seabury Press.

Greeff, M., Makoae, L. N., Dlamini, P. S., et al. (2008). Disclosure of HIV Status: Experiences and Perceptions of Persons Living with HIV/AIDS and Nurses Involved in Their Care in Africa. *Qualitative Health Research*, 18(3), 311–324.

http://www.comminit.com/.

Huesca, R. (2008). Tracing the History of Participatory Communication Approaches to Development: A Critical Appraisal, in Servaes, J. (ed.), *Communication for Development and Social Change*. Thousand Oaks, CA: SAGE Publications, pp. 189–198.

Jacobson, T. L. (2004, May). *Measuring Communicative Action for Participatory Communication*. Paper presented at the meeting of the International Communication Association, New Orleans, LA.

Jacobson, T. L. & Storey, J. D. (2004). Development Communication and Participation: Applying Habermas to a Case Study of Population Programs in Nepal. *Communication Theory*, 14(2), 99–121.

Jansen, C. & Janssen, I. (2010). Talk about It: The Effects of Cryptic HIV/AIDS Billboards. *Communicatio: South African Journal for Communication Theory & Research*, 36(1), 130–141.

Kincaid, D. L. (n.d.). *The Impact of AIDS Communication Programs on HIV Prevention Behavior*. Retrieved on September 28, 2010, from http://www.jhhesa.org/research/research_intro.html

Kothari, U. (2006), Power, Knowledge and Social Control in Participatory Development (excerpted from Participation: The New Tyranny, 2001), in Gumucio-Dagron, A. & Tufte, T. (eds.), *Communication for Social Change Anthology: Historical and Contemporary Readings*. South Orange, NJ: Communication for Social Change Consortium, pp. 925–927.

Kuhlmann, A. K. S., Kraft, J. M., Galavotti, C., Creek, T. L., Mooki, M., & Ntumy, R. (2008). Radio Role Models for the Prevention of Mother-to-Child Transmission of HIV and HIV Testing among Pregnant Women in Botswana. *Health Promotion International*, 23(3), 260–268.

Lerner, D. (1958). *The Passing of Traditional Society: Modernizing the Middle East*. Glencoe, IL: Free Press.

Lingappa, J. R., Lambdin, B., Bukusi, E. L., et al. (2008). Regional Differences in Prevalence of HIV-1 Discordance in Africa and Enrollment of HIV-1 Discordant Couples into an HIV-1 Prevention Trial. *PLoS One*, 3(1), e1411.

Malamba, S. S., Mermin, J. H., Bunnell, R., et al. (2005). Couples at Risk: HIV-1 Concordance and Discordance among Sexual Partners Receiving Voluntary Counseling and Testing in Uganda. *Journal of Acquired Immune Deficiency Syndromes*, 39(5), 576–580.

McClelland, D. (1964). Business Drive and National Achievement, in Etzioni, A. & Etzioni, E. (eds.), *Social Change*. New York: Basic Books, pp. 165–178.

McCombie, S., Hornik, R. C., & Anarfi, J. K. (2002). Effects of a Mass Media Campaign to Prevent AIDS among Young People in Ghana, in Hornik, R. C. (ed.), *Public Health Communication: Evidence for Behavior Change*. Mahwah, NJ: LEA, pp. 147–161.

McGrath, J. W., Celentano, D. D., Chard, S. E., et al. (2007). A Group-Based Intervention to Increase Condom Use among HIV Serodiscordant Couples in India, Thailand, and Uganda. *AIDS Care*, 19(3), 418–424.

Morrill, A. C. & Noland, C. (2006). Interpersonal Issues Surrounding HIV Counseling and Testing, and the Phenomenon of "Testing by Proxy." *Journal of Health Communication*, 11(2), 183–198.

Morris, N. (2003). A Comparative Analysis of the Diffusion and Participatory Models in Development Communication. *Communication Theory*, 13(2), 225–248.

Mubangizi, J., Downing, R., Ssebbowa, E., et al. (2000, July). *Couples at Risk: HIV-Concordance and Discordance among Partners Seeking HIV Testing in Uganda*. Paper presented to the International Conference on AIDS, Durban, South Africa.

Mundy, G. & Wyman, T. (2006). The Influence of HIV and AIDS Radio Public Service Announcements (PSAs): A Pan-regional Experience. *Impact Research*, 1(1). Retrieved September 27, 2010, from http://www.comminit.com/en/node/279591/307.

Noar, S. M., Palmgreen, P., Chabot, M., Dobransky, N., & Zimmerman, R. S. (2009). A 10-Year Systematic Review of HIV/AIDS Mass Communication Campaigns: Have We Made Progress? *Journal of Health Communication*, 14(1), 15–42.

Rogers, E. M. (1976). Communication and Development: The Passing of the Dominant paradigm, in Rogers, E. M. (ed.), *Communication and Development: Critical Perspectives*. Beverly Hills, CA: SAGE, pp 121–149.

Rostow, W. (1990). *The Stages of Economic Growth. A Non-communist Manifesto* (3rd ed.). Cambridge: Cambridge University Press.

Roth, D. L., Stewart, K. E., Clay, O. J., Van der Straten, A., Karita, E., & Allen, S. (2001). Sexual Practices of HIV Discordant and Concordant Couples in Rwanda: Effects of a Testing and Counseling Programme for Men. *International Journal of STD & AIDS*, 12(3), 181–188.

Schramm, W. L. (1964). *Mass Media and National Development: The Role of Information in the Developing Countries*. Stanford, CA: Stanford University Press.

Servaes, J. & Malikhao, P. (2008). Development Communication Approaches in an International Perspective, in Servaes, J. (ed.), *Communication for Development and Social Change*. Thousand Oaks, CA: SAGE Publications, pp. 158–179.

Steinberg, J. (2008). *Sizwe's Test: A Young Man's Journey through Africa's AIDS Epidemic*. New York: Simon & Schuster.

Tangmunkongvorakul, A., Celentano, D. D., Burke, J. G., De Boer, M. A., Wongpan, P., & Suriyanon, V. (1999). Factors Influencing Marital Stability among HIV Discordant Couples in Northern Thailand. *AIDS Care*, 11(5), 511–524.

Uganda AIDS Commission (2007). *Moving toward Universal Access: National HIV & AIDS Strategic Plan 2007/8–2011/12*. Republic of Uganda: Uganda AIDS Commission.

UNAIDS (2005). *Intensifying HIV Prevention. UNAIDS Policy Position Paper*. Retrieved September 25, 2010, from http://www.unaids.org/en/KnowledgeCentre/Resources/PolicyGuidance/UmbrellaPolicies/Prevention_Umbrella_Policies.asp.

_____ (2007). *Presentation of Policy Guidance to Address Gender Issues*. Retrieved on May 8, 2008, from http://data.unaids.org/pub/Presentation/2007/policy_guidance_address_gender_issues_item4_2_en.pdf.

_____ (2008). *Report on the Global AIDS Epidemic*. Geneva: Joint United Nations Program on HIV/AIDS (UNAIDS).

Van der Straten, A., King, R., Grinstead, O., Vittinghoff, E., Serufilira, A., & Allen, S. (1998). Sexual Coercion, Physical Violence, and HIV Infection among Women in Steady Relationships in Kigali, Rwanda. *AIDS and Behavior*, 2(1), 61–73.

Van Devanter, N., Thacker, A. S., & Arnold, B. M. (1999). Heterosexual Couples Confronting the Challenges of HIV Infection. *AIDS Care*, 11(2), 181–193.

Vaughan, P. W., Rogers, E. M., Singhal, A., & Swalehe, R. M. (2000). Entertainment-Education and HIV/AIDS Prevention: A Field Experiment in Tanzania. *Journal of Health Communication*, 5(Suppl), 81–100.

Vidanapathirana, J., Abramson, M. J., Forbes, A., & Fairley, C. (2005). Mass Media Interventions for Promoting HIV Testing: Cochrane Systematic Review. *International Journal of Epidemiology*, 35(2), 233–236.

Waisbord, S. (2001). *Family Tree of Theories, Methodologies and Strategies in Development Communication: The Rockefeller Foundation*. Retrieved on June 22, 2010, from http://www.comminit.com/en/node/1547/36.

Wawer, M. J., Gray, R. H., Sewankambo, N. K., et al. (2005). Rates of HIV-1 Transmission per Coital Act by Stage of HIV-1 Infection, in Rakai, Uganda. *Journal of Infectious Diseases*, 191(May), 1403–1409.

Were, W. A., Mermin, J. H., Wamai, N., et al. (2006). Undiagnosed HIV Infection and Couple HIV Discordance among Household Members of HIV-Infected People Receiving Antiretroviral Therapy in Uganda. *Journal of Acquired Immune Deficiency Syndromes*, 43(5), 91–95.

Witte, K. (1992). Putting the Fear Back into Fear Appeals: The Extended Parallel Process Model. *Communication Monographs*, 59(4), 329–349.

Chapter 18

Crime and Punishment: Infidelity in Telenovelas and Implications for Latina Adolescent Health

Tilly A. Gurman

Introduction

Although Latina teens are less likely to engage in sex compared to other teens, they are less likely to use condoms when having sex and more likely to parent a child once pregnant (Abma et al., 2004;Aneshensel et al., 1989; Eaton et al., 2011). Findings from the Youth Risk Behavior Surveillance System (YRBSS) results indicate that the percentage of Latina high school students who have ever engaged in sexual intercourse falls below their African American and White peers (43.9 percent versus 53.6 percent and 44.5 percent, respectively) (Eaton et al., 2012). Among sexually active high school students, however, Latinas are less likely to have used birth control pills, and other birth-control devices the last time they had sex (Eaton et al., 2012). It is not surprising, therefore, that Latinas have the highest teen birth rate in the United States (Guttmacher Institute, 2010; National Campaign to Prevent Teen Pregnancy, 2005).

Latinos, currently the largest ethnic minority population in the United States, are disproportionately affected by sexually transmitted infections (STIs), including HIV/AIDS (Centers for Disease Control and Prevention, 2012; Centers for Disease Control and Prevention, 2011; Centers for Disease Control and Prevention, 2005; Suro et al., 2002). Although Latinos comprise approximately 16 percent of the US population, they account for 20 percent of the estimated cumulative AIDS cases (Centers for Disease Control and Prevention, 2011). Compared to their White counterparts, Latinas experience more than three times the rate of infection for Chlamydia, syphilis, and HIV (Centers for Disease Control and Prevention, 2005; Centers for Disease Control and Prevention, 2011). Mutual monogamy is considered an effective strategy for the prevention of STIs, while infidelity may increase an individual's risk. Previous studies have documented that Spanish-language telenovelas contain large amounts of infidelity, with little emphasis on safer sex (Glascock & Ruggiero, 2004; Gurman, 2009). Moreover, for programs popular among Latino adolescents, telenovelas contain more infidelity compared to English-language programs (Gurman, 2009). Because Spanish-language telenovelas are among the highest rated programs among Latina adolescents in the United States (see Tables 18.1 and 18.2), it is plausible that Latina adolescents who watch telenovelas will be exposed to messages reinforcing infidelity.

Social Cognitive Theory (SCT) posits that individuals learn behaviors by watching others, including observing the resulting rewards and punishments (Bandura, 1986a, 1986b). Following SCT, television serves as an informal educator for adolescents about

Table 18.1: Spanish-language programs popular among Latina adolescents Ages 12–17*.

Network	Program Name	Type of Program	Nielsen Rating
Univision	Contra Viento Y Marea (Thursday)	Telenovela	13.3
Univision	Contra Viento Y Marea (Wednesday)	Telenovela	12.3
Univision	Contra Viento Y Marea (Tuesday)	Telenovela	12
Univision	Contra Viento Y Marea (Monday)	Telenovela	11.1
Univision	Piel de Otoño (Thursday)	Telenovela	10.3
Univision	Piel de Otoño (Tuesday)	Telenovela	10.3
Univision	Alborada (Thursday)	Telenovela	10.2
Univision	Alborada (Monday)	Telenovela	9.6
Univision	Alborada (Tuesday)	Telenovela	9.2
Univision	Piel de Otoño (Wednesday)	Telenovela	9.2
Univision	Bailando por un sueño	Game Show	9.2
Univision	Contra Viento Y Marea (Friday)	Telenovela	9.1
Univision	Alborada (Wednesday)	Telenovela	8.7
Univision	Piel de Otoño (Friday)	Telenovela	8.5
Univision	Piel de Otoño (Monday)	Telenovela	8.4
Univision	Casos de la Vida Real (Special edition)	Reality Drama	8.2
Univision	Alborada (Friday)	Telenovela	8
Univision	Cristina	Talk Show	7.7
Univision	Aqui y Ahora	News Show	5.8
Univision	Alborada (big finale)	Telenovela	5.4

*Nielsen data from December 15, 2005 through January 29, 2006.

a range of behaviors, including sexual behavior. Research literature supports SCT, as adolescents have reported learning about sexual health through television (Brown & Keller, 2000; Brown & Witherspoon, 2002; Brown et al., 2005; Collins et al., 2003; Sutton et al., 2002). Telenovela characters, especially those who appear regularly and are more similar to the viewer, have the ability, therefore, to teach Latina adolescent viewers about consequences of infidelity.

It is important to go beyond quantifying the frequency with which infidelity occurs in telenovelas and map the trajectory of cheating for female lead characters. Elucidating the way in which infidelity is contextualized will allow researchers to identify lessons learned from observing these virtual role models, infer sexual health implications for Latina adolescents, and determine strategies to promote healthy sexuality for Latina adolescents.

Table 18.2: English-language programs popular among Latina adolescents Ages 12–17*.

Network	Program Name	Type of Program	Nielsen Rating
WB	Supernatural	Drama	4.6
UPN	America's Next Top Model	Reality: Game Show	4.6
ABC	Desperate Housewives	Drama	4.5
ABC	Extreme Makeover: Home Edition	Reality	4.2
UPN	Everybody Hates Chris	Situation Comedy	3.9
UPN	Eve	Situation Comedy	3.8
UPN	Cuts	Situation Comedy	3.8
WB	Gilmore Girls	Drama	3.7
UPN	Veronica Mars	Drama	3.7
UPN	Girlfriends	Situation Comedy	3.6
UPN	Love, Inc.	Situation Comedy	3.4
FOX	Simpsons	Animated Comedy	3.2
FOX	Family Guy	Animated Comedy	3.2
WB	One Tree Hill	Drama	3.1
FOX	Prison Break	Drama	3.0
FOX	Trading Spouses	Reality	2.8
UPN	Half and Half	Situation Comedy	2.8
WB	Charmed	Drama	2.7
UPN	One on One	Situation Comedy	2.7
ABC	Grey's Anatomy	Drama	2.6

Nielsen data from August 29, 2005 through December 25, 2005.

Background

Telenovelas are Spanish-language serial dramas, which air for several months and then end with definite narrative closure (La Pastina et al., 2003; Lopez, 1995; Martín-Barbero, 1995). Telenovelas, as formulaic morality plays, focus on the struggle between good and evil. As a guiding principle, the primary component of telenovelas is a love story, "but the smooth passage of this love interest is always thwarted, traditionally by melodramatic tensions of infidelity, betrayal, and lies" (Pearson, 2005:402). Telenovelas – popular throughout Latin America and among Latinos in the United States – are primarily produced by Mexico, Brazil, and Venezuela (Hagedorn, 1995; La Pastina et al., 2003; Lopez, 1995; Pearson, 2005). In the

United States, the vast majority of telenovelas aired are imported from Grupo Televisa, a Mexican company that distributes telenovelas throughout Latin America as well (Barrera & Bielby, 2001).

Regardless of acculturation level, many Latinos in the United States view Spanish-language media, such as telenovelas, as a valid mechanism by which to maintain a connection with their culture of birth (Barrera & Bielby, 2001; Downey, 2006; Morales, 2006; Moran, 2003; Rios, 2003; Vargas, 2005; Mayer, 2003; Rivadeneyra, 2006; Rivadeneyra, 2011). For Latino adolescents, Spanish-language media can serve as a resource for "cultural continuity" (Vargas, 2005:46), helping them "envision past identities" (Mayer, 2003:135), whether or not they were born in the United States. Moreover, Latino adolescents view Spanish-language television as being more realistic in their portrayals of Latinos compared to the portrayals in English-language television (Rivadeneyra, 2006).

Telenovela story lines reinforce traditional Latino cultural norms, including the importance of Catholicism and gender roles (Rivadeneyra, 2011; Glascock & Ruggiero, 2004). In a nationally representative survey of Latinos living in the United States, approximately 76 percent of foreign-born Latinos and 59 percent of US-born Latinos reported being Roman Catholic (Suro et al., 2002). Latino adolescents similarly believe in the importance of religion. A US media industry survey of over 1,800 Latino youth similarly reported that 71 percent of respondents self-identified as religious and 52 percent wanted to raise their children according to religious values (Look-Look, 2006). Furthermore, previous research has illustrated that religion plays a role in Latina's interpretation of television content. In a qualitative study of 24 Latina adolescents attending Catholic school, Moran (2003) reported that respondents judged television characters' behaviors based on their religious upbringing and beliefs. The importance of Catholicism among Latina adolescents, however, has potential implications for STI prevention. For example, even though Catholicism encourages the protective behaviors of abstinence and monogamy, it concurrently denounces condom use. For youth who are unable to abstain and engage in concurrent sexual partnerships, not using condoms increases the risk of acquiring an STI. In addition, there is strong emphasis in Catholicism on penance for absolution of sins. Therefore, portrayals of religion within the context of infidelity may offer insight into the messages that Latina adolescents may receive from telenovelas regarding the possible rewards and punishments of infidelity.

Traditional female gender roles (*marianismo*) promote Latinas as nurturers, while simultaneously encourage chastity, fidelity, and sexual passivity. Such gender roles may disempower a Latina during sexual encounters or affect her ability to talk openly about sexuality with potential partners (Faulkner & Mansfield, 2002; Faulkner, 2003; Talashek et al., 2003; Vasquez, 1999). Male gender roles (*machismo*), on the other hand, are less disapproving of sexual activity and promote males as the protector, instigator of sex, and teacher of sex to women (Faulkner & Mansfield, 2002; Murphy & Boggess, 1998). One study of Mexican-American adolescents corroborated these beliefs, with 80 percent and 37 percent of participants agreeing that women and men, respectively, should remain virgins until marriage (Padilla & Baird, 1991). More recent studies have found associations between consumption of telenovelas and traditional gender roles (Rivadeneyra & Lebo, 2008; Rivadeneyra & Ward, 2005). For example, one study found that Latina adolescents who were high viewers of either Spanish-language television adhered to more traditional gender role attitudes, with no statistically significant association for males (Rivadeneyra & Ward, 2005). This finding suggests that the way in which telenovelas depict female characters' experience with infidelity may reinforce female viewers' notions of marianismo, including their perceptions of how they should react if faced with the possibility of engaging in infidelity.

According to SCT, individuals have the opportunity to learn about behaviors through ongoing interaction with environmental factors, including mass media (Bandura, 1986a). Observational learning is the process through which an individual uses her symbolic capacity to learn about behaviors vicariously from watching others in her environment (Bandura, 1986b; Bandura, 1986c). Models instruct, encourage, reinforce, and disinhibit individuals about specific behaviors. Observational learning can also influence an individual's self-efficacy, or confidence in her ability to engage in a particular behavior when needed (Bandura, 1986c). For example, observing a female character resisting another man's sexual advances and therefore remaining monogamous could reinforce a Latina adolescent's belief in her ability to behave similarly. Observational learning can be enhanced by increasing an individual's involvement and attention. Attentiveness can be increased via vicarious behavioral consequences, both rewards and punishments (Bandura, 1986b, 1986c). SCT suggests that observing models being rewarded for behavior increases the likelihood that viewers will engage in a similar behavior, above and beyond observing the same behavior without consequences. Observing a model receiving punishment for a behavior, on the other hand, can dissuade individuals from engaging in the behavior (Bandura, 1986c).

Outcome expectancies, according to Bandura (1986c), are the judgments made regarding potential risks and benefits of a given behavior. As individuals interact with their environment, they are confronted with its norms and values. For example, the way television depicts sexual content "conveys information about the importance and acceptability of sexual behavior" (Martino et al., 2005:916). Through their interaction with television content, individuals will determine their own beliefs about the benefits and costs of engaging in a particular behavior.

Outcome expectancies have been associated with condom use (Gomez & Marin, 1996; Norris & Ford, 1992) and sexual initiation (Christopher et al., 1993; Martino et al., 2005; O'Donnell et al., 2003). One recent study conducted surveys with adolescents, including Latinos, along with conducting a quantitative content analysis of sexual content among popular English-language programs. Content analysis findings indicated that sexual behaviors rarely resulted in negative repercussions. Moreover, survey findings for Latino adolescents demonstrated a relationship between exposure to sexual content and outcome expectancies, with greater exposure associated with fewer negative outcome expectations for sexual initiation (Martino et al., 2005).

The present qualitative study frames the analysis of sexual infidelity in telenovelas within the context of SCT, specifically observational learning, the vicarious consequences of reward and punishment, and outcome expectations. The overall aim of the present study was to elucidate messages about infidelity that may be derived from telenovelas by exploring the trajectories of infidelity, with a focus on the narrative development of the primary and secondary lead female characters in two telenovelas. Female characters, who reinforce sexual attitudes and behaviors as story lines unfold, were selected for analysis because character similarity aids observational learning (Bandura, 1986c). In other words, as a Latina adolescent engages with a Latina lead character in a telenovela, they participate in observational learning – with the modeled attitudes, behaviors, and interactions shaping the adolescent's sexual attitudes and beliefs. Such attitudes and beliefs may influence outcome expectancies and self-efficacy. Previous research and the above theoretical foundation, therefore, led to the following the three research questions:

RQ 1: How is infidelity portrayed across the different narratives?

RQ 2: What are the trajectories for female characters who engage in sexual infidelity, in terms of rewards and punishments?

RQ 3: How do cultural norms come into play within the depiction of infidelity and the outcomes of behavior?

Although the impact of telenovelas' portrayals of infidelity on actual Latino adolescent behavior cannot be deduced from a content analysis, a study that uncovers the depictions of rewards and punishments may, nevertheless, be a helpful preliminary step that can infer implications and inform audience studies.

Methods

Sample criteria

The present study is an ethnographic content analysis (ECA) of a larger, primarily quantitative content analysis, which analyzed sexual content of English-language ($n = 36$) and Spanish-language ($n = 34$) television programs popular among Latino adolescents (Gurman, 2009). Program selection for the overall study was informed by AC Nielsen ratings of English- and Spanish-language programs popular among Latino adolescents (ages 12–17). Within the larger sample, 47 percent of Spanish-language scenes ($n = 94$) and 12.4 percent of English-language scenes ($n = 29$) *with* any type of sexual content portrayed talk about either infidelity or unfaithful behavior. The data from the larger study were used to identify a subset for the present study.

The sample for the present study includes two telenovela programs, twenty episodes, and four female characters. The way in which the present study's sample was identified occurred in different stages. At the program level, the sample was first limited to Spanish-language programs, four Televisa telenovelas that aired primetime on the Univision network between February 28, 2006 and April 17, 2006. The author limited the sample to two of these telenovelas, *Barrera de Amor* and *Alborada*, because they provided the greatest number of episodes ($n = 20$) and scenes ($n = 138$) for data exploration. Among the 138 scenes including sexual content, 83 addressed sexual infidelity. While these 83 scenes were the primary scenes analyzed in the present study, the other 55 scenes were available to provide additional context. At the character level, the sample included the primary and secondary female lead characters for each of the telenovelas, all of whom were involved in infidelity. In *Alborada*, set in colonial Panama and Mexico, the female characters of interest were Hipólita and Esperanza. In *Barrera de Amor*, set in present-day Mexico, the female characters of interest were Maité and Manola.

Data collection and analysis

The present study uses ECA, a methodology that allows for the discovery of emergent patterns and themes in media. Of particular interest in ECA are the meanings and nuances of the who, what, where, and why depicted in mass media (Altheide, 1996). In order to explore these meanings and nuances in-depth, data collection for the present study occurred in three stages. First, during the data collection of the larger study, a team of three bilingual research assistants coded various content variables regarding sexual talk and behavior. Two of these variables identified the presence of sexual infidelity, either in a discussion or behavior. Talk about infidelity was identified when a discussion addressed a violation of a relationship between two people in a committed romantic relationship. The discussion did not necessarily need to occur between the actual participants of infidelity. The second variable, infidelity-related behavior, was identified when at least one of the characters involved in the sexual behavior at-hand was violating a committed relationship. The behavior could include flirting, passionate kissing, intimate touching, as well as sexual intercourse. Interrater reliability for identifying scenes that included infidelity was high for talk about infidelity (percent agreement: 92.89 percent; Scott's *pi* = .82) as well as infidelity-related behavior (percent agreement: 92.76 percent; Scott's *pi* = .86). Other variables provided additional context, including the gender of the individual who instigated the behavior and discussion of sexual risk/responsibility. Furthermore, research assistants provided a written description of the sexual content for each scene. The quantitative data were used to identify scenes containing infidelity, while the written description helped to understand the context of the content.

Second, the author obtained written descriptions of the four female lead characters as well as of all the episodes for *Alborada* and *Barrera de Amor* from *www.esmas.com*, the official website of Televisa, the production company for both telenovelas. These data enabled a more thorough exploration of the overall trajectory of infidelity, since the program- and scene-level data collected in the larger content analysis study did not span the entire run of the telenovelas.

Third, the author viewed the scenes identified by the research assistants as containing sexual infidelity, along with other scenes in the particular episode that included the female character of interest, to obtain additional context related to infidelity. Data analysis included "extensive reading, sorting, and searching" of the above information (Altheide, 1996:43) to identify repeated themes related to infidelity, including vicarious rewards and punishments.

Results

RQ 1: How is infidelity portrayed across the different narratives?

Among scenes with any type of sexual content in the larger study sample (n = 138), 60.1 percent (n = 83) included either talk about infidelity or unfaithful behavior. Of the 83 scenes with infidelity, 22.9 percent (n = 19) portrayed unfaithful behavior without talk about infidelity, 7.2 percent (n = 6) included both unfaithful behavior and talk about infidelity, and 69.9 percent (n = 58) included talk about infidelity without any depiction of unfaithful behavior. Approximately 9.6 percent of scenes with infidelity (n = 8) addressed sexual risk or responsibility. Most commonly, these scenes addressed unintended pregnancy (seven scenes), with other issues including abortion (two scenes, one of which also included unintended pregnancy) or virginity (one scene). Neither contraception nor condom use was portrayed in any of the scenes with infidelity. From these data, there appears to be little punishment for infidelity. At the same time, using ECA reveals that, for all four characters, infidelity resulted in an unintended pregnancy.

After further analyzing the data using ECA, it became evident that there were two types of infidelity portrayed. The first was one in which the act was not volitional and the female character had no personal motive for engaging in the behavior. Nonvolitional involvement included being fooled into the adulterous act or being sexually victimized. The second type of infidelity occurred when the female character had personal motives for engaging in the behavior. Motives included lust, greed, and the relentless desire to have a child. The rest of this section traces the trajectory of infidelity following the narrative development of the four female characters, by specific telenovela.

In *Alborada*, Hipólita's involvement in infidelity was nonvolitional, while Esperanza's involvement was driven by personal motives. Hipólita is depicted as an honest woman of simple means who was raised by a single mother. Her character is described on *Alborada's* website as "strong," "decisive," and a "rebel." Hipólita was brought into an arranged marriage with Antonio in exchange for an attractive dowry. Months after the wedding, the marriage had yet to be consummated because of Antonio's emotional scars of childhood sexual abuse. Desiring an heir for her family, Hipólita's mother-in-law blackmails a man to impersonate Antonio and hopefully impregnate Hipólita. This man, Luis, comes to Hipólita's bedroom at night. Believing that it is Antonio at her bedside, Hipólita states "I am so happy that you are with me," relieved to finally consummate their marriage. Throughout the scene, it is evident that Hipólita experiences pleasure from the physical intimacy, but she trusts that she is having sex with her husband, not some stranger. After they have sex, however, Luis confesses that he is not her husband and then flees without telling her his name or showing his face. This act of infidelity, therefore, was one in which the female character was unknowingly involved and had no personal motive.

Esperanza, on the other hand, follows the path of an adulterer with personal motive. Esperanza is described on *Alborada's* website as "uncultivated," "emotionally unstable," and "frigid." She is a devout Catholic and obsessed with becoming a mother, even though previous pregnancies have ended in miscarriage. It is this obsession with becoming a mother that drives her actions, which ultimately result in infidelity. After the last miscarriage she was warned by her physician that another pregnancy could be fatal. Yet she is determined to conceive again. Her husband, Luis (the same Luis as above), refuses to have sex with Esperanza for fear of her death. Esperanza falsely claims to have received visions of the Virgin who stated that she will bear a son. Esperanza later buys an aphrodisiac potion from a local *curandera* (witch doctor) to use on her husband. Diego (Luis' cousin) mistakenly drinks the potion, which overwhelms his libido and eventually rapes Esperanza.

During this rape scene, Diego says that she has a big problem and that he has a "solution." He continues by mentioning that the Virgin said that "she would send you a son, but whose son? ... What does it matter whose son it is?" As he continues, Esperanza pleads for him to stop and professes that what he is suggesting is a sin. Although her intention was not to have sex with Diego, Esperanza was unable to stop his advances. After the rape, her maid convinces her that perhaps it was a "miracle" and that Diego was "an instrument sent by that very Virgin." Esperanza, visibly shaken and disturbed, tries to console herself that perhaps it was a "sign from Heaven." She ultimately accepts the rape and decides not to disclose the rape to anyone else because what she cared about most was her desire to bear a child, whatever the cost.

In *Barrera de Amor*, Maité's involvement in infidelity was nonvolitional, while Manola's involvement was driven by personal motives. Maité's story begins with her being engaged to Luis Antonio, the veterinarian of the ranch owned by one of the town's wealthiest families, the Valladolids. Described on *Barrera de Amor's* website as a "hard-worker," "simple," and "generous," Maité works in the restaurant owned by the aunt who raised her.

One day Maité is out on the Valladolid ranch and meets Adolfo, the male heir of this ranch and best friend of Luis Antonio. Confusing Maité for hired help and thinking that he can treat her like a sexual object, Adolfo dismounts his horse, rushes over to her, and begins to grab her dress. She screams, "Let go of me! I don't want anything to do with you!" She slaps him and runs away, making her disinterest known to Adolfo. Angered by Maité, since his sexual advances had yet to be refused by any woman, Adolfo becomes obsessed with "making her mine." After another failed attempt, Adolfo eventually rapes Maité several weeks before his pending wedding to Manola. During the rape scene, which occurs at night in Maité's bedroom, she continues to make her disinterest clear to Adolfo, fighting him throughout the act.

Manola, in stark contrast to Maité, is described on *Barrera de Amor's* website as a "vain" and "superficial" woman with "few scruples" who is "concerned with appearances." As a result, for Manola, adultery is a "diversion" entirely about the physical pleasure, and she is a willing participant in an ongoing affair that lasts for many years. Although she does not love Adolfo, her fiancé, Manola wants to marry him for his wealth. Ultimately, Adolfo marries Maité, requiring Manola to find another rich man for her to marry, a task which she eventually accomplishes.

Throughout her relationships with wealthy men, Manola is involved in a sexual and clandestine relationship with Federico – refusing to engage in anything more than physical with him because of his lower socioeconomic status. One scene, which begins with her and Federico fixing themselves after an afternoon tryst in a hallway at Adolfo's house, illustrates this point. As Federico gives her a jewelry box, he states, "I don't make love with anyone like I do with you." Manola appears excited with her gift until she opens it. She looks at the brooch and asks, "What is this? Where did you buy this? At the market?" and proceeds to throw it on the floor. She continues, "I like expensive and fine things. Did you know that? If you want to give me a jewel, it needs to be gold. Those little colored rocks must be of glass. I want diamonds, rubies, real emeralds." Federico professes his love to her, to which she scoffs, "You want me to marry you. But you're nobody." When he pleads that he has fallen in love with her, she responds, "That is your problem." Later in the telenovela, Federico is able to afford finer jewelry. He hands her a gold broche decorated with rubies in a hidden alcove where they are passionately kissing in the daylight. This time, she doesn't discard the gift. Content, Federico states that he wants her to "enjoy your jewel like I enjoy you." Manola, nonetheless, continues to see Federico as a fling with no real prospect of offering her all that she feels she merits. Her greed and desire to be wealthy enables Manola to willingly remain in a loveless marriage and participate in a long-lasting affair.

RQ 2: What are the trajectories for female characters who engage in sexual infidelity, in terms of rewards and punishments?

As the narratives of the two telenovelas develop, the trajectories for female lead characters, in terms of rewards and punishments, evolve. Comparing the two lead female characters within each telenovela, it initially appears that the character who was unwillingly/unknowingly involved in infidelity suffers greater punishment, while the character with personal motive gains more rewards. As will be described under the findings for Research Question 3, the characters that ascribe more to the sociocultural norms of traditional gender roles and the importance of religion experience happy endings. Ultimately, the characters with personal motives for infidelity endure the most severe punishments of death and eternal damnation, while the characters that are willing to repent experience the most favorable rewards.

Through the majority of the narrative, the female lead characters who were unwilling/unknowing participants in infidelity endured physical and psychological punishments for their behavior. In Hipólita's case, not only does she get pregnant from the one act of infidelity, but she must live with the repercussions of an adulterer. These repercussions begin when Hipólita learns that she is pregnant and decides to flee from her husband in search of her son's father. This latter act will identify her as a single mother of an illegitimate son. Her servant, Adalgisa, tries to discourage her, stating, "the life of an illegitimate son is very difficult." During her quest, Hipólita endures difficulty securing employment eventually working as a maid – a profession much below her previous socioeconomic status. Furthermore, she experiences unwelcome advances due to the stigma of being a single mother, something men equate with sexually permissiveness. These trials and tribulations inevitably convince Hipólita to return home and attempt reconciliation with Antonio. This attempt ultimately fails because Hipólita realizes that, although Antonio promises to give her son a stable home and a legitimate last name, she cannot live in a loveless marriage with a man who does not truly care for her son. In the meanwhile, Diego discloses Hipólita's adultery and bastard son to the local authorities. Hipólita is ultimately found guilty of adultery and sentenced to endure public beating and humiliation. At the end of her pain and suffering, however, Hipólita experiences a happy ending, which will be further explored in the following section.

Similar to Hipólita, Maité adulterous event extolled many years of suffering and self-sacrifice. After the incident, a pregnant Maité seeks refuge in a nearby convent. Luis Antonio, her only true love, finds her, only to be told by a doctor and nun at the convent who tell him of her condition. Luis Antonio returns to town to confront Maité's aunt for more answers, and thereby learns of her rape. Furious, he physically assaults Adolfo to the point of hospitalization, coincidentally the day prior to Adolfo and Manola's wedding. Jacinta, Adolfo's mother and the Valladolid matriarch, uses her family's wealth and power to convince the authorities to jail Luis Antonio and wrongfully accuse him of financial fraud.

Maité states her commitment to "doing whatever it takes" in order to free Luis Antonio from jail. Due to Maité's lower social status, Jacinta quickly dismisses her pleas for Luis Antonio's release, calling her a "nobody," a "vulgar woman," and a "*descarada*" (brazen woman – negative connotation). In a desperate final effort to get Jacinta's attention, Maité disrupts Adolfo's wedding mid-ceremony and announces to the congregation and God that she is expecting Adolfo's baby – not disclosing that the pregnancy was a result of a rape. Jacinta, wanting to save her family name from further public humiliation, agrees to release Luis Antonio with the condition that Maité marry Adolfo. In order to save Luis Antonio from long-term imprisonment, Maité agrees to the marriage. Besides breaking the engagement to her true love and being coerced to marry the man who raped her, Maité's punishment lasts over twenty years. Maité endures a loveless marriage, coerced abandonment of her beloved child, and physical abuse from both her husband and mother-in-law. Similar to Hipólita, Maité experiences a happy ending – again to be explored in the next section.

Esperanza is possibly the most tragic character of the four analyzed in this study because she was unwillingly involved in the adultery; yet her greed leads to her eventual demise. Her selfish yet religious persona causes internalization of her guilt and silence about the rape. Esperanza is depicted as feebler than Hipólita, with her suffering taking place in the privacy of her bed chamber during and after the rape. In various scenes, Esperanza prays to God, begging for mercy. The only reward that Esperanza receives is that she does get the pregnancy she wished, although it eventually results in another miscarriage and her death. Esperanza, therefore, can be viewed as a character who suffers throughout the narrative as well as at the end of the narrative.

Manola, on the other hand, does not initially endure much punishment. Of the three other female characters, she is the only one who is successful hiding her affair. Most of her illicit encounters are in dark hallways or alleys and Federico's mother, who once witnesses them kissing, is the sole character who witnesses their infidelity. Moreover, Manola's infidelity is not only long-lasting but also pleasurable. Manola seems to enjoy the physical act as well as additional rewards, such as marrying a wealthy older man, Gustavo, who indulges her expensive tastes. Initially, it appears that she has the best of both worlds, since she is rich and simultaneously enjoys the physical pleasure from her lover. At the same time, she always seems displeased with what she has and tries to find ways to further her financial standing. For example, on multiple occasions, Manola tries to kill Gustavo so that she can obtain his inheritance without having to stay married to him longer. According to SCT, this modeled displeasure could reduce the impact of the vicarious rewards from the infidelity (Bandura, 1986c).

RQ 3: How do cultural norms come into play within the depiction of infidelity and the outcomes of behavior?

Traditional gender roles and religion intertwine and play important roles throughout the narratives' trajectories of infidelity. Overall, none of the 25 scenes with unfaithful behavior depicted the female as either the primary or mutual instigator. Males were the primary instigators in thirteen scenes, with the instigator for the remaining twelve scenes noted as unclear – a category selected when a scene begins mid-behavior. This finding suggests that traditional gender roles may be reinforced, with female characters depicted as the more passive participant in sexual encounters. Analyzing the female characters' narratives elucidates the reinforcement of traditional gender roles further. Specifically, the importance of motherhood and yearning for family among the female characters, with the exception of Manola, are depicted as strong motivators throughout the narratives. For example, Maité and Hipólita enact self-sacrifice and tolerate punishment for their infidelity in order to benefit their true love and their child, upholding their aspiration of family.

In both *Alborada* and *Barrera de Amor*, the presence and power of the Catholic Church is prominent throughout. In particular, the Catholic religion is almost treated as a separate character that contextualizes the ways in which female characters experience rewards or punishment. The remainder of this section follows each character to illustrate how both gender roles and religion surfaced throughout their respective narrative.

One might argue that Hipólita's character was created to challenge traditional gender roles. She is described on esmas.com as not accepting the "idea that the woman must be submissive to the man." In addition, during her sexual encounters with Luis, her facial expressions imply that Hipólita enjoyed sex. Nevertheless, Hipólita was impregnated because her mother-in-law wanted her to become a mother – a role that Hipólita readily accepted. Moreover, Hipólita is willing to endure personal hardship and self-sacrifice in order to ensure happiness for Rafael, her son. First, she leaves her husband in search of her son's father, hoping to legitimize Rafael's identity. During this quest she locates Luis and uncovers that he is Rafael's father. Inexorably they fall in love – something forbidden since both individuals are married to someone else. Realizing that her venture's success is bittersweet and unrealistic, Hipólita decides to reconcile with Antonio, with the hope of providing a safe and healthy home for Rafael, even though she feels no love for Antonio.

During the reconciliation attempt, Hipólita struggles with her acceptance of gender roles. For example, a dialogue between Hipólita and her maid, Adalgisa, illustrates that Hipólita doesn't want to challenge traditional female roles too much. In this discussion, Adalgisa reminds Hipólita that she can't keep turning down Antonio's advances, stating "he is your husband, you have to comply." Hipólita comments how she waited for months for Antonio to "make me a woman." Adalgisa replies that men are the ones who dictate sex, to which Hipólita retorts that, although she agrees, she wants "to decide who will be the man who has that control." Hipólita finally decides to leave Antonio and escape with Luis, no matter the risk. Hipólita declares to Adalgisa that she is "sick and tired of doing what others want" and that she doesn't want to "live a miserable life next to a man who doesn't care for Rafael." Reaffirming her love for Luis, Hipólita has sexual intercourse with him again, although this time she is aware of her actions and that, although in a loveless marriage, she is knowingly engaging in adultery. Although Hipólita gets pregnant a second time with Luis, she is able to keep the pregnancy a secret from everyone except Adalgisa, her faithful confidante.

As previously mentioned, Hipólita is punished by the Church for her adultery. It is important to note that because Hipólita has kept the second pregnancy a secret, her punishment is based only on her initial nonvolitional adultery. Friar Alvaro, who serves as the local judge and finalizes Hipólita's penalty, says that even though she seems like a "good mother" she must be beaten to "serve as an example to other women." In these public beating scenes, priests stand in the background to witness her penance. According to SCT, this depiction of punitive treatment may enhance rather than reduce Hipólita's social status, both in the eyes of the virtual community and the viewers at home (Bandura, 1986c). Soon after, the viceroy of New Spain proclaims the end of the inquisition, sparing Hipólita from further flagellation and humiliation.

At the end of the story, Luis and Hipólita's love triumphs, securing a happy ending. The punishments and sacrifices that Hipólita endured, including her public beating, make way for her happiness. She never received punishment for her second pregnancy and voluntary infidelity. On the contrary, Hipólita marries Luis, her true love, and gives birth to their second child. As for their spouses and Diego (the man who accused Hipólita of adultery), they have all died.

For Esperanza, her selfish desire for family drives her to risk death. While on the surface it may seem that Esperanza ascribes to the gender role of motherhood, she dismisses the role of being a good wife. Both Esperanza's family physician and husband have expressed concern that another pregnancy may result in her death, yet she ignores their concerns and persists with her goal of becoming pregnant. Esperanza eventually attains this goal, although the pregnancy inevitably yields another miscarriage and her untimely death.

Lying on her deathbed after the miscarriage, Esperanza suffers internal anguish for her sins, namely having sex outside of marriage and falsely claiming receiving visions of the Virgin who told her that her pregnancy was Godsend. In her final yearning for eternal salvation, Esperanza requests a priest be sent to her so that she may ask for forgiveness. She begs him for her absolution, stating "I am afraid of dying and going to Hell." After hearing about what happened, the priest responds that she has committed a "sacrilege" and that she will go to hell unless she confesses everything to Luis. At first she says that she cannot tell Luis what happened, to which the priest replies that he will not, therefore, be able to exonerate her sins. She beseeches him and cries "I have already received my punishment. The baby suffered an untimely end and perhaps I will die."

In another scene between a local judge and friar, the power and presence exerted by religion is further reinforced. The two are talking about Esperanza's rape and the fact that a priest was asked to absolve her sins. The judge comments "how barbaric" that Diego "took advantage" of his cousin's wife. The friar replies that the "biggest thing is the sacrilege," referring to his belief that Esperanza lying about receiving visions from the Virgin was worse than the fact that she was raped. They then agree to behave discretely in public discussions related to Esperanza because of Diego's standing. The friar comments that they may have to judge Esperanza if she lives, to which the judge replies "Well let's pray to God that in his infinite mercy he will take her."

Esperanza eventually tells Luis a portion of the truth – that Diego told her he was sent to her by the Virgin and later impregnated her. She fails, nonetheless, to disclose the rape. The priest absolves Esperanza's sins as he recites prayers in Latin and sprinkles holy water over her body. Esperanza shortly dies in a bedroom at a nearby convent, surrounded by Luis and other loved ones. It is uncertain, however, what becomes of Esperanza's soul – namely whether she will go to heaven or linger in purgatory – since her disclosure of the rape to Luis was not complete. A nun standing in the hallway outside the bedroom after Esperanza's death emphasizes this point. Glancing at a crucifix that hangs on the wall, she states that she hopes Esperanza's soul is not "condemned."

Maité is devoted both to religion – evident by the cross pendant she wears around her neck – and the importance of family. For Maité, the Church is where she finds refuge and solace. Throughout *Barrera de Amor*, Maité defers to God by willingly repenting and enduring suffering as penance. After discovering her pregnancy, Maité seeks refuge at a convent. While there, Maité asks God for guidance about handling her situation. She states, "I don't know what to do. Not for me, dear God, not for me. For Luis. For his children. For this child that I carry inside me. What should I do? Tell me." Later on, it is in a church where Maité is empowered to confront her rapist and demand attention. After agreeing to marry Adolfo in order to save Luis Antonio, Maité realizes that she feels only disgust for Adolfo. One night while lying in bed next to Adolfo, Maité again turns to God for guidance, asking to "give me the strength to tolerate this man." Although she repeatedly witnesses Adolfo coming home intoxicated with prostitutes at his side, Maité defers to religion and respects her marriage vows.

Not only does the Catholic Church provide Maité with solace and strength, but her desire to be a good mother grants her the strength to sacrifice her own personal happiness. For example, soon after the birth of her daughter, Maité ends up hospitalized because of intentional poisoning inflicted by Jacinta, her mother-in-law. While hovering near death, Maité experiences visions of Valeria (her baby daughter) and soon after miraculously recovers from the "crisis." When Maité's aunt comments that Maité kept mentioning her baby, the doctor, amazed at her recovery, states that Valeria "must have given you the strength for your life." Maité agrees, remarking, "I need to be with my girl." Upon returning home, Maité, unaware that her hospitalization was due to a poisoning inflicted by Jacinta, is convinced by Jacinta that she is unfit to be a mother. As a result, Maité agrees to flee and abandon Valeria, believing her sacrifice is what is best for her beloved daughter.

After many years away, Maité returns home – Valeria now a young woman. Initially, Maité is unable to disclose her identity to Valeria, for fear of being hated. At the end of the story, however, Maité is rewarded for her years of self-sacrifice and suffering. Adolfo and Jacinta, the two individuals who inflicted great suffering upon Maité, are dead. Valeria has also forgiven Maité's coerced abandonment. More importantly, Maité and Luis Antonio enjoy a double wedding, theirs and that of her daughter and his son.

In contrast, Manola is committed neither to the notion of having a family and being a good mother nor to the Church. It is in church on her wedding day where Manola experiences public humiliation and learns about Adolfo's infidelity with Maité. Horrified, she runs out of the wedding and refuses to go back, stating, "I will never forgive Adolfo for the humiliation." Her father tries to console her and reminds her that her marriage to Adolfo is their "only salvation," referring to financial stability. Manola replies, "I will never again enter that church." Furthermore, for Manola being a mother is only a means to an end and a way to maintain appearances in front of others. For example, when she finds out that she is pregnant with Federico's child, she realizes that she must have sex with Gustavo, her elderly husband, to fool him to believe that the child is his. One night, while in bed, she ponders that the only other solution would be to "get rid of the pregnancy" but then succumbs to engaging in sex with Gustavo, who she finds unappealing. Years later her lack of desire to assume the role of nurturer is depicted once again. Manola allows her son, now a grown man, to be wrongfully accused of a murder in order to protect herself. Not only did her son not commit the crime, but Manola was partially responsible for the murder.

Although Manola enjoys many apparent rewards throughout the telenovela, in the final episode she ends up dying. The police have finally discovered the multiple crimes (i.e., murder, torture, kidnapping, theft) she and Federico's committed throughout the years. They attempt to escape persecution, which results in their car being surrounded at the top of a cliff by police cars. Realizing there is no escape, they choose to drive off the cliff, plummeting to their death.

A scene earlier in the telenovela foreshadows the religious imagery evident in Manola's dramatic and tragic death. The scene is a flashback to Jacinta's youth, when she was in a small church watching her mother pray. Jacinta walks over to a painting on the wall and asks the church's caretaker about the significance of the people in the painting. He replies, "They are prisoners in Purgatory. They have to pay for their sin with suffering until the divine mercy reaches them and the day that their faults are forgiven, they will be able to go to Heaven." Although the earlier scene included a different character, the moral of the scene infers the fate of Manola's soul. Since she never repented for her sins, as Manola plummets off a steep cliff to her death, an interpretation derived from the previous scene's religious imagery suggests that she is plummeting toward Hell, or at least toward Purgatory. Moreover, Manola's persistent selfishness and unwillingness to save her son allows the viewer to feel no pity for her when she dies.

Discussion

While it is easy to dismiss telenovelas as melodramatic fantasies, these stories are heavily consumed by women, young and old, across the Latin American diaspora throughout Latin America and the United States (Morales, 2006). Furthermore, previous research documents that although Latinas acknowledge that telenovelas are exaggerations, they also believe that the stories represent some element of reality (de la Luz Casas Perez, 2005; Moran, 2003; Rivadeneyra, 2006). The present study, therefore, adds to the current literature by inferring lessons that multitudes of viewers may deduce from telenovelas' treatment of infidelity.

After analyzing the narratives of four lead female characters, four conclusions surface. First, these telenovelas imply that infidelity is practically inevitable, since all four characters participated in infidelity. Second, regardless of whether or not participation was voluntary, infidelity resulted in punishment and suffering, including an unintended pregnancy in all four cases. Although punishment is more common than reward overall, the characters initially involved in nonvolitional infidelity do ultimately enjoy happy endings. To obtain the happily-ever-after-ending, however, these characters endured much suffering and self-sacrifice – from forced abandonment of one's child, to public humiliation, to a loveless marriage. Where characters' infidelity was associated with personal motive, it was the long-term punishment that lingered – both Manola and Esperanza experienced tragic deaths, their souls' fate unknown.

Third, seeking guidance from religion and repenting one's sins are essential for alleviating suffering and reaping long-lasting rewards. Finally, following traditional gender roles, such as engaging in self-sacrifice to benefit a true love or beloved child, will be rewarded. Overall, characters that enjoyed happy endings embraced traditional gender roles, although Hipólita challenged that to a certain degree. Hipólita represented a slightly more assertive character that potentially exemplified a transitioning of telenovelas toward "social change" (Barrera & Bielby, 2001; de la Luz Casas Perez, 2005). At the same time, Manola, the only sexually assertive female, suffered a tragic death. The happy endings of Maité and Hipólita resulted in long-lasting rewards that reinforce traditional gender roles – marriage to the man they love and the reassurance of a family.

The present study offers implications for US Latina adolescent sexual health. Given the extensive reach of Televisa telenovelas throughout Latin America, however, these implications may also be relevant for young women in other countries throughout the region. First, given telenovelas' popularity, public health interventions with Latina adolescents should purposefully counter telenovela's potentially harmful content. For example, interventions could address the manner in which telenovelas depict sexual risk and responsibility and then foster discussions around safer sexual behavior, including condom use. Since telenovelas may not model safer sexual behavior, increasing young women's self-efficacy for using contraception is a critical component for ensuring improved reproductive health outcomes. Second, media literacy interventions could teach Latina adolescents to critically interpret portrayals of infidelity, gender roles, and sexuality. In combination with comprehensive sexuality education, media literacy interventions can empower Latina adolescents to become advocates for their own sexual health by teaching them to become critical mass media consumers. Third, parents or other adults can use telenovelas to initiate discussion about the depiction of sexual health issues and how they coincide with their family's values.

Although this study did not explicitly attempt to include monogamous characters, it is important to highlight that the characters studied were the telenovelas' female leads. Interestingly, Hipólita and Maité were the primary leads, while Esperanza and Manola were the secondary leads. The fact that the primary leads were involved in nonvolitional infidelity but through penance found happiness raises the question about whether these characters will be interpreted by female viewers as positive role models. Future research could explore whether Latina adolescents identify the primary lead characters as the preferred role models. Advocacy efforts should, nevertheless, encourage telenovela scriptwriters to construct positive monogamous role models, as opposed to role models that engage in infidelity but ultimately enjoy the benefits of true love and happiness. Such role models need not be perfect, but flawed behaviors can be complemented by responsible sexual behavior and healthy relationships. Because telenovelas are intended to entertain and not educate, such efforts must be handled by creative talents that can maintain telenovelas' essential melodramatic essence.

A limitation to this ECA is that it reflects an interpretation of data that may vary across individuals, especially since Latina adolescents may or may not interpret scenes similarly.

Therefore, a natural next step would be to conduct audience research to assess how viewers interpret telenovela content. Regardless, the current study findings offer interpretations that are informed by theoretical and cultural constructs and employ a well-grounded methodology. Another limitation stems from the fact that this analysis is based on telenovelas, which are no longer on air. This ECA is not intended to be generalizable to all telenovelas nor is it suggesting that all telenovelas treat female characters who engage in adultery similarly. Instead, this analysis hopes to introduce the value of analyzing these programs qualitatively to create more effective sexual health interventions.

Conclusion

The present qualitative study raises the caveat that although infidelity is prevalent throughout the popular genre of telenovelas, the vicarious lessons offered serve to discourage such behavior. Although STI prevention is not present in these storylines, multiple punishments were depicted. It is likely that future telenovelas will continue to portray infidelity and not regularly depict contraception or condom use. Given the reach of Televisa telenovelas throughout the Latin American diaspora, it is imperative to identify strategies to counter the depictions of female sexuality, which could be potentially harmful to Latina adolescent health. Convincing producers to model monogamy with greater frequency may be logistically difficult. As a result, the complicated trajectories depicted, which portray infidelity as a negative behavior with negative outcomes, should be used to initiate discussions with Latina adolescents. Engaging Latina adolescent consumers, along with their parents or other important adults, to question and challenge the portrayals of Latinas on television may eventually counter harmful reproductive health messages portrayed on these popular Spanish-language television programs.

References

Abma, J. C., Martinez, G. M., Mosher, W. D., & Dawson, B. S. (2004). *Teenagers in the United States: Sexual Activity, Contraceptive Use, and Childbearing, 2002.*

Aneshensel, C. S., Fielder, E. P., & Becerra, R. M. (1989). Fertility and Fertility-Related Behavior among Mexican-American and Non-Hispanic White Female Adolescents. *Journal of Health and Social Behavior*, 31, 56–76.

Altheide, D. L. (1996). *Qualitative Media Analysis.* Thousand Oaks: SAGE Publications, Inc.

Bandura, A. (1986a). Models of Human Nature and Causality. *Social Foundations of Thought & Action: A Social Cognitive Theory.* Englewood Cliffs: Prentice Hall, pp. 2–46.

——— (1986b). Observational Learning. *Social Foundations of Thought & Action: A Social Cognitive Theory.* Englewood Cliffs: Prentice Hall, pp 47–104.

——— (1986c). Vicarious Motivators. *Social Foundations of Thought & Action: A Social Cognitive Theory.* Englewood Cliffs: Prentice Hall, pp. 283–334.

Barrera, V. & Bielby, D. D. (2001). Places, Faces, and Other Familiar Things: The Cultural Experience of Telenovela Viewing among Latinos in the United States. *Journal of Popular Culture*, 34(4), 1–18.

Brown, J. D., Halpern, C. T., & L'Engle, K. L. (2005). Mass Media as a Sexual Super Peer for Early Maturing Girls. *Journal of Adolescent Health*, 36(5), 420–427.

Brown, J. D. & Keller, S. N. (2000). Can the Mass Media Be Healthy Sex Educators? *Family Planning Perspectives*, 32(5), 255–256.

Brown, J. D. & Witherspoon, E. M. (2002). The Mass Media and American Adolescents' Health. *Journal of Adolescent Health*, 31(6, Suppl 1), 153–170.

Centers for Disease Control and Prevention (2012). Diagnoses of HIV Infection and AIDS in the United States and Dependent Areas, 2010: HIV Surveillance Report, (22). Atlanta: US Department of Health and Human Services, CDC.

Centers for Disease Control and Prevention (2011). *HIV/AIDS among Latinos*. Atlanta: US Department of Health and Human Services, CDC.

Centers for Disease Control and Prevention (2005). *Sexually Transmitted Disease Surveillance, 2005*. Atlanta: US Department of Health and Human Services, CDC.

Christopher, F. S., Johnson, D. C., & Roosa, M. W. (1993). Family, Individual, and Social Correlates of Early Hispanic Adolescent Sexual Expression. *The Journal of Sex Research*, 30(1), 54–61.

Collins, R. L., Elliott, M. N., Berry, S. H., Kanouse, D. E., & Hunter, S. B. (2003). Entertainment Television as a Healthy Sex Educator: The Impact of Condom-Efficacy Information in an Episode of Friends. *Pediatrics*, 112(5), 1115–1121.

de la Luz Casas Pérez, M. (2005). Cultural Identity: Between Reality and Fiction: A Transformation of Genre and Roles in Mexican Telenovelas. *Television & New Media*, 6(4), 407–414.

Downey, K. (2006). Nielsen Ratings Prove Telenovelas Can Deliver. *Broadcasting & Cable*, 136(2), 24.

Eaton, D. K., Kann, L., Kinchen, S., et al. (2012). *Youth Risk Behavior Surveillance: United States, 2011* No. 61(SS04). Atlanta, GA: Centers for Disease Control and Prevention. Retrieved on June 19, 2012 from http://www.cdc.gov/mmwr/pdf/ss/ss6104.pdf.

Faulkner, S. L. (2003). Good Girl or Flirt Girl: Latinas' Definitions of Sex and Sexual Relationships. *Hispanic Journal of Behavioral Sciences*, 25(2), 174–200.

Faulkner, S. L. & Mansfield, P. K. (2002). Reconciling Messages: The Process of Sexual Talk for Latinas. *Qualitative Health Research*, 12(3), 310–328.

Glascock, J. & Ruggiero, T. E. (2004). Representations of Class and Gender on Primetime Spanish-Language Television in the United States. *Communication Quarterly*, 52(4), 390–402.

Gomez, C. A. & Marin, B. V. (1996). Gender, Culture, and Power: Barriers to HIV-Prevention Strategies for Women. *Journal of Sex Research*, 33(4), 355–362.

Gurman, T. (2009). Language Matters: Implications of Sexual Content in Fictional Narrative Television Programs Popular among Latino Adolescents. *Journal of Health and Mass Communication*, 1(3–4), 235–257.

Guttmacher Institute (2010). *U.S. Teenage Pregnancies, Births and Abortions: National and State Trends and Trends by Race and Ethnicity*. New York: Guttmacher Institute.

Hagedorn, R. (1995). Doubtless to Be Continued: A Brief History of Serial Narrative, in Allen, R. C. (ed.), *To Be Continued ... Soap Operas around the World*. London, England: Routledge, pp. 27–48.

La Pastina, A. C., Rego, C., & Straubhaar, J. (2003). The Centrality of Telenovelas in Latin America's Everyday Life: Past Tendencies, Current Knowledge, and Future Research. *Global Media Journal*, 2(2).

Look-Look (2006). *me2: Understanding the Young Latino in America.*

Lopez, A. M. (1995). Our Welcomed Guests: Telenovelas in Latin America, in Allen, R. C. (ed.), *To Be Continued ... Soap Operas around the World*. London, England: Routledge, pp. 256–275.

Martín-Barbero, J. (1995). Memory and Form in the Latin American Soap Opera, in Allen, R. C. (ed.), *To Be Continued ... Soap Operas around the World*. London, England: Routledge, pp. 276–284.

Martino, S. C., Collins, R. L., Kanouse, D. E., Elliott, M., & Berry, S. H. (2005). Social Cognitive Processes Mediating the Relationship between Exposure to Television's Sexual Content and Adolescents' Sexual Behavior. *Journal of Personality and Social Psychology*, 89(6), 914–924.

Morales, M. (2006). A Love Affair for Latino Viewers. *Broadcasting & Cable*, 136(2), 24–24.

Moran, K. C. (2003). A Reception Analysis: Latina Teenagers Talk about Telenovelas. [Electronic version]. Retrieved on October 10, 2012 from *Global Media Journal*, 2(2).

Murphy, J. J. & Boggess, S. (1998). Increased Condom Use among Teenage Males, 1988–1995: The Role of Attitudes. *Family Planning Perspectives*, 30(6), 276–280 & 303.

National Campaign to Prevent Teen Pregnancy (2005). *Change in Teen Birth Rates by Race/ Ethnicity.*

Norris, A. E. & Ford, K. (1992). Beliefs about Condoms and Accessibility of Condom Intentions in Hispanic and African American Youth. *Hispanic Journal of Behavioral Sciences*, 14(3), 373–382.

O'Donnell, L., Myint-U, A., O'Donnell, C. R., & Stueve, A. (2003). Long-term influence of sexual norms and attitudes on timing of sexual initiation among urban minority youth. *Journal of School Health*, 73(2), 68-75.

Padilla, A. M. & Baird, T. L. (1991). Mexican-American Adolescent Sexuality and Sexual Knowledge: An Exploratory Study. *Hispanic Journal of Behavioral Sciences*, 13(1), 95–104.

Pearson, R. C. (2005). Fact or Fiction? Narrative and Reality in the Mexican Telenovela. *Television New Media*, 6(4), 400–406.

Rios, D. I. (2003). U.S. Latino Audiences of 'Telenovelas'. *Journal of Latinos & Education*, 2(1), 59.

Rivadeneyra, R. (2006). Do You See What I Wee? Latino Adolescents' Perceptions of the Images on Television. *Journal of Adolescent Research*, 21(4), 393–414.

Rivadeneyra, R. (2011). Gender and Race Portrayals on Spanish-Language Television. *Sex Roles*, 65(3), 208–222.

Rivadeneyra, R. & Lebo, M. J. (2008). The Association between Television-Viewing Behaviors and Adolescent Dating Role Attitudes and Behaviors. *Journal of Adolescence*, 31(3), 291–305.

Rivadeneyra, R. & Ward, L. M. (2005). From Ally McBeal to Sabado Gigante: Contributions of Television Viewing to the Gender Role Attitudes of Latino Adolescents. *Journal of Adolescent Research*, 20(4), 453–475.

Suro, R., Brodie, M., Steffenson, A., Valdez, J., & Levin, R. (2002). *2002 National Survey of Latinos*. Menlo Park and Washington, D.C.: Kaiser Family Foundation and Pew Hispanic Center.

Sutton, M. J., Brown, J. D., Wilson, K. M., & Klein, J. D. (2002). Shaking the Tree of Knowledge for Forbidden Fruit: Where Adolescents Learn about Sexuality and Contraception, in Brown, J.D. J. R.

Steele & K. Walsh-Childers (eds.), *Sexual Teens, Sexual Media: Investigating Media's Influence on Adolescent Sexuality*. Mahwah: Lawrence Erlbaum Associates, Inc., pp. 25–58.

Suro, R., Brodie, M., Steffenson, A., Valdez, J., & Levin, R. (2002). *2002 National Survey of Latinos*. Menlo Park and Washington, D.C.: Kaiser Family Foundation and Pew Hispanic Center.

Talashek, M. L., Norr, K. F., & Dancy, B. L. (2003). Building Teen Power for Sexual Health. *Journal of Transcultural Nursing*, 14(3), 207–216.

Vargas, L. (2005). Media and Racialization among Working-Class Latina Immigrant Young Women, in Peacock, J., Watson, H., & Matthews, C. A. (eds.), *American South in a Global World*. Chapel Hill: University of North Carolina Press, pp. 39–58.

Vasquez, P. (1999). Culture: The Pervasive Context, in Koss-Chioino, J. D. & Vargas, L. A. (eds.), *Working with Latino Youth: Culture, Development, and Context*. San Francisco: Jossey-Bass Publishers, pp. 175–203.

Chapter 19

Conclusion: Communication for Sustainable Social Change Is
Possible, but not Inevitable

Jan Servaes

Change is not an end in itself, but a means to other objectives. The changes that are associated with development provide individuals and societies more control over their own destiny. Development enriches the lives of individuals by widening their horizons and reducing their sense of isolation. It reduces the afflictions brought on by disease and poverty, not only increasing lifespans, but improving the vitality of life.

(Stiglitz, 1998:3)

I stated at the outset that today's world has become increasingly complex and challenging to synthesize. The symbol of a mosaic or kaleidoscope, which, while focusing on certain colors and shapes, makes it difficult to focus on the whole, may come to mind again. Nevertheless, I remain convinced that sustainable development and communication for a sustainable future is possible, but not inevitable. Therefore, at the end of this journey, let me try to summarize the main points highlighted in the preceding chapters and provide some additional food for thought.

The transformation of society

As stated in the opening quote, we are, with many others, in search of a new paradigm for development and social change, one that looks at development and social change as a transformation of society.

Development is shaped and done by people – not for people. In order for people to be able to do so, they need to understand "how the system works." Therefore, development or social change should be equated with empowerment: the ability of people to influence the wider system and take control of their lives (Blewitt, 2008; Friedmann, 1992; Janssens, 2009).

It's obvious that people cannot do this entirely on their own. It also requires effort on the part of development change partners (agencies and agents) to help solve some of the dysfunctions in the system and create the enabling conditions. Therefore, this perspective argues that communication needs to be explicitly built into development plans and social change projects to ensure that a mutual sharing/learning process is facilitated. Such communicative sharing is deemed the best guarantee for creating successful transformations.

I have defined – see, for instance, Servaes (2012:64) – Communication for Development and Social Change as:

> Communication for social change is the nurturing of knowledge aimed at creating a consensus for action that takes into account the interests, needs and capacities of all concerned. It is thus a social process, which has as its ultimate objective sustainable development at distinct levels of society.

> Communication media and ICTs are important tools in achieving social change but their use is not an end in itself. Interpersonal communication, traditional and group media must also play a fundamental role.

This new starting point is examining the processes of "bottom-up" change, focusing on self-development of local communities. The basic assumption is that there are no countries or communities that function completely autonomously and that are completely self-sufficient, nor are there any nations whose development is exclusively determined by external factors. Every society is dependent in one way or another, both in form and in degree.

A new cultural concept of humanism with a cosmopolitan challenge

This also implies, as explicitly argued by Southern scholars like Lalatendu Acharya and Mohan Dutta in this volume, Appiah (2006), Dissanayake (2006), Gunaratne (2005), Sen (2004), or Tehranian (2007) that a *cultural perspective* has to be fully embraced.

Dissanayake (2006:6), for instance, presents it as a *new concept of humanism*: "Humanism as generally understood in Western discourse ... places at the center of its interest the sovereign individual – the individual who is self-present, the originator of action and meaning, and the privileged location of human values and civilizational achievements. However, the concept of the self and individual that is textualized in the kind of classical works that attract the attention of Asian communication theorists present a substantially different picture. The ontology and axiology of selfhood found in Buddhism differs considerably from those associated with European humanism. What these differences signpost is that there is not one but many humanisms."

Many humanisms may lead to what Appiah (2006:174) calls *the cosmopolitan challenge*: "If we accept the cosmopolitan challenge, we will tell our representatives that we want them to remember those strangers. Not because we are moved by their suffering – we may or may not be – but because we are responsive to what Adam Smith called 'reason, principle, conscience, the inhabitant of the beast.' The people of the richest nations can do better. This is a demand of simple morality. But it is one that will resonate more widely if we make our civilization more cosmopolitan."

And, as the 2010 Human Development Report (UNDP, 2010:12) concludes, "Fully realizing the human development agenda requires going further. Putting people at the centre of development is much more than an intellectual exercise. It means making progress equitable and broad-based, enabling people to be active participants in change and ensuring that current achievements are not attained at the expense of future generations. Meeting these challenges is not only possible – it is necessary. And it is more urgent than ever."

Sustainable development, power, and communication

Therefore, attention is also needed to critically analyze the *content of development agendas* (Nederveen Pieterse, 2010; Neumayer, 2010; Servaes, 2008). An understanding of the way in which development and social change projects both encounter and transform power relationships within (and between) the multiple stakeholders who are impacted by such projects and an understanding of the way in which communication plays a central part in building (or maintaining or changing) power relationships is needed (Espinosa & Walker, 2011; Omoto, 2005; Papa et al., 2006; Sikes et al., 1989).

Three streams of action are important:

1. Media must be activated to build public support and upward pressure for policy decisions.
2. Interest groups must be involved and alliances established for reaching a common understanding and mobilizing societal forces. This calls for networking with influential individuals and groups, political forces and public organizations, professional and academic institutions, religious and cause-oriented groups, business and industry.
3. Public demand must be generated and citizens' movements activated to evoke a response from local, national, and international leaders. It may not always be easy to build up a strong public movement around development issues – but even a moderate display of interest and effort by community leaders could stimulate the process for policy decisions and resource allocation for combating the problem.

Two of the ongoing concerns that were touched upon by several contributors in this volume were related to (a) the attitude and behavioral change component in transformative processes, and (b) the search for the "best" communication instrument/channel to achieve social change.

In today's discussion, as exemplified in the chapters by Polk, Norman and others, the discussion often breaks down in opposites: new versus old media, technology versus human interaction. It is no surprise that these days the outcome is often tipped in favor of the former. For instance, Christine Ogan and her graduate students (2009) conclude that, after a detailed analysis of the literature between 1997 and 2007, studies have moved away from mass communication toward ICTs' role in development, that they infrequently address development in the context of globalization (Elliott & Lemert, 2006; Milliot & Tournois, 2010) and often continue to embrace a modernization paradigm despite its many criticisms:

> We believe that the more recent attention to ICTs has to do with the constant search for the magic solution to bringing information to people to transform their lives, allowing them to improve their economic condition, educate their children, increase literacy and the levels of education and spread democracy in their countries. Despite years of research that tells us that information is necessary but insufficient to bring about this change, ICTs have become the most recent iteration of the holy grail for development. And even if communication scholars know better because critical scholarship written over the last 30 years has told them so, newcomers to this field from other information-based disciplines may not have such close acquaintance with that literature. Furthermore, because of the appeal of the modernization paradigm, there is a tendency to forget that it cannot work (Ogan et al., 2009:667–668).

However, the empirical study into the emerging effects of instantly available social media on collective environmentally sustainable behavior by Langley & van den Broek (2010) is also interesting in this regard. They found that most people appreciate the need to address environmental issues in everyday life but lack the motivation to change their behavior for mainly two reasons: fatalism and busyness. People are held back by a lack of knowledge or interest, other priorities, or plain skepticism that one person's choices can really make a difference.

When social media helps tackle barriers to adopting a sustainable lifestyle, for a myriad of reasons, good intentions don't automatically translate into action, Langley and van den Broek found. In particular, social media takes what would normally be small, invisible actions and broadcasts them to the rest of the world. When pooled with the actions of thousands of others, suddenly one initiative is seen to have a significant impact. The effect quickly snowballs as people are more likely to take part in initiatives that have already attracted a critical mass of participants; large numbers send a signal that this is socially appropriate behavior.

In other words, when people are encouraged to share their commitments and achievements with others online, the foundation is set for making actual behavior change. The caveat is that *social media is best for encouraging small steps*; as Langley and van der Broek found that online initiatives that call for a significant change in lifestyle will have trouble recruiting large numbers of participants.

So are social media campaigns the panacea for the planet? Of course not, Myers (2012) concludes: "The fight against global warming won't be won simply by consumers voting for their favorite sustainability project on Nokia's Climate Mission mobile game. However, these digital initiatives do impart pro-environmental values and help shape consumer preference for greener lifestyles." In other words, social media on its own won't necessarily save the planet. But it might just encourage a more sustainable future.

Participation and power

As documented in this volume, the reaction against modernization (and to some extent the realization of global structural imbalances) gave birth to various participatory approaches. They shared the common intent of actively involving people who were the "subjects" of development in shaping the process. But in most cases this is where similarity ends and a diversity of differences begin. People's participation became defined in many different ways and this in turn led to numerous unresolved disagreements (for an overview, see Carpentier, 2011; Jacobson & Servaes, 1999).

Uphoff (1985), for instance, identified four different ways of participation, which can be observed in most development projects claiming to be participatory in nature:

1. *Participation in implementation:* People are actively encouraged and mobilized to take part in the actualization of projects. They are given certain responsibilities and set certain tasks or required to contribute specified resources.
2. *Participation in evaluation:* Upon completion of a project, people are invited to critique the success or failure of it.
3. *Participation in benefit:* People take part in enjoying the fruits of a project, this maybe water from a hand-pump, medical care by a "bare-foot doctor," a truck to transport produce to market, or village meetings in the new community hall.
4. *Participation in decision-making:* People initiate, discuss, conceptualize, and plan activities they will all do as a community. Some of this may be related to more common development areas such as building schools or applying for land tenure. Others may be more political, such as removing corrupt officials, supporting parliamentary candidates, or resisting pressures from the elites. Yet others may be cultural or religious in nature – organizing a traditional feast, prayers for an end to the drought, and a big party just to have a good time.

Jules Pretty (1995) offers a more detailed typology of participation:

1. *Passive participation:* People participate by being told what is going to happen or has already happened. It is a unilateral announcement by an administration or project management without any listening to people's responses. The information being shared belongs only to external professionals.
2. *Participation in information giving:* People participate by answering questions posed by extractive researchers using questionnaire surveys or similar approaches. People do not have the opportunity to influence proceedings, as the findings of the research are neither shared nor checked for accuracy.
3. *Participation by consultation:* People participate by being consulted, and external agents listen to views. These external agents define both problems and solutions, and may

modify these in the light of people's responses. Such a consultative process does not concede any share in decision-making, and professionals are under no obligation to take on board people's views.

4. *Participation for material incentive:* People participate by providing resources, for example, labor, in return for food, cash or other material incentives. Much on-farm research falls in this category, as farmers provide the fields but are not involved in the experimentation or process of learning. It is very common to see this called participation, yet people have no stake in prolonging activities when the incentives end.

5. *Functional Participation:* People participate by forming groups to meet predetermined objectives related to the project, which can involve the development or promotion of externally initiated social organization. Such involvement does not tend to be at early stages of project cycles of planning, but rather after major decisions have been made. These institutions tend to be dependent on external initiators and facilitators, but may become self-dependent.

6. *Interactive participation:* People participate in joint analysis, which leads to action plans and the formation of new local institutions or the strengthening of existing ones. It tends to involve interdisciplinary methodologies that seek multiple objectives and make use of systematic and structured learning processes. These groups take control over local decisions, and so people have a stake in maintaining structures or practices.

7. *Self-mobilization:* People participate by taking initiatives independent of external institutions to change systems. Such self-initiated mobilization and collective action may or may not challenge existing inequitable distributions of wealth and power.

Most will agree that participation in decision-making in Uphoff's categorization, or self-mobilization in Pretty's typology, is the most important form to promote. It gives people control of their lives and environment. At the same time, the people acquire problem-solving skills and acquire full ownership of projects – two important elements that will contribute toward securing the sustained development of their community.

Sparks (2007) offers two broad variants of the participatory paradigm in communication for social change. The first he terms the negotiated variant in which local participants are no longer the pure passive objects in a process which sets goals in which they have no input, but rather it is one in which they act as initiators in both their knowledge of situation and the problems it contains and in the formation of a communication strategy designed to overcome them. The state, aid agency, and expert are no longer accorded a superior status in defining the problems, identifying the solutions or formulating communication strategies and managing change, although they are defined as outsiders defining the change.

The radical variant of the participatory paradigm, according to Sparks, acknowledges that communities in developing countries are marked by inequalities and seeks to find ways of allowing these communities of disadvantaged women, poor peasants, and agricultural laborers to effect social change by empowering themselves, organizing through social force and achieving developmental changes that improve their conditions. In this way, according to Sparks, the radical variant emphasizes empowerment, political strategies, and social action that are more visible in NGO's and new social movements (see also Esteva & Prakah, 1998; Nash, 2005).

The impact of change

The perspective on "impact," used by Oxfam America and explained by Adinda Van Hemelrijck – "*A significant and sustainable change in power relations that enables excluded and marginalized people to realize their rights to access and manage the resources, services and knowledge they need for strengthening their livelihoods, improving their well-being, and influencing and holding accountable the institutions that affect their lives*" –, is of particular importance here. It implies that development efforts – and thus its monitoring, evaluation, and learning processes – should focus on both building people's capabilities to understand and work the system (agency) and strengthening the enablers that help them doing so (the institutions and complex webs of societal relationships).

Van Hemelrijck correctly argues that systemic change can only be realized if there is a strong collaborative and long-term commitment of all key stakeholders, persistently focused on specific rights issues in a specific context over a long period of time.

A core premise therefore is that monitoring, evaluation, and learning can and should serve and strengthen these collaborative efforts (rather than satisfying merely donor interests), and by doing so, directly and indirectly, contribute to empowerment.

Hence the importance of robust impact measurement and learning systems, which

a) Proactively can produce convincing arguments showing key stakeholders that their contributions "can" make a difference, and that "together" they are more likely to achieve their goals; and therefore

b) Can reveal the complex (*nonlinear*) systemic relationships between changes at different levels and at different moments in times, and make them understandable (without fragmenting or overly simplifying things) particularly for the people themselves;

c) Can create the appropriate spaces at various levels for ongoing constituency feedback and debate among the key stakeholders through which new and concrete options for alternative action and behavior are shaped;

d) Can thwart a digression into a standard broad "integrated" and/or "sectoral" approach that is nothing more than a basket of loosely connected initiatives, and instead, can keep stakeholders laser-focused on a particular rights issue and the specific leverage points that, at particular moments in time, likely will foster large changes;

e) In the long run, can deal with the *unpredictability* of changing contexts, shifting alliances, and transforming power configurations due to increased understanding and influence by key stakeholders;

f) Are simple, flexible, and cost-effective enough to last for many years, and can help build the case for plausible contributions to fighting poverty and injustice (rather than try to attribute such changes to any single actor, or any single project, or any single intervention).

Measurement and evaluation for "social usefulness"

Evaluation and impact assessments should include participatory baseline formulations and communication needs assessments (Parks, 2005; Servaes & Arnst, 1999). They should also include self-evaluation by the communities themselves and the concept of "social usefulness." They should be used to feedback at the policy level. There is a need for effective and convincing evaluation models and data to show evidence of the impact of communication for development. Sustainability indicators based on qualitative dimensions of development need to be emphasized, involving the potential of ICTs to collect feedback interactively. Research should also be reinforced in order to better identify communication needs (Lie, 2003).

While many successful small-scale examples of communication for development exist, these need to be scaled up, thus improving practice and policy at every level. A focus on small-scale projects (pilot projects) is acceptable, but evidence-based and properly researched benchmarks need to be set.

These impact measurement systems, therefore, need to be integrated with ongoing *collective sense-making and learning processes*, combined with *independent impact evaluations* using mixed methods, appropriate to the context and learning needs of partners and key stakeholders *at the various levels* in the development process (Kennedy, 2008; Lesca, 2011; McIntyre, 2008). In these processes, however, we are dealing with fluid configurations of stakeholders with divergent views and interests, organizational capacities and learning abilities, roles and (legal) responsibilities, and probably also quite diverging degrees of allegiance to the change goals. None of these stakeholders, moreover, are homogeneous and stable entities in themselves. If their engagement is part of the trajectory of systemic-transformational change, however, then individual and collective learning through feedback, critical reflection, and debate at the various levels is essential. Learning is needed for several purposes: practical improvements of individual contributions or interventions, strategic adjustments at the aggregated levels where synergies are created, and improving the (individual and collective) learning processes themselves. The distinction between primary stakeholders, clients, constituencies, allies, targets, donors, and grantees is turning blurry, as all are becoming partners is a collective endeavor to understand and create systemic change.

From a rights-based development perspective, all are equally and mutually accountable *"to act, observe/measure, reflect, improve, and learn"* for properly addressing the rights issue at stake, since all are part of the same system that needs to be changed.

References

Appiah, K. A. (2006). *Cosmopolitanism: Ethics in a World of Strangers*. London: Allen Lane.

Blewitt, J. (ed.) (2008). *Community, Empowerment and Sustainable Development*. Devon: Green Books.

Carpentier, Nico (2011). *Media and Participation. A Site of Ideological-Democratic Struggle*. Bristol: Intellect.

Dissanayake, W. (2006). Postcolonial Theory and Asian Communication Theory: Towards a Creative Dialogue. *China Media Research*, 2(4), 1–8.

Elliott, A. & Lemert, C. (2006). *The New Individualism: The Emotional Costs of Globalization*. London: Routledge.

Espinosa, A. & Walker, J. (2011). *A Complexity Approach to Sustainability. Theory and Application*. London: Imperial College Press.

Esteva, G. & Prakah, M. S. (1998). *Grassroots Post-modernism: Remaking the Soil of Cultures*. London: Zed Books.

Friedmann, J. (1992). *Empowerment: The Politics of Alternative Development*. Cambridge, MA: Blackwell.

Gunaratne, S. (2005). *The Dao of the Press: A Humanocentric Theory*. Cresskill, NJ: Hampton Press.

Jacobson, T. & Servaes, J. (eds.) (1999). *Theoretical Approaches to Participatory Communication*. Cresskill, NJ: Hampton.

Janssens, Maddy (ed.) (2009). *Sustainable Cities: Diversity, Economic Growth and Social Cohesion*. Cheltenham, UK: Elgar.

Kennedy, T. (2008). *Where the Rivers Meet the Sky: A Collaborative Approach to Participatory Development*. Penang: Southbound.

Langley, David & Tijs van den Broek (2010). *Exploring Social Media as a Driver of Sustainable Behaviour: Case Analysis and Policy Implications*. Paper 'Internet Politics and Policy Conference', 16–17 September, Oxford.

Lesca, N. (ed.) (2011). *Environmental Scanning and Sustainable Development*. Hoboken NJ: Wiley.

Lie, R. (2003). Spaces of Intercultural Communication: An Interdisciplinary Introduction to Communication, Culture, and Globalizing/Localizing Identities. Creskill: Hampton.

McIntyre, A. (2008). *Participatory Action Research*. Thousand Oaks, CA: SAGE.

Milliot, Eric & Nadine, Tournois (2010). *The Paradoxes of Globalization*. New York: Palgrave Macmillan.

Myers, Stephanie (2012). "How Social Media Really Can Produce Social Change on *TriplePundit. People, Planet, Profit*. Retrieved on February 15, 2012 from http://www.triplepundit.com/2012/02/social-media-really-producesocial-change/

Nash, J. (ed.) (2005). *Social Movements: An Anthropological reader*. Masden, MA: Blackwell.

Nederveen Pieterse, J. (2010). *Development Theory* (2nd ed). Los Angeles: SAGE.

Neumayer, Eric (2010). *Weak versus Strong Sustainability: Exploring the Limits of Two Opposing Paradigms*. Cheltenham, UK: Elgar.

Ogan, C. L., Bashir, M., Camaj, L., et al. (2009). Development Communication: The State of Research in an Era of ICTs and Globalization. *The International Communication Gazette*, 71(8), 655–670.

Omoto, A. (2005). *Processes of Community Change and Social Action.* Mahwah, NJ: Lawrence Erlbaum.

Papa, M. J., Singhal, A., & Papa, W. (2006). *Organizing for Social Change. A Dialectic Journey of Theory and Praxis.* New Delhi: SAGE Publications.

Parks, Will with D. Gray-Felder et al. (2005). Who Measures Change? An Introduction to Participatory Monitoring and Evaluation of Communication for Social Change. Orange, NJ: CSC Foundation.

Pretty, Jules et al. (1995). *Participatory Learning and Action: A Trainer's Guide.* London: International Institute for Environment and Development.

Sen, A. (2004). Cultural Liberty and Human Development, in Fukuda-Parr, S. (ed.), *Human Development Report: Cultural Liberty in Today's Diverse World.* New York: United Nations Development Programme.

Servaes J. (ed.) (2008). *Communication for Development and Social Change.* London: SAGE.

Servaes J. (1999). *Communication for Development: One World, Multiple Cultures.* Creskill, NJ: Hampton.

———(2012). Comparing Development Communication, in Frank Esser & Thomas Hanitzsch (eds.), *The Handbook of Comparative Communication Research.* New York: Routledge, pp. 64–80.

Servaes, J. & Arnst, R. (1999). Principles of Participatory Communication Research: Its Strengths(!) and Weaknesses(?), in Servaes, J. & Jacobson, T. (eds.), *Theoretical Approaches to Participatory Communication.* Creskill, NJ: Hampton Press, pp. 107–127.

Sikes, W., Drexler, A., & Gant, J. (eds.) (1989). *The Emerging Practice of Organizational Development.* Alexandria VI: NTL Institute for Applied Behavioral Science.

Sparks, C. (2007). *Globalization, Development and the Mass Media.* Thousand Oaks, CA: SAGE.

Stiglitz, J. (1998). Towards a New Paradigm for Development: Strategies, Policies, and Processes. Prebisch Lecture at UNCTAD, Geneva, 19 October 1998.

Tehranian, M. (2007). *Rethinking Civilization: Resolving Conflict in the Human Family.* London: Routledge.

UNDP (2010). *Human Development Report 2010. The Real Wealth of Nations: Pathways to Human Development.* New York: United Nations Development Programme.

Uphoff, Norman (1985). Fitting Projects to People, in Cernea, M. (ed.), *Putting People First: Sociological Variables in Rural Development.* New York: Oxford University Press.

Contributors

Editor

Jan Servaes (PhD, 1987, Catholic University of Louvain, Belgium) is Chair Professor and Head of the Department of Media and Communication at the City University of Hong Kong (http://www6.cityu.edu.hk/com/); UNESCO Chair in Communication for Sustainable Social Change at the University of Massachusetts Amherst (USA, http://www.csschange.org); Honorary Guest Professor at the Huazhong University of Science and Technology (HUST), Wuhan, China; Researcher at the "Brussels Center for Journalism Studies (BCJS)," Belgium (http://www.hubrussel.be/eCache/IEE/18/733.html); Editor-in-Chief of *Telematics and Informatics: An Interdisciplinary Journal on the Social Impacts of New Technologies* (Elsevier, http://www.elsevier.com/locate/tele), Editor of the Southbound Book Series *Communication for Development and Social Change* (http://www.Southbound.com.my), and Editor of the Hampton Book Series *Communication, Globalization and Cultural Identity*.

He has been President of the European Consortium for Communications Research (ECCR, http://www.ecrea.eu) and Vice-President of the International Association of Media and Communication Research (IAMCR, http://www.iamcr.org), in charge of Academic Publications and Research, from 2000 to 2004. He chaired the Scientific Committee for the World Congress on Communication for Development (Rome, 25–27 October 2006), organized by the World Bank, FAO, and the Communication Initiative.

Servaes has taught International Communication and Development Communication in Australia (Brisbane), Belgium (Brussels and Antwerp), the United States (Cornell), The Netherlands (Nijmegen), and Thailand (Thammasat, Bangkok) in addition to several teaching stints at about 100 universities in 43 countries.

Servaes has undertaken research, development, and advisory work around the world and is known as the author of journal articles and books on such topics as international and development communication; ICT and media policies; intercultural communication and language; participation and social change; and human rights and conflict management. Some of his most recent book titles include: (2008) Servaes J., *Communication for Development and Social Change*, SAGE, Los Angeles, London, New Delhi, Singapore; (2007) Servaes J. & Liu S. (eds.), *Moving Targets. Mapping the Paths Between Communication, Technology and Social Change in Communities*, Southbound, Penang; (2006) Thomas P. & Servaes J. (eds.), *Intellectual Property Rights and Communications in Asia*, SAGE, New Delhi; (2006) Servaes J. & Carpentier N. (eds.),

Towards a Sustainable European Information Society, ECCR Book Series, Intellect, Bristol; (2005) Shi -Xu, Kienpointner M. & Servaes J.(eds.), *Read the Cultural Other. Forms of Otherness in the Discourses of Hong Kong's Decolonisation*, Mouton De Gruyter, Berlin; (2003), Servaes J. (ed.), *The European Information Society: A Reality Check*, ECCR Book Series, Intellect, Bristol; (2003) Servaes J. (ed.), *Approaches to Development. Studies on Communication for Development*, UNESCO Publishing House, Paris; (2002) Servaes J., *Communication for Development. One World, Multiple Cultures*, Hampton Press, Cresskill (Foreword by Jan Pronk).
E-mail: 9cssc9@gmail.com

Authors

Lalatendu Acharya (MBA, 1991; PhD, 2011, Communication, Purdue University) is an Assistant Professor in the Department of Consumer Sciences and Retailing, Purdue University. Lala has worked extensively with corporate, government, and development sectors and has extensive experience of working with children as a Communications Officer for UNICEF. Lala conducts research in Participatory approaches, Consumer participation, Health communication campaigns with vulnerable populations, Consumer Issues in Health care, and Health care relationship sales and marketing. Lala has presented his work in National and International conferences and has published his research in journal articles and book chapters.
E-mail: lacharya@purdue.edu

K. Kovacs Burns, MSc, MSHA, PhD, Associate Director, Health Sciences Council and Director of Interdisciplinary Health Research Academy, University of Alberta. Her research focuses on public engagement in local, national, and international health and social policy and program decisions, and the impact of policies on the public.
E-mail: kathy.kovacsburns@ualberta.ca

J. Chaw-Kant, MSc, is a Research Project Coordinator in the Faculty of Nursing, University of Alberta. She is currently involved in several research projects with topics such as the homeless and homelessness; access to health services by persons living with HIV; and clinical mentorship of nurses in HIV care.
E-mail: jean.chaw-kant@ualberta.ca

Betty Chirchir (BDS, 1988 University of Nairobi; MPH, 1996 University of Nairobi) is the Director of Bon Santé Consulting in Nairobi, Kenya and undertakes consultancy work for several local, national, and international organizations in the East and Southern African region. Dr. Chirchir works to strengthen public, private, and community-based responses to HIV in the areas of communication, human resources for health,

382

and workplace programming using innovative methods and has contributed to the development of numerous national HIV policies, training manuals, and strategic plans in the region. Dr. Chirchir has undertaken several research projects, program evaluations, and documentation assignments in the health sector.

E-mail: bchirchir@bonsante.co.ke

Joelle Cruz (PhD, Texas A&M University) is an Assistant Professor in the Communication Studies Department at Clemson University. Her work is nourished by her upbringing in Côte d' Ivoire, West Africa. Her research lies at the intersections of organizing for social change and development communication. She explores issues of power by examining the construction of development aid and its beneficiaries by organizations such as USAID and the World Bank. She also focuses on social change strategies deployed by African women's organizations. Such is the case for her dissertation research, which looks at women's grassroots organizations working toward economic empowerment in postconflict Liberia.

E-mail: joellecruz@neo.tamu.edu

Mohan Jyoti Dutta (PhD, 2001, Communication, University of Minnesota) Professor and Head of the Department of Communications and New Media at the National University of Singapore. At NUS, he is the Founding Director of the Center for Culture-Centered Approach to Research and Evaluation (CARE), directing research on culturally-centered, community-based projects of social change. He teaches and conducts research in international health communication, critical cultural theory, poverty in healthcare, health activism in globalization politics, indigenous cosmologies of health, subaltern studies and dialogue, and public policy and social change.

Currently, he serves as Senior Editor of the journal *Health Communication* and sits on the editorial board of seven journals. He was the Associate Dean for Research and Graduate Education in the College of Liberal Arts at Purdue University, a Service Learning Fellow, and a Fellow of the Entrepreneurial Leadership Academy at Purdue University. Mohan has published over 100 journal articles and book chapters, and authored the books *Communicating Health: A Culture-Centered Approach* and *Communicating Social Change: Structure, Culture, Agency*, and co-edited *Emerging Perspectives in Health Communication: Meaning, Culture, and Power* and *Communicating for Social Impact: Engaging Communication Theory, Research, and Pedagogy*.

E-mail: mohanjdutt@gmail.com

Tilly A. Gurman (DrPH, 2007, Johns Hopkins University Bloomberg School of Public Health) is an Assistant Professor in the Department of Global Health at George Washington University School of Public Health and Health Services, with expertise in health communication, reproductive health, patient-provider communication, program evaluation, and mass media content analysis. A Venezuelan native, Dr. Gurman has focused her research on the Latin American diaspora, including the United States, Guatemala, El Salvador, and

Mexico. For example, in one project she surveyed healthcare providers and interviewed Spanish-speaking mothers of infants about barriers to accessing infant healthcare services in the United States. In addition to publishing the research findings, Dr. Gurman developed trainings for healthcare providers and coproduced a video – in the style of Spanish-language soap operas – for patients. More recently, she researched the potential of combining income-generation projects with health education to improve indigenous women's reproductive health in Guatemala.

E-mail: tgurman@gwu.edu

Fadia Hasan is a PhD Candidate in the Communication Department at UMass Amherst. She earned her BA from Hampshire College with an undergraduate thesis titled, "The Politics of Femininity in Mainstream Indian Films." Her MA was in Communications from University of Massachusetts, Amherst. Fadia's focus in her Masters has been Global Consumer & Class Cultures and Alternative Economies. Her Masters thesis is titled, "Fair Trade Practices in Contemporary Bangladeshi Society: Community Development, Cultural Revival and Sustainability through a Participatory Approach." Currently, her PhD work is in the area of Environmental Communications, with a focus on Grassroots Movements and Trans-(national) Policy Frameworks.

E-mail: fhasan@comm.umass.edu

Patchanee Malikhao received a PhD in Sociology from the University of Queensland in Australia, a Master's of Arts degree in Mass Communication from Thammasat University in Thailand, a Master's of Science degree in Printing Technology from Rochester Institute of Technology (RIT), Rochester, New York, and a Bachelor of Science (Hons.) in Photographic Science and Printing Technology from Chulalongkorn University in Thailand. She has worked and received extensive trainings in the fields of Communication for Social Change, Imaging Technology, Social Science Research Methods and Data Analyses in Belgium, Australia, and the United States. She was a recipient of many scholarships and awards, including the Fulbright Scholarship, the Australian Postgraduate Award, and the Outstanding Teacher Award. She worked from August 2008 to July 2011 as a researcher and a lecturer in the School of Public Health at the University of Massachusetts, Amherst, USA. Afterwards she joined Thammasat University in Bangkok, Thailand, and became a Senior Fellow in the CSSC Center at UMass Amherst. Her most recent book *Sex in the Village: Culture, Religion and HIV/AIDS in Thailand* is published by Southbound/Penang and Silkworm Books/Chiang Mai.

E-mail: pmalikhao@gmail.com

Ramadimetja Shirley Mogale, MCur, RN, is a PhD Candidate in the Faculty of Nursing, University of Alberta, Canada. Her research program focuses on the culture of prosecution of violence against women and related issues such as homelessness.

E-mail: mogale@ualberta.ca

Verity Norman (MEd, 2011, University of Massachusetts, Amherst, USA) is the Program Development Manager at Boston University's African Presidential Center, which tracks issues of democracy and development in Africa. She is a recent graduate from the Center for International Education at the University of Massachusetts, Amherst. She is also a Junior Fellow of the Center for Communication for Sustainable Social Change, also at the University of Massachusetts. Verity is an educator-activist whose work has focused on arts-based education, and has collaborated with students and teachers in southern Africa, North America, Europe, and Southeast Asia. Her academic research centers on participatory education and communication, and how hip hop and music can be used as emancipatory educational tools. She continues her work with teen musicians and grassroots organizers in developing music education models that engage youth in global issues of social justice. Verity recently started working as the Academic Outreach Director for Nomadic Wax, a fair trade international record label and multimedia events production company, specializing in hip hop and underground music from around the world.
E-mail: veritynorman@gmail.com

Tokunbo Ojo (PhD, University of Queensland, Australia) teaches at the School of Journalism and Communication, Carleton University, Ottawa, Canada. His teaching and research interests include development and international communication, journalism studies, political economy of the media, and global media governance. His published works have appeared in *Journalism: Theory, Practice & Criticism*; *Communication for Development and Social Change*; *Canadian Journal of Communication*; *Journal of Information Technology Impact*; *International Journal of Education and Development Using ICT*; and *Information Development*.
E-mail: ojotoks@yahoo.com

Toks Dele Oyedemi (PhD, University of Massachusetts, Amherst) is currently a fellow at Communication for Sustainable Social Change (CSSC) and at the National Center for Digital Government (NCDG) both at the University of Massachusetts, USA. He was a member of NetTel@Africa, a transnational working group on developing training programs on ICT policy and regulation in Africa. He has taught at universities in South Africa and the USA. His research and publications broadly focus on technology and society. His publications have appeared in journals such as *International Journal of Communication* and *Telematics and Informatics*.
E-mail: toks.umass@gmail.com

David J. Park (PhD, University of Wisconsin-Madison, 2003) is Graduate Assistant Professor in the School of Journalism and Mass Communication at Florida International University. In 2005, he was named a Howard Hughes Research Sabbatical Scholar and Honorary Fellow at the University of Wisconsin-Madison in the School of Journalism and Mass Communication. He has been a Fulbright-Hayes Scholar to the Caribbean, an ENDA

Tiers-Monde Intern in Senegal, and a Tinker-Nave grant recipient to conduct research in Argentina. In 2009, he received the Outstanding Faculty Contributions to Service-Learning Instruction in Higher Education Award from the Executive Committee of the Gulf-South Summit for Service-Learning and Civic Engagement in Higher Education for his work in New Orleans. His publications include his recent book *Conglomerate Rock: The Music Industry's Quest to Divide Music and Conquer Wallets*, published by Lexington Books, a division of Rowman and Littlefield publishers.
E-mail: djpark@fiu.edu

Katrina Phillips (MSc Development Management, Open University, UK) is a consultant specializing in using communication for social change in Africa. She creates interactive communication strategies and tools, from initial research to delivery, using TV, radio, mobile telephones, the web, print, and community networks to enable and support conversations and development. Katrina works with government ministries, UN agencies, international donors, NGOs, and local community organizations among others in southern and East Africa; she is based in Zimbabwe.
E-mail: phillips.katrina@gmail.com

Emily Polk is a PhD Candidate in Communication at the University of Massachusetts at Amherst (MA, 2006, Columbia University) and a Junior Fellow at the Center for the Communication for Sustainable Social Change. She has worked as a human rights journalist around the world and as a senior editor at CSRwire, a global source of corporate social responsibility news. Her own writing and radio documentaries have appeared in National Geographic Traveler, The Boston Globe, NPR, AlterNet, The Indian Express, Central America Weekly, the Ghanaian Chronicle, and Whole Earth Magazine, among others. Her academic articles have been published in *Global Media Journal*, *Media Development*, and *Development in Practice*.
E-mail: epolk@comm.umass.edu

Jyotika Ramaprasad is Professor and Vice Dean for Graduate Studies and Research in the School of Communication at the University of Miami. She has published her research in the *International Communication Gazette, Journalism Quarterly, Newspaper Research Journal, Asian Journal of Communication, Mass Communication & Society, The Harvard International Journal of Press/Politics, Journal of Advertising, Journal of Advertising Research, Journal of Current Issues & Research in Advertising*, and *Social Marketing Quarterly*. Her research interests are currently focused on the use of communication for social change in developing countries and on journalist profiles.

Ramaprasad has consulted for disaster preparedness in Southeast Asia and for journalism/communication education in East Africa. She has received several US State Department grants for capacity building in journalism and communication for social change in South Asia and

East Africa. She has run workshops, given talks, and taught as well as provided curricular advice in several institutions around the world including Europe, Africa, and Asia.
E-mail: jyotika@miami.edu

Leslie Richardson (PhD, Tulane University) is the Director of the Center for the Advancement of Teaching at Florida International University. She taught English and Women's Studies at Xavier University before and after Hurricane Katrina. While her previous scholarship and publications focused on eighteenth-century literature, after Katrina her interest shifted to community-based pedagogy and social-justice pedagogy. She advocates a learning-centered approach to teaching, and finds much compelling evidence that the needs of learners and the needs of communities can be made fruitfully mutual with a thoughtful approach to course design.
E-mail: laricha@fiu.edu.

M.S. Richter, DCur, RN, Associate Professor in the Faculty of Nursing, University of Alberta. Her research interest focuses on the social determinants of health, and more specifically research on homelessness to inform public policies and frontline practices that protect and promote health of the low socioeconomic and homeless populations. In this research, she focused on the capacity for health professionals, media personnel, and the public to influence public policy on global homelessness.
E-mail: solina.richter@ualberta.ca

Song Shi is a PhD Candidate in Communication Department at the University of Massachusetts, Amherst. He is also a junior fellow at the Center of Communication for Sustainable Social Change at UMass. His research interest includes three interrelated fields: the influences of new media on social change and development in developing countries; digital divide, new media, and Information and Communications Technology (ICT); digital copyright and new media. His recent research focused on the use of the Internet and the development of Chinese civil society organizations, Internet policy in China and broadband policy in the United States. In his research, he employed both qualitative methods and quantitative methods in communication studies.
E-mail: sshi@comm.umass.edu

Rachel Stohr (MA, 2009, University of New Mexico) is a PhD Candidate and Graduate Teaching Assistant in the Department of Communication Studies at the University of Nebraska- Lincoln. Her research and teaching reflect her interests in organizational rhetoric and cosmopolitan theory. Her work explores, critiques, and seeks to improve the organizational and rhetorical processes through which disempowered citizens might gain voice in global public discourse.
E-mail: rstohr84@gmail.com

Boonlert Supadhiloke received a PhD in mass communication and an MA in journalism from the University of Wisconsin-Madison, USA. He graduated with a BA in journalism (Hon.) from Thammasat University, Thailand. He became the first Dean of the Faculty of Journalism and Mass Communication at Thammasat. He was transferred to the Government Public Relations Department, serving as Director of Radio Thailand, Deputy Director-General and Inspector-General. He was on deputation to serve the Food and Agriculture Organization of the United Nations as a development communication consultant. He has worked as: Research Fellow at East-West Communication Institute, Hawaii and Minister-Counselor for Information, Royal Embassy of Thailand, Washington D.C., USA He has published books and articles on various research topics including Human Rights and Right to Communicate, Participatory Communication and Sustainable Development, Community and Public Broadcasting Systems, Political Communication and Democracy. He is currently an Associate Professor and researcher at Bangkok University, Thailand.
E-mail: boonlert.s@bu.ac.th

Adinda Van Hemelrijck (MA Comparative Cultural Sciences & International Relations, 1995/2005, University of Ghent, Belgium) is a PhD candidate at the Institute for Development Studies (Participation, Power and Social Change Team) in the UK. She is currently working as an independent advisor, among others, with International Fund for Agricultural Development (IFAD) and the Bill & Melinda Gates Foundation (BMGF) on the design of a participatory impact assessment and learning approach combining PRA-based methods such as participatory statistics, constituency voice and most significant change. Until February 2012 she worked as a senior global advisor at Oxfam America. She assists local development actors worldwide in building empowering measurement and learning systems and strengthening their capacity for running these systems. In the past 14 years, she has undertaken research, design, and advisory work with various grassroots organizations, governments, international research institutions, and development and integration agencies. Her passion is about learning and accountability in collaborative settings (e.g., strategic partnerships, coalitions, movements, networks) in areas of smallholders' productive water rights, farmer-driven agricultural development, rural communities' livelihood rights in the face of foreign land investments and extractive industries, and gender and cultural identity. She contributed to publications on gender in agricultural development, total quality management in development education, and communication for social change and development.
E-mail: a.vanhemelrijck@ids.ac.uk

Author Index

Subject Index